An Anthology of Critical Works

Gifted & ADVANCED BLACK STUDENTS IN SCHOOL

An Anthology of Critical Works

Gifted & Advanced Black Students in School

Edited by
Tarek C. Grantham, Ph.D., Donna Y. Ford, Ph.D., Malik S. Henfield, Ph.D.,
Michelle Trotman Scott, Ph.D., Deborah A. Harmon, Ph.D.,
Sonya Porchèr, Ed.D., and Cheryl Price

PRUFROCK PRESS INC.
WACO, TEXAS

DEDICATION

This is book is dedicated to the late Dr. Mary M. Frasier who unselfishly sowed seeds for the editors of this book to grow the area of multicultural gifted education. We all owe Mary a great deal of gratitude for her unwavering and tireless efforts to call attention to the needs of gifted Black students in schools throughout the nation.

Mary galvanized people from all walks of life to pave a way for each of us to have a voice, to embrace a broader conceptualization of giftedness, and to join the fight against social injustices toward Black and other ethnic minority gifted students. Through her grace, wisdom, and tenacity, Mary's advocacy on behalf of gifted ethnic minority students showed us how more bees are attracted and battles are fought and won with honey versus vinegar. With poise, integrity, hard work, and resilience, Mary modeled professionalism, demonstrating how to pursue purpose with vigor, to rise above adverse circumstances to achieve one's goals, and to help others along the way. She taught us to believe in ourselves as Black people and Black scholars. She had high hopes for us to carry on the work of investing resources, time, and attention to identifying gifted Black children and developing their potential to the fullest. She also charged us to expect you to do the same.

Although we celebrate her contributions in gifted education, we also take pride in and honor the fact that Mary was not only a brilliant scholar, she was a gifted wife, a gifted mother of two gifted daughters, and a grandmother. The field of gifted education owes a great deal of gratitude to Mary and her family for all of the sacrifices that she made so that we can understand and appreciate how the field of education can and should respond to gifted and advanced Black students in schools.

Thank you Mary, and thank you Mack and Frasier families for all of the wonderful seeds that you have sown!

Library of Congress Cataloging-in-Publication Data

Gifted and advanced Black students in school : an anthology of critical works / edited by Tarek C. Grantham ... [et al].
  p. cm.
ISBN 978-1-59363-700-2 (pbk.)
1. Gifted children--Education--United States. 2. African American students. 3. African Americans--Education. I. Grantham, Tarek C.
LC3993.2.G54 2011
371.829'96073--dc23
                          2011017475

Copyright ©2011, Prufrock Press Inc.

Edited by Jennifer Robins

Cover and layout design by Raquel Trevino

ISBN-13: 978-1-59363-700-2

No part of this book may be reproduced, translated, stored in a retrieval system, or transmitted, in any form or by any means, electronic, mechanical, photocopying, microfilming, recording, or otherwise, without written permission from the publisher.

Printed in the United States of America.

At the time of this book's publication, all facts and figures cited are the most current available. All telephone numbers, addresses, and websites URLs are accurate and active. All publications, organizations, websites, and other resources exist as described in the book, and all have been verified. The editors and Prufrock Press Inc. make no warranty or guarantee concerning the information and materials given out by organizations or content found at websites, and we are not responsible for any changes that occur after this book's publication. If you find an error, please contact Prufrock Press Inc.

Prufrock Press Inc.
P.O. Box 8813
Waco, TX 76714-8813
Phone: (800) 998-2208
Fax: (800) 240-0333
http://www.prufrock.com

TABLE OF CONTENTS

XI FOREWORD
Alexinia Y. Baldwin, Ph.D.
Professor Emeritus University of Connecticut

XIII PROLOGUE

1 SECTION I
Historical Context and Background
Tarek C. Grantham, Donna Y. Ford, and Malik S. Henfield

3 CHAPTER 1
Rethinking the Issues Regarding the Culturally Disadvantaged Gifted
Mary M. Frasier

13 CHAPTER 2
I'm Black but Look at Me, I Am Also Gifted
Alexinia Y. Baldwin

23 CHAPTER 3
Desegregating Gifted Education: A Need Unmet
Donna Y. Ford

39 SECTION II
Creativity, Black Children, and Torrance
Tarek C. Grantham

41 CHAPTER 4
Creativity and Its Educational Implications for the Gifted
E. Paul Torrance

55 CHAPTER 5
Creative Positives of Disadvantaged Children and Youth
E. Paul Torrance

65 CHAPTER 6
The Role of Creativity in Identification of the Gifted and Talented
E. Paul Torrance

73 CHAPTER 7
Understanding the Challenge of Creativity Among African Americans
Alexinia Young Baldwin

81 SECTION III
Discovering Gifted Potential in Black Students
Tarek C. Grantham, Donna Y. Ford, and Malik S. Henfield

85 CHAPTER 8
Undiscovered Diamonds: The Minority Gifted Child
Alexina Y. Baldwin

99 CHAPTER 9
Disadvantaged and Culturally Diverse Gifted Students
Mary M. Frasier

109 CHAPTER 10
Gifted and Talented Black Children: Identifying Diamonds in the Rough
Donna Y. Ford and J. John Harris III

TABLE OF CONTENTS

121 CHAPTER 11
Toward a New Paradigm for Identifying Talent Potential
Mary M. Frasier and A. Harry Passow

137 CHAPTER 12
Core Attributes of Giftedness: A Foundation for Recognizing the Gifted Potential of Minority and Economically Disadvantaged Students
Mary M. Frasier, Scott L. Hunsaker, Jongyeun Lee, Sandra Mitchell, Bonnie Cramond, Sally Krisel, Jaime H. Garda, Darlene Martin, Elaine Frank, and Vernon S. Finley

155 SECTION IV
Highly Gifted Black Students
Malik S. Henfield

157 CHAPTER 13
A Socio-Psychological Study of Negro Children of Superior Intelligence
Martin D. Jenkins

175 CHAPTER 14
Case Studies of Negro Children of Binet IQ 160 and Above
Martin D. Jenkins

185 CHAPTER 15
The Upper Limit of Ability Among American Negroes
Martin D. Jenkins

189 CHAPTER 16
Intellectually Superior Negro Youth: Problems and Needs
Martin D. Jenkins

201 SECTION V
Assessment of Black Students
Donna Y. Ford, Malik S. Henfield, and Tarek C. Grantham

203 CHAPTER 17
On Black Intelligence
Robert L. Williams

211 CHAPTER 18
Assessment and Identification of African-American Learners With Gifts and Talents
James M. Patton

227 CHAPTER 19
What Good Is This Thing Called Intelligence and Why Bother to Measure It?
Asa G. Hilliard

243 CHAPTER 20
Addressing Underrepresentation of Gifted Minority Children Using the Naglieri Nonverbal Ability Test (NNAT)
Jack A. Naglieri and Donna Y. Ford

253 CHAPTER 21
Nondiscriminatory Assessment: Considerations for Gifted Education
Laurice M. Joseph and Donna Y. Ford

271 SECTION VI
Recruitment and Retention of Black Students in Gifted Education
Donna Y. Ford, Tarek C. Grantham, and Malik S. Henfield

TABLE OF CONTENTS

273 CHAPTER 22
The Underrepresentation of Minority Students in Gifted Education: Problems and Promises in Recruitment and Retention
Donna Y. Ford

295 CHAPTER 23
Recruitment Is Not Enough: Retaining African American Students in Gifted Education
James L. Moore III, Donna Y. Ford, and H. Richard Milner

323 CHAPTER 24
Culturally and Linguistically Diverse Students in Gifted Education: Recruitment and Retention Issues
Donna Y. Ford, Tarek C. Grantham, and Gilman W. Whiting

349 SECTION VII
The Future of Gifted Education for Black Students
Donna Y. Ford, Tarek C. Grantham, and Malik S. Henfield

351 CHAPTER 25
Underrepresentation in Gifted Education: How Did We Get Here and What Needs to Change? Straight Talk on the Issue of Underrepresentation: An Interview With Dr. Mary M. Frasier
Tarek C. Grantham

357 CHAPTER 26
African American Experiences Conducting Cross-Cultural Research: Controversy, Cautions, Concerns, and Considerations
Donna Y. Ford, James L. Moore III, Gilman W. Whiting, and Tarek C. Grantham

377 EPILOGUE
Tarek C. Grantham, Donna Y. Ford, and Malik S. Henfield

381 ABOUT THE EDITORS

FOREWORD

Alexinia Y. Baldwin, Ph.D.
Professor Emeritus University of Connecticut

When I first began my job as a teacher, I was aware of the variety of abilities of the children in my class. It was during segregation, so programs that were provided to White gifted students did not exist for Black gifted students. This inadequacy disturbed me greatly because there were many students in my classes who exemplified gifted characteristics. The articles in this anthology by Martin D. Jenkins (1936, 1943, 1948, 1950) show that concern for giftedness among Black students was addressed very early in publications that focused on Black issues. Although there was evidence of giftedness in this population, very few published articles were available that emphasized possibilities and the urgency for attention to this concern in public schools and teacher training institutions.

In 1965, preceding the desegregation of schools, I became the teacher of the first class for gifted Black students in grades 5–8 in a large school district. For many years, there had been classes and programs for gifted students who were White, but none had been provided for Black students. The data collected on identification procedures and program activities for these students while they were in the classes, along with longitudinal data on their development into adults, showed how important it was to provide opportunities for Black students to be identified and included in programs for the gifted. This anthology draws attention to the continued lack of inclusion of Black students in programs for the gifted throughout the last century. It gives those who are working to make a change in program planning a philosophical approach for influencing the processes for identifying and planning for the inclusion of gifted Black students in programs for the gifted.

The increased interest in the status of minority pupils in programs for the gifted makes this anthology an excellent source to relay the decades of thoughts, dreams, and recommendations for future recognition of giftedness within the Black population. The articles included are not based solely on the timeline when authors began to express concerns about this lack of attention to gifted Black students. They are a compendium of articles based on the range of discussion in which each gives a flavor of the concern and demand for attention to this valuable and overlooked ability source. In the current explosion of written materials and documents, it is easy for the articles included here to become archived and left out of the current discussion. This anthology is a valuable resource because it gives the reader a range of thoughts over a period of 72 years.

The articles included here have been selected to give a broad range of areas in which there has often been resistance to change in thinking regarding the inclusion of Black students in programs for the gifted. These areas are identification, curriculum design, administrator and teacher attitudes, creativity, the definition of giftedness, and parental and community roles. These are articles and thoughts from authors who themselves are minorities, thus lending credence to the professional observations that have been made through the years. The articles that are included in this publication have been featured in reputable publications both within the field of gifted education and outside of the field.

The editors of this compendium are to be commended on the organization of the anthology, which gives the reader a chance to select the time, author, and area of concern without having to go through the entire publication. It is my hope that the attention that this anthology draws to the concerns of the various authors will inspire further research and planning ideas for new scholars of all racial groups who are just becoming involved in education—and particularly education of the gifted.

PROLOGUE

In late 2009, the coeditors of this anthology met prior to the National Association for Gifted Children's annual conference to discuss—and vent about—the impact of our efforts to address the underidentification of Black students as gifted and their subsequent underrepresentation in gifted education programs. No one knew what outcomes to expect; there was no meeting agenda nor any individual or collective goals to build upon, but many concerns about the status of Black youth and their achievement consumed our conversation. We were all frustrated that too little progress was being made to reverse underrepresentation and increase Black student enrollment in gifted programs; our efforts to address these issues over the years seemed to have been in vain. It became clear that although we had worked together in dyads or triads in workshops and on publications (e.g., articles, chapters, studies), our efforts needed to be combined and become more formalized. With this agreement in mind, the Consortium of African American Scholars (CAAS) in gifted education was formed. We are saddened to say that no such group has existed in gifted education; one was long overdue. Yet we are proud and happy to take on the challenges needed to redress inequities in gifted education for Black students.

The members of CAAS, all coeditors of this anthology, come from many walks of life, but we all share the desire—personal and professional—to desegregate gifted education and to recruit and retain African American students in gifted education programs. We have been raised and educated in urban and suburban communities; as children, our family demographics ranged from low income to high income and included married, single, and divorced parents—some with only a high school diploma, and others with advanced or terminal degrees from colleges and universities. Regardless of our backgrounds, we have all overcome insurmountable odds to achieve career success, and we believe that many other Black students from all walks of life can overcome and experience greater school success, which leads to greater career success.

This book, an anthology of seminal works focusing on gifted Black student issues, represents a labor of love. In the midst of frustration triggered by education's slow progress to meet the needs of gifted Black students, members of CAAS paused to galvanize our collective strengths to begin to capture in a new way a culmination of our gifted education experiences, which represent a range of a few years to two decades. At our meeting in 2009, we rightfully vented much of our frustration over the years, and shared recommendations, solutions, and resources to address inequities related to Black students in gifted education. We are exhausted with feeling vexed and frustrated, as too little progress has been and is being made regarding underrepresentation among Black students in gifted education. Therefore, this anthology represents our collective desire to help the field of education move purposefully and deliberately forward to experience greater success in recruiting and retaining Black students in gifted education.

Black students' inequitable representation in gifted education has a relatively long history, as evidenced by the studies of Martin D. Jenkins, perhaps the first (and only) scholar to consistently focus on Black students with extremely high IQ test scores. His work has mostly been overlooked in the history of gifted education. His scholarship on gifted Black students is not the only work to be neglected, as research by Drs. E. Paul Torrance, Asa G. Hilliard, III, and Robert L. Williams, to name a few, has also tended to be excluded from discussion. Further, the field of gifted education owes much to the scholarship of Drs. Alexinia Y. Baldwin and Mary M. Frasier, who devoted their lives to the issue of underrepresentation. These "mothers" of gifted education for Black students have given the field a legacy that helps keep CAAS members focused and committed to gifted education. Standing on the shoulders of Baldwin and Frasier, no one has been as vocal, prolific, and consistent in calling attention to concerns and recommendations than our senior colleague, Dr. Donna Y. Ford. She is the creator of what we proudly call multicultural gifted education. These three great women have indeed given birth to scholarship on gifted Black students and raised our field to another level in its capacity to understand and meet their needs. Baldwin, Frasier, and Ford have mentored thousands of teachers, counselors, administrators, parents, policy makers, and undergraduate and graduate students, as well as Black students in K–12 schools. The articles in this anthology of scholarship—historical and contemporary—comprise a one-of-a-kind tribute to their legacy. There is no other work that takes readers through a journey that tells the story of Black students' participation (or lack thereof) in gifted education. In sharing scholarly articles, we focus on topics, issues, and challenges associated with being culturally responsive and equitable. This includes various aspects of identification, assessment, characteristics of atypical giftedness, creativity, and more.

A number of assumptions and propositions guided this selection of readings. Specifically, we believe without apology, that:

- ❖ underrepresentation is inequitable and unnecessary;
- ❖ all groups are equally endowed in intelligence, academic ability, and creativity; thus, no group should have a monopoly on being identified and served as gifted;

- underrepresentation can decrease when the focus is on recruitment and retention;
- teachers and educators (due to low expectations and deficit thinking) are the major contributors to underrepresentation, but substantive and purposeful professional development and courses can change this;
- creative strengths reveal gifted potential;
- traditional tests and instruments are a major contributor to underrepresentation, and alternative tests and instruments can increase Black students' representation;
- policies and procedures that contribute to and sustain underrepresentation must be interrogated and changed; and
- underrepresentation can be corrected.

Of course, not every piece of scholarship could be included in this book. Thus, we developed a few criteria for inclusion, with the most important being that the author had shown *consistent* commitment to fighting underrepresentation. It was also the opportunity to showcase neglected scholars such as those listed above. This volume, divided into seven sections and totaling 26 works, by no means tells the entire story of Black children and gifted education. Recognizing that there is so much more to understand and explain, we intend for this to be the first of a series of volumes on understanding and educating gifted Black students.

Section I provides a historical context and background regarding Black students and gifted education, relying on the voices of Frasier, Baldwin, and Ford to set the stage. Section II focuses on creativity, intelligence, and Black students, paying considerable attention to the extensive work of E. Paul Torrance. In this section, we argue that the field's focus on Torrance's contributions in creativity has neglected his call for attention to gifted Black students.

Section III, Discovering Gifted Potential in Black Students, informs readers what must be done to get beyond deficit thinking in order to discover, value, and nurture gifts and talents in Black students. Highly gifted Black students are the focus of Section IV. Here, Martin D. Jenkins' extensive and neglected body of work is showcased. Not surprisingly, Section V covers the assessment of Black intelligence. In it, we tackle the thorny issue of the pitfalls and promises of testing and assessing Black students. Particular attention is given to equitable assessment policies and practices and nonverbal measures. Section VI focuses on a concept that Donna Y. Ford introduced to the field in the early 1990s—recruitment *and* retention. Her rationale is clear—not only must we find ways to increase access to gifted education, but we must also ensure Black students' success once identified and placed. The final section builds upon and goes beyond our past and current status, and is titled The Future of Gifted Education for Black Students. It is important for us to learn from the past: What has not worked? What is not working? What things did and do work? What can be tweaked to work more effectively? What research questions and issues must be considered that contribute to our current knowledge base? What frameworks and methods show promise for future scholarship on gifted Black students? The future rests extensively on honest reflections, the will to change, and taking action to improve the education for gifted Black students in terms of excellence and equity. To wit, as Ford has stressed in a number of ways, "A mind is not only a terrible thing to waste" (The United Negro College Fund's motto), and a mind is a terrible thing to erase. *Everyone* suffers when gifted Black students are overlooked or denied, regardless of the reason—*all* students should be given an opportunity to reach their potential and to participate in high-quality gifted programs.

When compiling this volume, the editors and publisher took care to reproduce the content of each article as it originally appeared, including the form, grammar, style, and so forth. The only changes to the original text were for consistency within and between chapters related to the formatting style (i.e., making headings, subheadings, and titles for figures and tables aligned with current APA style).

SECTION I

Historical Context and Background

Tarek C. Grantham, Donna Y. Ford, and Malik S. Henfield

In 1954, the landmark case of *Brown v. Board of Education*, which overturned the long-standing 1896 *Plessy v. Ferguson* decision that allowed state-sponsored segregation, legislated that Black students were entitled to an equal opportunity to learn, and that, with all due speed, schools must desegregate. Handed down on May 17, 1954, the Warren Court ruled that "separate educational facilities are inherently unequal." Consequently, de jure segregation based on race was ruled a violation of the Equal Protection Clause of the Fourteenth Amendment of the U.S. Constitution. How did educators interpret this ruling for the field of gifted education? *All* programs were required to desegregate, to break down barriers! In gifted education, perhaps the most equitable legislation is the Jacob K. Javits Gifted and Talented Students Education Act of 1988, which sought to open gifted education's doors to underrepresented groups.

Of course, it is one thing to pass a law that declares injustices illegal in education; it is another thing to implement it. In other words, attitudes are nearly impossible to legislate; thus, constant monitoring is necessary. As the scholars highlighted in this section have written about extensively, gifted programs remain very racially segregated, with Black students being the most invisible. Unfortunately for Black students and our nation, despite the unwavering efforts of scholars who have devoted their life's work to desegregating gifted education, underrepresentation has been and remains pervasive in programs for the gifted.

As editors of this book, our frustration is evident, and unapologetically so; our frustration rests with the conviction that underrepresentation is unnecessary, preventable, *and* solvable. When attitudes about and expectations for Black students are strength-based and unclouded by deficit thinking, it is easy to see their gifts and talents—regardless of the instrument and criteria.

In the 1970s, Alexinia Baldwin and Mary Frasier set the groundwork for others, especially the editors of this volume, to focus their professional careers on following the mandate of *Brown v. Board of Education* more than 60 years ago. Like Frasier and Baldwin, we urge readers to ensure equal access to high-quality education and gifted programs for Black students. Given the strong rhetoric imploring educators to produce a more skilled and talented workforce moving forward, doing so represents a win-win situation for gifted Black students, as well as the nation as a whole. Additional context and recommendations presented in the works that follow speak directly to this point.

References

Brown v. Board of Education of Topeka, 347 U.S. 483 (1954).
Plessy v. Ferguson, 163 U.S. 537 (1896).
Title V, Part D. [Jacob K. Javits Gifted and Talented Students Education Act of 1988], Elementary and Secondary Education Act of 1988 (2002), 20 U.S.C. sec. 7253 et seq.

CHAPTER 1

Rethinking the Issues Regarding the Culturally Disadvantaged Gifted

Mary M. Frasier

    This discussion shall focus on issues relative to providing programs that meet the needs of the disadvantaged gifted population. The term *disadvantaged* shall be used generically to symbolize all of the numerous designations that have been used to refer to this population.

    That there might be gifted children among disadvantaged populations was relatively unheard of prior to the 1960's. With the exception of a few studies such as Witty and Jenkins (1934) and Jenkins (1948), the emphasis on disadvantaged populations had largely been on their academic and social difficulties. Attendant to this emphasis had been efforts that were primarily directed toward remediation.

    Heralded by those who began to suggest that the provision of appropriate educational opportunities indeed allowed students from impoverished backgrounds and racial and ethnic minorities to achieve (McClelland, 1958), the era of the disadvantaged gifted might be said to have begun. Reissman's (1962) writings about the culturally deprived gifted child were symbolic of the discussions that began to recognize that among the disadvantaged population there were those who had above average potential to succeed.

    Many questions arose for which answers are still being sought. Who are the disadvantaged gifted? How should they appropriately be designated (e.g., culturally deprived, culturally disadvantaged, culturally different)? In what ways do they differ from their nongifted counterparts and from the advantaged gifted? How

---

Reprinted from Frasier, M. M. (1979). Rethinking the issues regarding the culturally disadvantaged gifted. *Exceptional Children, 45,* 538–542. Reprinted with permission of the Council for Exceptional Children.

should they be identified (i.e., should traditional identification criteria be used with modifications or should supplementary measures be developed)?

Definition of Population

Numerous writers have suggested various ways to define the population that would be included in the category of the disadvantaged gifted. Brickman and Lehrer (1972) reflected the feelings of those who have suggested that the interpretation of disadvantaged be broad enough "to include a variety of persons who have not been able to enjoy culture and education to the fullest on account of various disabilities, whether social, ideological, and religious or of any other origin" (p. 2). Thus, the approach represents those who would suggest that this group would include not only racial ethnic minorities, but also women, handicapped individuals, and underachievers.

Frost and Hawkes (1971) summarized the conclusions of those who felt that the common denominator for membership in a disadvantaged population would be that the candidates are poor. Therefore, the economically deprived of any racial group would be classified as disadvantaged.

A recent discussion by Baldwin (1978) suggested a more plausible way of defining this group. Viewing the disadvantaged as those who are deprived of the opportunity to develop their mental capacities, she described three sets of external influences that define who should be in this group. The influences or variables named by Baldwin (1978, p. 1) are:

> *Cultural diversity* [as] a condition of racial, ethnic, language, or physical differences from a dominant culture.
> *Socioeconomic deprivation* [as] a condition of legal or *de facto* denial of social interaction combined with substandard housing and jobs.
> *Geographic isolation* [as] a condition of being geographically located away from the mainstream of society.

In defining the disadvantaged gifted, then, it may be concluded that within any group—be it determined by ethnic group membership, sex, physical disabilities, or economics—external and environmental influences represent a most powerful factor in discriminating between the advantaged and the disadvantaged. However, as these external and environmental factors appear to have more perversely affected Blacks, Puerto Ricans, American Indians, and Mexican Americans, the evidence suggests that the use of the term *disadvantaged* more frequently refers to these populations.

Appropriate Designation

Should the gifted among this group be called culturally "disadvantaged," "different," "deprived," or "diverse"? Several writers (Baldwin, 1978; Passow, 1972; Renzulli, 1971; Sato, 1974) have supported the notion by Frost and Hawkes (1971) that the real war should not be an attack on the jargon but rather a systematic effort that is focused on the alleviation of the problems that are denying large segments of disadvantaged populations the right to be recognized for their potential to achieve.

Despite the valiant efforts of researchers such as Torrance (1974) to demonstrate that differences are not necessarily deficits, Good and Brophy (1977) observed, for example, that "a remarkable number of otherwise well-informed people believe that most of the disadvantaged are blacks and that most blacks are disadvantaged or both" (p. 197).

Differences should be celebrated for their contribution to diversity, the very trait that has brought gifted children to our attention. The challenge in educating disadvantaged gifted youth should be to develop potential, not to wish conformity to one model of giftedness with all else being deficient.

Identification

Identification of disadvantaged gifted individuals is the area that has received the most attention. Some of the more important research in this area has been that conducted by Taylor and Ellison (1966/1968), Grant and Renzulli (1971), Torrance (1971), Bruch (1971), Stallings (1972), Meeker and Meeker (1973), Bernal and Reyna (1974), Mercer (1978), and Gay (1978).

The Alpha Biographical Inventory developed by Taylor and his associates (1966/1968) is a 300-item life experience inventory that has proven to be useful in identifying gifted individuals among the disadvantaged population. Significant among the findings from research studies involving this inventory are indications that there are no racial differences on the creativity index and quite small racial differences on the academic index.

Grant and Renzulli (1971) developed the Sub-Cultural Indices of Academic Potential (SCIAP), now called Relevant Aspects of Potential (RAP) (Grant, 1974). On this inventory students indicate how they feel about themselves and how they would react in situations that are common to their everyday experiences. The instrument yields a profile indicative of high potential among minority group students.

The analysis of results from 20 independent studies of the effects of race and socioeconomic status on performance on the Torrance Tests of Creative Thinking indicated that there was either no difference or difference in favor of the culturally different groups (Torrance, 1971). Disadvantaged groups tended especially to excel on figural tests.

The Abbreviated Binet for Disadvantaged (ABDA) devised by Bruch (1971) yields a score derived from selected items in the Stanford-Binet that are biased toward disadvantaged Black children. Culture specific indications of giftedness among native Spanish speaking Mexican Americans have been the subject of research conducted by Bernal and Reyna (1975). Gay (1978) is doing similar research with Black children.

Stallings (1972) has developed an instrument that can be used to discover giftedness among urban children whose experiences are limited by an 8 to 10 block radius in their community. Called the Stallings' Environmentally Based Screen (SEBS), the goal is to identify gifted children based on their ability to respond to environmental matters.

Two especially promising procedures have been pursued by Meeker and Meeker (1973) and Mercer and Lewis (1978). In their efforts to find a more appropriate way of interpreting the Stanford-Binet results of disadvantaged Black, Chicano, and Anglo boys, Meeker and Meeker (1973) developed a Test of Learning Abilities that would yield specific patterns of strengths and weaknesses based on Structure of Intellect (SOI) analyses.

Mercer and Lewis (1978) were concerned with the development of procedure to identify disadvantaged gifted children that allows their performance to be compared with their own sociocultural group. The System of Multicultural Pluralistic Assessment (SOMPA) is based on the notion that one's own sociocultural group is a more appropriate yardstick for determining whether performance is below normal, normal, or supranormal.

CREATING AN EFFECTIVE LEARNING ENVIRONMENT

A problem that still remains is one that relates to the attitudes and values held by teachers of these children.

Frasier (1977) suggested that administrators and teachers can work together to destroy this negative association by demonstrating a commitment to:

1. *Accept* the fact that all children from disadvantaged backgrounds are not deficient in their ability to achieve academically; that some *can* be found who deviate upward from the behavior of the nongifted within their groups.
2. *Recognize* observable indications of potential giftedness among this population. Findings from a study by Glaser and Ross (1970) will help with this problem, for they identified several qualities that distinguish gifted disadvantaged children and youth from their nongifted peers.

3. *Search* for gifted children from among disadvantaged populations with a specified goal (e.g., the location of 3% to 5% of a disadvantaged population as gifted).
4. *Plan* educational experiences that allow gifted disadvantaged children to develop skills not provided by their environment such as test taking and study habits.
5. *Develop* appropriate guidance and other ancillary serves to help these pupils with affective matters such as peer, family, and [self] attitudes toward them as "being different" and the recognition of options (Passow, 1972, p. 30).

Appropriate Educational Programming

Many factors unique to disadvantaged gifted children should be considered when planning appropriate educational experiences for them. Several writers (Baldwin, 1978; Blanning, 1978; Passow, 1972; Renzulli, 1971; Sato, 1974; Stallings, 1972; Torrance, 1977; Witt, 1971; Wrightstone, 1960) have addressed themselves to the general issue of building on strengths rather than weaknesses.

A combined counseling and instructional approach seems to work best to upgrade academic skills and help develop the personal skills of self direction and control. Such an approach should have among its objectives the development of (a) communication skills of reading, writing, listening, and questioning; (b) skills that enhance the ability to distinguish between relevant and irrelevant information; (c) questioning skills for seeking assistance not readily available in the home, the community, and the school; and (d) familiarity with information sources that could provide options not readily apparent or considered.

Two strategies that are especially appropriate in this respect are Decision Making Skills for Life Planning (DLP) (Frasier, 1974) and Future Problem Solving Bowl (Torrance, 1976).

The rationale behind the DLP is embedded in Bloom's Taxonomy. However, it begins by combining "knowledge of self" activities with analysis and evaluation activities. The premise is that disadvantaged gifted youth, especially, must be assisted in recognizing and understanding what they know about themselves and their abilities and how this information affects decisions that they make about their future. Through a series of structured steps they are led to the establishment of their own directions. The teacher serves as a supportive facilitator. DLP is based on the fact that at critical junctures during their formative years, the individual learns how to ask: Who am I? Where am I going? How will I get there? How will I evaluate my progress toward a goal? This is the individual who is developing the skills necessary to take charge of his or her own future. This type of approach is critical to helping disadvantaged students examine the options available to them. It also helps them plan how to take advantage of those options without sacrificing either self or culture.

The procedure is as follows:
1. Using the song "I've Gotta Be Me" and the poem *A Dream Deferred* by Langston Hughes, students are led in a discussion of the possible fates of dreams.
2. The next step involves an analysis of the student's present ability to make decisions. They examine their powers within the setting of their home, their school, and their community.
3. Then, using exercises from Simon, Howe, and Kirschenbaum (1972), they are assisted in understanding their personal wishes, beliefs, and values. In addition, they are assisted in describing the kind of person they are and then the kind of person they would like to become.
4. Assistance is given in helping each student develop a goal that might be attained in a short period of time.
5. The plan is put into action after they have developed all of the resources—people and things they need to accomplish their goal.
6. Periodic followup is made to see how well the students are doing in meeting the contract they have set with themselves.
7. Evaluation during a followup session is conducted for the purpose of analyzing the behaviors that caused the goal to be met or determining why the goal was not met.

Through this procedure systematic skills are developed that aid these students in making relevant decisions about and for themselves.

Futuring is the science, art, and maybe even game of trying to learn about the future in order to best cope with and live in it (Agel, 1974). Developing appropriate skills for anticipating and coping with the future is a critical need of disadvantaged gifted children, for often they can quickly be consumed by attitudes of apathy or indifference when the future appears hopeless. Future Problem Solving, an approach developed by Torrance (1976), is a technique that is recommended to teach disadvantaged students the skills they need to anticipate and solve problems of the future.

Future problem solving would allow gifted disadvantaged children to practice the much needed skills for imagining, exploring, and rehearsing both imaginable and unimaginable events related to the problems they may face in realizing goals.

A Final Word

These final points are offered as information that should be followed or considered when developing curricula for the disadvantaged gifted child:

1. The fact that a family is economically disabled does not necessarily mean that love and affection do not prevail in the home. The poor, ragged child may be rich in love and affection, which are significant determinants of school success.
2. Bereiter and Engelmann (1966) pointed out that low income children do not necessarily suffer from sensory deprivation or a lack of stimulation. They are surrounded by sensory stimulation. What they may lack are experiences that have definite educational value and that lay the groundwork for future academic growth.
3. Ginsburg (1972) reminded us that in many fundamental ways poor children's cognition is quite similar to that of middle class children. He maintained that there are cognitive universals or modes of language and thought shared by all children. There may exist social class differences in cognition, yet these differences are rather superficial. One must not make the mistake of calling them deficiencies.
4. According to Labov, Cohen, Robins, and Lewis (cited in Ginsburg, 1972), language is merely one element of a cultural orientation that clashes with the school's values, and it is the conflict, not a deficit in language, which largely accounts for poor performance in school.
5. Finally, Ausubel (1964) succinctly pointed out that "frequently the best way of motivating an unmotivated pupil is to ignore his motivational state for the time being and to concentrate on teaching him as effectively as possible. Much to his surprise and to his teacher's, he will learn despite his lack of motivation; and from the satisfaction of learning he will characteristically develop the motivation to learn more" (p. 17).

Only in recent years have the gifted and talented among disadvantaged populations received the deliberate attention of educators. The problem has been one of identification, and then of appropriate education. Previous remediation approaches exemplify the first part of the old Chinese proverb (cited in Tripp, 1970), "Give a man a fish, and you feed him for a day." Future problem solving and decision making skills exemplify the option expressed in the last line of this proverb, "Teach a man to fish, and you feed him for a lifetime." Use of these types of approaches would allow disadvantaged gifted children and youth the opportunity to develop commensurate with their above average potential.

References

Agel, J. Futuring: Is today the tomorrow you planned yesterday? *Learning: The Magazine for Creative Teaching.* February 1974, pp. 41–42; 55–56.

Ausubel, D. P. How reversible are the cognitive and motivational effects of cultural deprivation? Implications for teaching the culturally deprived child. *Urban Education,* 1964, *1,* 16–38.

Baldwin, A. Y. Introduction. In A. Y. Baldwin, G. H. Gear, & L. J. Lucito (Eds.) *Educational planning for the gifted: Overcoming cultural, geographic, and socioeconomic barriers.* Reston VA: The Council for Exceptional Children, 1978.

Bereiter, C., & Engelmann, S. *Teaching disadvantaged children in the preschool.* New York, NY: Prentice-Hall, 1966.

Bernal, E. B., & Reyna, J. Analysis and identification of giftedness in Mexican American children: A pilot study. In B. O. Boston (Ed.), *A resource manual of information on educating the gifted and talented.* Reston, VA: The Council for Exceptional Children, 1975.

Blanning, J. M. Gifted adolescents in urban independent study programs. In *Ideas for urban/rural gifted/talented: Case histories and program plans.* Ventura, CA: Ventura County Superintendent of Schools, 1978.

Brickman, W. M., & Lehrer, S. *Education and the many faces of the disadvantaged: Cultural and historical perspectives.* New York, NY: Wiley, 1972.

Bruch, C. B. Modifications of procedures for identification of the disadvantaged gifted. *Gifted Child Quarterly,* 1971, *15,* 267–272.

Frasier, M. M. (1974). Decision-making skills for life planning (DLP). *Talents and Gifts,* 1974, *17*(1), 25–26.

Frasier, M. M. *Help for organizing productive experiences (HOPE) for the culturally diverse gifted and talented.* Athens, GA: University of Georgia, 1977. (ERIC Document Reproduction Service No. Ed 141 981)

Frost, J. L., & Hawkes, G. R. *The disadvantaged child: Issues and innovations* (2nd ed.). Boston: Houghton-Mifflin, 1971.

Gay, J. E. A proposed plan for identifying black gifted children. *Gifted Child Quarterly,* 1978, *22,* 353–360.

Ginsburg, H. *Myths of the deprived child: Poor children's intellect and education.* Englewood Cliffs, NJ: Prentice-Hall, 1972.

Glaser, E. M., & Ross, H. L. *A study of successful persons from seriously disadvantaged backgrounds* (Final Report, Office of Special Manpower Programs, Contract No. 82-05-68-03). Washington, DC: US Department of Labor, March 1970.

Good, T. L, & Brophy, J. E. *Educational Psychology: A realistic approach.* New York, NY: Holt, Rinehart & Winston, 1977.

Grant, T. E. *Relevant aspects of potential.* Marlborough, CT: RAP Researchers, 1974.

Grant, T. E., & Renzulli, J. S. *Subcultural indices of academic potential.* Storrs, CT: The University of Connecticut, 1971.

Jenkins, M. D. (1948). The upper limit of ability among American Negroes. *Scientific Monthly,* 1948, *66,* 339–401.

McClelland, D. C. *Talent and society.* New York, NY: Van Nostrand-Reinhold Books, 1958.

Meeker, M., & Meeker, R. Strategies for assessing intellectual patterns in Black, Anglo, and Mexican-American boys—or any other children—and implications for education. *Journal of School Psychology,* 1973, *11,* 341–350.

Mercer, J. B., & Lewis, J. G. Using the system of multicultural assessment (SOMPA) to identify the gifted minority child. In A. Y. Baldwin, G. H. Gear, & L. J. Lucito (Eds.), *Educational planning for the gifted: Overcoming cultural, geographic and socioeconomic barriers*. Reston, VA: The Council for Exceptional Children, 1978.

Passow, H. A. The gifted and the disadvantaged. *The National Elementary Principal, 1972, 51*, 22–31.

Reissman, F. *The culturally deprived gifted*. New York, NY: Harper & Row, 1962.

Renzulli, J. S. Talent potential in minority groups students. *Exceptional Children*, 1971, *39*, 437–444.

Sato, I. S. The culturally different gifted child—The dawning of his day? *Exceptional Children*, 1974, *40*, 572–576.

Simon, S. B., Howe, L. W., & Kirschenbaum, H. *Values clarification: A handbook of practical strategies for teachers and students*. New York, NY: Hart, 1972.

Stallings, G. *Gifted disadvantaged children* (Technical paper). Storrs, CT: The University of Connecticut, March 1972.

Taylor, C. W., & Ellison, R. L. *Manual for alpha biographical inventory*. Salt Lake City, UT: Institute for Behavioral Research in Creativity, 1966. (Revised, 1968.)

Torrance, E. P. Are the Torrance Tests of Creative Thinking biased against or in favor of disadvantaged groups? *Gifted Child Quarterly*, 1971, *15*, 75–80.

Torrance, E. P. Differences are not deficits. *Teachers College Record*, 1974, *75*, 472–487.

Torrance, E. P. *Handbook for training future problem solving teams and conducting future problem solving bowls*. Athens, GA: Georgia Studies of Creative Behavior, February 1976.

Torrance, E. P. *Discovery and nurturance of giftedness in the culturally different*. Reston, VA: The Council for Exceptional Children, 1977.

Tripp, R. T. *The international thesaurus of quotations*. New York, NY: Crowell, 1970.

Witt, G. The life enrichment activity program, inc.: A continuing program for creative, disadvantaged children. *Journal of Research and Development in Education*, 1971, *4*(3), 67–73.

Witty, P., & Jenkins, M. D. The educational achievement of a group of gifted Negro children. *Journal of Educational Psychology*, 1934, *45*, 589–597.

Wrightstone, J. W. (1960). Demonstration guidance project in New York City. *Harvard Educational Review*, 1960, *30*, 3.

MARY M. FRASIER *is Assistant Professor, Educational Psychology, and Co-coordinator, Programs for the Gifted, University of Georgia, Athens.*

CHAPTER 2

I'm Black but Look at Me, I Am Also Gifted

Alexinia Y. Baldwin
State University of New York at Albany

Abstract

The lack of representation of black gifted children in educational programs for the gifted is a cause for great concern. Historical precedents and lack of empirical data on appropriate identification processes and educational planning techniques have been noted as part of the reason for the lack. A discussion of research data to date indicates that observation techniques, community involvement, and peer, parent, and teacher nominations are viable techniques to use in identifying the black gifted child. The data also show that leadership skills, creativity, and mental processing abilities, are good indicators of giftedness among the black students. Identification, curriculum, the instructional environment (teacher, setting, strategies), and evaluation are discussed as important aspects of a total plan for the black gifted child. Alternatives for program planning are recommended.

Problem in Perspective

The low representation of black children in programs for the gifted is a frustrating phenomenon. Heritability reasons for this condition have been alluded to by persons such as Jensen (1969) and Eysenck (1973). However, research by

Reprinted from Baldwin, A.Y. (1987). I'm Black but look at me, I am also gifted. *Gifted Child Quarterly, 31*, 180–185. Reprinted with permission of Sage Publications.

Baldwin (1977), Hilliard (1976), and Torrance (1971) shows that IQ and achievement tests cannot be depended upon to assess the capabilities of these children. There are many intervening variables which are rooted in historical and environmental precursors. Variables such as socioeconomic deprivation, cultural diversity, social and geographic isolation, and a relative perception of powerlessness, require assessment or identification techniques which cut across these variables to locate the hidden talents of the black child.

According to a report on poverty (one of the intervening variables) Malcolm (1985) indicates that 48 percent of all black children live in poverty and they represent 32 percent of all poor children. This startling statistic highlights the importance of using restructured processes for locating and developing abilities of gifted black children. The task is not an easy one because a single answer regarding characteristics or required curriculum cannot be generalized to all black students. The experiential groupings within the black ethnic structure are quite diverse although the common ingredients of parentage or physical features identify the individual as black. These common ingredients have compounded the effects of the intervening variables listed above.

Historically, giftedness among black students has been a long-standing concern. The need to recognize and develop the giftedness of blacks was a concern of black leaders who were early agents of change. During the late 19th and early 20th centuries, Booker T. Washington and W.E.B. DuBois espoused philosophies which placed emphases on developing the talents and gifts of black students. DuBois (1903) talked about the "talented tenth" and strongly urged that identification and development of this talent be pursued with vigor. His philosophy reflected a concern for the development of academic abilities; whereas Washington's (1900) often repeated statement, "Cast down your buckets where you are," reflected his philosophical approach highlighting the need to develop academic as well as creative and other non-academic specific talents. Historians have tried to draw sharp distinctions between these two educators, but while they differed in their philosophical emphases, their common concern was the recognition and nurturance of the potential or evidenced ability of black people—a group of Americans who were struggling to develop and overcome the indignities that had been imposed upon them through the centuries.

Related Research

During the first half of the twentieth century, concern for or interest in the black gifted child within institutions of public education was practically non-existent. Although studies by Witty and Jenkins (1934–36) and by Proctor (1929) indicated that giftedness existed among black students, very little systematic planning or research to include these children in gifted programs occurred whether

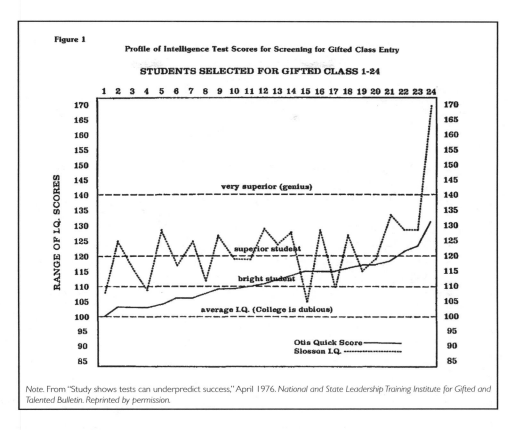

Note. From "Study shows tests can underpredict success," April 1976. *National and State Leadership Training Institute for Gifted and Talented Bulletin.* Reprinted by permission.

they were housed in segregated or integrated school systems. Theories and concepts regarding the identification of gifted black students have been proposed, but there is a dearth of empirical studies from which to draw for decision-making purposes. Studies that are cited in this article represent a cross-section of reported data regarding identification and educational planning for gifted students.

Federal funds that became available during the mid-sixties for innovative educational programming provided an opportunity for the development of a program for gifted black elementary students (Baldwin, 1977). Longitudinal data from this program highlight the importance of alternative approaches to locating and providing educational experiences for gifted black children.

Figure 1 shows a profile of the IQ scores of 24 fifth grade boys and girls who were selected from a pool of 100 black children representing six schools within a large southern city in 1966. The Otis Quick Scoring Mental Abilities Test was the first source of IQ scores. Paragraph meaning, arithmetic, and word meaning scores of the Stanford Achievement tests taken at the end of the fourth grade were used. Those students scoring 100 IQ or above on the Otis-Lennon Quick Score IQ Test plus those showing grade equivalent scores (GE) of 3.5 or above on the achievement tests were placed in the identification pool. The Slosson Intelligence Test was

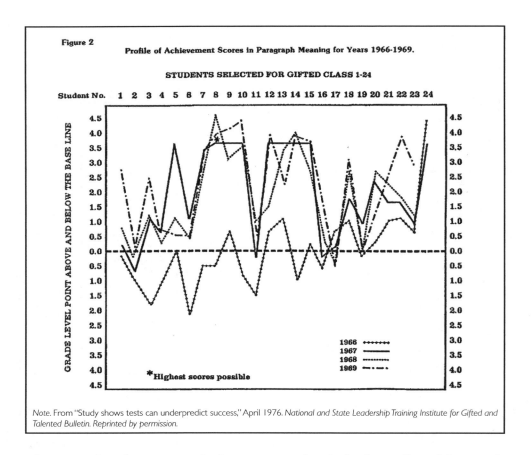

Note. From "Study shows tests can underpredict success," April 1976. *National and State Leadership Training Institute for Gifted and Talented Bulletin.* Reprinted by permission.

administered to the entire pool of nominees, and with the data collected from each of these sources, 24 students were selected. The age range was 9.5–10.7. The IQ scores ranged from 100 to 160+ with a GE range from 2.5–4.0. Strict adherence to the scores, which are represented in Figure 1, would have eliminated all but two or three of the students because the city-wide cut-off IQ score for programs for the gifted was 132.

Figure 2 shows the achievement scores in paragraph meaning which were used as part of the identification process in 1966. It is obvious by the line representation for 1966 that many of these children were working far below grade level. Lines on the graph representing subsequent years indicate the outstanding change in achievement of approximately 19 out of the 24 students and the evidence of improved achievement for all of them. The original IQ scores did not indicate this type of potential. A six-year follow-up study indicated that all of the students were in college in various parts of the country with some on substantial scholarships. The educational awards earned by this group included a first place award in a national science competition, a senior year scholarship to study in France, and National Merit Award first and second place winners.

As has been illustrated in the preceding case study, the use of designated score ranges on the IQ or achievement tests as the only criteria for giftedness can significantly affect the black child's ranking for inclusion in programs for the gifted. In this case the use of criteria other than IQ scores proved to be effective.

Hilliard (1976) proposed the use of behavioral styles found in music, religion, and language as vehicles through which intelligence among black children can be discovered. The theoretical framework for his proposition was taken from the behavioral styles research of Cohen (1971) and Shapiro (1965). The item answers on the prescreening test which Hilliard designed clustered around behavioral characteristics usually associated with giftedness. Among these characteristics were alertness, confidence, sense of humor, expressiveness, verbal creativity, and risk-taking. Hilliard's research suggests that these characteristics can be significant indicators of high level ability.

Another attempt to identify black students was done by Davis (1978). Although longitudinal data to verify the effectiveness of this technique are not yet available, Davis has presented a strong argument for community-based identification. A development framework for nomination was designed for black and white community persons to use as one aspect of the identification process. Fifteen students were nominated by this process and placed in programs for the gifted. The areas of giftedness identified for these children included psychosocial ability; talent specific areas such as math, science, or music; and general cognitive processing ability separately or in combination with other abilities. The report of the study indicated that these students were quite successful in the educational experiences which were planned for them. Davis' small study capitalized on the importance of a significant identification strategy which is often overlooked in school; that is, using community recommendations regarding the giftedness of students.

Analysis of data gathered on an identification process used for 205 black students in the Washington, DC area was reported by Blackshear (1979). She found that nominations from peers, parents, and teachers were most predictive of selection for the program. Of those who were successful and continued in the program after one year, the strongest predictor variable was creative thinking. Items used on the identification matrix for this group of students included informal creative thinking tests, reading and math tests, school grades, and peer, parent, and teacher nominations.

Along these same lines, Dabney (1980) reported in a four year study of black adolescents, that among those children identified as gifted, high level leadership skills appeared to be most predictive of success in the program for the gifted and in their ability to meet college entry requirements at prestigious colleges.

The role of observation strategies for identifying gifted black students has not been fully explored; however, observation of everyday performances as these children interact with their peer group or environment in school and outside of school, can play an important role in the identification process of black gifted children. This assumption has not been verified by controlled research techniques; however, corroborating information from black teachers who have observed black students in class and an analysis of the relationship of these sample behaviors in relation to existing intelligence models, lend credence to the assumption.

An indication of intellectual acuity, for example, can be demonstrated in the child's ability to understand and explain relationships using content common to the child's environment. An elaborate story told in non-standard English might not be acceptable as evidence of ability; unfortunately, the focus becomes the English usage, not the detailed plot or figurative language ability displayed. High levels of intellectual processing abilities such as divergent production, transformation of a variety of content, and flexibility of thought can, for example, be displayed through the ability to use commonplace items for purposes other than what they were intended. The ability to recall and accurately report detailed information on events which occurred in the community can be a sign of high levels of memory skills and the ability to organize and classify information. These are just a few examples of observable performances that can be used as indicators of exceptional ability. A table of common descriptors (Baldwin, 1985) and a supplemental checklist (Baldwin, 1984) have been designed to help observers recognize behaviors that can be indicative of intellectual acuity.

The black gifted child might bring to the learning environment many skill weaknesses, but he or she might also have strengths which could be used to develop the skills necessary for continued development of all of their abilities. The use of familiar experiences to encourage the growth of abilities in order to accomplish the goals of the curriculum will be crucial.

Music or graphic arts might be the child's area of interest or strength. Cognitive skills in area such as math, science, language development, or history, and skills in research techniques, or synthesis of information can be generated through music or the arts. For junior high students, for instance, parallels in politics and the changing characteristics of jazz can afford a great motivation for the development of basic skills. Students can be challenged to find connections or parallels between the type of political or economic atmosphere (conservative or liberal; depression or boom) and "raw or cool jazz." They can be encouraged to listen to recordings of jazz to determine differences and to search the literature for historical landmarks in politics and economics. As was stated in a previous article (Baldwin, Gear, and Lucito, 1978),

> I think it is important to explain that our goals for the population concerned here are both cognitive and affective in nature. It is imperative that we plan precisely for these children because we have assumed that there are gaps in their previous school train-

ing, and new plans should involve them in a vertical movement in acquiring knowledge while involving them in a horizontal movement where they increase depth of knowledge. (p. 19)

The teaching strategies, the teacher, and the environment are important aspects of the program for the black gifted child. The attitude of the teacher is a crucial element in the child's development. This attitude must be one which is free of prejudice or preconceived stereotypes. There must be acceptance of the child as person who is potentially capable of high achievement. Teachers will need training in recognizing and interpreting these behavioral patterns and the relationship of these patterns to giftedness.

Educational Planning

The discussion in this article is not intended to suggest that there is a distinct and totally different program which should be designed for black gifted students. It is intended to show how important it is that program planning, from identification through evaluation of the student, integrate those aspects that are necessary to recognize and enhance the abilities of the black gifted child.

After the process of identification has taken place the appropriate educational plan for the black gifted child that includes the same elements of a design for all children, is crucial. To operationalize a plan, attention must be given to each element of the total program framework and the relationship of this plan to the needs of this population. This framework includes: (1) Defining the Population—identification; (2) Deciding the Goals—curriculum; (3) Instructional System—teaching strategies, the teacher, the environment; (4) Evaluation—quality of program, processes, and products.

The first concern in developing curriculum for the gifted black child is that it must be differentiated as for all gifted students. Within this context, the curriculum and instructional system, which are designed to meet the needs of the black gifted child will be reflected in the plans designed for all gifted students. Differentiation will focus upon more depth and breadth in content, process, product, and teaching strategies. Further ideas for differentiation can be found in Maker (1982a, 1982b) and Kaplan (1986).

The integration of personal development goals such as improved self-concept is important for a program for the gifted. Exum and Colangelo (1979) have recommended the use of a Black Identity Facilitation (BIF) model which includes several components which other programs often ignore. The model includes a cognitive portion which represents a psychohistorical examination of the black experience, a developmental reading portion which includes readings which refer to black gifted children, and laboratory experiences which examine cross-cultural interactions. Along these lines, Frasier and McCannon (1981) have recommended the use of bibliotherapy which involves children in reading about characters much like themselves in race and socioeconomic levels, who have made significant accomplishments.

The next important aspect of teacher behavior is the ability to understand and to have a higher level of tolerance for behavioral characteristics which don't fit the usual conception of giftedness. The teacher must also play a leadership role in developing harmony and acceptance among the children within the classroom. The teacher must be accepting but also plan with the students to set criteria and expectancies for cognitive and non-cognitive behaviors.

The evaluation of the success of activities and student development must, in the case of the black gifted child, be primarily formative. Formative evaluation will give the teacher a chance to adjust or alter procedures to meet the needs of the black child. This evaluation must not be solely dependent upon grades achieved but on a combination of behaviors which are important in the total development of the child. It is important that the children themselves become contributors to the evaluation process.

Conclusion

The problem of finding and meeting the needs of the black gifted child, as discussed in the preceding paragraphs, has highlighted the importance of additional research and application of appropriate processes for identifying gifted black children. The importance of the role of the teacher and the environment in which the black child will be placed has also been stressed. Although it is important that generalizations not be made for all black children who might be gifted, a good understanding of the variables which might intervene in the process of providing the appropriate educational environment for these children is important. The experience of black gifted students within the total grouping of gifted students should be one where aspects of the black culture will be a part of the lesson explored by all of the children. When ethnic groups have knowledge and understanding of another cultural group, the self-concept and sphere of experience for all groups is broadened and enriched. It is clear that there is a need for an increased understanding of the large pool of gifted or potentially gifted black children who need encouragement and guidance in the development of their abilities.

References

Baldwin, A. Y. (1977). Tests do underpredict: A case study. *Phi Delta Kappan, 58*(8), 620–621.

Baldwin, A. Y. (1984). *The Baldwin Identification Matrix 2 for the identification of the gifted and talented: A handbook for its use.* New York, NY: Trillium Press.

Baldwin, A. Y. (1985). Programs for the gifted and talented: Issues concerning minority populations. In F. D. Horowitz & M. O'Brien (Eds.), *The gifted and talented: Developmental perspectives* (pp. 223–247). Washington, DC: American Psychological Association.

Baldwin, A. Y., Gear, G., & Lucito, L. (Eds.). (1978). *Educational planning for the gifted: Overcoming cultural, geographic, and socio-economic barriers.* Reston, VA: Council for Exceptional Children.

Blackshear, P. (1979). *A comparison of peer nomination and teacher nomination in the identification of the academically gifted, black, primary level student.* Unpublished doctoral dissertation, University of Maryland, College Park.

Cohen, R. (1971). *The influence of conceptual role-sets on measures of learning ability. Race and intelligence.* Washington, DC: American Anthropological Association.

Dabney, M. (1980). *The Black adolescent: Focus upon the creative positives,* Paper presented at the annual meeting of the Council for Exceptional Children, Philadelphia, PA. (ERIC Document Reproduction Service No. ED 189 767).

Davis, P. (1978). *Community-based efforts to increase the identification of the number of gifted minority children.* Ypsilanti, MI: Eastern Michigan College of Education. (ERIC Document Reproduction Service No. ED 176 487).

DuBois, W. E. B. (1903). The talented tenth. In *The Negro Problem.* New York, NY: James Pott Company.

Eysenck, H. L. (1973). *Measurement of intelligence.* Lancaster, England: Medical and Technical Publishing Company Ltd.

Exum, H., & Colangelo, N. (1979). Enhancing self-concept with gifted black students. *Roeper Review, 1,* 5–6.

Frasier, M., & McCannon, C. (1981). Using bibliotherapy with gifted children. *Gifted Child Quarterly, 25,* 81–85.

Hilliard, A. G. (1976). *Alternative to IQ testing: An approach to the identification of the gifted "minority" children* (Report No. 75 175). San Francisco, CA: San Francisco State University. (ERIC Document Reproduction Service No. ED 147 009).

Jensen, A. (1969). How much can we boost IQ and scholastic achievement? *Harvard Educational Review, 39,* 1–123.

Kaplan, S. (1986). Qualitatively differentiated curricula. In C. J. Maker (Ed.), *Critical issues in gifted education: Defensible programs for the gifted* (pp. 121–134). Rockville, MD: Aspen Publishers.

Maker, C. J. (1982a). *Curriculum development for the gifted.* Rockville, MD: Aspen Publishers.

Maker, C. J. (1982b). *Teaching models in education of the gifted.* Rockville, MD: Aspen Publishers.

Meeker, M. & Meeker, R. (1979). *SOI Learning Abilities Test* (rev. ed.). El Segundo, CA: SOI Institute.

Malcolm, A. A. (1985, October 20). Poverty: New class of youthful poor, less educated, politically silent. *New York Times,* p. B5.

Proctor, L. (1929). *A case study of thirty superior colored children of Washington, D.C.* Unpublished master's thesis, University of Chicago, IL.

Shapiro, D. (1965). *Neurotic styles.* New York, NY: Basic Books.

Torrance, E. P. (1971). Are the Torrance tests of creative thinking biased against or in favor "of disadvantaged groups?" *Gifted Child Quarterly, 15,* 75–80.

Washington, B. T. (1971). *Up from slavery: An autobiography* (rev. ed.). Williamstown, MA: Comer House Publishers.

Witty, P. & Jenkins, M. (1934). The educational achievement of a group of gifted Negro children. *Journal of Educational Psychology, 25,* 585–597.

CHAPTER 3

Desegregating Gifted Education: A Need Unmet

Donna Y. Ford
The University of Virginia

Abundant data suggest that gifted programs are the most segregated educational programs in the United States. Minority children, particularly African Americans, economically disadvantaged students, and underachievers are severely underrepresented in gifted programs but overrepresented in special education programs for the learning disabled, behaviorally disordered, and mentally retarded. The author advocates that concerted efforts must be launched by educators and parents to ensure that African American students who exhibit exceptional talent receive the education to which they are entitled. After discussing the conditions that have led to this underrepresentation, this article suggests ways to desegregate gifted education programs and redress educational inequities in this area. It then appraises the promise and effectiveness of contemporary definitions of giftedness, theories of intelligence, and assessment practices in identifying a more representative array of students for gifted programs. Finally, the article discusses what is required to retain more African American students in gifted programs.

Few educators would disagree that the 1954 *Brown v. Board of Education of Topeka, Kansas* decision represents the most significant U.S. Supreme Court ruling on equal educational opportunity. Indeed, as Russo, Ford, and Harris (1993) maintain, it is the very cornerstone of all subsequent legal developments ensuring the rights of disenfranchised groups in the past 40 years. In the absence of any specific controlling Supreme Court precedent or mandatory federal legislation entitlements, however, one can only extrapolate the implications of *Brown* for gifted education. Abundant data suggest that gifted programs are the most segregated educational programs in this nation, and that concerted efforts must be made to ensure that minority students, economically disadvantaged students, underachievers, and other nontraditional students receive the education to which they are entitled.

Recent years have seen increased attention and efforts devoted to identifying and placing minority students in gifted education programs. This response reflects an insistence in the professional and scholarly literature that minority children, particularly African American children, are severely underrepresented in gifted programs (Alamprese & Erlanger, 1988; Ford & Harris, 1991; Richert, 1987; U.S. Department of Education, 1993), but overrepresented or overenrolled in special education programs for the learning disabled, behaviorally disordered, and mentally retarded (Chinn & Selma, 1987; Kunjufu, 1993; Patton, 1992).

The most far-reaching legislation affecting gifted education thus far has been the Jacob K. Javits Gifted and Talented Students Act of 1988, the passage of which marked the culmination of the efforts of many dedicated gifted education proponents. The Javits Act provides both financial assistance to state and local educational agencies charged with developing and maintaining gifted programs, and it gives highest priority to the identification of gifted racial minority, economically disadvantaged, limited-English-proficient, and disabled students. Despite the altruistic prescience of this legislation, a disconcerting underrepresentation of nontraditional students persists in gifted programs. For example, in 1993, the U.S. Department of Education (USDE) noted that African American males were disproportionately placed in special education programs, more so than any other racial or ethnic group. Earlier, Alamprese and Erlanger (1988) reported that African American males were three times more liable than White American males to be placed in classes for the mentally retarded, and one-half less likely to appear in gifted programs. Taking a national perspective, they also reported that whereas approximately 16% of the U.S. school population was African American, African Americans comprised only 8% of gifted programs.

Several reasons help explain the dearth of African Americans in public school programs for the gifted. Among these are: abstract and disparate definitions of giftedness, inequitable practices of identifying gifted students, educators' lack of understanding about cultural differences in learning styles and achievement aspirations, inadequate preparation of teachers to recognize giftedness among students from diverse cultural backgrounds, the lack of encouragement given to African American parents to become involved in the processes related to identification and selection of students for gifted education, definitions of underachievement that are particularly disparaging to African American students, and a paucity of funding and funding sources for efforts aimed at making the gifted education population look more like America.

This article begins by focusing on the issues surrounding the underrepresentation of African American students in gifted education programs, positing various explanations for this phenomenon. It further suggests ways to address the problem—that is, how to "desegregate" gifted programs and otherwise redress inequities in this area of education. These suggestions range from the application of new definitions and theories of giftedness to the implementation of promising new identification and assessment practices that might serve to increase the numbers of African American students who can benefit from the enhanced opportunities gifted education provides. Lastly, recommendations for retaining African American students in gifted programs will be offered.

Factors in the Underrepresentation Equation

Definitions of Giftedness

Definitions of giftedness abound, but little consensus exists regarding how best to define the term. Cassidy and Hossler (1992) note that most states continue to follow the federal government's 1978 or older definitions of "gifted" outright or in modified form. The 1978 definition describes gifted students as those who possess demonstrated or potential ability, intellectually or creatively, in specific academic areas, the performing or visual arts, and leadership. It succeeded a 1972 USDE definition that included psychomotor ability as a category of giftedness. Thirty states have made no definitional revisions in at least a decade, and only 15 had made revisions in the last five years (Cassidy & Hossler, 1992).

The most encouraging aspect of the federal definition is its inclusion of the "potentially" gifted among those to be considered for exceptional educational regard. It thus appears to recognize the need to serve those students who have yet to manifest their gifts for various reasons—that is, gifted students who might otherwise go unrecognized. These students tend to include underachievers, minority students, economically disadvantaged students, learning and behaviorally disordered students, and disabled students who might not be identified and placed in gifted programs whose definitions of giftedness rely primarily on student scores on standardized intelligence or achievement tests. As Ford, Harris, and Winborne (1990) and Patton (1992) contend, such instruments often fail to capture the true abilities of these students.

A major shortcoming of the USDE definition is that students whose gifts lie in other areas may still be overlooked. For instance, Gardner's (1983) theory of "multiple intelligences" proposes at least seven types of intelligence, five of which are not measured by traditional standardized or norm-referenced tests. According to Gardner, only two types of intelligence, logical-mathematical and linguistic intelligence, are measured by such tests. The other five forms—interpersonal, intrapersonal, bodily-kinesthetic, spatial, and musical intelligence—are not. A related concern associated with defining giftedness is that the states that apply the USDE definitions tend to focus their searches on students who display gifts in the intellectual and specific academic ability areas as opposed to those whose strengths reside in the creative, visual and performing arts, and leadership areas.

According to Sternberg (1988), the educational needs of many gifted students often go unmet because most states continue to define giftedness from a unidimensional perspective, primarily as a function of high IQ scores. Such unidimensional assessments identify only some students as gifted and miss the rest. This definition also ignores those students who consistently perform poorly on paper-and-pencil tasks and other tests (standardized or not) because of cultural bias, learning style differences, and test anxiety (Cummins, 1989; Ford, Winborne, & Harris, 1991; Hilliard, 1987, 1989). Following Whitmore (1980), Ford (1992) and others have found that many gifted students underachieve because of a lack of effort and poor motivation. This underachievement phenomenon among the gifted appears paradoxical, but as many as 20% of gifted students have been reported to perform poorly in school, drop out, or otherwise fail to reach their academic potential (National Commission on Excellence in Education, 1983).

IDENTIFICATION PRACTICES

School districts often rely solely on norm-referenced intelligence or achievement tests as their primary assessment instruments for determining student placement in gifted programs. VanTassel-Baska, Patton, and Prillaman (1989) report that 88.5% of states rely primarily on such instruments to identify gifted students, including those from underrepresented socioeconomic, racial, and ethnic groups. Multidimensional, multi-modal assessment strategies are utilized much less often, even though numerous researchers have emphasized the importance of these methods (Ford & Harris, 1991; Harris & Ford, 1991; Patton, 1992; Tuttle, Becker, & Sousa, 1988). Moreover, holistic assessment strategies, culturally and learning-style sensitive tests, parent and peer nominations, creativity checklists, student portfolios, and performance assessments have been recognized as promising strategies for identifying underrepresented student populations for gifted programs (Ford & Harris, 1991; Harris & Ford, 1991).

Coleman and Gallagher (1992) note that some, but not all, states have begun to institute several measures to expand the pool of gifted students. These include screening the files of all students for indications of giftedness, requiring staff development of regular education teachers to increase their ability to recognize non-traditional students who may be gifted. Staff development might include training teachers to use checklists, interviews, and autobiographies for additional assistance in identifying giftedness; and to refer students for further assessment if they obtain scores at the 85th percentile or above on standardized tests. Nonetheless, a cut-off number, IQ score, or percentile ranking continues to be the mainstay of identification practices for gifted education placement.

Cultural Differences in Learning Style

A number of researchers have noted differences in learning styles between African American and White American students (i.e., Hilliard, 1989; Dunn & Griggs, 1990). These differences have several implications for giftedness identification and teaching practices. For example, Dunn and Griggs suggest that the extent to which students are global versus analytical, visual versus auditory, highly mobile versus less mobile, or less peer-oriented versus more peer-oriented learners will affect their learning, achievement, motivation, and school performance. If misunderstood, they claim, teachers will not recognize the strengths that African American students bring into the classroom, resulting in decreased opportunities for these students to be recognized and identified as gifted.

Few teachers, particularly those who have taught for some time, have received extensive and continuous preparation in education that is multicultural in its scope. This experiential shortcoming makes it difficult, if not impossible, for teachers to understand the ways in which culturally and racially diverse groups of students manifest their talents and abilities. Research showing that African American students tend to be concrete and global rather than abstract and analytical thinkers, and tend to prefer group rather than individual learning experiences stands in stark contrast to traditional mainstream teaching and testing methods. Those teachers who recognize and accept such differences are more likely to identify gifted African American students than those who perceive such differences as culturally and educationally irrelevant or even detrimental.

The Teacher's Role in the Recognition of Giftedness

Tuttle, Becker, and Sousa (1988) note that the most prevalent method of identifying gifted learners in the U.S. is to ask for teacher recommendations. However, research findings suggest that teachers may not be the most reliable sources for identifying gifted learners, particularly those from culturally or racially diverse groups, and then referring them for gifted programs. Early research by Pegnato and Birch (1959) concludes that junior high school teachers not only failed to nominate over 50% of the gifted students in their school, but they also identified many average students as gifted. According to Jacobs (1971), primary teachers surveyed could identify only 10% of the students who had scored high on individual IQ tests. Cox and Daniel (1985) report that almost 38% of the teachers in their public school sample had unidentified gifted students in their third- and fourth-grade classrooms, the grades at which gifted programs tend to begin. Other studies indicate that teachers frequently emphasize such behaviors as cooperation, answering correctly, punctuality, and neatness when identifying gifted students (Patton, 1992; VanTassel-Baska et al., 1989). Thus, teachers are likely to refer the "model" child for gifted education services.

Issues related to the lack of teacher certification and endorsement in gifted education also arouse concern when discussing equity in this educational arena. Many states lack laws requiring certification for teachers of the gifted. Karnes and Whorton (1991) report that only 5 states have statements of competencies for teachers of gifted education. Half the states, they found, require no teacher certification or endorsement in gifted education, only 14 require practicum experiences, and only 8 require that teachers of the gifted have teaching experience in the regular classroom prior to teaching gifted students; 3 states make training in gifted education optional. Sixty-one percent of the teachers surveyed by Archambault et al. (1993) had received no staff development in the area of gifted education.

Parental Influence and Involvement

Many researchers have concluded that family background and associated parental influences may be the primary forces affecting students' achievement over time, and that parents provide primary sources of information concerning the educational welfare of their children. Ample data indicate that substantive parental involvement in the educational process enhances student achievement (Ford, 1993). Specifically, Karnes, Shwedel, and Steinberg (1984) report that 90% of the parents of gifted children they surveyed involved themselves directly in their children's schooling by taking part in the teacher selection process and in parent organizations.

African American parents, particularly those from low-SES groups, have been shown to face numerous barriers to schooling involvement. Marion (1981) notes Black parents' concern that public school teachers often fail to acknowledge the giftedness within the minority student population. He notes further their apprehension that school personnel may view them with suspicion because they often work in menial occupations, are less affluent, and have lower educational attainment levels and different family values. So many African Americans parents experience such continuous distress regarding their children's education that they have developed what Slaughter and Kuehne (1988) describe as a "crisis of confidence" in the benefits of public education per se (p. 60). Though the majority of African American parents still favor public education, their widespread concern about the schools' treatment of and influence on their children's learning and development often inhibits their participation or presence in formal school settings. These parents tend to further distrust school systems when they become aware of the overrepresentation of African American youth in special education programs. These concerns, real or perceived, cause African American parents to fear that their children stand a better chance of being labeled "trouble makers" than "gifted."

Underachievement and Giftedness

Many factors inhibit gifted students from "acting gifted" and thereby inhibit their very identification. The term "gifted underachiever," while it appears paradoxical, represents a disturbingly high proportion of high school dropouts, with estimates ranging from 10% to 20% (Davis & Rimm, 1989; Lajoie & Shore, 1981). More than half of all gifted students are routinely identified as underachievers (National Commission on Excellence in Education, 1983). However, depending upon which definitions of giftedness and underachievement are utilized, the percentages may be even higher (Ford, 1992).

The many definitions of underachievement that have been applied to gifted students frequently reflect a discrepancy between some standardized measure and actual school performance. Less often has underachievement been defined as a function of effort, even though few would disagree that low effort often begets low achievement. The definitions also assume that only students who score highly on standardized intelligence, ability, or achievement tests, and who perform lower than expected in school (achieving, for example, low grades) are underachievers. By implication, these definitions ignore the fact that many capable learners do not necessarily perform optimally on standardized instruments.

Ford (1991) reports that of the 48 gifted African American students she surveyed, 38 reported exerting low levels of effort in school, and all 38 had been identified as underachievers. Far too many African American children perform poorly in school not because they lack basic intellectual capacities or specific learning skills, but because they have low expectations, feel helpless, blame others, or give up in the face of failure (Tomlinson, 1992).

Minority and poor children may face test bias or experience test anxiety disproportionately (Ford et al., 1990). Well-supported findings suggest that the inherent bias found in standardized tests causes many gifted African American students to produce mediocre or low scores on these measures (Hilliard, 1987). Because test results do not always accurately reflect the ability of gifted African American students, the identification of underachievement becomes more complicated. One wonders what happens to the gifted African American student who scores poorly on such tests, but who is fully capable of performing well in programs for the gifted. This hypothetical student poses a serious educational dilemma when standardized testing is the sine qua non of gifted identification procedures.

The influence of peer pressure on African American students' achievement and effort should also be taken into account. A good deal of data indicate that pressures from peers to forego achievement can undermine the academic success of African

American students. The fear associated with losing friendships and being isolated from peers because of outstanding achievement has been reported to wreak special havoc on the motivation and efforts of gifted African American students (USDE, 1993). According to Tomlinson (1992):

> Peer pressure profoundly influences the academic behavior of students. . . . Typically, peer pressure motivates students to stay in school and graduate, but even as they frown on failure, peers also restrain high achievement. . . . Some student cultures actively reject academic aspirations. In this case, high grades can be a source of peer ridicule; and when effort is hostage to peer pressure, those high achievers who persist may face strong social sanctions. (p. 2)

A lack of consensus also exists over whether underachievement should be assessed by comparing (1) IQ test scores with grades, (2) IQ test scores with ability test scores, (3) achievement test scores with grades, (4) achievement test scores with ability test scores, (5) ability test scores with grades, or (6) any combination of the preceding. Further, a student may be labeled gifted in one state or school district but not in another, depending upon the identification procedures followed or the IQ cut-off scores in a state or school district. Thus, whether a student is identified as gifted or an underachiever is relative and therefore suspect. A child who, based on multidimensional assessment procedures, has a high capacity for achievement, but who exerts a weak effort in school-related tasks, must also be viewed as an underachiever (Ford, 1992).

Like traditional definitions of giftedness, underachievement definitions are usually based on the norms for White middle-class students and, as such, do not necessarily match characteristics common among African American students. This further complicates the arduous task of defining underachievement among the latter group of students. If African American children do not manifest achievement in the same way as White students, they may go unidentified as gifted and/or underachieving. Nevertheless, promising practices and strategies have been described in the research literature regarding strategies to identify and place more representative numbers of African American learners in gifted programs. These practices are described in the following sections.

Recommendations for Desegregating Gifted Programs

Redefining Intelligence and Giftedness

While passé educational definitions and achievement tests ignore this nation's changing demographics and increasing diversity as well as individual and cultural differences among students, at least two recent theories of intelligence and giftedness promise to capture the strengths and abilities of greater numbers of gifted African American learners. Sternberg's (1988) triarchic theory of intelligence proposes that intelligence can be revealed in at least three ways: contextually, experientially, and componentially. Componential learners are analytical and abstract thinkers who do well on standardized tests and in school. Experiential learners value creativity and like to deal with novelty; they dislike rules and have few of their own because they view rules as inconveniences meant to be broken. Contextual learners adapt to their environments, a skill not measured by IQ tests. They are "street smart," socially competent and practical, but they may do poorly in school. They are survivors and fairly unconventional. They dislike others' rules, are indifferent to detail, and enjoy analyzing and criticizing.

Gardner's (1983) theory of multiple intelligences defines intelligence as the capacity to solve problems or to fashion products that are valued in one or more cultural settings. Gardner argues that fair intelligence tests based on culturally valued activities should be used to determine giftedness. Moreover, he contends that assessments for placement in gifted programs should take place within familiar contexts because performance inevitably depends on a person's familiarity with the materials and demands of the assessment experience. Thus, meaningful assessment of intelligence is impossible if students have had little or no experience with a particular subject matter or type of material.

Redefining Underachievement

Just as Gould (1981) maintains that educators and psychologists must redefine intelligence and move beyond reifying this construct, they must also move beyond reifying underachievement by placing more emphasis on characteristics of underachievement that standardized tests fail to measure. Accordingly, underachievement should be analyzed relative to sociopsychological factors and how these factors affect (inhibit or enhance) achievement (Ford et al., 1991). These factors include locus of control, fears and anxieties (particularly relative to tests), self-concept, self-esteem, motivation, and effort. Underachievement among gifted African American students should also be examined in conjunction with additional social barriers to achievement such as overt discrimination, low teacher expectations, and cultural barriers to achievement (e.g., home and community values that differ from school values).

Increased Multicultural Training for Teachers of the Gifted

Current forecasts project that by the end of the 20th century, half the U.S. student population will be comprised of racial minorities (Hodgkinson, 1988). Such projections underscore the need for multicultural education training among the nation's current and future teachers. Perspectives on individual differences attributable to race, gender, socioeconomic status, and geographic locale must be infused throughout the curriculum for gifted teacher education to reeducate educators and school personnel and replace inaccurate deficit models that impede learning and leave many gifted minority students unrecognized. In-service and continuing professional education and development for teachers of gifted students would include learning focused on comparative education issues, the sociology of education, urban education, Black and other racial/ethnic group studies, individual and cultural differences in learning styles, and bias-free identification and assessment techniques.

Enhanced Parental Involvement

Scott-Jones (1987) maintains that academically successful African American children have mothers who provided more books, set clearer academic goals for their children, and are more involved in their children's schoolwork than other African American parents. Indeed, the tendency in American schools to provide African American children with a biased learning environment practically forces parents to involve themselves in the formal learning process. With regard to special education, Harry (1992) recommends that African American parental involvement should be manifested in four indispensable and substantive roles. These roles are equally relevant for African American parents of gifted children. They include the following:

1. becoming members of the official assessment teams that determine students' placement in special or gifted education programs;
2. assisting in the preparation of reports on issues affecting the educational status of minority, gifted, and underachieving students;
3. serving on local educational agency committees or boards, on school site-based management teams, and other educational advisory committees;
4. working in the school as teachers' aides, parent liaisons, and in peer support positions from which they can more directly offer advice and input to school personnel on the assessment and placement of their children.

Additionally, African American parents can lobby their school boards and other school officials to ensure that gifted program assessment and selection boards include parents and community leaders who reflect the demographics of the community relative to race, gender, and socioeconomic status.

INCREASED USE OF MULTIDIMENSIONAL AND MULTIMODAL ASSESSMENTS

Traditional unidimensional instruments such as standardized intelligence and achievement tests cannot reliably measure a multidimensional construct like intelligence. However, multidimensional and multimodal assessment instruments and techniques can increase the prospects of identifying and placing more representative numbers of African Americans and other minorities—including potentially gifted students, underachievers, and nontraditional students—in gifted programs. Such assessments more readily accommodate multiple and contextual definitions of intelligence inherent in the worldviews of diverse groups of learners, while valuing the culture, values, and customs of these groups (Patton, 1992).

Multidimensional, multimodal assessments take different forms; however, their essential components include both quantitative and qualitative assessment strategies. Culturally sensitive quantitative instruments include the Coloured, Standard, and Advanced Progressive Matrices, the Matrix Analogies Test (expanded or short forms), the Kaufman Assessment Battery for Children, and the Torrance Tests for Creative Thinking (Patton, 1992). Other assessment models that result in more inclusive profiles of giftedness across racial/ethnic and cultural lines include the Baldwin Identification Matrix; the Frasier Talent Assessment Profile; the Program of Assessment, Diagnosis, and Instruction; and the Potentially Gifted Minority Student Project (Patton, 1992).

Promising qualitative assessments include the Scales for Rating the Behavioral Characteristics of Superior Students (Renzulli, 1983), and the Multidimensional Screening Device (Kranz, 1978). Also useful are methods that employ portfolio assessments; reviews of students' transcripts; observational or performance-based assessments; nominations by parents, teachers, peers, or the students themselves; interviews; and biographical inventories (Coleman & Gallagher, 1992; Hadaway & Marek-Schroer, 1992; Tuttle et al., 1988).

Portfolios and biographical inventories represent two of the most promising contemporary qualitative indices for identifying giftedness in students standardized measures usually disavow. Portfolios are purposeful collections of student work and records, amassed over time, that reflect the student's ability to produce, to perceive, and to reflect (Simmons, 1990). Their contents can be written, behavioral, or oral, and may include artwork, journals, writing samples, projects, teacher observations of student use of free time, audiotapes or videotapes of class discussions, samples of student work done outside of school (e.g., hobbies, collections, leadership or conflict-resolution experiences, family duties) (Hadaway & Marek-Schroer, 1992). Similarly, biographical inventories acknowledge that gifted students often display more of their superior abilities or strengths outside of school or only in particular areas within the school. For instance, students may have developed community organizations that demonstrate leadership, or participated in drama clubs outside of school rather than in school. Such inventories may take the form of multiple-choice items, checklists, open-ended questions, or any combination thereof.

Increasing the Retention of African American students in Gifted Education Programs

The majority of efforts have been aimed at the identification and placement (i.e., recruitment) of African American students in gifted programs. Rarely have issues surrounding retention received attention. However, once placed, gifted African Americans derive particular benefit from support services designed to ensure their goodness-of-fit with gifted programs.

Counseling strategies for helping gifted African American students cope with the difficulties inherent in being a part of gifted programs must address the heightened peer pressures and feelings of isolation from their friends that these students often face, as well as their concerns over being viewed as "different" from the traditional students in such programs (Ford, Harris, & Schuerger, 1993; Ford, Schuerger, & Harris, 1991). Attention to problems associated with test anxiety is a particularly important aspect of retention efforts for African American students if schools rely on grades or performance to determine continued placement in gifted programs. Depending on students' particular strengths or weaknesses, tutoring by older, high-achieving African Americans may also enhance gifted Black students' academic performance. Additionally, financial support for learning enrichment opportunities outside of school (for example, on weekends, after school hours, and during the summers) would certainly promote success among gifted African Americans whose families are of limited means. Such support might include scholarships to attend residential and nonresidential summer programs and institutes, as well as grants to facilitate students' participation in out-of-state competitions or other challenging and enriching learning opportunities.

Conclusion

Recognizing the potentials and talents of all children requires a broadened vision of giftedness that reflects the understanding that talent and creativity vary markedly among individuals of varying cultural, ethnic, socioeconomic, and linguistic backgrounds. Accordingly, gifted education professionals must ensure that programs for exceptional students are inclusive rather than exclusive, and that minority, economically disadvantaged, and underachieving students have equal opportunity to excel in stimulating and nurturing educational environments. The recommendations offered in this article for desegregating gifted programs are not exhaustive. Rather, they suggest a point from which the nation can begin ensuring the success of all gifted students, including those who have yet to reveal their true capabilities. To continue relying on unidimensional rather than multidimensional assessment strategies, to reify intelligence, and to perceive cultural differences and diversity as inconsequential to learning and academic success is to ignore one of the basic tenets of education: that all children must be encouraged to learn and achieve at optimal levels, and that those who exhibit exceptional gifts will be recognized and challenged to realize even higher promise.

References

Alamprese, J. A., & Erlanger, W. J. (1988). *No gifts wasted: Effective strategies for educating highly able, disadvantaged students in mathematics and science* (Volume 1). Washington, DC: Cosmos Corporation.

Archambault, F. X., Jr., Westberg, K. L., Brown, S. W., Hallmark, B. W., Zhang, W., & Emmons, C. L. (1993). Classroom practices used with gifted third- and fourth-grade students. *Journal for the Education of the Gifted, 16*(2), 103–119.

Brown v. Board of Education of Topeka, Kansas, 347 U.S. 483 (1954).

Cassidy, J., & Hossler, A. (1992). State and federal definitions of the gifted: An update. *Gifted Child Quarterly, 15*(1), 46–53.

Chinn, P. C., & Selma, H. (1987). Representation of minority students in special education classes. *Remedial and Special Education, 8,* 41–46.

Coleman, M. R., & Gallagher, J. J. (1992). State policies for identification of nontraditional gifted students. *Gifted Child Today, 23*(1), 15–17.

Cox, J., & Daniel, N. (1985). The Richardson survey concludes. *Gifted Child Today, 16*(2), 103–119.

Cox, J., Daniel, N., & Boston, B. (1985). *Educating able learners.* Austin, TX: University of Texas Press.

Cummins, J. (1989). Institutionalized racism and the assessment of minority children. In R. J. Samuda & S. L. Kong (Eds.), *Assessment and placement of minority students* (pp. 95–198). Toronto: C. J. Hogrefe.

Davis, G. A., & Rimm, S. B. (1989). *Education of the gifted and talented* (2nd ed.). Englewood Cliffs, NJ: Prentice-Hall.

Dunn, R., & Griggs, S. A. (1990). Research on the learning style characteristics of selected racial and ethnic groups. *Reading, Writing, and Learning Disabilities, 6,* 261–280.

Education Commission of the States. (1989, May). A close look at the shortage of minority teachers. *Education Week,* p. 29.

Ford, D. Y. (1991). *Self-perceptions of social, psychological, and cultural determinants of achievement among gifted Black students: A paradox of underachievement.* Unpublished doctoral dissertation, Cleveland State University, Cleveland, OH.

Ford, D. Y. (1992). Determinants of underachievement as perceived by gifted, above-average, and average Black students. *Roeper Review, 14*(3), 130–136.

Ford, D. Y. (1993). Black students' achievement orientation as a function of perceived family achievement orientation and demographic variables. *Journal of Negro Education, 62*(1), 47–66.

Ford, D. Y., & Harris, J. J., III. (1991). On discovering the hidden treasure of gifted and talented African American children. *Roeper Review, 13*(1), 27–33.

Ford, D. Y., Harris, J. J., III, & Schuerger, J. M. (1993). Racial identity development among gifted Black students: Counseling issues and concerns. *Journal of Counseling and Development, 71*(4), 409–417.

Ford, D. Y., Harris, J. J., III, & Winborne, D. G. (1990). The coloring of IQ testing: A new name for an old phenomenon. *Urban League Review, 13*(2), 99–111.

Ford, D. Y., Schuerger, J. M., & Harris, J. J., III. (1991). Meeting the socio-psychological needs of gifted Black students. *Journal of Counseling and Development, 69*(6), 577–580.

Ford, D. Y., Winborne, D. G., & Harris J. J., III. (1991). Determinants of underachievement among gifted Black students: Learning to underachieve. *Journal of Social and Behavioral Sciences, 35*(3), 145–162.

Gardner, H. (1983). *Frames of mind.* New York: Basic Books.

Gould, S. J. (1981). The mismeasure of man. New York: W. W. Norton.

Hadaway, N., & Marek-Schroer, M. F. (1992). Multidimensional assessment of the gifted minority student. *Roeper Review, 15*(2), 73–77.

Harris, J. J., III, & Ford, D. Y. (1991). Identifying and nurturing the promise of gifted Black students. *Journal of Negro Education, 60*(1), 3–18.

Harry, B. (1992). Restructuring the participation of African American parents in special education. *Exceptional Children, 59*(2), 123–131.

Hilliard, A. G., III. (Ed.). (1987, April-July). Testing African American students [Special Issue]. *Negro Education Review, 38*(2–3).

Hilliard, A. G., III. (1989, December). Cultural style in teaching and learning. *Education Digest,* 20–23.

Hodgkinson, H. (1988, October). An interview with Harold Hodgkinson: Using demographic data for long-range planning. *Phi Delta Kappan,* 166–170.

Jacobs, J. C. (1971). Effectiveness of teacher and parent identification of gifted children as a function of school levels. *Psychology in the Schools, 8,* 140–142.

Karnes, M. B., Shwedel, A. M., & Steinberg, D. (1984). Styles of parenting among young gifted children. *Roeper Review, 6*(4), 232–235.

Karnes, F. A., & Whorton, J. F. (1991). Teacher certification and endorsement in gifted education: Past, present, and future. *Gifted Child Quarterly, 35*(3), 148–150.

Kranz, B. (1978). *Multidimensional Screening Device (MSD) for the Identification of Gifted and Talented children.* Grand Forks, ND: University of North Dakota Bureau of Educational Research.

Kunjufu, J. (1993, February 5). *Maximizing African American male academic achievement.* Paper presented at the 5th Annual Equal Educational Opportunity Conference, "Positive Challenges and Approaches to Educating the African American Male," Louisville, KY.

Lajoie, S. P., & Shore, B. M. (1981). Three myths? The over-representation of the gifted among drop-outs, delinquents, and suicides. *Gifted Child Quarterly, 25*(3), 138–141.

Marion, R. L. (1981). Working with parents of the disadvantaged or culturally different gifted. *Roeper Review, 3,* 32–34.

National Commission for Excellence in Education. (1983). *A nation at risk: The imperative for educational reform*. Washington, DC: U.S. Department of Education.

Patton, J. M. (1992). Assessment and identification of African American learners with gifts and talents. *Exceptional Children, 59*(2), 150–159.

Pegnato, C. W., & Birch, J. S. (March, 1959). Locating gifted children in junior high school: A comparison of methods. *Exceptional Children, 25,* 300–304.

Renzulli, J. S. (1983). Rating the behavioral characteristics of superior students. *Gifted Child Today, 14*(5), 30–35.

Richert, E. S. (1987). Rampant problems and promising practices in the identification of disadvantaged gifted children. *Gifted Child Quarterly, 31*(4), 149–154.

Russo, C. J., Ford, D. Y., & Harris, J. J., III. (1993). The educational rights of gifted children: Lost in the legal shuffle? *Roeper Review, 16*(1), 67–71.

Scott-Jones, D. (1987). Mother-as-teacher in the families of high- and low-achieving low-income Black first graders. *Journal of Negro Education, 56*(1), 21–34.

Simmons, J. (1990). Portfolios as large-scale assessments. *Language Arts, 67*(3), 262–268.

Slaughter, D. T., & Kuehne, V. S. (1987/1988) Improving Black education: Perspectives on parent involvement. *Urban League Review, 11*(1–2), 59–75.

Sternberg, R. J. (1988). *The triarchic mind: A new theory of human intelligence*. New York: Viking.

Tomlinson, T. (1992). *Issues in education. Hard work and high expectations: Motivating students to learn*. Washington, DC: U.S. Department of Education, Office of Educational Research and Improvement.

Tuttle, F. B., Jr., Becker, L. A., & Sousa, J. A. (1988). *Characteristics and identification of gifted and talented students* (3rd ed.). Washington, DC: National Education Association.

U.S. Department of Education. (1993). *National excellence: A case for developing America's talent*. Washington, DC: U.S. Department of Education.

VanTassel-Baska, J., Patton, J., & Prillaman, D. (1989). Disadvantaged gifted learners at-risk for educational attention. *Focus on Exceptional Children, 22*(3), 1–16.

Whitmore, J. R. (1980). *Giftedness, conflict, and underachievement*. Boston: Allyn & Bacon.

SECTION II

Creativity, Black Children, and Torrance

Tarek C. Grantham

When you look at Black children, what do you see? When Black children look at you, what do they see? What do you want them to see in you? What do you want Black children to know and understand about themselves? When you listen to Black children's ideas and conversations, what stands out in your mind? When Black children listen to you, what do they hear? When you have the opportunity to encourage innovation in Black children, how do you communicate your expectations of them? When you teach Black children, do you expect to learn something meaningful from them as well? When you observe Black children expressing their feelings of joy or sorrow, how is it similar or different to how you express yours? In what ways do you celebrate things that you have in common with Black children? How do you handle differences you observe in Black and other children? Who are the smartest Black children that you know or have seen? How do you determine who is smart and who is not so bright? If you were to ask Black children about their futures, what criteria would you use to determine their likelihood for school-related success? In what ways have you encouraged Black children to reach their academic and creative potential? What evidence do you have that your encouragement worked?

Each of us might ask ourselves these questions when we take seriously the need to empower Black children to reach their full potential. Given the diminishing state of education for Black children, we should question our thoughts and actions and how they impact Black children and their creative accomplishment.

Imagine living during a segregated era in the 1960s when many, if not most, Whites saw inferiority rather than intellectual gifts and creative potential in Black children. In E. Paul Torrance, we have an exception. As the readings in this section vividly illustrate, Torrance—the most prolific scholar on creativity—encouraged, admonished, and dared people not to overlook creativity and intellectual promise among Black children. Compassion for culturally diverse and disadvantaged people, coupled with serious and unmatched scholarship, was the powerful combination that allowed Dr. Torrance to see the brilliance in Black children when most were blind to it. His belief that creativity, one of the highest manifestations of intelligence, exists in all cultural groups, including Blacks, and his findings from empirical research that found the same, helped Black children to be viewed and assessed as intelligent, creative, and full of potential.

In the year 2011, we are reminded of the early and risky pioneering efforts made by Dr. Torrance to awaken a nation of people to the nature of creativity in Black children, the wonder of Black culture, and the power and promise of Black people's creative contributions to American culture. A gentle giant of a scholar, and a creative genius himself, Dr. Torrance was a Southern boy who brought with him a Northern influence on his scholarship that helped to open the eyes of educators and communities around the world to the creative genius in Black children. Baldwin (2001) celebrated Torrance as the "most prolific in his discussion of creativity among [Black] children. . . . His work has been a guide, and he has provided significant exposure to both the quality of creativity and the lack of understanding about its presence in [Black] students" (p. 123). Let's all learn from Torrance and his research on creativity using a slice of scholarship in what follows.

Reference

Baldwin, A. Y. (2001). Understanding the challenge of creativity among African Americans. *Journal of Secondary Gifted Education, 12,* 121–125.

CHAPTER 4

Creativity and Its Educational Implications[1] for the Gifted

E. Paul Torrance[2]

After studying, experimenting, exploring, talking, and writing for over ten years about the educational implications of creativity for the gifted, it would seem that I should be able to set forth these implications clearly and neatly. In fact, I have been looking forward to doing this.

Now, I find the task an impossible one. As I sat down to look back at the work of the past ten years, no such encompassing synthesis would come. Instead, new and incomplete but exciting and absorbing ideas possessed me. I kept trying to fight them off and started to list the implications of one of my earliest findings concerning the identification of the creatively gifted (Torrance, 1962): if one uses only an intelligence test and thereby identifies the upper twenty percent as gifted, he would miss seventy percent of those who would be identified as falling in the top twenty percent on tests of creative thinking ability. In spite of many attempts by high status authorities in several fields to explain this fact away, it remains virtually unchanged. The seventy percent figure is surprisingly constant in hundreds of studies, at different age levels, in different subcultures, using different tests of intelligence, and with different measures of creative thinking ability. Educators have not yet dared to dream of even the most obvious implications of this single finding. In fact, I found my own mind blocked and unwilling to continue my listing of implications.

Suddenly, I realized that my predicament was a very predictable one. Creativity is something infinite and its possibilities can never be exhausted! Finally, I relaxed

---
[1] Based on keynote address to 15th Annual Meeting of The National Association for Gifted Children, Chicago, Illinois, May 1, 1968.
[2] Dr. Torrance is Chairman, Department of Educational Psychology, The University of Georgia.

Reprinted from Torrance, E. P. (1968). Creativity and its educational implications for the gifted. *Gifted Child Quarterly, 12,* 67–78. Reprinted with permission of Sage Publications.

and allowed five of the most persistent and urgent of the implications that kept fighting for expression to take possession of me. Then, I became afraid.

I know that these implications will not be widely accepted. At best, I can formulate them only incompletely. In expressing these implications at a meeting like this, I invite new criticism, ridicule, slander, and further excommunication from the scientific fraternity of educational researchers.

I have been toying with these five ideas for several years, however, and they will not let me alone. Therefore, I give them to you incomplete, only partially tested, and controversial.

Necessary to Look to Creatively Gifted Disadvantaged

I am especially hesitant to express the most persistent and urgent of the implications that have possessed me. For some time, I have been experiencing a dawning realization that in the future we shall have to depend upon creatively gifted members of disadvantaged and minority cultures for most of our creative achievements. In a way, this may have been true all along. To be a part of the advantaged, dominant culture, a person frequently has to sacrifice too much of his perception of reality and his search for the truth to make much of a creative contribution. Our creative achievers will be those who accept only those parts of the dominant culture which are true and who hold on to their individuality and their minority or disadvantaged culture. It will be they who possess the "different" element, the "divine discontent," and the clearness of vision to see that "the king wears no clothes."

I could cite famous examples from history to show how creative breakthroughs have come from disadvantaged groups. Critics would say immediately that this could never occur in our modern, technological, space age culture. Almost daily, however, dramatic examples quietly find their way into the news. Let me review three recent ones.

The March 25, 1968, *National Observer*, reports an interesting item from Birmingham, Alabama, that seems to have been ignored by newspapers in the South. The bold experiments of a 17-year old Negro boy, Bracie Watson, had stirred cautious excitement among scientists of the University of Alabama Medical Center. Bracie is confident that an animal ovum can be fertilized and develop as an embryo outside the mother animal's womb.

Bracie Watson is the son of a mechanic and a schoolteacher. He first attracted attention in Birmingham as a ninth grader when he won a science contest with a successful skin graft involving chickens. He could not enter the regional contest then because Negroes were barred from competition. Later, by telephone and personal calls he sought laboratory space at the University Medical Center to transplant a kidney from one dog to another. Members of the Center staff recognized Bracie's unusual creative scientific potential and approved his request. His kidney-transplant experiments eventually succeeded and one dog with a transplanted kidney has since had puppies.

In the eleventh grade Bracie went to work on developing an artificial womb. He had read of the problem some mothers have in bringing their babies to full term. He speculated that in some instances a baby's chances would be improved if it could be moved to an artificial womb.

The embryologist with whom Bracie worked pronounced the whole approach as brazenly naive. This did not stop Bracie, however. He kept rat embryos alive as long as 14 hours in an artificial womb. They normally would have died within minutes after removal from the mother's womb. "He's unusual," said Dr. Ed Weller, the embryologist. When he is graduated from high school, Bracie plans to accept a full-four-year scholarship to the University of Alabama and to pursue a doctorate in biochemistry.

The March 17, 1968, issue of the *Los Angeles Times*, in one of its articles on the "Brown Beret" or "Brown Power" movement in the high schools, tells some of the story of Dr. Julian Nava, the only Mexican-American on the Los Angeles Board of Education. One of the major complaints of the "Brown Beret" leaders was that Mexican-Americans and Negroes in the Los Angeles schools have been and still are being shunted by counselors and administrators into industrial arts classes and not permitted to enroll in college preparatory classes.

When asked if there is any validity to these complaints, Dr. Nava replied, "I was graduated from Roosevelt High in 1945. I was told to take auto shop. And I did. I did as I was told. Then I went into the Navy—and I wasn't a Mexican anymore, I was just Julian. It opened my eyes."

Dr. Nava continued, "But then in the Navy I was an auto mechanic—so I can't say that the advice was all bad. A lot of those decisions were based on what the high school counselors considered a 'realistic assessment of the chances of success.' They realized the chances, then, of a Mexican-American getting through college. I'm just worried for fear they're still making those 'realistic assessments.' I just wonder how many other Julians have ended up in auto shop, somewhere, and stayed there."

Dr. Nava, now 40, attained his Ph.D. in history at Harvard.

The members of the "Brown Beret" are asking that they be given a chance to know their history and their culture. They are asking for compulsory bilingual and bicultural education and for teachers who know something of the Mexican cultural heritage and recognize their cultural traditions. They are asking for textbooks that show Mexican contributions to society, show the injustices they have experienced, and concentrate on Mexican folklore. They are asking for more effective testing procedures to identify potentialities for purposes of grouping and guidance. They are asking for more library materials in Spanish and that all school facilities be made more fully available to them for educational purposes.

The April 7, 1968, issue of the *Atlanta Constitution* reported a story about a Georgia native, Negro singer James Brown. Only a few years ago, James Brown had been a shoeshine boy in Augusta, Georgia. During the rioting following the death of Martin Luther King, Jr., Brown had gone on television and radio in the nation's capital to appeal for an end to looting and rioting. He pled, "Don't burn, give the kids a chance to learn. Don't terrorize—organize."

He continued, "I used to shine shoes on the steps of station WRDW in Augusta. I think we started at three cents, then five cents and six cents, never did get a dime. But today I own that station. That is Black Power. I didn't get a chance to finish the seventh grade, but I made it. I made it because you were with me and because I had honesty, and dignity, and pride."

There are many problems involved in implementing implications concerning creatively disadvantaged children. There are many problems of identification. The facts are that we do not do a very good job of identifying the gifted among disadvantaged groups of all kinds—Negroes, Mexican-American, Navajos, Zunis, Chippewas, Cherokees, hillbillies, the deaf, and the blind. Even the Torrance Tests of Creative Thinking (Torrance, 1966) are sensitive enough to make one aware of otherwise unnoticed potentialities among them. For example, I believe that populations of deaf children harbor many unusually creative persons. It took that wild and discredited "science" of phrenology to conquer the superstitious belief that deaf mutes were utterly beyond the reach of human aid (Bakan, 1968). A phrenological analysis of Laura Bridgman's skull "proved" that she had an active, intelligent brain and as a consequence she became the first deaf-mute to be systematically educated. It is my hope that another set of discredited techniques, the Torrance Tests of Creative Thinking, may play a role in showing that deaf mutes can think creatively and can make useful creative contributions. I believe a start has been made. Dr. Rawley Silver has administered the figural tests of creative thinking to some of his deaf art students and I would describe many of their performances as being phenomenal. Silver, however, has been unable to obtain much cooperation from rehabilitation authorities in helping these gifted youngsters receive training. Their scores on verbally-oriented intelligence and achievement tests are so low that they are regarded as uneducable.

Not only are there difficulties in identifying creatively gifted children among disadvantaged groups, there are still more serious difficulties in providing them with professional help that will make more frequent the happy accidents of the Bracie Watsons, the James Browns, and the Julian Navas. In fact, there have been almost no sustained, systematic professional attempts to do this. One such pioneering effort is Dr. George Witt's LEAP or Life Enrichment Activity Program for creatively gifted, disadvantaged Negro children. Now, Witt says that it was nothing but a miracle that any of the original 16 children in the program remained (Golden, 1967). He observed, "We had nothing but trouble at first. The kids teased and berated each other." He described how one of the little girls came in the first day and looked at her reflection in the mirror and said, "You're nothin and nobody, and you're always gonna be nothin and nobody." They could not believe it when someone selected them because they were special and that they are somebodies. These children have made amazing strides in learning and in creative achievement. Critics maintain that any child, given as much attention as Witt's youngsters have been given, would develop their creative talents. To this criticism, Witt replied, "They say of course that it can be done but no one has ever done it. I'm interested in proving that it can be done." For his attention, Witt chose creatively gifted disadvantaged children. At the University of Georgia, Dr. Catherine Bruch, the coordinator of our programs in the area of the gifted, has chosen the gifted disadvantaged as an area of emphasis.

CREATIVELY HANDICAPPED AND SPECIAL EDUCATION

As my second implication, I am suggesting that the "creatively handicapped" be adopted as a new category in the field of Special Education of Exceptional Children. I know that it will impress even this sympathetic audience as a wild idea. Actually, the logic for this implication is rather clear. There are many children whose behavior problems stem from the differences their abilities create between them and other children and between them and their teachers. Their learning difficulties arise from the incompatibility between their abilities and learning preferences on one hand and the teaching methods and system of rewards of the school on the other. If brought together with other creatively gifted youngsters, they would no longer be misfits. If taught in ways compatible with their abilities and interests their achievement might soar.

Those of us who have been interested in special provisions for gifted children have frequently been told that it is hopeless to expect support for improved programs of education for them. Critics have said that the plight of the mentally retarded, the blind, the deaf, and the crippled arouses sympathy. They argue that the gifted are well endowed and can take care of themselves. Apparently they have been blinded to the countless tragedies of gifted children who are powerless to help themselves and are the object of hate and aggression. The letters I receive from creatively gifted young people and parents of creatively gifted children tell me that they are wrong.

Recently, Robert E. Samples (1967) in *Saturday Review* gave us the tremendously sensitive and disturbing story of Kari, whose handicap was her creativity. Samples wrote that Kari appears strange to the conformity-cloistered society around her. He said that she creates a guilt in the cliché-makers which they transform to resentment. They pressure her in the direction of the norm and her resistance is interpreted as immaturity and stubbornness that must be overcome. Kari was the one student in her class who defended the heroine in Hawthorne's *The Scarlet Letter* for having the courage to be apart from the society and at the same time damned her for being dishonest to herself. In the ensuing argument, she contended that virtue was in doing what had to be done, rather than "obeying like a starved rat the corridors of a maze somebody else built." The frightened teacher gave her a "D" for her participation. Samples concluded that "We need the Karis, all of them, but how can they be saved? The simplicity of the answer is as frightening as it is demanding: We must be more like Kari" (p.74).

My response to Samples' solution is that it is too idealistic. It will be too long before we can develop any large number of teachers who can become like Kari, teachers who can be truly empathetic with creatively handicapped children. In programs of special education, I believe that it is reasonable to expect that we can develop enough teachers for special programs for creatively handicapped-gifted children who are serious misfits in regular classrooms and school programs.

Although the logic of this idea is quite reasonable to me, I realize that most educators will place it in the category of science fiction. In fact, a recent issue of *Analog Science Fiction* (Foray, 1968) gives us an excellent idea of how a school for creatively handicapped-gifted children might be established and implemented. The children in Thorley School of the *Analog* story were ESP gifted. The teachers were also gifted and trained in ESP. This was not known to the public, however, and the school was privately endowed. Public school psychologists and counselors referred to Thorling the children they could not get through to, especially the kindergarteners they did not even wish to try to get through to. Thorling School accepted some of these and rejected others. When asked to explain the school's criteria for acceptance, the principal explained, "We take the children we can help." The children they could help, of course, were the ESP gifted. Their behavior problems usually came from the differences their ESP abilities created between them and other children. There were, of course, problems with accreditation and the *Analog* story revolves about a visit from the accrediting board. All of the children cooperated to conceal the fact that Thorling was a school for the ESP gifted and used their ESP abilities to do so. Their conclusion, however, was that people lacking this sensitivity were so unaware of the ESP abilities of others that no efforts are required to hide such abilities.

NEED FOR A TIME OUT OF SCHOOL

At a time when there is national concern about reducing school dropouts, it is perhaps dangerous to suggest that any group of children or adolescents be encouraged or permitted to dropout, even temporarily. Therefore, I shall use the term

"Time-Out" and suggest that we institutionalize it in such a way that such children would still be in school, just outside of the curriculum.

A number of people who have studied the school experiences of people who have made historically important creative achievements have noted that many of these eminent people had had time-outs. These time-outs are periods when the normal activities of school were suspended and the boy or girl had a free period in which to think, plan, read unrestrainedly, or meet a new group of people under new circumstances. Goertzel and Goertzel (1962) estimated that at least ten percent of the 400 notables in their study described a "time-out" period which significantly influenced their later development. They specifically cited Winston Churchill, John F. Kennedy, H. G. Wells, Charles Evans Hughes, William Randolph Hurst, Richard Byrd, Edna St. Vincent Millay, Louis Brandeis, Marie Curie, and others. Among present day notables, Edwin Land is one who dropped out of school and came up with a number of inventions, including Polaroid.

I have long been impressed with the high incidence of time-outs in the lives of the world's notables and I can even claim a time-out of my own of about six months to recover from the aftermath of a ruptured appendix at age ten. I have known many creatively gifted children and adolescents in trouble for whom I would like to have prescribed a time-out. As a consequence, I have wondered how such time-outs could be institutionalized in such a way that chances of success would not be ruined for the child or adolescent involved.

I must admit that I was too fainthearted to suggest such a procedure until I learned about Elizabeth Drews' (1968) experience with Fernwood in Oregon. In the Colton (Oregon) Consolidated School, 24 students were randomly selected from grades 7, 8 and 9. Two very capable teacher-counselors told these young people as they sat in their bare classroom that they could make theirs the kind of school they wanted. "They could find out what was important to them and then work on what was important." The arrangement of the room and what it was to contain was up to them. Since the experiment began in September, the out-of-school environment proved to be irresistible. When the students realized that they were really free to choose, they reveled in it. Only one or two of the students would sit through even the most dynamic lecture prepared by the teachers. In the free environment of Fernwood, they sought out personal refuges, sometimes in groups, but often singly.

The most confirmed low achiever and general misfit, according to Drews, was a boy of 16—a non-reader with a tested IQ that placed him in the moron category. He was generally belligerent and was mean to younger students. He had been thrown out of school repeatedly and had come back more resistant to learning each time. He had been a habitual truant but his attendance at Fernwood was perfect. At first he spent all of his time outdoors. Gradually he gained enough peace of mind to overcome his aversion to school to enter the classroom. Then, as Drews wrote, "By dint of alchemy or miracle (and perhaps with the aid of a stack of 200 plus or minus comic books) he learned to read. Next he began to become social. He learned to play chess, occasionally beating his teachers. By the time the experiment was abandoned in December because of cancellation of funds, he had become an excellent conversationalist who could talk about war and peace as well as the vagaries of the weather. A year after the program ended, he was spending half of each day helping mentally retarded children in a special room and he is known for his gentleness and loving ways."

At Fernwood, there was time to listen to music, build things, plan trips and go on them, read books and talk about them, and form natural and meaningful interpersonal relationships. At home, these youngsters had usually been engaged in endless chores. At school, relentless bells had dictated when the mind was to be turned on and off and what words their eyes were to focus upon. The curriculum was text-centered and fact-oriented. Talk, except in recitations, was regarded as idle chatter, discouraged in the classrooms, and forbidden in the halls. At Fernwood, there was freedom to dream and envision what one might be and become. The warmth and trust of the teachers finally won over the more reluctant students.

Many exciting things occurred during Fernwood's four-month existence. A nonreader began to read without the pressure of applied methods and scheduled class periods. Those who had habitually failed English discovered that they could speak fluently and well when they could talk about something of interest. A boy who had been indifferent to mathematics did four months of work in three days and ended up six weeks ahead of his former classmates. They became aware of changes in themselves and near the end of the term commented that they had not destroyed property at Fernwood—not even those who had been the most hardened marauders. One of them said, "I was not closed in at Fernwood. I wasn't in a cage or cell, so I didn't need to destroy." These students did not "lose ground" by being out of the regular school program for four months. All except two of them did better work and received higher grades upon return to school than they had done prior to the free experience.

Free to learn in their own ways about things that they wanted to know, the students made almost all of the suggestions of things to do. Some of them became so addicted to reading that parents complained. Four girls decided to go to England to widen their horizon and searched diligently and in vain for jobs for 14-year olds. They decided to become columnists and began writing a teen-age column which they sold to the local paper. Later a publisher of a teen-age paper "discovered" their talent and one of them was asked to become his editor. Only history will reveal what else is yet to come from this rather bold experiment.

I am sure that not all students—or even all creatively gifted students—need time-outs. I suspect, however, that many of them do and would profit thereby. Neither am I saying that it must be set up as Elizabeth Drews described in the

Oregon experiment. Time-outs can be provided in many ways. For Fannie Hurst (1967), it was provided by her assistant principal. She was frequently "sent up to his office" for many minor misdemeanors such as prompting other students, reading extraneous books during study hours, and writing essays for classmates in exchange for geometry homework. The assistant principal showed little interest in her violations but, as she described, "he diagnosed and articulated for her much of the groping confusion that must have been responsible for her itchy malaise" (p. 26). He talked with her about her major interest, writing, and gave her guidance in her reading. He read the "literary efforts" she produced in his office as disciplinary measures and encouraged her to follow her inclinations to write. She continued to devise misdemeanors so that she would be "sent up to his office." These experiences gave her a kind of time-out.

Sponsors and Patrons Outside the School

Almost always wherever independence and creativity occur and result in outstanding creative achievement, there has been some other individual who played the role of "sponsor or patron." This role is played by someone who is not a member of the peer group, but who possesses prestige and power in the same social system. He does several things. Regardless of his own views, the sponsor encourages and supports the creative young person in expressing and testing his ideas and in thinking through things for himself. He protects the individual from the reactions of his peers and of authorities long enough for him to try out some of his ideas and become productive.

In the past, I have suggested to school psychologists, school counselors, and principals that they were in positions to play the role of sponsor or patron to creatively gifted children. After much thought and over twelve years of experience trying to play this role as major adviser to certain graduate students, I have developed doubts that professional personnel within the school can really play this role very successfully. Graduate advisers and other school and university personnel may occasionally have to go to bat for a creatively gifted student. Many times they may succeed. I doubt, however, that the sponsor role can be sustained successfully by professional personnel within a school without damage to the school and the child. What I believe would be more productive would be for professional personnel to help creatively gifted children find sponsors or patrons in the community.

Dr. George Witt, in his project with creatively gifted disadvantaged children, has demonstrated the feasibility of this idea. In his first summer program, Witt found community sponsors for each of his creatively gifted disadvantaged children, (Torrance and Witt, 1966). One boy worked with an architect at his office once a week. One girl met three hours a week with a creative clothing designer to design and make her own clothes. One boy met once a week with the head of an audiovisual center; another visited a professor of zoology once a week to learn how to write a poem. One girl visited a newspaper reporter and identified herself as a "woman of the press." One boy met weekly with an attorney to discuss some of his interesting cases.

In Witt's continuing programs, arrangements have been made for a creative family to sponsor each child. These families invited the creative disadvantaged children to do creative things with them during week-ends. This program has now been expanded and many exciting and worthwhile outcomes have resulted. I believe that such experiences can be integrated into school programs. If not, perhaps the provision of sponsors for highly creative children might become a challenging task for local chapters of the National Association for Gifted Children!

USING THE BUILT-IN MOTIVATION OF CREATIVE LEARNING

Now that many American schools have seriously assumed the task of educating all children, we are suddenly aware that there is a "motivation gap." There is a gap between what children want to learn and what the schools want to teach them. This motivation gap is perhaps especially acute for many creative youngsters. What they need most of all, of course, is the built-in motivation of creative ways of learning. The education of all children could be vastly improved, in my opinion, by making much greater use than there now is of the built-in motivation power of creative ways of learning. For creative children, it is essential.

We can usually improve almost any kind of human functioning, increase learning rates, or change undesirable behavior to more desirable behavior in most persons by increasing or decreasing motivation in the form of external pressures (rewards and punishments). Most educators think of motivation only in this sense. With unmotivated learners and low achievers, especially the highly creative ones, it has been my observation that external pressures, whether in the form of reward or punishment, rarely promote desirable behavior. In fact, we can seldom "make" a creative student learn, achieve, or work harder, if he chooses not to do so. With some children and adults, the more we reward them the worse they behave and the less they learn, and likewise the more we punish them, the worse they behave. I am convinced that this is frequently true of highly creative children.

Even when reward and/or punishment succeed temporarily, they do not supply the inner motivation necessary for continued achievement. Such motivation is short-lived and requires continuous reapplication. The inner stimulation from creative ways of learning makes the reapplication of rewards and punishments unnecessary. Although rewards are less erratic as motivators than punishment, they are still quite erratic in motivating learning.

Man is an inquisitive, exploring kind of being, who cannot keep his restless mind inactive even when there are no problems to be solved. He seems to be unable to keep from digging into things, turning ideas over in his mind, trying out new combinations, searching for new relationships and struggling for new insights. Man's search for beauty—the aesthetic—is almost as relentless. A particular individual may not search for beauty in a painting or in a sonata. Maslow (1954) learned from a young athlete that a perfect tackle could be as aesthetic a product as a sonnet and could be approached in the same spirit of creativity and achievement. From a housewife, he says that he learned that a first-rate soup is more aesthetic and represents a higher level of achievement than a second-rate painting. From a psychiatrist, he learned of the aesthetic delight in his everyday job of helping people create themselves.

I have tried to identify the most essential characteristics of educational methods that provide the self-motivating influences of creative ways of learning. Perhaps the most essential of these is incompleteness or openness. Many outstanding creative people have commented upon the power of incompleteness in motivating achievement. Ben Shahn (1959), in discussing his creativity in painting, described how he traps images like some inventors trap ideas. He explained that these images are not complete, saying, "If I had a complete image I think I would lose interest in it." To him, the most rewarding thing about painting is the exploration and discovery that he finds. Compton (1953), in his case studies of Nobel prize winners in science, concluded that it is not the love of knowledge but the love of adding to knowledge that is important in motivation for achievement.

A pupil may encounter incompleteness outside of school and this may motivate his achievement or he may encounter incompleteness in the classroom. The incompleteness may be encountered in pictures, stories, objects of instruction, the behavioral settings of the classroom, or in structured sequences of learning activities. In my current work with five year olds, I encourage children to see all knowledge as incomplete. I show them a picture or read them a story and then I ask them to think about all of the things that the picture or the story does not tell about the events described and then to ask questions about these things. In answering their questions, information is frequently given as incomplete. The incompleteness and changing nature of the objects presented are emphasized.

Perhaps my own favorite strategy of building-in motivation in a learning activity through creative processes is to have the learner produce something—a drawing, a story, a papier mache animal, etc.—and then to do something with what they have produced. This is a central feature in the ideabooks for elementary and junior high school pupils created by Myers and me (1965abcd, 1966) and the Imagi/Craft materials created by Cunnington and me (1965). This is also a central feature of the JUST SUPPOSING exercises I am developing now for use with pre-primary children.

Educational and psychological literature is filled with successful experiences in which creative writing has motivated still other kinds of learning. Maya Pines (1967), after surveying the leading programs for teaching pre-primary children to read, concluded that all of the most successful ones had one thing in common. They all elicit the child's creativity by letting him make up his own words and stories almost from the beginning.

Just why educational methods in which children produce something that leads to doing other things are so powerful in motivating additional learning and creative achievement is not altogether clear. Some people maintain that the power of such methods comes from the fact that human life is meaningless without creativity and that consequently creativity excites creativity. Truly creative poetry can stimulate the scientist and the creative insight of the scientist can stimulate the poet. Others (Flanagan, 1959) have explained that the more creative acts we experience, whether they are our own or those of others, the more we live and anything that makes a person more fully alive is likely to facilitate creative achievement. Some creative products, however, are far more powerful than others in motivating achievement. May O'Neill's (1961) *Hailstones and Halibut Bones*, for example, seems almost always to impel children to write poems about color, experiment with color, and find out things about color. The creative productions of one child also seem to impel others to similar efforts. Perhaps this is because they present a challenge that is within attainment. It may be that their very imperfections motivate achievement.

A third kind of built-in motivation is to be found in the questions children ask. The child's "wanting to know" is reflected in the number and kinds of questions he asks.

By the time a child enters school for the first time he is on his way to learning the skills of finding out by asking questions. When he enters school, however, the teacher begins asking all the questions and the child has little chance to ask questions. Furthermore, the teacher's questions are rarely asked to gain information. The teacher almost always knows the answer. Real questions for information are rare. Questions asked in the classroom are usually to find out whether the child knows something that the teacher knows.

Just imagine how stimulating it would be if teachers really asked children for information! If teachers did this, children would ask questions far more freely and with greater skill and excitement. Pupils and teachers would be kept busy finding out what they want to know.

Even if motivation for learning and achievement is intense and sustained, there is still a need for guidance. Unless there is some guidance and direction from the teacher, most children will cease to develop after a certain stage and will become discouraged. Creative ways of learning, in fact, call for the most sensitive kind of guidance and direction possible. They call for intense listening and observing and giving the kind of guidance that will make all honest efforts to learn and achieve rewarding enough to sustain motivation. The teacher must deal with the disparagement, ridicule, and criticism of the other children.

Perhaps the most important thing for the teacher or parent of a creative child to remember, however, is that once learning and achievement have been motivated, it is dangerous to stop them. The teacher's aim should be to seek out the child's own best motivations and possibilities and guide these to the most fruitful development. Halting strongly motivated learning is like caging a bird in the act of migration. It is useless to offer him crumbs and berries. He will leave them untouched and beat his wings against the bars of the cage until he is given the free air and sky. Rewarding desirable behavior and punishing undesirable behavior in creative children are to no avail!

References

Atlanta Journal Washington Bureau. "Georgia Soul Singer Pleads for Race Peace." *Atlanta Journal - Constitution,* April 7, 1968.

Bakan, D. "Is Phrenology Foolish?" *Psychology Today*, 1968, 1(2), 44–51.

Compton, A. H. "Case Histories: Creativity in Science." In *The Nature of Creative Thinking.* New York: Industrial Relations Institute, 1953.

Cunnington, B. F. and E. P. Torrance. *Imagi/ Craft Series.* Boston: Ginn and Company, 1965.

Drews, Elizabeth M. "Fernwood: A Free School." (Mimeographed). Portland: Portland State College, 1968.

Flanagan, D. "Creativity in Science." In P. Smith (Ed.) *Creativity.* New York: Hastings House, 1959. Pp. 103–109.

Foray, V. "Practice!" *Analog Science Fiction,* February, 1968, 139–160.

Goertzel, V. and Mildred G. Goertzel. *Cradles of Eminence.* Boston: Little, Brown and Co., 1962.

Golden, T. "LEAP: An Experiment in Creativity for Gradeschoolers." *Sunday Pictorial, New Haven (Conn. Register,* February 19, 1967. Pp. 6–9.

Hurst, Fannie. "The Melody Lingers On." In M. L. Ernst (Ed.) *The Teacher.* Englewood Cliffs, N.J.: Prentice-Hall, 1967. Pp. 23–28.

McFadden, J. M. "Bracie's Science Project Startles the Professionals." *The National Observer,* March 25, 1968.

Maslow, A. H. *Motivation and Personality.* New York: Harper & Row, 1954.

Myers, R. E. and E. P. Torrance. *Can You Imagine?* Boston: Ginn & Co., 1965a.

Myers, R. E. and E. P. Torrance. *Invitations to Thinking and Doing.* Boston: Ginn & Co., 1965b.

Myers, R. E. and E. P. Torrance. *Invitations to Speaking and Writing Creatively.* Boston: Ginn & Co., 1965c.

Myers, R. E. and E. P. Torrance. *For Those Who Wonder.* Boston: Ginn & Co., 1965d.

Myers, R. E. and E. P. Torrance. *Plots, Puzzles, and Ploys.* Boston: Ginn & Co., 1966.

O'Neill, Mary. *Hailstones and Halibut Bones.* Garden City, N.Y.: Doubleday & Co., 1961.

Pines, Maya. *Revolution in Learning.* New York: Harper & Row, 1967.

Samples, R. E. "Kari's Handicap—The Impediment of Creativity." *Saturday Review,* July 15, 1967. Pp. 56–57, 74.

Shahn, B. "On Painting." In *The Creative Mind and Method.* Cambridge, Mass.: WGBH-FM, 1959. Pp. 20–21.

Torgerson, D. "Start of a Revolution?: 'Brown Power' Unity Seen Behind School Disorders." *Los Angeles Times,* March 17, 1968. Section C, pp. 1–5.

Torrance, E. P. *Guiding Creative Talent.* Englewood Cliffs, N.J.: Prentice-Hall, 1962.

Torrance, E. P. *Torrance Tests of Creative Thinking: Norms-Technical Manual (Research Edition).* Princeton, N.J.: Personnel Press, Inc., 1966.

Torrance, E. P. and G. P. Witt. "Experimental Grouping on the Basis of Creative Abilities and Motivations." *Gifted Child Quarterly, 1965, 10, 9–14.*

Witt, G. P. *The Life Enrichment Activity Program: A Community Children's Culture Center.* Hamden, Conn.: George P. Witt, 1965.

CHAPTER 5

Creative Positives of Disadvantaged Children and Youth

E. Paul Torrance

Dr. Torrance is Chairman and Professor, Department of Educational Psychology, The University of Georgia.

How realistic is our dream of educating to the extent of their potentialities children who live in poverty?

Reading some of the recently published accounts of what happens in classrooms in big city ghettos and other disadvantaged areas gives one a feeling of hopelessness. Just try reading such accounts as Bel Kaufman's *Up the Down Stair Case* (1964), Robert Kendall's *White Teacher in a Black School* (1964), Elizabeth M. Eddy's *Walk the Chalk Line* (1965), James Herndon's *The Way It Spozed to Be* (1965), Margaret Anderson's *The Children of the South* (1966), Herbert Kohl's *36 Children* (1967), Jonathan Kozol's *Death at an Early Age* (1967), and Robert Coles' *Dead End School* (1968). Even though I fear that the picture presented by these accounts is fairly realistic insofar as the great bulk of the education of disadvantaged children is concerned, I do not believe that our dream is an impossible one or one that we should surrender easily. Certainly we get a glimmer of what might result from a more optimistic assessment of the potentialities of disadvantaged children from such work as E. R. Braithwaite's *To Sir, With Love* (1959), Robert Rosenthal and Lenore Jacobson's *Pygmalion in the Classroom* (1968), and Robert Glasser's *Schools Without Failure* (1969).

It is not possible to estimate accurately the amount of unawakened and unrecognized potential lost each year. Joseph H. Douglass (1969), Staff Director of the 1970 White House Conference on Children and Youth, recently estimated that

Reprinted from Torrance, E. P. (1969). Creative positives of disadvantaged children and youth. Gifted Child Quarterly, 13, 71–81. Reprinted with permission of Sage Publications.

some 80,000 of the youth who drop out each year have I.Q.'s within the top 25 percent of the population—that is, 110 or better. He also estimated that this potential will never be tapped and will be irretrievably lost. Douglass also reported that very few school systems throughout the country have instituted programs for the identification of the talented and that there is no follow through in the few programs that have been initiated. He reports further that programs for the retrieval of talent among the disadvantaged are practically nonexistent. Douglass further challenges that "no satisfactory method yet has been devised to discover or predict talent potential among individuals who, for economic and cultural reasons, are not in the mainstream of American life."

Issues Concerning Unrecognized Potential

I am optimistic about the possibilities of discovering talent potential among disadvantaged children and youth. In several sources, I (1963, 1968, 1969) have suggested possible approaches and given information about my own very limited work on this problem. I believe that George Witt's (1968) LEAP Project in New Haven, Connecticut, and Kay Bruch's (1969) work in Athens, Georgia, indicate that the possibilities are indeed exciting and that the idea of awakening and recognizing extraordinary potentialities among disadvantaged children is much more than "an impossible dream."

I must admit, however, that the dream is an impossible one as long as we insist on identifying and cultivating only those kinds of talent that the dominant, advantaged culture values. We must also look for and cultivate talents of the type that are valued in the various disadvantaged subcultures of our country. Can't we see that this is what the youth in disadvantaged subcultures have been trying to tell us during the past two or three years? Why do you suppose Mexican-American students strike to get more books written in Spanish in school libraries and to protest the tendency for high school counselors to insist that they concentrate on shop courses? Why do you suppose black students sit in at colleges and demand departments for the study of black culture and a hand in awarding scholarships? Why do you suppose young Indian leaders are calling for "Red Power" and demanding the right to develop a separate Indian way of life? Why do you suppose Puerto Ricans are joining with blacks to get control of neighborhood schools?

Obviously, all of these movements represent efforts by disadvantaged groups in our society to gain more power over their lives. They are trying to develop pride in themselves and their heritage. They are searching for more favorable and more realistic self images. James Brown, the black soul singer pleads, "Say It Loud, I'm Black and I'm Proud." I see underneath all these movements a plea that educators recognize and cultivate talents of the type that are highly valued in the various disadvantaged subcultures of our country.

My position (Torrance, 1969) is that not only should we identify and cultivate the talents valued by a particular subculture but that we shall be more successful if we do. Criticisms of our established talent assessment procedures when applied to disadvantaged children and youth are too well known to be enumerated. On the positive side, we can point with some degree of success in the identification and cultivation of talent among disadvantaged groups in instrumental and vocal music, dancing, dramatics, visual art, and athletics. Even here, there has been gross neglect of talent. There has always been far more of this kind of talent than we have been willing to recognize and use. These are kinds of talents that are valued among disadvantaged cultures in the United States and I believe a survey would show that we could locate a higher proportion of high level talent in these areas among disadvantaged than among advantaged groups.

I have offered two suggestions for finding hidden talent among disadvantaged children and my colleague, Kay Bruch, has offered a third. It seems to me that a part of the difficulty, but only a part of it, lies in the nature of the talent tests whatever their nature. Most of them require that the child respond in terms of the experiences common in our dominant, advantaged culture. The disadvantaged child is not permitted to respond in terms of his own experiences, the experiences common in his culture or unique to himself. Most tests of creativity—and the *Torrance Tests of Creative Thinking* (Torrance, 1966) in particular—permit disadvantaged children to respond in terms of their own experiences. This increases the chances of obtaining responses and makes it possible to evaluate the responses in terms of the child's experiences whatever they might be.

Other problems of talent identification lay almost completely outside the nature of the instruments used in the process. In order to obtain an indication of potentiality from a child, it is necessary to motivate him to display that potentiality and to feel psychologically safe in doing so. In my own work with disadvantaged black children, I have used the creativity workshop as a format for accomplishing this goal. In this format, I have found that tests of creative thinking ability take on more power than in typical situations (Torrance, 1968). Even in formal situations, disadvantaged children perform rather well on the figural tests of creative thinking ability (Torrance, 1967). Their performance on the verbal tests, however, is quite poor in the formal school testing situation. This is, of course, in line with numerous findings concerning the generally poor performance of disadvantaged children on almost all kinds of verbal tests and on speeded or timed tests.

In the creativity workshop, three procedures were used to elicit the hidden verbal abilities for which we were searching. No tests were given until there had been time for the creative processes of the children to become awakened. No time limits were imposed. The examiners offered to record the children's ideas. These procedures were generally quite effective. No one observing these activities or the resulting products could have said that these children were nonverbal.

Bruch (1969) has made another important point. She contends that for the disadvantaged the identification question cannot be whether they perform on tests of intelligence or achievement at a currently high level, but whether there are indices of probable development to higher levels than those at which they now function. She offers as an example a youth who had demonstrated exceptional talent in music, a culturally valued talent among the black disadvantaged. She argues that this youth may also be able to function more fully through latent abilities in academic areas. She suggests that through his specific culturally valued talent, music, a developmental program could be built for the needed abilities in vocabulary fluency and comprehension, mathematical symbolic thinking, and other thinking processes.

On the basis of both published (Torrance, 1964, 1967) and unpublished studies of disadvantaged groups, I believe I have identified a set of creative positives that occur to a high degree among disadvantaged children and upon which I believe we can build successful educational programs for awakening many potentialities. The following is a list of these creative positives:

1. *High non-verbal fluency and originality.* On the figural forms of the *Torrance Tests of Creative Thinking* (1966) disadvantaged groups almost always hold their own or even excel similar advantaged groups. This seems to hold true in a variety of localities throughout the United States and for Negroes, American Indians, Mexican-Americans, and Caucasians. Frequently, however, their figural flexibility and elaboration are less outstanding. I have also noticed high fluency and originality, and sometimes flexibility and elaboration as well, in creative movement or dance. It also comes out in games, problem-solving activities, and the like.

2. *High creative productivity in small groups.* In my experience, I have found disadvantaged children to be more highly productive in small groups than in individual or large group situations. They even become quite verbal in small group creative problem-solving situations and seem less inhibited than more advantaged children. Leaders emerge and are given support by the rest of the group.

3. *Adept in visual art activities.* In every disadvantaged group with which I have worked there have been surprisingly large numbers of gifted artists. In some cases, they have persisted in being copyists rather than trusting their originality. This seems to be more characteristic of the Negro than of the American Indian and Mexican-American groups on which we have data. Even the gifted Negro artists become more imaginative and inventive as they become involved in group activities such as puppetry, making giant murals, and the like.

4. *Highly creative in movement, dance, and other physical activities.* Disadvantaged children seem to take naturally to work in creative movement, dance, and

other physical activities. Many of them will work hard at these activities and develop considerable discipline. In our workshop last summer we gave some emphasis to hula hoop activities. Two of the girls in the workshop won district championships and one of them later won the city championship and was second place winner in the state contest. None of the boys in our workshop showed the discipline to practice with hula hoops to attain championship form. If we had encouraged them to enter the Frisbee contest, they might have developed such discipline.

5. *Highly motivated by games, music, sports, humor, and concrete objects.* The warm-up effects of games, music, sports, humor, and the like seem to enable disadvantaged children to achieve a higher level of mental functioning than otherwise attained.
6. *Language rich in imagery.* In telling stories, making up songs, and producing solutions to problems, their language is rich in imagery.

Although we must obtain data from other disadvantaged groups and complete additional analyses of the data we already have, the findings seem clear enough to warrant a few rather gross implications. First, if you are searching for gifted children among disadvantaged populations, you will be assured of greater success if you seek them in the areas I have identified than in traditional ways. Second, more serious consideration should be given to careers in the creative arts and sciences for disadvantaged youth than we have in the past. When asked about their aspirations, almost no disadvantaged children express choices in the creative fields, (Torrance, 1967). Yet many disadvantaged persons who have attained success have done so in the creative fields, especially where talent has known no limits.

Awakening Unrecognized Potential

I know of no large-scale, deliberate attempts to identify and awaken creative talent among disadvantaged groups. Frank Standage in Project Talent Search in Eastern Kentucky has administered 10,000 Appalachian youngsters the *Torrance Tests of Creative Thinking* and has launched a program for recognizing and awakening the potentialities indicated by the results of this particular talent search. It is too early even to speculate about the outcomes of this project except to say that a wealth of outstanding talent is being found among these rather disadvantaged youths. The only sustained project of which I am aware in which creatively gifted disadvantaged children have been identified through tests, then recognized, and provided a program designed to awaken their potentialities is the Life Enrichment Activity Program or LEAP initiated and sustained by George Witt at New Haven, Connecticut.

Preliminary Results of the Life Enrichment Activity Program

George Witt (1968) initiated a program over three years ago for a group of 16 highly creative, lower-class Negro children in a ghetto setting. He believed that highly creative children are injured more in such settings than are their less creative peers. Witt selected his 16 highly creative children from the second through fourth grade of a ghetto school solely on the basis of tests of creative thinking *(The Torrance Tests of Creative Thinking* and one test task that Witt himself devised).

Twelve of the original 16 children have continued in the program for over three years and all of them have manifested high level creative skills in such fields as music, art, science, and writing. Much work has been done with the families. In many instances, the high creative talents of siblings have been recognized and opportunities have been provided for them to have music, art, ballet, and other kinds of lessons from outstanding teachers. In a few instances, it has been possible to help parents of the children upgrade their job skills and acquire better jobs. In fashioning a program for highly creative, inner-city children, Witt attempted to incorporate the following major characteristics:

1. be clearly structured but flexible;
2. provide for opportunities to be rewarded for solving problems;
3. be viewed by one and all in a positive light;
4. be tangible; and have many activities conducted in the homes;
5. have enough competent adults in charge to minimize the need for the ubiquitous instant jeering and quarreling;
6. continue controls indefinitely;
7. involve exciting people from the inner and non-inner city;
8. design all learning experiences so that exciting perceptual-motor experiences precede, accompany, and follow cognitive growth;
9. be intimately coordinated by a director expert in individual, group, and community dynamics;
10. provide for the support, control, and involvement of the children's families, parents, and siblings.

Each year, Witt reports, new structural elements have been added to the program as the children, their families, and the programs have grown. During the first part of the program the specialists who worked with the program began to doubt that the children who had been selected had any kind of creative potentialities. Witt encouraged them to keep working, however, and he continued working with the children and involving their families. Before the end of the first summer, all of the children had exhibited outstanding promise in at least one creative field and many of them had shown unusual promise in two or more areas. It would be hazardous to predict the adult futures of the twelve children who have continued in the program devised by Witt and called "LEAP" (Life Enrichment Activity Program). The present indications, however, are that these children are developing talents that are highly valued both in their own subcultures and in the dominant culture, that their families are supporting their development and in most cases developing along with them. There are indications that such talents can be identified at least as early as age eight and that there is a bountiful supply of such talent in almost all disadvantaged groups.

In my search for imaginative projects at the high school level, I came across a promising one (Howe, 1969) in which girls from Goucher College taught poetry in a vocational-technical high school in the inner-city area of Baltimore. This experience demonstrates how creativity development can awaken unrecognized potentialities under what would appear to be very improbable situations. The Goucher undergraduates had not been trained as teachers but they knew and loved poetry and they knew about "open questions" that provoke deep, creative thinking about poetry. The students were tenth-grade boys in the auto mechanics curriculum. The school faculty was quite skeptical about what would happen with untrained teachers. The teaching was in small groups of five or six students. The poems selected by the Goucher girls ranged from very brief "pop" poetry to a relatively long narrative poem by Robert Frost called "Out, Out." They taught the boys about open and closed questions and that they did not have to play the traditional game of closed, single answer questions. As the boys discovered that they could actually determine curriculum, they became less shy about saying what they liked. They enjoyed solving the puzzles posed by some of the poems. They liked poems that were difficult but not too difficult. They thought that a poem had to have "something to say". There were serious discussions about the way the students lived, about such matters as race, policemen, drugs, war, religion, etc.

How can we evaluate such experiences? How do we know that such creative experience awakened unrecognized potentialities? The project participants had several discussions about how they could get an evaluation without testing the students. Finally, they decided to give the boys four poems that they had not previously seen. The boys were asked to write on one of the four poems that they particularly liked and to explain why they did and what the poem was saying. Most of them wrote freely, assured that their papers would not be corrected or graded. One of the school's regular teachers who had been skeptical all along conducted her own experiment. She gave the same writing assignment to other classes in the school which had not had this kind of creative experience in poetry. She admitted that by any standards the boys taught by the Goucher students were superior to the others. This may sound like a miracle but it isn't. I do not think that this experience tells us that teachers do not need to learn methods. They do. I think the Goucher undergraduates had learned some good methods. They knew the methods of open-ended questions. They understood that poems communicate feelings and that the teacher's method must help students get to the poem's words by encouraging and permitting open response to feelings. Even when we do not share ideas or values, we share feelings. We also share the language of feeling—sadness, joy, suffering, anger, wonder. Perhaps this is a way into language for deprived children and young people who are labeled as non-verbal.

In stressing the importance of creativity development in awakening unrecognized potential, I must make it crystal clear that I do not see it as a panacea or cure-all. We all know that much else is necessary. Certainly we must see that basic physiological and psychological needs are satisfied. Unrecognized potential in children will not be awakened as long as they are hungry, cold, inadequately clothed and housed—as long as their lives are unsafe—as long as they feel that they do not belong—as long as their dignity is not respected—as long as they experience no love, respect, or self-esteem. If this unrecognized potential is to be awakened, children must be supplied with what Maslow (1968) calls B-values—love, truth, beauty, and justice. Maslow points out the well known fact that if you take away all love from children, it can kill them. Children need truth in the same way. The child deprived of truth becomes paranoid, mistrusting everybody, searching for hidden meanings. Deprivation of beauty also causes illness. Children become very depressed and uncomfortable in ugly surroundings. It affects their whole being—memory, thinking, creativity, judgment. Deprivation of justice also sickens and history tells what happens to people deprived of justice for a long time.

For unrecognized potential to become awakened there must be a feeling of purpose—a feeling of destiny. The Hippies in California told me that I am too achievement-oriented in my thinking about creativity. Perhaps I am, but I have always insisted upon the importance of the intrinsic motivation inherent in creative ways of learning and creative activities. Extrinsic motivations may be effective in many instances but both rewards and punishment are quite erratic in their effects. Even when they are effective, they must be applied again and again to keep learning going. Maslow (1968) tells the amusing anecdote of a psychology class which played a prank on their professor by secretly conditioning him while he was delivering a lecture on conditioning. The professor, without realizing it, began nodding more and more. By the end of the lecture he was nodding continually. As soon as the class told the professor what he was doing, he stopped nodding. After that no amount of smiling on the part of the class could make him nod again. Truth had made the learning disappear. The very essence of creativity development is the search for the truth. Such learning is enduring, and there is built-in motivation that keeps the process going.

Another thing we all know is that we must be willing to pay the price of awakening unrecognized potential. It takes energy, imagination, hard work, and money. We are reminded of this on every hand. In reviewing Ronald Goldman's (1968) book, *Breakthrough*, which analyzes the life experiences of a number of eminent people who came up through poverty, Brian Jackson (1968) states the problem as follows:

> "... Every wretched primary school in the rundown centers of our big cities has as much latent talent in it as any Hampstead kindergarten. But we shall see little evidence of it, and that distorted, till we civilize our priorities, and begin by spending most money on those children who had least to start with."

REFERENCES

Anderson, M. *The Children of the South*. New York: Farrar, Straus and Giroux, 1966.
Braithwaite, E. R. *To Sir, With Love*. Englewood Cliffs, N.J.: Prentice-Hall, Inc., 1959.
Bruch, C. "A Proposed Rationale for the Identification and Development of the Gifted Disadvantaged." Athens, Ga.: Department of Educational Psychology, University of Georgia, 1969.
Coles, R. *Dead End School*. Boston: Atlantic-Little, Brown, 1968.
Douglass, J. H. "Strategies for Maximizing the Development of Talent among the Urban Disadvantaged". Paper prepared for the 47th Annual Convention of the Council for Exceptional Children, April 9, 1969, Denver, Colorado.
Eddy, E. M. *Walk the White Line*. Garden City, N.Y.: Doubleday & Company, Inc., 1967.
Glasser, W. *Schools Without Failure*. New York: Harper & Row, 1969.
Goldman, R. J. *Breakthrough*. London: Routledge & Kegan Paul, Ltd., 1968.
Herndon, J. *The Way It Spozed to Be*. New York: Simon and Schuster, 1965.
Howe, F. "Untaught teachers and improbable poets." *Saturday Review*, March 15, 1969, 52 (11), 60–62, 79.
Jackson, B. *"Going through the mill." The Guardian (Manchester)*, December 20, 1968.
Kaufman, B. *Up the Down Staircase*. Englewood Cliffs, N.J.: Prentice-Hall, Inc., 1964.
Kendall, R. *White Teacher in a Black School*. Chicago: Henry Regnery Company, 1964.
Kohl, H. *36 Children*. New York: New American Library, 1967.
Kozol, J. *Death at an Early Age*. Boston: Houghton Mifflin Company, 1967.
Maslow, A. H. "Goals of Humanistic Education." (Tape Recording) Esalen Institute, Big Sur, Calif., 1968.
Rosenthal, R. & L. Jacobson. *Pygmalion in the Classroom*. New York: Holt, Rinehart and Winston, Inc., 1968.
Torrance, E. P. *Education and the Creative Potential*. Minneapolis: University of Minnesota Press, 1963.
Torrance, E. P. *Rewarding Creative Behavior*. Englewood Cliffs, N.J.: Prentice-Hall, Inc., 1965.
Torrance, E. P. *Torrance Tests of Creative Thinking: Norms-Technical Manual (Research Edition)*. Princeton, N.J.: Personnel Press, Inc., 1966.
Torrance, E. P. *Understanding the Fourth Grade Slump in Creativity*. Athens, Ga.: Georgia Studies of Creative Behavior, 1967.

Torrance, E. P. "Finding hidden talents among disadvantaged children." *Gifted Child Quarterly*, 1968, 12, 67–78.

Torrance, E. P. "Issues in the identification and encouragement of disadvantaged Children." *TAG Gifted Children Newsletter*, March, 1969, 11(2) 48–55.

Witt, G. *The Life Enrichment Activity Program: A Brief History.* New Haven, Conn.: LEAP, Inc., 363 Dixwell Avenue, 1968. (Mimeographed).

CHAPTER 6

The Role of Creativity in Identification of the Gifted and Talented

E. Paul Torrance

For more than 40 years I have maintained that creativity should always be one of the criteria considered in identifying gifted and talented students. I welcome this opportunity to review briefly some of the events that led me to this conclusion and have continued to reinforce it and to restate what I regard as the most important principles that should guide school systems in their identification policies and procedures.

THE PROBLEM

Throughout history, a common characteristic of those who have made outstanding artistic and scientific contributions, social improvements, technological breakthroughs, and the like has been their creativity. The importance of identifying and developing creative talent has been argued by historians such as Toynbee (1964), futurists (Polak, 1973), scientists (Seaborg, 1963), educators (Torrance, 1979). Today there are additional reasons why it is necessary to give a fair chance to creative children, young people, and adults. We are living in an age of increasing rates of change, depleted natural resources, threats of nuclear war, interdependence, and destandardization. All of these forces require us to utilize increased ingenuity and creativity.

These matters are widely acknowledged facts, yet legislators, educational leaders, and even scholars of gifted education express a peculiar ambivalence about

Reprinted from Torrance, E. P. (1984). The role of creativity in identification of the gifted and talented. *Gifted Child Quarterly, 28,* 153–156. Reprinted with permission of Sage Publications.

using creativity as a criterion in identifying gifted and talented students and applying the technology we have developed to facilitate this process and the development and improvement of creative functioning.

For centuries, Buddhists have used a kind of creativity test (*koans*) to select gifted candidates for training. The ancient Chinese and Japanese identified their geniuses by having them create poems on such topics as plum blossoms in the moonlight. Although Western societies have been generally ambivalent and often opposed to identifying and deliberately developing creative talent, patrons and sponsors in the Golden Ages of creative achievement in Italy, Greece, and France did it.

Perhaps the most difficult and fundamental problem in identifying creatively gifted and talented children is that of dealing with a national climate that is generally unfavorable to creative achievement. This is further complicated by a national climate that rather generally discourages the full development of potentialities, except for certain types of athletics. The problem is especially severe in the South. This problem was described rather eloquently some years ago by Lillian Smith (1949) in *Killers of the Dream*. She pointed out such paradoxes as the fact that we value beautiful things but import them from Asia and Europe to derogate our native sons who aspire to create beautiful things. We have feared hands that create but have accepted and honored hands that destroyed. In the South, as perhaps nowhere else, creativity has been considered sinful. We went through a long period in which the new learning, science, was considered sinful. I grew up in Georgia in such an environment. I can recall vividly, when I was thinking of going to college and hopelessly searching for the resources to do so, many of my friends were afraid that I would be exposed to this sinful science. Curiosity was sinful. Humor was sinful. Dancing was sinful. *Anything* creative was sinful.

This paradox, however, is not limited to the South, the creation of beautiful things, or to the time prior to 1957. Even now in these times of economic crisis, our inventors and researchers are treated rather shabbily and many of our corporations prefer to purchase high technology from Japan or Germany rather than permit our inventors and researchers to develop their own. As a consequence the number of patents and inventions by citizens of the United States has been dropping since 1978. Since 1967, Japan has been increasing its lead over the United States in the number of patents and inventions each year (Orkin, 1974). Orkin (1981) and others attribute this lag to laws that do not protect the rights of inventors and rob them of their just rewards.

My Personal Odyssey

When I began teaching eighth and ninth graders in 1936 after completing only two years of college, I wondered why I had so much trouble with a few creatively gifted students I tried to teach. (There was no problem of identification. Their creativity was richly manifest in the thousands of strategies they invented to defeat me.) I punished them and punished them, about the only thing that I knew then to do. This bothered me, as I knew they were gifted and that I was not able to meet their needs. (Incidentally, these creatively gifted troublemakers later became school superintendents, labor negotiators, ministers, and one of them Secretary of Labor in the Ford Presidential Cabinet.)

My problem became even more severe during my second year of teaching at Georgia Military College High School, a local high school for boys and a boarding school primarily for boys who were unable to adapt to their local high schools. Generally, their creative giftedness was at the seat of their behavior and learning problems. Somehow, I developed some teaching strategies and methods that worked. I was especially successful in teaching students who failed certain courses like geometry during the first semester. I taught them for the second semester, and generally most of them outachieved their classmates in the original classes who had passed the first semester. When I began teaching these special classes, my teaching colleagues pitied me for being assigned so many "unteachable" students. However, they became angry when my students outachieved their own at the end of the year on standardized achievement tests. Somehow, I had been able to use the creative strengths of these students and they had overcome unfavorable attitudes about the subject matter, learning more in one semester than their peers had learned in two semesters.

It was during this period that I developed in 1943 my first creativity test. By that time, I had become involved in counselor training, tests and measurements, and the like. It seemed to me that the available tests did not identify the kinds of giftedness that I sensed in so many of my students.

This work was interrupted in 1945 by my military service in World War II, counseling disabled veterans following World War II, studying how to train aircrews to survive emergencies and extreme conditions, and trying to find out what made some fighter pilots aces. My military assignment in World War II was to interview and prepare classification summaries for men who had been courtmartialed and later to develop a program to prepare them to re-enter life outside of prison. Again, it was clear to me that many of these men were in trouble on account of their creativity and that their successful adaptation to society would depend upon their management of this creativity. Many times, I was painfully aware that a lack of measure of creative talent made it difficult for me to support adequately a disabled veteran's plans for the future. As I began to study the psychology of survival in emergencies and extreme conditions, it soon became clear to me that training for survival should include training in creative problem solving. Thus, many of the assessment instruments we developed and the training procedures we suggested revolved around this insight. As my associates and I completed our intensive personality studies of the United States jet aces in Korea, it also became clear that a distinguishing characteristic of these aces was their creativity.

When I became director of the Bureau of Educational Research at the University of Minnesota in 1958, the advisory committee recommended that we initiate a pioneering program of research on giftedness. College of Education Dean Walter W. Cook was firmly committed to the concept of a variety of kinds of giftedness and the advisory committee was approving. It was then easy for me to make the decision to begin work on the identification of creatively gifted and talented students and the cultivation of this kind of giftedness.

Development of Tests of Creative Talent

My research assistants and I began work almost immediately with students at all educational levels. I had been taught that almost all scientific progress is dependent upon the development and calibration of instruments for measuring the phenomena under investigation. We developed a variety of tests of creative thinking ability, creative motivation scales, and biographical inventories based upon our theories about the life experiences through which creative thinking skills and creative motivations and commitment develop. Most of our predictive validity studies, however, were targeted to test the validity of a general purpose battery of creative thinking ability tests that could be used from kindergarten through graduate and professional education.

Our first major predictive validity study (Torrance, Tan, & Allman, 1970) was with elementary education majors who were followed up eight years later. Tan and I developed a checklist of creative behavior exhibited by elementary teachers and this yielded a measure of creative behavior for 114 of the subjects who had become elementary school teachers and returned our follow-up questionnaire. Coefficients of correlation of .62 and .57 were obtained between the indices of creative teaching behavior and two measures of verbal creativity obtained at the time they were juniors in elementary education.

At the same time I initiated the elementary teacher study, I also began longitudinal studies with both elementary and high school students. The high school students were followed up in 1970 (Torrance, 1972), 12 years later, and the elementary school students were followed up in 1980 (Torrance, 1981), 22 years later. In my opinion, both of these studies have yielded encouraging results and have shown clear relationships between creativity test performances in elementary and high school and "real life" creative achievements.

In the high school study, follow-up data were obtained from 230 subjects. These data included: information about publicly recognized and acknowledged creative achievements (such as patents and inventions, new products developed and marketed, books published, scientific discoveries, awards in the arts and sciences, new businesses initiated, and the like); descriptions of their three highest creative achievements; and future career images. An overall validity coefficient of .51 was obtained for the creativity measures and these criteria. For males, this validity coefficient was .59 and for females it was .46 (Torrance, 1972).

In the elementary school study, follow-up data were obtained for 220 subjects. The same kinds of follow-up data were obtained for them as had been obtained for their older counterparts. In addition, data were obtained about their more personal, not publicly recognized, creative achievements. Even though this study covered a span of 22 years, the validity coefficients were equally as good as in the 12-year study. For males, the overall validity coefficient was .62; for females, it was .57. For the total sample, an overall validity coefficient of .63 was obtained. Although the creativity test predictors leave considerable unexplained variance, it is unusual to find higher predictive validity for intelligence and achievement tests or other predictor variables in similar studies. In the present study, validity coefficients for measures of intelligence ranged from -.02 to .34 and averaged .17. In the present study, it was found that additional variance could be explained by such things as having certain teachers known for encouraging creativity, having a mentor, having a future career image during the elementary school years, and having experiences with foreign study and living. Thus, I believe that the predictive validity is as good as we have any right to expect for almost any kind of predictor of adult achievements (Torrance, 1981).

Although there have been several predictive validity studies with the *Torrance Tests of Creative Thinking*, as well as with other creativity predictors, except for two by Howieson (1981, 1984), all of them have been for relatively short periods (usually about five years). Howieson (1981) reported a 10-year follow-up study covering the period from 1965 to 1975 in Australia. Her subjects were 400 seventh graders and the criterion data consisted of responses to the Wallach and Wing (1969) checklist of creative achievements outside of the school curriculum. The total score on the *Torrance Tests of Creative Thinking* correlated .30 with the total criterion score. As in the Torrance studies, the predictions were more accurate for the males than for the females. Howieson (1984) has just completed a 23-year follow-up study using predictor data collected in 1960 by Torrance in Western Australia. Although the verbal measures derived from the *Torrance Tests of Creative Thinking* failed to predict adult creative achievements at a satisfactory level for the 306 subjects who returned their questionnaires, the figural measures fared rather well. For her measure of quality of publicly recognized creative achievements, Howieson obtained a multiple correlation coefficient of .51; for quantity of personal (not publicly recognized) creative achievements, a multiple coefficient of correlation of .33; and for quality of personal creative achievements, one of .44.

It is not possible to estimate accurately the extent to which creativity tests are now being used to identify the gifted and talented. Yarborough and Johnson

(1983) reported a survey of 36 state departments of education which resulted in the identification of 109 outstanding programs for the gifted and talented. In 31% of the 87 programs supplying appropriate data, creativity tests had been used in identification. In some states, creativity tests are listed among the acceptable criteria for identifying the gifted; in some, creativity tests are not mentioned as acceptable criteria; and in still others, creativity tests are explicitly named as unacceptable criteria. In most instances, the *Torrance Tests of Creative Thinking* and other measures of creative talent are used as a part of multiple criteria selection, employing some device such as the *Baldwin Identification Matrix* (Baldwin & Wooster, 1977) wherein several indicators of giftedness are weighted and a composite index developed. In some instances, a group intelligence test is used for initial screening and a creativity test is administered to students who attain a certain cutoff score (such as an IQ of 115 or higher) but do not achieve a higher cut-off score such as 130, 135, or 140.

Documentation of Validity of Creativity as a Criterion

Students in the IQ range of 115 to 130 who are identified as creatively gifted (generally Creativity Indices of 130 or higher) seem to hold their own quite well in academically-oriented gifted programs and achieve as well as their less creative peers who have IQs of 130 or higher. In defending this position, I have cited my earlier studies (Torrance, 1962) and the Getzels and Jackson (1962) study which showed that creatively gifted students missing such cut-off points as 130 IQs, achieve as well as their classmates with IQs in excess of 130 who would be classified as creatively gifted by similar standards.

More convincing, however, is my comparative longitudinal study of the adult creative achievements of elementary school children identified as highly intelligent and highly creative (Torrance and Wu, 1981). On all four of the criteria of adult creative achievement (number of publicly recognized creative achievements, number of personal creative achievements, quality of highest creative achievements, and quality of future career images), the highly creative group excelled over the highly intelligent group and equaled those who were highly intelligent and highly creative. They also achieved as many post high school degrees, honors, and other academic attainments as their more intelligent (higher IQ) counterparts.

Recommended Principles for Identification Policies and Procedures

In summary, I suggest the following five policies and procedures regarding the identification of the gifted and the talented on the basis of the experiences and research described herein:

1. Creativity should almost always be one of the criteria, though not the sole criterion. In general, when creativity indicators are used, students who might otherwise be missed, should be included rather than to exclude anyone.
2. Different kinds of excellence (multiple talents) should be evaluated. Society needs many different kinds of talent and schools should encourage them.
3. Where disabilities and sensory handicaps are involved and where young children (3 to 6 years) are involved, attention must be given to procedures that permit responses in a modality possible for the student.
4. Where disadvantaged and culturally different children are involved, attention must also be given to the selection of test tasks that assess the kinds of excellence that are valued by the particular culture or subculture of the children being evaluated.
5. Even in using creativity tests, select one that considers a wide variety of indicators rather than a single one. For example, the new streamlined scoring of the figural forms of the *Torrance Tests of Creative Thinking* (Torrance & Ball, 1984; Howieson, 1984) which considers five norm-referenced and thirteen criterion-referenced indicators, yields better predictive validity than does the earlier scoring system which considers only four norm-referenced indicators.

REFERENCES

Baldwin, A. Y., & Wooster, J. *Baldwin identification matrix inservice kit for the identification of gifted and talented students.* Buffalo, NY: DOK Publishers, 1977.

Getzels, J. W., & Jackson, P. W. *Creativity and intelligence.* NYC: John Wiley, 1962.

Howieson, N. A longitudinal study of creativity: 1965–1975. *Journal of Creative Behavior,* 1981, *15,* 117–135.

Howieson, N. The prediction of creative achievement from childhood measures: A longitudinal study in Australia, 1960–1983. *Unpublished doctoral dissertation,* University of Georgia, 1984.

Orkin, N. Legal rights of the employed inventor: New approaches to old problems. *Journal of the Potent Office Society,* 1974, *December.*

Orkin, H. The legal rights of the employed inventor in the United States: A labor management perspective. In J. Phillips (Ed.), *Employees' inventions: A comparative study.* Sunderland, England; Fernsway Publications, 1981.

Polak, F. L. *The image of the future.* NYC: Elsevier, 1973.

Seaborg, G. T. Training the creative scientist. *Science Newsletter,* 1963, *83,* 314.

Smith, L. *Killers of the dream.* NYC: Norton, 1949.

Torrance, E. P. *Guiding creative talent.* Englewood Cliffs, NJ: Prentice Hall, 1962.

Torrance, E. P. Career patterns and peak creative achievements of creative high school students 12 years later. *Gifted Child Quarterly,* 1972, *16,* 75–88.

Torrance, E. P. *The Torrance tests of creative thinking: Norms-technical manual.* Bensenville, IL: Scholastic Testing Service, 1974.

Torrance, E. P. *The search for satori and creativity.* Buffalo, NY: Creative Education Foundation, 1979.

Torrance, E. P. Predicting the creativity of elementary school children (1958–80)—and the teacher who "made a difference." *Gifted Child Quarterly, 1981, 25,* 55–62.

Torrance, E. P., & Ball, O. E. *Torrance tests of creative thinking: Streamlined (revised) manual, figural A and B.* Bensenville, IL: Scholastic Testing Service, 1984.

Torrance, E. P., Tan, C. A., & Allman, T. Verbal originality and teacher behavior: A predictive validity study. *Journal of Teacher Education,* 1970, *21,* 335–341.

Torrance, E. P., & Wu, T. H. A comparative longitudinal study of the adult creative achievements of elementary school children identified as highly intelligent and as highly creative. *Creative Child and Adult Quarterly,* 1981, *6,* 71–76.

Toynbee, A. Is America neglecting her creative minority? In C. W. Taylor (Ed.), *Widening horizons of creativity.* NYC: John Wiley, 1964.

Wallach, M., & Wing, C. W., Jr. *The talented student.* NYC: Holt, Rinehart & Winston, 1969.

Yarborough, B. H., & Johnson, R. A. Identifying the gifted: A theory-practice gap. *Gifted Child Quarterly,* 1983, *27,* 135–138.

E. Paul Torrance, Alumni Foundation Distinguished Professor of Educational Psychology. Address: The University of Georgia, Aderhold Hall, Athens, Georgia 30602.

CHAPTER 7

Understanding the Challenge of Creativity Among African Americans

Alexinia Young Baldwin

The relationship between creativity and intelligence, the recognition of creativity in students (a process that can be empirically documented), and the basic construct of creativity are the basis for much discussion. In adding a special population to the discussion, such as African Americans, who, as a group, have a special approach to creativity or method of exhibiting creativity, raises the level of discourse. As Banks (1988) has indicated, cultural behaviors can be distinct within an ethnic group, yet have an overlay from other cultures from the environment in which they exist. Many creative behaviors shown by African Americans overlap those of other cultures. The basic premise of creativity and its underlying principles exists in all populations, but the representation, manifestation, or melding of these principles varies within and among groups.

WHAT ARE WE SAYING ABOUT CREATIVITY?

Clark (1988) outlined an integrated concept of creativity that includes: thinking (can be developed and measured); sensing (creation of new products or talent in a particular area); feeling (emotional energy from the creator); and intuition (high consciousness or high awareness of elements in the environment). Torrance, on the other hand, titled his book *The Searcher Satori & Creativity*. The Japanese meaning of satori translates into what Americans might call an "a-ha" experience. Torrance (1979) explained satori as the highest point attainable, a sudden flash of enlightenment. Satori evolves when there has been "intensive, long-term, one-to-one relationship to a 'sensei'" (teacher). Above all, satori requires persistence, hard work, self-discipline, diligence, energy, effort, competence, expertness" (p. ix). This fits into what Clark called the thinking part of creativity.

Historical reports of the last decades are revealing more and more about the creative endeavors of African Americans. Unique problem-solving skills helped members of this population survive in the face of many inequities. Little attention, however, has been paid to the relationship of these skills to creativity and, thus, to intelligence.

Hughes (1969), Kurtzman (1967), Stein (1962, as referenced in Clark, 1988) subscribed to several traits for the rationally thinking creative individual. Although the traits listed could apply to all populations, there are several that can be found most often among African American students. These are:

- often anti-authoritarian;
- zany sense of humor;
- more adventurous;
- little tolerance for boredom; and
- high divergent thinking ability.

Clark's (1988) explanation of sensing, feeling, and intuition draws attention to similar characteristics or traits that also coincide with those found among African American children. These include:

- a special kind of perception;
- more spontaneous and expressive;
- openness to experience and new ideas;
- skilled performance of the traditional arts; and
- when confronted with novelty of design, music, or ideas, gets excited and involved (less creative people get suspicious and hostile; Clark, 1988).

Baldwin (1985) has listed some common characteristics and indicators that reflect creative traits. Her list coincides with those given above and reflects the integrated concept suggested by Clark (1988). Baldwin's list includes:

- language rich in imagery, humor, symbolism, and persuasion;
- logical reasoning, planning ability, and pragmatic problem-solving ability;
- sensitivity and alertness to movement; and
- resiliency to hardships encountered in the environment.

These traits are often exhibited in unusual and unacceptable classroom behaviors. Consequently, many teachers do not capitalize on these qualities to develop appropriate classroom activities that can develop new ideas through many media, become a catalyst for enhancing academic weaknesses, be a means for developing leadership skills, and promote a positive self-concept (Baldwin, 1985).

A negative self-concept has been a big issue that has been discussed over and over again as an important deterrent to the expression of giftedness or creativity among African American students. Torrance (1968) warned about discontinuity that can occur among children of minority groups when they lack a positive self-concept or are not seen as having true potential. He referred to this as a disruption of a child's experiences, thus causing him or her to feel out of place and creative activities to cease or become diminished.

Vygotsky's (1978) writings have caused psychologists to focus on the influence that environmental stimulation has on cognitive capabilities such as the language and intellectual development of children. Drawing upon this position, helping African American students to develop their creativity should also include providing environmental supports such as a stimulating environment, continual guidance, critical judgments of creative efforts, the use of manipulative or other nonverbal materials, and a chance to work independently or in small groups.

Piirto (1992) has reviewed several authors' concept of creativity. As a way of pulling together ideas that affect the rationale for placing creativity at a much higher level of importance for African American students, I have selected only a few to reference in this article.

In their 1976 ground-breaking study of problem finding in visual artists, Getzels and Csikszentmihalyi thought that creativity was an attempt to reduce tension that may not be perceived consciously. The way artist did this was to seek problems that could be solved symbolically through human imagination. When the problem was identified and a temporary solution found, the tension was released, but this differed from the simple concept of equilibration, which Piaget had described years earlier (Piirto, 1992, p. 20).

Gardner's book, *Frames of Mind* (1983), has given educators another way of looking at the traits that can be classified within a wide range of intellectual abilities. These abilities or intelligences are: (1) linguistic intelligence (use of language); (2) musical intelligence (thinking in musical terms); (3) logical-mathematical intelligence (thinking in terms of manipulation of numbers); (4) spatial intelligence (thinking and responding to the concept of space); (5) bodily-kinesthetic intelligence (use of the body to communicate ideas or concepts); (6) inter-personal intelligence (sensitivity to, and the ability to, relate to other people); (7) intra-personal intelligence (awareness of self with assurance); and (8) naturalistic intelligence (sensitivity to the features of the natural world). Creativity is an aspect of each of these intelligences. In addition, according to Gardner, creative individuals are often marked by an anomalous pattern of intelligences, by a tension between intellectual and personality styles, and by a striking lack of fit between personality and domain, intelligence and field, and biological constitution and choice of career. Indeed, it sometimes appears as if the very lack of fit served as a primary motivation for the individual to strike out in a new direction and, ultimately, to fashion a creative product (Gardner, 1988). Perhaps, as Gardner has theorized, "to conceptualize lifetime achievements of great magnitude, a new approach to the study of creativity [is] necessary" (Gardner, 1993 p. 299). Gardner has argued that it is important for educators to recognize the different ways in which individuals can express their mental processing abilities. For creativity to flourish with students presently enrolled in our classes, as well as those of generations to come, attention must be paid to the connections that creativity has with intelligence in general and Gardner's intelligences in particular.

Sternberg (1997) has listed in his triarchic view of giftedness three individual differences that might be found in a classroom. These are: analytic giftedness (the ability to dissect a problem and understand its parts); synthetic giftedness (reflected in a show of insight, intuition, or creativity and the ability to effectively handle new situations); and practical giftedness (the ability to apply analytic and synthetic intelligence to the solution of problems in various context). Those students who would score high in synthetic giftedness would probably do poorly on traditional intelligence tests. This applies significantly to many African American students, especially males.

Gardner and Sternberg have both emphasized the presence of creativity in all aspects of our daily lives and those of the children we teach. The inherent benefit of these positions is the recognition and the development of links from creativity to all aspects of our lives.

A study by Clasen, Middleton, and Connell (1994) sought to assess artistic and problem-solving performance in minority and nonminority students. In one part of the assessment, the researchers involved the students in problem-solving scenarios. They found that fluency and flexibility were the two constructs of problem solving on which minority students scored much higher than their nonminority peers. Peer identifications were a part of the total assessment technique, and the results were consistent across the home and school problem-solving scenarios. Several talented minority art students were discovered through the process that these authors used. However, it is meaningful for teachers to know the depth of feeling these students had about art. They all thought art was "fun," but also that it didn't matter in the whole scheme of school activities. They reasoned that the other subjects they studied were considered real "work" and more important to school performance. The researchers noted that, "At a time when school dropout rates of minorities, especially minority males, is of national concern, it would seem that systematic recognition and development of diverse talents is one way of convincing students that education can be meaningful" (p. 31).

As Piirto (1992) suggested, although theories of creativity have been proposed by many different philosophers and theoreticians, very little has been done to synthesize these theories. And, few individuals have had recommendations or insights about creativity among African American youngsters.

Torrance (1971) has been most prolific in his discussion of creativity among minority children (at the time of his writings referring to Black children). His work has been a guide, and he has provided significant exposure to both the quality of creativity and the lack of understanding about its presence in minority students. He used the statement of a 5-year-old Black student as a title of one of his conference papers: "I was a Block and Nobody Builded Me!" From this title, Torrance built a case for providing minority youth an educational program based upon their creative positives. His list of creative positives is one that has been presented over and over because it does not fall prey to the typical focus on deficits and negatives. Torrance's list includes:

- ability to express feeling and emotions;
- ability to improvise with commonplace materials;
- articulateness in role-playing and story telling;
- enjoyment of and ability in visual arts (drawing, painting, sculpture, etc.);
- enjoyment of and ability in creative movement, dance, dramatics, etc.;
- enjoyment of and ability in music, rhythm, etc.;
- expressive speech;
- fluency and flexibility in nonverbal media;
- enjoyment of and skills in group activities, problem solving, etc.;
- responsiveness to the concrete;
- responsiveness to the kinesthetic;
- expressiveness of gesture, body language, etc.;
- humor;
- richness in imagery in informal language;
- originality of ideas, problem solving;
- problem-centeredness;
- emotional responsiveness; and
- quickness of warm-up (Torrance, 1971).

Whereas Torrance called these positives, many teachers would see them as deficits because there are no state-wide evaluation tools to assess these qualities or textbooks that refer to these as proper content or behaviors. As a beginning teacher, I failed at first to see the creative giftedness in one of my students. Leonard was a child who did not fit (in my mind) the qualities of the gifted child. His homework was never finished, he was never on time to school, he was never selected first for participation on the baseball team, and his assignments were torn and generally unpresentable. After rejecting many of his assignments with a mark of "unsatisfactory," Leonard decided to do something different—not what I wanted, but what he wanted. When I saw that he had illustrated all of his language assignments in cartoon form with characters portraying the answers, I knew that I had a "block" that needed to be built. My eyes were opened to the many faces of giftedness and the importance of teachers allowing these faces to be shown. Leonard became a track star (competing singularly instead of in groups) and finished his senior year at the Sorbonne in France before returning to Georgetown University to complete a degree in international relations. There are many more cases out there where teachers fail to recognize the positives and build on them in the classroom.

Conclusions

Creativity will continue to be a difficult construct to define accurately, as is the case with its close associate, intelligence. Piirto (1992) has tried to give her readers a list of theoretical thoughts from 50 or more philosophers, psychologists, psychoanalytic theorists, and domain specific theorists (pp. 318–321) about creativity. This long list shows how uncertain the field is about a definition of creativity. However, it is an important variable to be considered when we think of parenting, teaching, testing, and rewarding excellence. The culture of an individual can influence his or her approaches to stimuli. For the African American student, expressions of creativity can be similar to those shown by children of other ethnic groups, but the interpretation of these behaviors will vary according to the ingrained opinion of what behaviors can be considered creative positives instead of deficits.

Piirto (1992) has offered several suggestions to help parents and teachers nurture creativity. They include parents providing a private place for creative work to be done. The place might be very small, but it belongs to the child even if it is for a short period of time. In the classroom, there should be a corner designed for a quiet getaway. Children should have an opportunity to have some musical experience with an instrument or in participatory activities. A sketch pad, crayons, and other art tools should be available. At school, the classroom should be filled with books, music, posters, and miscellaneous objects with which children can experiment. There should be a display of the child's work and encouragement to continue. Parents and teachers should show students that they appreciate creative activities and serve as role-models for them. Historical information about those African Americans who have been or are creative in various fields should be included in the curriculum for all children but especially for African American students.

The future, with new and ever expanding technological sources, will provide an avenue for African American students to experiment with their ideas without the stigma that might be attached to their behaviors in class. Teachers must be ready to channel this energy by incorporating creative explorations as part of the content to be studied. Locating information on the Internet is just one step toward channeling this creative energy. Inventing challenges and counterarguments as part of the strategy for learning is another. Lynch and Harris (2000) have suggested that refutational processes be used to stimulate creativity for the teacher and the student. An example of this technique could be to give students in a social studies class a story about the Civil War with several errors included (such as the Civil War was fought to protect the South's interest in the stock market, especially the markets in Europe and Asia). Students can be encouraged to refute this statement with a rationale for doing so. Lynch and Harris cite scholars who claim that teachers who have been able to understand this concept and work with their children in such a manner help students take risks, challenge ideas, and experiment with creative hypotheses.

Torrance's early concerns in the 1960s about creativity in minority students and his continuing concern in the 1990s about the lack of understanding and the manner in which creativity in minorities is recognized and enhanced highlights the slow recognition of this aspect of ability among African Americans. Hopefully, during the next century, educational theories will include as part of its facts and generalizations these creative positives that educational planners must recognize.

REFERENCES

Baldwin, A. Y. (1985). Programs for the gifted and talented: Issues concerning minority populations. In F. Horowitz & M. O'Brien (Eds.), *The gifted and talented: Developmental perspectives* (pp. 223–249). Washington DC: American Psychological Association.

Banks, J. (1988). *Multiethnic education: Theory and practice* (2nd ed.). Boston: Allyn and Bacon.

Clark, B. (1988). *Growing up gifted* (3rd ed.). Columbus, OH: Merrill.

Clasen, D., Middleton, J., & Connell, T. (1994). Assessing artistic and problem-solving performance in minority and nonminority students using a nontraditional multidimensional approach. *Gifted Child Quarterly, 38,* 27–32.

Gardner, H. (1983). *Frames of mind.* New York: Basic Books.

Gardner, H. (1988). Creative lives and creative works: A synthetic scientific approach. In R. Steinberg (Ed.) *The nature of creativity* (pp. 288–321). New York: Cambridge University Press.

Gardner, H. (1993). *Creating minds: An anatomy of creativity seen through the lives of Freud, Einstein, Picasso, Stravinsky, Eliot, Graham, and Gandhi.* New York: Basic Books.

Getzels, J., & Csikszentmihalyi, M. (1976). *The creative vision: A longitudinal study of problem finding in art.* New York: Wiley.

Lynch, M., & Harris, C. (2000). *Teaching the creative child, K–8.* Needham, MA: Allyn and Bacon.

Piirto, J. (1992). *Understanding those who create.* Dayton, OH: Ohio Psychology Press.

Sternberg, R. J. (1997). A triarchic view of giftedness: Theory and practice. In N. Colangelo & G. A. Davis (Eds.). *Handbook of gifted education* (2nd ed.; pp. 43–53). Boston: Allyn and Bacon.

Torrance, E. P. (1968). *Education and the creative potential.* Minneapolis: University of Minnesota Press.

Torrance, E. P. (1971, April). "I was a block and nobody builded me!" Paper presented at the meeting of the Council on Exceptional Children, Miami Beach, FL.

Torrance, E. P. (1979). *The search for satori and creativity.* Great Neck, NY: Creative Synergetic Associates, Ltd.

Vygotsky, L. (1978). *Mind in society: The development of higher mental processes.* Cambridge, MA: Harvard University Press.

SECTION III

Discovering Gifted Potential in Black Students

Tarek C. Grantham, Donna Y. Ford, and Malik S. Henfield

In 1993, the coeditors of this anthology, like other equity-minded educators, celebrated a new, visionary, philosophical, and proactive federal definition (presented below) that focused on potential and talent development. As a member of the steering group that provided counsel to the U.S. Secretary of Education, Dr. Mary Frasier contributed to the shift in terminology that gave rise to much discussion and rethinking of the notion of being gifted and/or talented and the role of the environment.

> Children and youth with outstanding talent perform or show the potential for performing at remarkably high levels of accomplishment when compared with others of their age, experience, or environment.
>
> These children and youth exhibit high performance capability in intellectual, creative, and/or artistic areas, possess an unusual leadership capacity, or excel in specific academic fields. They require services or activities not ordinarily provided by the schools.
>
> Outstanding talents are present in children and youth from all cultural groups, across all economic strata, and in all areas of human endeavor. (U.S. Department of Education, Office of Educational Research and Improvement, 1993, para. 6–9)

A number of definitions exist for the word *potential*. The term is about possibility and promise; it is about the importance of investing in students for growth; it refers to a latent excellence or ability that may or may not be developed; and it is about the reality that, regardless of the amount of training one has in gifted education, no one will ever know what students are fully capable of doing. Thus, the notions of potential and development of talent are fundamentally about giving students a chance to achieve at higher levels and demonstrate outstanding talent. This opportunity comes with gifted education. As the National Association for Gifted Children recognized (2008), discovering potential and developing talent is a lifelong process—it takes open-mindedness, time, faith, and commitment.

Frasier's commitment to addressing the "quiet crisis" was carried out, in part, by her research conducted as part of The National Research Center on the Gifted and Talented. In two published executive summaries, Frasier and Passow (1994) called for a paradigm shift in how we identify potential giftedness, and Frasier and colleagues (1995) defined core attributes of giftedness to explain ways in which it manifests among Black students. Unlike any other work in the field of gifted education at the time, Frasier's (1991) comprehensive study of characteristics associated with giftedness helped gifted education teachers, administrators, and professional development specialists throughout the nation to discover potential in Black students. Echoing the same sentiment of discovering potential, Baldwin's (1987) and Ford's (Ford & Harris, 1990) research brought unprecedented attention to the idea of affirming gifted Black children as the jewels they are. Their work placed value on the discovery process, and they confronted barriers with the goal of empowering people to see Black children through the brilliance of diamonds. This anthology would be incomplete if we had ignored or discounted in any way works surrounding the discovery of potential and talent development. It is clear that we must both discover and nurture talent in Black students. If not, everyone pays a price.

References

Baldwin, A. Y. (1987). Undiscovered diamonds: The minority gifted child. *Journal for the Education of the Gifted, 10,* 271–285.

Ford, D. Y., & Harris, J. J., III. (1990). Gifted and talented Black children: Identifying diamonds in the rough. *Gifted Child Today, 13*(3), 17–21.

Frasier, M. M. (1991). Disadvantaged and culturally diverse gifted students. *Journal for the Education of the Gifted, 14,* 234–245.

Frasier, M. M., Hunsaker, S. L., Lee, J., Mitchell, S., Cramond, B., Krisel, S., . . . Finley, V. S. (1995). *Core attributes of giftedness: A foundation for recognizing the gifted potential of minority and economically disadvantaged students* (Research Monograph No. 95210). Storrs: University of Connecticut, The National Research Center on the Gifted and Talented.

Frasier, M. M., & Passow, A. H. (1994). *Toward a new paradigm for identifying talent potential* (Research Monograph No. 94112). Storrs: University of Connecticut, The National Research Center on the Gifted and Talented.

National Association for Gifted Children. (2008). *Redefining giftedness for a new century: Shifting the paradigm.* Retrieved from http://www.nagc.org/index.aspx?id=6404

U.S. Department of Education, Office of Educational Research and Improvement. (1993). *National excellence: A case for developing America's talent.* Washington, DC: U.S. Government Printing Office. Retrieved from http://www2.ed.gov/pubs/DevTalent/part3.html

CHAPTER 8

Undiscovered Diamonds: The Minority Gifted Child

Alexina Y. Baldwin

A disproportionately low number of minority students have been identified and placed in programs for gifted students. The realities of the situation relate to the attitudes of planners and teachers, the identification process itself, inadequate research verifying the use of appropriate identification tools, and an inadequate picture of how a program should be designed.

Empirical research on identification and planning for the minority gifted child is sparse but that which is available highlights the need for more extensive research in this area. Exploratory research using The Raven Matrices and chronometric devices as part of the identification process appear to hold promise for developing new hypotheses and proving or disproving those that are presently proposed. More flexibility of planning, more funding for research, more dissemination of information, and improved teacher training on how to recognize clues for identifying exceptional intellectual processing abilities are among the recommendations proposed here to alleviate the problem of discovering the gifted among minority populations.

The intersection of the four words—undiscovered, diamonds, minority and gifted establishes a focal point from which one can view the loss of value to the world, our country, and the individual when attention is not given to the discovery and nurturance of the minority gifted child.

The paradigm used for discussing this issue is one which could be used as a framework for discussing the lack of proportionate representation of other minorities in programs for the gifted. The elements of the paradigm are as follows:

1. Statement of the problem
2. Definition of terms

3. Realities on concerns of the situation
4. Conceptualization and research
5. Recommendations for action

Statement of the Problem

There is an increasing concern about the lack of minorities in programs for the gifted. Many proponents of the gifted such as Passow (1977), Gallagher (1985), and Baldwin (1985) have addressed the problem through books, conferences and articles. There are few easy answers to the problem because established norms for identifying and planning for the gifted are hard to alter in light of the paucity of supportive data for recommending substantive changes.

Definition of Terms

For purposes of this discussion, minority gifted children will be defined as those who are Black, Hispanic, or American Indian. The undiscovered diamonds among these groups of children are those who because of cultural differences, socioeconomic deprivation, or geographic isolation, do not respond to the standard educational stimuli.

The term gifted as used here is perceived to be evidence of above average ability, creative-processing ability and task commitment in one or a combination of four areas: Cognitive, Creative Products, Psychosocial, and Psychomotor (Baldwin, 1984). This perception is based on the following assumptions:
1. That giftedness can be expressed through a variety of behaviors.
2. That giftedness expressed in one area, as defined above, is just as important as giftedness expressed in another, and
3. That all populations have gifted children who exhibit behaviors that are indicative of giftedness.

The term "undiscovered diamonds" is used as a simile to express the idea that among the minority populations there are ability resources of high value which are being untapped. According to census information and predictions by demographers concerning population growth, by the year 2000, one out of three Americans will be nonwhite and at least 53 U.S. cities will have become predominantly nonwhite (Education Week, 1986). The amount of attention given to finding the diamonds among minority groups and the type of educational experiences given them today will determine their creative and productive levels in the future.

REALITIES TO CONSIDER

Among the many considerations that are directly related to the problems of inclusion of minorities in programs for the gifted are: attitude, identification, and program/curriculum.

ATTITUDES

The attitude of those individuals who have the responsibility for designing educational programs for gifted students, the attitude of some minority communities toward the concept of giftedness, and the attitude of some legislators regarding constituent priorities can negatively affect the process of discovering these diamonds.

The attitudes of program planners is, in part, based upon the degree of acceptance of the foregoing assumptions regarding giftedness. Concomitantly, attitudes are shaped by the degree of knowledge concerning the variables which affect the ability of many minorities to respond to traditional identification criteria. It is important to realize that attitudes toward planning for the development of unique abilities among minority students are often derived from the realities planners face in attempting to adjust the organizational patterns of educational settings to the unique needs and abilities of these children. These organizational patterns often do not allow the flexibility of planning or the necessary resources for adequately meeting the requirements of programs for gifted minorities. A minority child whose school achievement scores are low but who possesses exceptionally creative ability in the graphic or performing arts, for instance, may well need special attention directed to a weakness in the academic area as well as special attention to the development of the special gifts of creativity. Many schools cannot provide this type of educational plan, consequently, little attention will be given to considering these areas of giftedness. Very often creativity is the dimension through which minority gifted children express their exceptional abilities.

The attitude of persons and groups, external to the immediate school environment, toward education of the gifted can also affect programs for minority gifted students. In minority communities of large urban areas, programs for the gifted are considered "elitist." Their assessment of gifted programs is based upon their observance that these programs include very few minority children. As a result of this perception, many legislators who represent the constituents of these communities find it necessary to argue against the use of state funds for developing programs for the gifted (G. Poshard, personal communication, November 25, 1986).

Identification Procedures

Although identification is a separate aspect of the concern for minority gifted students, it is inextricably tied to the attitudes of program planners as pointed out in the previous paragraphs. Subjective as well as objective techniques for identification of minority students is often necessary in order to diminish the effect of external variables on their ability to do well on objective tests. If program planners consider objective tests of cognitive ability as the most effective means of identifying gifted students, many minority students will not be identified.

In many states the problem of identification is exacerbated because state funding for gifted programs is based upon the number of students identified at or above certain IQ or academic achievement scores. These quantitative data are more easily defended and explained by and for the legislators but the need for this type of data erodes efforts to use qualitative measures to locate minority gifted students. Furthermore, school districts and legislators argue that the curriculum for the gifted student is based upon evidence of their ability to excel in the "regular" courses offered in educational institutions.

In spite of these restrictive criteria for state funding, the use of subjective measures in the identification of gifted students has been recommended by many professionals. This technique has been shown to be successful in its use with minority students (Baldwin, 1977). In the last few years, however, evidence of the increased need to satisfy legal complaints regarding inclusion or exclusion of children in programs for the gifted has made the process of identification a cause for concern. In some school districts such as San Antonio, TX and Seattle, WA program planners have even been called upon to prepare a legal defense of the identification techniques used. The reality of expenses and time involved will tend to cause school districts to eliminate subjective techniques as part of their identification process. If school districts revert to using only standardized tests for the identification of gifted students, the problem of locating minority gifted children will unfortunately increase.

Program and Curriculum Planning for the Minority Gifted

The realities to be discussed under program planning and curriculum are related to both the student attitude and the identification process. If a minority student is selected for the program for the gifted, problems of appropriately designed curriculum often surface. While some students of the minority population will have little or no difficulty with a program which stresses academic giftedness, some will need special planning which will accommodate their special strengths. Thus, a child whose profile shows strengths in leadership and creativity might not be able to use these strengths if a program is not designed to enhance these abilities.

Disenchantment on the part of the teacher and student regarding the student's progress could then result.

PRESENT CONCEPTUALIZATIONS AND RESEARCH FINDINGS

Having faced these realities and concerns, it is important that some conceptualization and research strategies which are related to attitude, identification, and programs be discussed.

ATTITUDES

The changing concept of intelligence as measured by IQ scores has positively affected attitudes concerning the presence of abilities among minorities even when standardized scores indicate differently. Raven & Summers (1986), for example, have explained that:

> use of deviation IQs tends to give users the impression that the concept of IQ has a greater explanatory, diagnostic, and prescriptive power than it has.... assignment of an IQ tends to give users the impression that there is much greater stability and uniformity in human development than there is.... the closer we get to unidimensional measures, the more we discover that human, and particularly educated, abilities are distributed in this way. (p. 7)

Sternberg (1984) admonishes us to look at the test we use with an eye toward analyzing the relationship of these tests to the people we are serving. In his words,

> Tests work for some people some of the time, but they do not work for other people much of the time. Moreover, the people for whom they do not work are often the same again and again. Applied conservatively and with full respect to all of the available information, tests can be of some use. Misapplied or overused, they are worse than nothing... In the meantime, we must remember that the fact that test score is (or appears to be precise) does not mean that it is valid (p. 14).

Gardner (1983) has proposed that we look for multiple intelligences. Gardner's proposal is far-reaching in view of the traditional use of much more limited standardized criteria which relates primarily to basic skills in school.

A review of the conceptualizations which generated these writings point to an attitudinal change in the perception of abilities which in turn should affect positively the attitudes of planners toward the identification of gifted minority students and provisions made for the development of these abilities.

Minority Dropouts

Attitudes toward the idea that there are gifted students among school dropouts is slowly changing. For those persons who tend to be more conservative in their definition of giftedness the presence of giftedness among minority dropouts is antithetical to their thinking. Douglas (1969), however, indicated that 20% of the dropout students included in his study were gifted. Today the dropout rate among minorities is at an all time high. Data show that in New York for instance, this rate for African Americans is 53%, Latinos 62%, and Native Americans 46 % (African American Institute of SUNY, 1986).

Even so, New York's dropout rate is not the highest in the country. Unfortunately empirical data are not available to replicate Douglas' finding using 1980–86 dropout statistics. However, if a rule of thumb is applied to existing dropout data to estimate the number of gifted minorities among the dropouts, this number would be significant. The loss of this talent alone is enough cause for concern without considering those students who have remained in school but are underachieving.

The concept of developing the abilities of minorities and the importance of attention being focused on academic as well as nonacademic abilities were recommended by Dubois (1903) and Washington in his recently reprinted book *Up From Slavery* (1971). Quite often the exceptional abilities other than those traditionally recognized as legitimate areas of giftedness are not included in the regular program for the gifted. This lack of recognition does not, however, apply to those minorities who show exceptional athletic ability!

A plausible yet untested assumption about giftedness is that this quality of ability will be expressed in some manner within or outside of the traditional educational setting. In an effort to explain the reason for the lack of minorities in the programs for the gifted one might be tempted to equate this lack of inclusion with the lack of females in mathematics. An attempt to justify this comparison could be done by attributing the presence of more males than females in programs for mathematics, the presence of more blacks than whites in team sports, or the presence of more whites than minorities in programs for the gifted, to the amount of practice each included group devoted to the skills needed for the particular area. This type of justification tends to perpetuate the myths regarding each group. Instead, a closer look at the expectations or lack of expectations of these comparative groups should be taken. Herein could lie the actual cause of unequal representation.

The manner in which this ability will be exhibited will vary according to the type of academic and nonacademic experiences the child had during its formative years. The challenge for the school is to harness and develop this ability.

Attitudes about the additional time and thought necessary for insuring the inclusion of minority gifted students in programs are shaped by the new pressure on school districts to become paragons of excellence. This pressure had decreased the flexibility in planning that many schools would need in order to adequately plan and develop programs for many of the gifted minority students.

New York State for instance, has increased the number of required hours in specified subject areas. Other states have made similar adjustments to satisfy these needs (Mueller and McKeown, 1986). In the opinion of Futrell (1986),

> Our schools today are structurally decrepit, still shaped by an organizational model appropriate to 19th century industry. That model does little to enliven the imagination. It does much to stifle innovation. . . . It does much to intensify isolation." (p. 6)

IDENTIFICATION STRATEGIES

There is increasing interest in the appropriate identification strategies that should be used to select minority gifted students. In the last decade, there has been a general consensus that multi-dimensional screening is the preferred method for identifying gifted students. This acceptance opens the possibility for the selection of instruments and techniques which will more appropriately identify the gifted among minorities.

Although multidimensional screening holds great promise for selecting minority students, it does not guarantee that they will be identified. The Baldwin Identification Matrix (BIM) for example was designed to include a wide array of assessment strategies which would tap a wide range of gifted behaviors. The first edition of the BIM did not outline the categories of gifted behaviors to be assessed nor did it provide a mechanism for giving equal weighting to these areas. It was left to the planners to include these categories and select the appropriate instrument for assessment. An analysis of data received from the research in progress (Baldwin, 1985) on the use of the BIM revealed that in spite of the wide array of inclusions, the BIM users had placed more emphasis on the traditional academic areas. The data show that the most predictive instruments for selection were: Standardized Achievement Test scores, IQ scores, Teacher ratings, and the Cognitive Processing tests (Raven Progressive Matrices and the SOI Abilities Test).

In school districts where minorities were well represented in programs for the gifted, creativity and leadership were good predictors of selection. Tests of creativity, teacher, parent, and peer rated leadership scales were used as part of the identification process (Blackshear, 1979; Dabney, 1983). The design of the second edition of the BIM—Baldwin Identification Matrix 2 Baldwin, (1984)—specifies more clearly the categories which should be included in the BIM profile and provides a mechanism for giving equal weight to each of these categories. Subjective as well as objective measures are recommended for use. (A compendium of optional test selections under each category of the definition used is available from the author.) There has been an increased use of the Raven Progressive Matrices (RPM) as a measure of intellectual processing skills. The most recent research supplement (Raven & Summers 1986) included American norming data. Populations of Blacks, Hispanics, Navajo Indians, and Asians were included in the norming process although limitations in selecting the sample groups was noted by the authors.

A preliminary review of the data secured by Baldwin and Start (1986) using children (N = 51) from a socioeconomically disadvantaged black population indicates that aside from the 10 children who were included in the academically talented class 11 others had equivalent or higher scores on the RPM. Additional measures on these 11 children will be analyzed. It appears, however, that the use of this test can certainly bring to the attention of planners, children who might be missed using other means. This is an example of the type of data which can be included on the BIM profile.

Another aspect of this project by Baldwin and Start included the use of Reaction Time (RT) as an analytic chronometric technique in cognition. This research ties into the increasing number of studies on reaction time in the analysis of individual differences and the relationship of the speed of encoding to the mental ability of the individual. Phillip Vernon (1986) among others has been actively involved in the renewal of this concept. This research will hopefully hold promise for identifying the mental abilities of individuals exclusive of their experiences or ethnic backgrounds. Since little research is available on the identification of gifted minority students a few studies that have pointed out some of the problems are referenced again and again. Stallings (1970) developed an environmentally sensitive testing instrument whose items were derived from the radius of the urban child's community. Thus, street signs, churches, barber-shops, store fronts, etc., were used to measure recall. Data from the attempts to standardize the strategies used are not available but the concept of Stallings' project developed from his theory that since traditional methods of testing use recall of facts in manipulating data, the assessment of this ability to recall information should be tested using familiar objects. Stallings emphasizes the use of this approach for teacher-made assessment strategies along with the regular standardized techniques for identification.

As a result of his research, Hilliard (1976) has suggested that identification criteria for the minority student include qualities such as alertness, energy, confidence, humor, expressiveness, experimentation, social control, verbal creativity, and risk-taking. Hilliard did not suggest the type of instrumentation that could be used for surfacing these traits merely that it is important to include these qualities as part of the observations strategies used by teachers.

Mercer (1971) developed the System of Multipluralistic Assessment (SOMPA), an instrument designed to accommodate the variables which might affect the functioning level of Mexican-American children. SOMPA has been successful in giving the minority child the equivalent IQ scores needed for entering programs for the gifted.

Meeker (1979) has developed the Atypical Screening Form of the SOI Learning Abilities Test. Unpublished research by Baldwin (1985) indicated that the use of this test with minority students who were highly verbal penalized them if this was the only test being used. The test did, however, locate some children who would not have been identified by using other processes.

Additional articles concerning strategies used for identifying the gifted minorities can be found in articles written by Bernal & Reyna (1974), Blackshear (1979), Boothy & Lacoste (1977), and Bruch (1972).

Programs and Curriculum

The research literature on programs and curriculum designed or adapted for use with gifted minority students is sparse. Practices in this area are based mainly on conceptualizations of curricula and program designs which are most appropriate for these children.

The programmatic needs of these children would be more adequately met through a total program plan instead of, for example, a limited pull-out program. The model for this program should not be a deficit model but one focused on the positive talents of the gifted children. Curriculum should include opportunities for developing positive self concepts. This would include an opportunity to learn about and share the history and artifacts of their culture with other students. Higher level thinking skills can be developed through the use of their strengths in creativity, music, or leadership skills. They could for instance explore the parallels between the various sociopolitical periods of this country and the types of music, poetry, and paintings done by minorities. As a part of this project, they could be asked to project future representations of these areas based on data they would have collected.

The use of bibliotherapy has been suggested by Frasier and McCannon (1981). This activity coupled with the use of mentors or role models from minority groups will help develop positive self concepts.

The Empire State Institute for the Performing Arts is an example of the type of program that can be used to discover and develop the abilities of minority children. This institute's teacher/performers contract with school districts of the state of New York where they involve the children in drama and various roles of the theater from the actor to the technician. During these training sessions, students are encouraged to use or develop their reading skills and knowledge of history, literature and many other subjects. From this experience, high school students have been able to work as interns with the theater. They use the theater as their school base having signed a contract with the home school to complete the requirements necessary for completion of their degrees. The exciting stories of the exceptionally high ability exhibited by many underachieving students in this program make this type of network a viable resource for discovering and nurturing the talent of the minority gifted student.

There are increasing numbers of resources of materials becoming available for use in schools. Local libraries, museums, and state and local government documents are good sources. There is a need for a more complete portrait of the appropriate program to meet the needs of the minority gifted student. Examples of what has worked will need to be shared with program designers including short-range units of study.

It is the opinion of this author that programs for the gifted minority cannot be codified because the programmatic needs of individuals within this gifted minority population can be quite different. A general structure to follow would include the following: a variety of individual or small group projects based on the students' interests, community exploration and service, creative physical expression, one-to-one and group counseling, challenging courses including interdisciplinary ones, outside class experiences with research strategies of archeologists, museum curators, scientist, etc., and the involvement of parents or guardians in understanding the roles they can play in the development of these exceptional abilities.

Recommendations for Action

The recommendations to be made for meeting the needs of the gifted minority child must be closely tied to attitudes and the conceptualization of the problem. Based upon these factors, the following recommendations are made.

1. National research and training centers that would provide the type of concentrated effort and information for development and dissemination.

    These research and training centers would bring together persons who would seek answers to many research questions such as:
    - ❖ What percentage of the national dropout rate among minorities are gifted?
    - ❖ What identification techniques are most effective to use in locating gifted minority students?
    - ❖ Are there behaviors which are unique to minority students that should be included in the identification process?

- ❖ Are there differences in the innate capabilities of minority students when compared to other population groups?
- ❖ What teaching strategies or models are most effective in meeting the needs of the gifted minority student?

The training aspects of the research center should include the development of links between demonstrated behaviors and intellectual processing abilities. Teachers and planners should then be trained to use observation techniques to determine significant clues of potential giftedness.

Another aspect of this training should include techniques of using one discipline to develop a skill in another. For example, a child who is gifted in music might have little motivation to develop skills in mathematics. Introducing the child to the use of mathematics in music and art will create motivation to study mathematics. The subsequent lessons in mathematics could be designed using music or art as the beginning point. Each aspect of training should be designed so that it can become a part of preservice and inservice requirements for teachers, psychologists, and counselors.

2. Parents must be included in the plan for developing the skills of the young child. Special curriculum for the parent and child must be developed and special training activities planned for parents in order for them to give their youngsters a head start.
3. There is a need for professionals in the field of education of the gifted to reach out to businesses for assistance in using technology to develop teaching materials and processes for efficiently identifying the child from a minority group. There is a need for continuing research in the use of computers and interactive disks for the development of reading skills, creative problem-solving techniques, and creative product development strategies. Education divisions of these businesses are willing to work with educators in developing new strategies for discovering and enhancing intellectual abilities. These professionals can also be used as mentors and consultants who are given the responsibility of exposing student to many career trajectories.
4. National and international groups should develop a network which would provide examples of curriculum materials used with minority students who have strengths in certain areas, but also need to develop the areas where they have weaknesses.
5. There should be greater flexibility in school scheduling to allow children to benefit from more than a cursory involvement with the many cultural and educational resources outside of the school room. These resources can help in discovering certain talents and using those talents for the development

of the child's abilities. The benefits to the minority student of becoming a participant in the acquisition of knowledge within or outside of the regular school environment will be enormous.

6. Support for longitudinal studies and evaluations of programs which have been instituted is crucial for long-range decision making. This will require program planners and teachers to maintain data regarding the effects of the processes used to identify and plan for minority children.
7. Funding through the federal government or through matching grants from community organization, foundations, or corporation is crucial if effective and significant research regarding the discovery and nurturance of talent among minorities is to be done. The investment of time, effort, and funds in creative and meaningful answers to the processes for discovering "diamonds" among minority students is an investment in the future of our society.
8. There is a need for a repository or organized network for sharing information and ideas regarding activities that have worked. Telecommunications networks have been used, for instance, to assist participants in special interest areas to continue the development of new strategies to share with others who are connected to the system. Special Talk, a Logo group in special education has used this technique successfully (Cockran & Bull, 1986). This type of network would also develop a "buddy system" among planners and teachers.

Conclusions

An indepth review of the five aspects of the paradigm suggested that if we intended to address the concerns of the "undiscovered diamonds" then we need systematic and sincere planning to address these concerns. These five aspects point to the fact that (a) we are missing some major sources of talent in our society; (b) that we have uncertain ways to try to discover that talent; and (c) there is no clear picture of the nature of differentiated program strategies that should be used for these students. Futrell, (1986) has noted that, "the new student population, which consists increasingly of minorities, children of poverty, children from nontraditional homes and children with limited English proficiency will become exiled from the mainstream of American society. These students will form our nation's new disenfranchised class" (p. 5). It is safe to assume that some of the children among this group are gifted. Therefore, it is imperative that a major investment both human and monetary, be made to support efforts to discover and develop the abilities of these students.

The outcome of such a massive undertaking would provide models which would generate ideas for strategies to be used with all minority students and will establish clearer guidelines for discovering and developing the tremendous amount of talent which would otherwise be lost to the nation.

REFERENCES

Baldwin, A. Y. (1977). Tests can underpredict: A case study. *Phi Delta Kappan, 58*(8), 620–621.

Baldwin, A. Y. (1984). *Baldwin Identification Matrix 2 for the identification of gifted and talented.* New York: Trillium Press.

Baldwin, A. Y. (1985). Programs for the gifted and talented: Issues concerning minority populations. In F. Horowitz & M. O'Brien (Eds.), *The gifted and talented: developmental perspectives* (pp. 223–249).

Bernal, E. & Reyna, J. (1974). *Analysis of giftedness in Mexican-American children and design of a prototype identification instrument.* Final Report, Contract DEC-47-0621130307, USOE (Austin, Texas: Southwest Education Development Laboratory, 1974).

Blackshear, P. (1979). *A comparison of peer nomination and teacher nomination in the identification of the academically gifted, black, primary level student.* Unpublished doctoral dissertation, University of Maryland.

Boothy, P. & Lacoste, R. J. (1977). *Unmined gold: Potentially gifted children of the inner city.* San Antonio Texas: University of Texas. (ERIC Document Reproduction Service No. ED 154 076)

Bruch, C. B. (1972). *The ABDA: Making the Stanford-Binet culturally biased for black children.* Unpublished manuscript. University of Georgia, Department of Education Psychology, Athens.

Cockran, P. & Bull, G. (1986). Specialtalk. *Logo Exchange, 5*(3), 17–18.

Dabney, M. (1983, July). *Perspectives and directives in assessment of the black child.* Paper presented at the meeting of the Council for Exceptional Children, Atlanta, GA.

Douglas, J. H. (1969, April). *Strategies for maximizing the development of talent among the urban disadvantaged.* Paper presented at the annual meeting of the Council for Exceptional Children, Denver, CO.

DuBois, W. E. B. (1903). The talented tenth. In, *The Negro Problem.* New York, NY: James Pott Company.

Gallagher, J. (1985). *Teaching the gifted child: 3rd Edition.* Boston: Allyn & Bacon, Inc.

Gardner, H. (1983). *Frames of mind: The theory of multiple intelligences.* New York: Basic Books.

Frasier, M. & McCannon, C. (1981). Using bibliotheraphy with gifted children. *Gifted Child Quarterly, 25*(2), 81–85.

Futrell, M. (1986). Restructuring teaching: A call for research. *Educational Researcher, 15*(10), 5–8.

Hillard, A. G. (1976). *Alternative to IQ testing: An approach to the identification of the gifted "Minority" Children (Report No. 75 175).* San Francisco, CA: San Francisco State University. (ERIC Document Reproduction Service No. ED 147009).

Meeker, M. & Meeker, R. (1979). *SOI Learning Abilities Test (rev. ed.).* El Segundo, CA.: SOI Institute.

Mercer, J. R. (1971 September). *Pluralistic diagnosis in the evaluation of black and Chicano children: A procedure for taking sociocultural variables into account in clinical assessment.* Paper presented at the meeting of the American Psychological Association, Washington, D.C.

Mueller, V. & McKeown, M. (Eds.), (1986). *The fiscal, legal and political aspects of state reform of elementary and secondary education. Sixth Annual Yearbook of the American Education Finance Association.* Cambridge, MA: Ballinger Publishing Co.

New York State African-American Institute of the State University of New York (1986). *Dropping out of school in New York: The invisible people of color.* (Available from [State University of New York, State University Plaza, Albany, NY]).

Passow, A. H. (1977). The gifted and the disadvantaged. In J. Miley, I. Sato, W. Luche, P. Weaver, J. Curry, & R. Ponce (Eds.), *Promising practices: Teaching the disadvantaged gifted and talented* (pp. 51–57). Ventura, CA: Office of the Superintendent of Ventura County Schools.

Raven, J., & Summers, B. (1986). *Manual for Raven's Progressive Matrices and Vocabulary Scales research supplement no. 3: A compendium of North American normative and validity studies.* San Antonio, TX: The Psychological Corporation.

Stallings, C. (1970). *Techniques for identification and development of potentials for gifted disadvantaged children.* Unpublished manuscript.

Sternberg, R. (1984). What should intelligence tests test: Implications for a triarchic theory of intelligence for intelligence testing. *Educational Researcher, 13*(1), 5–15.

Today's numbers, tomorrow's nation. (1986, May). *Education Week*, p. 14.

Vernon, P. (1986). Relationships between speed-of-processing, personality and intelligence. Personality, Cognition and Values. London: The Macmillan Press Ltd.

Washington, B.T. (1971). *Up from slavery: An autobiography. (rev. ed.).* Williamstown, MA.: Corner House Publishers.

CHAPTER 9

Disadvantaged and Culturally Diverse Gifted Students

Mary M. Frasier

The low number of gifted students identified in disadvantaged and culturally diverse groups has been, and continues to be, problematic. Why has this problem persisted? Why do we know, think we know, and need to know about resolving identification issues? This paper provides responses to these questions and proposes a possible solution. A profile system is presented that describes a viable way to utilize data from test and non-test sources to identify these children.

The issue of identifying gifted disadvantaged and culturally diverse students has long been problematic. The low number of these children being identified for gifted programs attests to the fact that identification problems have not been solved. Talent loss among them continues virtually unabated. The homogeneity of the population in gifted programs, in and of itself, is not necessarily the problem *if* the identified students can truly be said to represent all those who are gifted.

Why then are there so few disadvantaged and culturally diverse students enrolled in gifted programs? The purposes of this discussion are (a) to briefly review what we know, what we think we know, and what we need to know about the identification of gifted disadvantaged and culturally diverse students; and (b) to present a system designed to facilitate the use of multiple criteria in identifying giftedness.

Mary M. Frasier is an Associate Professor in the Department of Educational Psychology, 323 Aderhold Hall, The University of Georgia, Athens, GA 30602. She is also a Principal Investigator for the National Research Center on the Gifted and Talented project at Georgia.

Reprinted from Frasier, M. M. (1991). Disadvantaged and culturally diverse gifted students. *Journal for the Education of the Gifted, 234–245.* Reprinted with permission of Prufrock Press Inc.

WHAT WE KNOW

A major challenge is to discover bright disadvantaged and culturally diverse children so that they, too, can take advantage of programs and services designed to assist children in realizing their potential for achievement. What we know about finding those children will be discussed in this section.

While we do know that gifted children may be found in all cultural groups and at every socioeconomic level, we also know that, thus far, attempts to find them have not been successful. We know that current identification procedures present major difficulties when attempting to identify gifted disadvantaged and culturally diverse children. Reliance on teacher nominations and the use of I.Q. cut-off scores has effectively precluded the identification of the gifts and talents of these students (Frasier, 1990). Abbott (1982) has aptly observed that "examining I.Q. scores for the purpose of identifying giftedness . . . amounts to viewing intelligence in terms of English fluency" (p. 8).

We know that accurate assessment of ability requires that data from multiple sources be collected and evaluated. According to current research on intelligence and the assessment of intellectual capacity, an intelligence test provides a very narrow view of abilities (Gardner, 1983; Sternberg, 1986; Treffinger & Renzulli, 1986). Its sole use reduces the multifaceted, complex phenomenon called giftedness to a single factor.

We know that some disadvantaged and culturally diverse children are identified when traditional identification procedures are used. Most do not fare well in the process. As Bernal (1982) has noted:

> Many gifted minority and white students, if lacking in psychometric sophistication or command of standard English, will score below their actual achievement or aptitude levels. Such students cannot be identified by traditional means, especially early in their school careers (p. 52).

We know that there must be a reevaluation of current practices if there are to be improvements in the identification of students currently underrepresented in gifted programs.

Passow (1982) succinctly described three factors affecting the identification of gifted disadvantaged children: (a) experiential deprivations, especially in early childhood; (b) limited language development; and (c) socioeconomic or racial isolation. We know that implicit or explicit knowledge of these factors fosters the attitude that gifted children cannot be found in groups defined as disadvantaged. Such attitudes affect these children's access to gifted programs; the search may be limited by the notion that none will be found.

We know that numerous solutions have been suggested to address the underrepresentation of disadvantaged and culturally diverse students in gifted programs. These solutions have included: (a) soliciting nominations from persons other than the teacher (Blackshear, 1979; Davis, 1978); (b) using checklists and rating scales specifically designed for culturally diverse and disadvantaged populations (Bernal, 1974; Gay, 1978; Hilliard, 1976; Torrance, 1977); (c) modifying or altering traditional identification procedures (Fitz-Gibbon, 1975); (d) developing culture specific identification systems (Mercer & Lewis, 1978); (e) using quota systems (LaRose, 1978); (f) developing programs designed to eliminate experiential and language deficits prior to evaluation for gifted programs (Johnson, Starnes, Gregory & Blaylock, 1985); (g) using a matrix to weight data from multiple sources (Baldwin & Wooster, 1977; Baldwin, 1984); and (h) modifying assessment procedures by providing students with instruction before administering test tasks (Feuerstein, 1979).

We know that none of these solutions has solved the problem. Few culturally diverse and disadvantaged students are being identified for participation in gifted programs.

What We Think We Know

A frequent conclusion is that disadvantaged children come from environments that do not support academic endeavors. The perceived value and motivational discrepancies between the home and the school are felt to be the major factors affecting their achievement (Passow, 1982). The problem is that all children from low-income homes are felt to be deprived of the experiences needed to adequately prepare them to succeed in school. What is frequently not recognized is the wide variation in the kinds and amounts of environmental stimulation provided by families in different socioeconomic, ethnic, and racial groups.

Findings from research suggest that it would be more profitable to focus on characteristics of the home environment; the traditional focus on educational level and occupation of parents has not provided a complete picture. Hess and Holloway (1982) concluded that investigations into verbal interaction between parents and children, expectations of parents for achievement, affective relationships between parents and children, discipline and control strategies, and parental beliefs are better variables to study.

There should be a recognition of the differences within disadvantaged and culturally diverse populations. Indiscriminately applying stereotypical descriptors to each minority or low-income child must be avoided (Kitano & Kirby, 1986). There are many well-adjusted, well-cared for children, even in inner city environments, who are encouraged and supported in their intellectual pursuits (Frasier, 1980). Adverse conditions of life may hamper academic achievement, but there is no conclusive evidence that such conditions preclude academic success (Gordon & Wilkerson, 1966).

We think we know that characteristics of gifted disadvantaged and culturally diverse children are more similar to those of nongifted members of their group than to those that typical describe gifted children. In actuality, when traits used to describe gifted advantaged children are compared with traits describing gifted disadvantaged children, there is little difference except in semantics (Frasier, 1983). Traits common to gifted children, regardless of group membership, include the ability to: (a) meaningfully manipulate some symbol system held valuable in the subculture; (b) think logically, given appropriate data; (c) use stored knowledge to solve problems; (d) reason by analogy; and (e) extend or extrapolate knowledge to new situations of unique applications (Gallagher & Kinney, 1974). We need to know more about how these abilities are manifested differently in various cultural groups.

What We Need to Know

If we are to succeed in identifying gifted children from all cultures we must resist the tendency to compare them to dominant culture standards. Rogoff and Morelli (1989) have suggested the use of a sociocultural context of development:

> Not only is the diversity of cultural backgrounds in our nation a resource for the creativity and future of the nation, it is also a resource for scholars to study how children develop. To make good use of this information, cultural research with minorities needs to focus on examining the process and functioning of the cultural context of development. . . . The potential from research on cultural groups around the world as well as down the street lies in its challenge to our system of assumptions and in the creative efforts of scholars to synthesize knowledge from observations of different contexts of human development. Such challenge and synthesis is fruitful in the efforts to achieve a deeper and broader understanding of human nature and nurture (pp. 346–347).

To achieve this deeper and broader understanding, it would be helpful to focus attention on those children we are missing when traditional identification procedures are used. The goal should not be to find ways to fit these children into the existing paradigm. The goal should be to develop an identification paradigm that accommodates both the children we are missing and the children we are finding.

An important place to start is to study those students from disadvantaged and culturally diverse backgrounds who were nominated but never made it into the gifted program. Was their nomination a fluke? What attributes of giftedness did they exhibit that caused them to be nominated? What definition of giftedness was in the mind of the nominator? What can we observe about these children, beyond test scores, that would provide us with information that should be considered in determining their potential for gifted performance?

A very useful list of characteristics developed by Hagen (1980) places the emphasis on gifted behaviors; her list deemphasizes a test score as the "sine qua non" of giftedness. Behavioral characteristics include observing such behaviors as a student's use of language, the quality of questions, problem solving strategies, and the students' breadth and depth of information. This list provides a useful way for classroom teachers and parents to understand gifted behaviors they can observe in the classroom and in the home.

Present identification procedures provide no effective way to collect and use this information. There is a need to find a way to use data, in addition to test scores, to assess giftedness.

DeHaan and Havighurst (1961) cautioned against relying on test data alone to identify and select students with gifts and talents. They asserted that the very complex, multidimensional nature of mental abilities suggests that above-average ability can be described more adequately as a group of independent factors than as a general ability expressed by an I.Q. Specifically, they noted that "A profile, rather than an I.Q., would seem to be more suitable as an expression of these patterns of abilities" (DeHaan & Havighurst, 1961, p. 41). They further asserted that:

> The conclusions that can be drawn from scientific studies of tests is that although objective tests are good, and the I.Q. a valuable concept, they need to be used with a good deal of caution. There is not mechanical formula that can be applied. Every decision concerning a gifted child has to be made in light of *all* available data (DeHaan & Havighurst, 1961, p. 44).

Current discussions concerned with the measurement of intelligent behavior emphasize more and more the use of multiple criteria. Cronbach (1984, p. 339) noted that "Whatever test is used, information of other kinds, . . . should be taken into account." Summarizing viewpoints from several authors concerned with the identification of gifted cultural and ethnic minority students, Maker and Schiever (1989) noted two consistent recommendations: (a) use multiple assessment procedures, including objective data from a variety of sources (p. 295); and (b) use a case study approach, in which a variety of assessment data is interpreted in the context of a student's individual characteristics, and decisions are made by a team of qualified individuals (p. 296).

The Frasier Talent Assessment Profile (F-TAP)

The Frasier Talent Assessment Profile system (See Figure 1) was designed to facilitate the use of test and non-test criteria to identify students with extraordinary gifts and talents. It is based on four assumptions:

1. Methods to locate gifted children from diverse cultural backgrounds can be developed without eroding quality and without requiring excessive data collection or excessive expenditures of time.
2. Identification methods should rely on assessing dynamic rather than static displays of gifted behaviors.
3. A profile, rather than cut-off scores or weighting systems, provides the most effective and efficient way to display data for interpretation from test and non-test sources.
4. Results from identification procedures should be used to design programs and develop curricula for gifted students.

Structure of the Frasier Talent Assessment Profile

The F-TAP provides a way to collect, display, and interpret data from test and non-test sources. Data are never reduced to a single score; rather, the use of multiple scales provide a way to interpret data from diverse sources.

The five scales on the horizontal axis reflect the most commonly used ways to describe test and non-test results: (a) percentile, (b) deviation I.Q., (c) stanine, (d) standard deviation, and (e) Likert scale. Points on these scales are aligned so that data from different sources can be viewed in relationship to each other.

The vertical axis contains the categories in which data are collected. The five categories were selected to reflect the talent areas specified in the 1978 Federal definition of gifted children: (a) academic, (b) creativity, etc. Both aptitude and achievement data are collected in the first four categories; self-report and observational data are collected in the fifth category.

Data Collection and Evaluation

Data are collected in those categories relevant in determining the strength and quality of gifted behaviors for the talent area under consideration. A blank category is provided so that decision-makers can exercise some flexibility in including data not covered by the categories listed.

Interpretations of data collected on the profile are recorded on a summary sheet. In addition, factors that may impact the development of programs, curricula, and counseling activities are recorded. These factors include descriptions of students' personal characteristics, special language considerations and mediating

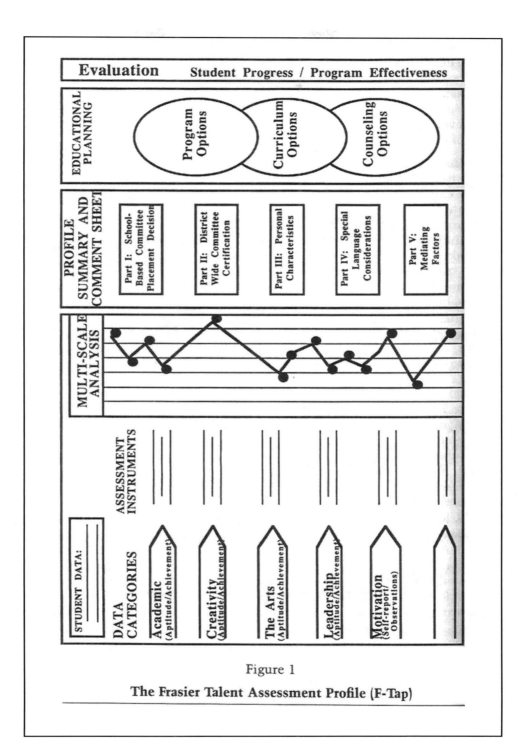

Figure 1
The Frasier Talent Assessment Profile (F-Tap)

factors that influence curriculum decisions, e.g., physical, visual, auditory, and emotional circumstances, and environmental decisions.

Implementing the F-TAP

Collecting data on the F-TAP proceeds in three stages: (a) screening, (b) assessment, and (c) placement. During screening, nominations are sought from sources inside and outside the school. The goal is to involve anyone who has knowledge about a child's behavior. The surest way to achieve equity is to provide numerous ways for talented children to be included, regardless of background or group membership. Qualifying levels are set as liberally as possible; all recommendations are considered. Every possible way is sought to involve every segment of the community in the nomination process.

During the assessment stage, data are collected and plotted on the profile. During the placement stage, data are interpreted. Decision-makers review each student's profile according to guidelines and make recommendations for placement or non-placement. This stage conforms to the best practice that no decisions are made until all data can be reviewed and evaluated.

Key Considerations

Staff development is critical to the implementations of the F-TAP. A staff development program must include all groups that should be informed regarding giftedness and the process used to certify students for placement. These groups might consist of: (a) regular classroom teachers and teachers for the gifted; (b) other school personnel, including principals, media specialists, and Central Office administrators, e.g., subject area coordinators, curriculum coordinators; and (c) students, parents, and peers. In other words, any person with knowledge about a student should be provided with information about the gifted program and invited to submit nominations.

Staff development programs should include information on behavioral characteristics of gifted students; the definition of giftedness, especially the state's definition; and a thorough understanding of the identification process. Information on the process should include a description of the type student sought, when nominations can be made, the process by which decisions are made for placement, and the appeals process. The most important emphasis should be on explaining behavioral characteristics that indicate gifted potential. Careful attention should be paid to helping nominators understand how these behaviors may be exhibited in different groups.

Summary

The F-TAP transcends the practice of using cut-off scores by providing a way of collecting, displaying, and interpreting data from test and non-test sources. It provides an effective way for decision-makers to evaluate student strengths and needs when making program, curriculum, and counseling decisions. In addition, it provides an effective framework for evaluating student growth in the gifted program. Further information on the use of the F-TAP is available from the author.

The mandate before us is to identify and nurture gifted potential wherever it is found. The challenge before us is to find an equitable way to allow *all* gifted children the opportunity to participate in experiences designed to maximize the development of their potential. This challenge can best be met by placing our emphasis on the analysis, synthesis, and evaluation of the diverse ways in which gifted potential is exhibited.

References

Abbot J. (1982). An anthropological approach to the identification of Navajo gifted children. In *Identifying and educating the disadvantaged gifted/talented*. Selected proceedings from the fifth national conference on disadvantaged gifted/talented. Los Angeles, CA: The National/State Leadership Training Institute on the Gifted and the Talented.

Baldwin, A. (1984). *The Baldwin identification matrix 2 for the identification of the gifted and talented: A handbook for its use.* New York: Trillum Press.

Baldwin, A., & Wooster, J. (1977). *Baldwin identification matrix inservice kit for the identification of gifted and talented students.* Buffalo, NY: D.O.K.

Bernal, E. (1974). Gifted Mexican American children: An ethno-scientific perspective. *California Journal of Educational Research, 25,* 261–273.

Bernal, E. (1982). Identifying minority gifted students: Special problems and procedures. In *Identifying and educating the disadvantaged gifted/talented*. Selected proceedings from the fifth national conference on disadvantaged gifted/talented. Los Angeles, CA: The National/State Leadership Training Institute on the Gifted and the Talented.

Blackshear, P. (1979). *A comparison of peer nomination and teacher nomination in the identification of the academically gifted black, primary level student.* Unpublished doctoral dissertation, University of Maryland, College Park.

Cronbach, L. (1984). *Essentials of psychological testing* (4th ed.). New York: Harper & Row.

Davis, P. (1978). *Community-based efforts to increase the identification of the number of gifted minority children.* Ypsilanti, MI: Eastern Michigan College of Education. (ED 176 487)

DeHaan, R., & Havighurst, R. (1961). *Educating gifted children.* Chicago: University of Chicago Press.

Education Amendments of 1978, Pub. L No. 95-561, 92 Stat. 2143 (1978).

Feuerstein, R. (1979). *The dynamic assessment of retarded performers.* Baltimore: University Park Press.

Fitz-Gibbon, C. (1975). The identification of mentally gifted "disadvantaged" students at the eighth grade level. *Journal of Negro Education, 43*(1), 53–66.

Frasier, M. (1980). Programming for the culturally diverse. In J. Jordan & J. Grossi (Eds.), *An administrator's handbook on designing programs for the gifted and talented* (pp. 56–65). Reston, VA: Council for Exceptional Children.

Frasier, M. (1983). *A comparison of general traits and behaviors attributed to the gifted with traits and behaviors attributed to the gifted disadvantaged.* Unpublished manuscript, The University of Georgia, Athens, GA.

Frasier, M. (1990, April). *The equitable identification of gifted and talented children.* Paper presented at the annual meeting of the American Educational Research Association, Boston, Massachusetts.

Gallagher, J., & Kinney, L. (1974). *Talent delayed-talent denied: The culturally different gifted child. A conference report.* Reston, VA: The Foundation for Exceptional Children.

Gardner, H. (1983). *Frames of mind: The theory of multiple intelligences.* New York: Basic.

Gay, J. (1978). A proposed plan for identifying black gifted children. *Gifted Child Quarterly, 22*(3), 353–360.

Gordon, E., & Wilkerson, D. A. (1966). *Compensatory education for the disadvantaged. Programs and practices: Pre-school through college.* New York: College Entrance Board.

Hagen, E. (1980). *Identification of the gifted.* New York: Teachers College, Columbia University.

Hess, R., & Holloway, S. (1982). Family and school as educational institutions. *Review of Child Development Research, 7,* 179–222.

Hilliard, A. (1976, June). *Alternatives to I.Q. testing: An approach to the identification of gifted "minority" children* (Final report). Sacramento, CA: California State Department of Education, Sacramento Division of Special Education. (ED 147 009)

Johnson, S., Starnes, W., Gregory, D., & Blaylock, A. (1985). Program of assessment, diagnosis, and instruction (PADI): Identifying and nurturing potentially gifted and talented minority students. *The Journal of Negro Education, 54*(3), 416–430.

Kitano, M., & Kirby, D. (1986). *Gifted education: A comprehensive view.* Boston: Little, Brown.

LaRose, B. (1978). A quota system for gifted minority children: A viable solution. *Gifted Child Quarterly, 22,* 394–403.

Maker, C., & Schiever, S. (Eds.). (1989). *Critical issues in gifted education: Defensible programs for cultural and ethnic minorities.* Austin, TX: Pro-Ed.

Mercer, J., & Lewis, J. (1978). Using the system of multicultural pluralistic assessment (SOMPA) to identify the gifted minority child. In A. Baldwin, G. Gear & L. Lucito (Eds.), *Educational planning for the gifted* (pp. 7–14). Reston, VA: Council for Exceptional Children.

Passow, A. (1982). The gifted disadvantaged: some reflections. In *Identifying and educating the disadvantaged gifted/talented.* Selected proceedings from the fifth national conference on disadvantaged gifted/talented. Los Angeles, CA: The National/State Leadership Training Institute on the Gifted and the Talented.

Rogoff, B., & Morelli, G. (1989). Perspectives on children's development from cultural psychology. *American Psychologist, 44,* 343–348.

Sternberg, R. (1986, February). Identifying the gifted through I.Q.: Why a little bit of knowledge is a dangerous thing. *Roeper Review, 8*(3), 143–147.

Torrance, E. (1977). *Discovery and nurturance of giftedness in the culturally different.* Reston, VA: Council for Exceptional Children.

Treffinger, D., & Renzulli, J. (1986, February). Giftedness as potential for creative productivity: Transcending I.Q. scores. *Roeper Review, 8*(3), 150–154.

CHAPTER 10

Gifted and Talented Black Children: Identifying Diamonds in the Rough

Donna Y. Ford
J. John Harris III

> Giftedness is not something we invent, not something we discover. It is what one society or another wants it to be (Sternberg & Davidson, 1986, p. 3).

Our history swells with the accounts of people with superior abilities. As early as 2200 B.C. the Chinese had developed an elaborate system of competitive examinations to select outstanding persons for government positions (DuBois, 1970). In A.D. 618, early China, gifted children were sent to the imperial court to have their gifts recognized and nurtured. In ancient Sparta, fighting skills and leadership defined giftedness (Davis & Rimm, 1989). In fact, the records of practically every culture reveal a special fascination for their ablest citizens (Renzulli, 1986, p. 53).

Even today, education tailored to the needs of the gifted and talented generates consuming interest and enthusiasm so that the literature includes an abundance of information about these students—and especially about middle-class white children.

One cannot, however, say the same about the research devoted to minority—and particularly black—gifted and talented children. In fact, an examination of the relevant literature between 1924 and 1989 reveals that of 4,109 articles found on the gifted and talented, a paltry 75 (only 1.8 percent) address minority group members. The percentage would be lower still if one counted only those articles about gifted and talented blacks.

Reprinted from Ford, D.Y., & Harris, J.J., III. (1990). Gifted and talented Black children: Identifying diamonds in the rough. Gifted Child Today, 13(3), 17–21. Reprinted with permission of Prufrock Press Inc.

Educators now find this proportion discouraging, in that less information means less understanding of gifted and talented blacks. Of course, less comprehension means inadequate identification procedures, definitions, theories, and programs—all of which results in an underrepresentation of blacks in programs for the gifted and talented. Equally unsettling, *all* 75 articles on minorities bear the stigmatic heading *disadvantaged* gifted and talented, the term either implying or stating that race itself limits the development of such intelligence. But Passow (1986) pointed out that while one finds considerable overlap between minority students and disadvantaged conditions, by no means are the two synonymous.

This article will (1) examine the barriers to the effective recognition of and assistance for gifted and talented blacks, (2) discuss rationales for reexamining the current definitions and for broadening the theories of gifted and talented to include blacks, and (3) offer prescriptions for change and a list of considerations for educators, particularly those in urban areas.

The difficulty of defining, identifying, and then helping gifted and talented blacks lies largely in the current overreliance upon standardized tests, the reification of intelligence and IQ, and the use of unidimensional instruments to assess the *multidimensional* construct called intelligence.

This overreliance on, misuse of, and perhaps even abuse of standardized tests is confounded by inattention to the influence of one's culture and environment upon the development and manifestation of giftedness and talent in different racial groups.

In essence, we must study more carefully gifted and talented blacks so that they will no longer remain, as Passow (1984) called them, "the largest untapped resource of human intelligence and creativity."

Shortcomings of the Traditional Identification Procedures

Since the pioneering work of Martin Jenkins and Allison Davis demonstrated measureable talent and intelligence among young black people, educators have sought to develop reliable ways to identify giftedness and talent within minorities (Johnson, Starnes, Gregory, & Blaylock, 1985). Unfortunately, a number of barriers still discourage equal and equitable educational opportunities for gifted and talented blacks.

One such barrier, the identification process itself, helps produce an underrepresentation of blacks in gifted and talented programs (Baldwin, 1977, 1987; Harty, Adkins, & Sherwood, 1984; McKenzie, 1986). Data published by the U.S. Department of Education's Office of Civil Rights indicate that minority groups (that is to say, blacks, Hispanics, and Native Americans) are underrepresented in from 30 to 70 percent of the gifted programs nationally and are overrepresented by between 40 and 50 percent in the special education programs (Richert, 1987).

Identifying gifted and talented blacks has been difficult for several reasons:

- ❖ The process is influenced negatively by attitudes and expectations of educators who do not believe the gifted exist in culturally different groups.
- ❖ Sterile IQ-based definitions hinder the process. (Giftedness is primarily defined and identified by performance on intelligence tests whose implicit analogy is "the higher the score, the higher the intelligence." Because, on average, blacks score lower on these standardized measures, they are perceived as less intelligent than their white counterparts. Davis and Rimm [1989] state that low IQ and achievement test scores may be misinterpreted to "prove" absence of giftedness.)
- ❖ Some educators rely indiscriminately on intelligence tests and unidimensional instruments to assess intelligence levels. (Moreover, educators who use standardized tests to identify the giftedness among blacks, either consciously or subconsciously, reify IQ scores and ignore the fact that the tests can and do misinterpret intelligence. As Baldwin [1987] states, the use of designated score ranges on an IQ or achievement test as the only criterion for giftedness can significantly affect the black child's chances for inclusion in gifted and talented programs.)
- ❖ There is a gap between research and practice. (Although there are different ideas on how identification should take place, few identification models systematically put into operation the findings. More often than not, in practice, the identification systems do not reflect the research results. For example, some educational preparation programs teach about cultural diversity, but we know that many educators fail to practice what they teach.)
- ❖ Theories to account for giftedness and talent among blacks are inadequate. (In brief and in fact, no theories exist to account for giftedness among blacks. Hence, they must express their giftedness exactly as white middle-class students do. Generally, deviations from norms are not identified as giftedness.)
- ❖ There is a failure to acknowledge both the culture and environment within which blacks function. (A general resistance to the heterogeneity of culture leads educators to overlook individual needs and, hence, fail to meet them.)
- ❖ Professionals lack agreement on a universally accepted definition of "gifted and talented." (Bernal [1981], Passow [1972], Renzulli [1978], Richert [1987], Sternberg [1985], Torrance [1977a], and Yancey [1983] suggest that broad, diverse, vague, and indefensible definitions compound the identification problems and, thus, increase the already high probability that blacks will be underrepresented in gifted and talented programs. Davis and

Rimm [1989] state that so many definitions of gifted and talented exist that even the gifted mind would get boggled.)

These difficulties illustrate the controversy over whether IQ alone can accurately identify giftedness. On the one side, traditional educators argue that IQ, by itself, can do the job perfectly well. On the other side, contemporary educators oppose identification based solely on IQ scores and argue for pluralistic definitions and theories of giftedness as well as for the inclusion of characteristics other than cognition during the identification process. The following sections discuss these issues in greater detail.

Definitions of the Gifted and Talented

If the definition of giftedness is not a useful one, it can lead to unfavorable consequences of many kinds, both for society and its individuals. If the definition of giftedness is not valuable, talents may be wasted, and less valuable ones fostered and encouraged (Sternberg & Davidson, 1986, p. 4).

Since Terman (1925) presented his unidimensional definition of giftedness (the top one percent in general intelligence ability, as measured by performance on the Stanford-Binet Intelligence test), traditional definitions of giftedness have been generated primarily in two ways: (1) by high scores on IQ tests, and (2) by high scores on achievement tests (Bernal, 1981; Renzulli & Stoddard, 1980; Torrance, 1977a; Yancey, 1983). Both of these practices equate giftedness with high scores on standardized instruments and, thereby, maximize the probability that blacks will fare poorly when (and if) assessed for gifted and talented programs.

The literature presents an abundance of data and criticism indicating that such tests, standardized as they are on white middle-class norms, show bias in favor of whites (Baldwin, 1987; Renzulli & Stoddard, 1980; Yancey, 1983).

In 1972, the U.S. Office of Education defined gifted and talented children as those identified by professionally qualified persons who, by virtue of outstanding abilities, are capable of high performance (U.S. Commissioner of Education, 1972). These abilities, either potential or manifest, include (1) general intellectual ability, (2) specific academic aptitudes, (3) creative or productive thinking, (4) leadership ability, (5) visual and performing arts, and (6) psycho-motor ability (Bernal, 1981; Cremins, 1987; Tannenbaum, 1986). But in Public Law 95-561 of the Education Amendments of the Elementary and Secondary Education Act, the *most* recent definition (1978), omits the sixth category, *psychomotor ability*.

Dissatisfied with the USOE definition, Renzulli (1986) offered an alternative definition that educators may find more useful because it acknowledges that giftedness has many manifestations:

> Giftedness consists of an interaction among three basic clusters of human traits—the clusters being above-average general abilities, high levels of task commitment, and high levels of creativity. Gifted and talented children are those possessing or capable of developing this composite set of traits and applying them to any potentially valuable area of human performance . . . (p. 73).

This definition is more likely than previous definitions to identify gifted and talented blacks. What is needed is a definition of gifted and talented that rests on the idea that a variety of talents and abilities contribute to a person's accomplishments (Renzulli, 1973). Such a definition would rest also on the assumption that rather than trying to identify a universally gifted child, we should look for those aspects of giftedness valued by the child's culture (Torrance, 1978). A review of the literature so far fails to produce an example of such a broadly ideal definition.

PLURALISTIC PROCEDURES FOR IDENTIFYING GIFTED AND TALENTED BLACKS

Traditional identification procedures have disillusioned blacks for more than a century—a reality that prompts an emphasis here on pluralistic views that show the effectiveness of incorporating culture and context into identification procedures. These procedures and subsequent prescriptions hold out the promise of overcoming the identification problems and thereby decreasing the underrepresentation of blacks in gifted and talented programs.

A pluralistic view of giftedness and talent requires educators to adopt a multicultural, multi-modal, multidimensional view of giftedness. In general, the perspective uses three strategies to improve the identification process: (1) modify the giftedness "standards"; (2) seek new, culturally "fair" instruments; and (3) include other criteria beyond standardized test scores for the operational definitions (Gallagher & Courtright, 1986). Such a perspective would identify students with gifted potential.

Other helpful indices include the *Baldwin Identification Matrix 2* (Baldwin, 1984), the *Alpha Biographical* (1968), the *Torrance Tests of Creative Thinking* (Torrance, 1977b), the *System of Multicultural Pluralistic Assessment: SOMPA* (Mercer & Lewis, 1977), and the *Relevant Aspects Potential* (Grant & Renzulli, 1976).

Identification should also incorporate nominations from teachers, parents, peers, and or the applicants themselves. Such inventories as the Khatena-Torrance Creative Perception Inventory (1976), the *SOI Learning Abilities Test* (Meeker & Meeker, 1985), the Multidimensional Screening Device (Kranz, 1978), and the Self Concept and Motivation Inventory (Farrah, Milchus, & Reitz, 1967) may also help identify giftedness among blacks.

The most recent instrument to depart from psychometrics is the Sternberg Multidimensional Abilities Test (Sternberg, in press), which examines intelligence more comprehensively than the traditional IQ tests. The Sternberg instrument suggest manifestations of giftedness inadequately revealed by existing tests.

PRESCRIPTIONS FOR CHANGE

Throughout the first half of the twentieth century, the educational establishment expressed only slight concern for the gifted and talented black child; however, the 1960s may well be recalled as the time when educators noticed and began to countermand the inferior opportunities that beset a large segment of the minority population. Unfortunately, it was a period plagued by uncoordinated attempts simply to "do something" for the culturally different—attempts that amounted to little more than the proverbial "drop in the bucket" compared to the number of black youngsters "whose daily school experience is nothing less than an educational disaster" (Renzulli, 1973).

This history reflects, quite clearly, inadequate identification procedures, definitions, and theories for accommodating gifted and talented blacks. It reinforces the need to reexamine current definitions, theories, and practices for gifted and talented blacks who will otherwise continue to represent our largest untapped source of intelligence (Passow, 1984).

All educators—and particularly those in urban areas—must collaborate to create definitions, theories, and identification procedures that help rather than hinder blacks by taking into account the interaction of the environment and the person. When one considers the many possible interactions among these factors, one can easily see why so much disagreement exists over the definition of giftedness (Renzulli, 1986).

The following prescriptions delineate the essence of giftedness without relying on standardized instruments, and they may further help to nurture the gift and the talent. Both proactive and reactive, these prescriptions represent a progress from the zealous reliance on unidimensional identification procedures to measure the multidimensional, multicultural, multi-modal construct called giftedness. Moreover, these prescriptions present culture-based definitions of, pluralistic (cultural and contextual) theories about giftedness and talent. In addition, seven comprehensive programs for gifted and talented blacks are set forth as prescriptions for change.

DEFINITIONS OF GIFTEDNESS APPROPRIATE FOR BLACKS

> We have carried with us into the 1980s a 1900 definition of intelligence and an IQ test largely unchanged since 1930 (Hatch & Gardner, 1986).

Contemporary definitions must acknowledge that giftedness results from an interplay among culture, language, world view, conceptual style, values, and personality. Perhaps most importantly, these kinds of definitions recognize that every cultural group has its exceptionally capable members (Bernal, 1981). They must emphasize the black child's potential (Davis & Rimm, 1989). Combining the Renzulli (1978) definition and the U.S. Department of Education 1972 definition—which includes the "psychomotor ability" criterion—may yield one of the most operational of definitions.

THEORIES OF INTELLIGENCE AND INTELLIGENCES

Sternberg (1984b) and Gardner (1983) developed modern and insightful theories of intelligence and intelligences, respectively, more sensitive than traditional theories to varying kinds of giftedness. Both suggest that cognition by itself can neither fully nor adequately describe giftedness. For example, Hatch and Gardner dismiss IQ tests as narrow instruments used primarily for assessing the kinds of giftedness and talent valued in western society and school settings (Hatch & Gardner, 1986).

With his Triarchic Theory of Intelligence, Sternberg (1985) proposes that (a) intelligence cannot be understood outside of a sociocultural context so that what is "gifted" in one culture or environment may be irrelevant in another; (b) intelligence is purposeful, goal-oriented, relevant behavior consisting of the ability to learn from experience and the ability to adapt to one's environment; and (c) intelligence depends on information processing skills and strategies (Weinberg, 1989). Moreover, Sternberg (1984a) suggests that gifted individuals shape their environments and, perhaps more important, they do not necessarily possess high IQs. Thus, without the inclusion of non-cognitive factors like those just described, many gifted students will continue to suffer the stigma of mediocrity (Renzulli, 1986).

Gardner's Theory of Multiple Intelligences (1984) suggests that intelligence resembles a constellation of at least seven discrete competencies: linguistic, logical-mathematical, spatial, bodily kinetics, musical, inter-personal, and intra-personal. In addition, Gardner believes that a person can be gifted in one area and average or below average in the others.

Hatch and Gardner (1986) advanced the idea that competencies in the "non-cognitive" domains may be just as valuable and praiseworthy as competencies in those called intelligent. For example, among the Puluwat Islanders in the South Seas, spatial intelligence is critical for those able to navigate canoes by attending to stars and constellations. In other societies, interpersonal intelligence is valued in literary endeavors. Hatch and Gardner also note that, in our society, the ability to write poetry, to play sports, to present a convincing argument, or even to demonstrate a general language ability is not reflected by standardized tests.

At the risk of stating the obvious, the two theories just discussed mutually support and complement rather than contradict one another. They both tend to prove that it is much better to specify the nature of intelligence in terms of the external world, the internal world, and the interrelationship between them (Sternberg, 1985).

Before the 1980s, few theories departed from the customary to address giftedness in the black community. Those educators who would understand and help gifted and talented blacks must support these new and comprehensive theories, for they hold the greatest promise for enhancing identification procedures and subsequently increasing the participation of blacks in gifted and talented programs.

Comprehensive Programs for Gifted and Talented Black Students

Continuing professional education. Few schools can offer its students personnel instantaneously skilled and knowledgeable in gifted education, or qualified enough to put research into practice. Educators must understand the culture and basic needs of black students. Once teachers understand that giftedness is individually and culturally unique, they are more able to draw upon the strengths of children in teaching and choosing curricular materials.

Administrators, meanwhile, would assume responsibility for appointing and training personnel who accept the idea that not everyone thinks alike (Cooper, 1980). Consideration for this diversity requires administrators and teachers to become more accountable, skillful, and creative in meeting the exceptional needs of gifted and talented black students. As such, staff development must focus on altering traditional expectations and assumptions regarding gifted and talented blacks.

Public education. Public education must ultimately meet the needs of all students, but this message often gets lost in the pious rhetoric of excellence, equality, and equity. McDaniel (1989) observes that schools are "incremental" in nature and consequently lag behind social change, but if they do not actively promote gifted and talent development, they neglect their underlying purpose.

Community involvement. A community should involve itself in the practice of educational excellence, not just in movement advocacy. Moreover, school personnel must actively involve parents, community educators, and the school's efforts.

Philosophy of pluralism. As this article suggests, a philosophy of pluralism must pervade our schools and society before any modern definition, theory, or program will be effective. Given the nation's changing demographics, it can no longer afford to ignore cultural diversity. Moreover, more minority leaders are needed to serve as role models.

Assessment. To repeat, non-traditional and pluralistic instruments are critical to identifying gifted and talented black students. Marked departures from traditional practices are now virtually analogous to sound, futuristic educational perspectives. The systematic pupil identification needed requires modern definitions and theories, and the wise and careful participation of educators, administrators, parents, and the community. This identification must (obviously) begin in the early years and the primary grades. Just as important, it must be continuous, for giftedness can manifest itself at different times.

Curriculum. Educational programs must acknowledge non-cognitive, non-academic skills so that blacks may enjoy increased opportunities for reaching their potential. The organization, content, and methodology of the curriculum must be defined and implemented against an awareness of the total environment, and, at the same time, the acknowledgement of the affective and cognitive elements of giftedness. In addition, a teacher's instructional style must match and complement that of the students, and instructional patterns must be flexible.

Parental involvement. Because the first six years of life are critical in the development and manifestation of giftedness, parents must become active participants in this special educational process. A partnership with educators, initiated by either side, can provide a gifted student with a supportive, nurturing environment. Neither parent nor educator can effectively "go it alone."

*****

The phenomenon of giftedness continues to fascinate contemporary educators and researchers, and new definitions and theories promise a fuller appreciation of and attention to children. The prescriptions listed above are intended to increase this appreciation and to enhance the recognition of inherent intellectual skills, giftedness, and talent among blacks. We must continually search for a clearer understanding of this valued abstraction we call giftedness because as so cogently stated by Arnold Gessell:

> The current knowledge of a child's mind is comparable to a fifteenth century map of the world—a mixture of truth and error, and 'vast areas remain to be explored' (Cited in Renzulli, 1986).

REFERENCES

Alpha Biographical (1968). Greensboro, NC: Predictive Press.

Baldwin, A. Y. (1977). Tests do underpredict: A case study. *Phi Delta Kappan, 59*(8), 620–621.

Baldwin, A. Y. (1987). I'm black but look at me, I am also gifted. *The Gifted Child Quarterly, 31*(4), 180–185.

Bernal, E. M. (1981). *Special problems and procedures for identifying minority gifted students.* Texas: Creative Educational Enterprises. (ERIC Document Reproduction Service No. ED 203 652).

Cooper, G. C. (1980). Everyone does not think alike. *English Journal, 69*(4), 45–50.

Cremins, M. A. (1987). *A rationale for reexamining definitions, identification, and programs for the gifted disabled/disadvantaged.* Arlington, MA. (ERIC Document Reproduction Service No. ED 289 284).

Davis, G. A., & Rimm, S. (1989). *Education of the gifted and talented* (2nd edition). New Jersey: Prentice Hall.

Dubois, P. H. (1970). *A history of psychological testing.* Boston: Allyn & Bacon.

Farrah, G. A. Milchus, N. J. & Reitz, W. (1967). Self Concept and Motivation Inventory. Dearborn Heights, MI: Person-O-Metrics, Inc.

Gallagher, J. J., & Courtright, R. D. (1986). The educational definition of giftedness and its policy implication. In R. J. Sternberg & J. E. Davidson (Eds.) *Conceptions of giftedness.* Cambridge: Cambridge University Press.

Gardner, H. (1983). *Frames of mind.* New York: Basic Books.

Gardner, H. (1984). Assessing intelligences: A comment on testing intelligences without I.Q. tests. *Phi Delta Kappan, 65*(10), 699–700.

Grant, T. E., & Renzulli, J. S. (1976). *Relevant aspects of potential.* RAP Researchers.

Harty, H., Adkins, D. M., & Sherwood, R. D. (1984). Predictability of giftedness identification indices for two recognized approaches to elementary school gifted education. *Journal of Educational Research, 77*(6), 337–342.

Hatch, T. C., & Gardner, H. (1986). From testing intelligence to assessing competencies: A pluralistic view of intelligence. *Roeper Review, 8*(3), 147–150.

Johnson, S. T., Starnes, W. T., Gregory, D., & Blaylock, A. (1985). Program of assessment, diagnosis, and instruction PADI: Identifying and nurturing potentially gifted and talented minority students. *Journal of Negro Education, 24,* 416–430.

Khatena, J., & Torrance, E. P. (1976). Khatena-Torrance Creative Perception Inventory. Chicago: Stoelting Co.

Kranz, B. (1978). *Multidimensional Screening Device (MSD) for the identification of gifted and talented children.* Grand Forks: University of North Dakota Bureau of Educational Research.

McDaniel, T. R. (1989). Mainstreaming the gifted: Historical perspectives on excellence and equity. *Roeper Review, 24*(3), 112–14.

McKenzie, J. (1986). The influence of identification practices, race and SES on the identification of gifted students. *The Gifted Child Quarterly, 30,* 93–95.

Meeker, M., & Meeker, R. (1985). *SOI-Learning Abilities Test: Screening Form for Atypical Gifted.* Vida, OR: M & M Systems.

Mercer, J. R., & Lewis, J. (1977). *System of Multicultural Pluralistic Assessment (SOMPA).* New York: The Psychological Corporation.

Passow, A. H. (1972). The gifted and the disadvantaged. *The National Elementary Principal, 51*(5), 24–41.

Passow, A. H. (1984). *Education of the gifted in world perspective.* New York: Teachers College Columbia University. (ERIC Reproduction Service No. ED 292 239).

Passow, A. H. (1986). *Educational programs for minority/disadvantaged gifted students.* New York: Teachers College Columbia University. (ERIC Reproduction Series No. ED 268 190).

Public Law 95-561 (1978). *Educational Amendments of 1978.* 92 Stat. 2143, 95th Congress, 2nd session.

Renzulli, J. S. (1973). Talent potential in minority group students. *Exceptional Children, 39,* 437–444.

Renzulli, J. S. (1978). What makes giftedness: Reexamining a definition. *Phi Delta Kappan, 60,* 108–184.

Renzulli, J. S. (1986). The three-ring conception of giftedness: A developmental model for creative productivity. In R. J. Sternberg & J. E. Davidson (Eds.). *Conceptions of giftedness.* Cambridge: Cambridge University Press.

Renzulli, J. S., & Stoddard, E. P. (1980). *Gifted and talented education in perspective.* Reston, VA: The Council for Exceptional Children.

Richert, E. S. (1987). Rampant problems and promising practices in the identification of disadvantaged gifted children. *The Gifted Child Quarterly, 31*(4), 149–154.

Sternberg, R. J. (1984a). Toward a triarchic theory of human intelligence. *Behavioral and Brain Sciences, 7,* 269–315.

Sternberg, R. J. (1984b). What should intelligence tests test? Implications for a triarchic theory of intelligence for intelligence testing. *Educational Researcher, 13*(1), 5–15.

Sternberg, R. J. (1985). *Beyond IQ: A triarchic theory of human intelligence.* Cambridge: Cambridge University Press.

Sternberg, R. J., & Davidson, J. E. (1986). *Conceptions of giftedness.* Cambridge: Cambridge University Press.

Tannenbaum, A. J. (1986). Giftedness: A psychosocial approach. In R. J. Sternberg & J. E. Davidson (Eds.). *Conceptions of giftedness.* Cambridge: Cambridge University Press.

Terman, L. (1925). Mental and physical traits of a thousand gifted children. In L. Terman (Ed.), *Genetic studies of genius* (Vol. 1). Stanford, CA: Stanford University Press.

Torrance, E. P. (1977a). *Discovery and nurturance of giftedness in the culturally different.* Virginia: Council on Exceptional Children.

Torrance, E. P. (1977b). *Torrance Tests of Creative Thinking.* Bensenville, IL: Scholastic Testing Services.

Torrance, E. P. (1978). Ways of discovering gifted black children. In A. Y. Baldwin, G. H. Gear, & L. J. Lucito (Eds.). *Educational planning for the gifted: Overcoming cultural, geographic, and socioeconomic barriers.* Reston, VA: Council for Exceptional Children.

U.S. Commissioner of Education (1972). *Education of the gifted and talented: Report to the Congress of the United States by the U.S. Commissioner of Education.* Washington, D.C.: U.S. Government Printing Office.

Weinberg, R. A. (1989). Intelligence and IQ: Landmark issues and great debate. *American Psychologist, 44*(2), 98–104.

Yancey, E. (1983). *Increasing participation of minority and culturally diverse students in gifted programs.* Washington, D.C.: The American University Mid-Atlantic Center for Race Equity. (ERIC Document Reproduction Series No. ED 244 010).

CHAPTER 11

Toward a New Paradigm for Identifying Talent Potential

Mary M. Frasier
The University of Georgia
Athens, Georgia

A. Harry Passow
Teachers College, Columbia University
New York, New York

Executive Summary

Introduction

In its 1950 statement on the education of the gifted, the Educational Policies Commission (EPC) asserted that "the educational needs of individuals who have superior intellectual capacity and of those who possess special talents in high degree differ in some important respects from the needs of other individuals" and that "gifted members of the total school population constitute a minority which is too largely neglected" (p. iii). Furthermore, the Commission deplored America's waste of talent noting: "That a large amount of human talent possessed by individuals now living is lost through stultification and isolation can be convincingly demonstrated—although admittedly the precise dimensions defy measurements" (p. 14).

The EPC contended it was important to know the causes—economic, social, psychological, and educational—as well as the groups in which the waste

---

Reprinted from Frasier, M. M., & Passow, A. H. (1994). *Toward a new paradigm for identifying talent potential* (Research Monograph No. 94112). Storrs: University of Connecticut, The National Research Center on the Gifted and Talented. Reprinted with permission of The National Research Center on the Gifted and Talented.

occurred. Pointing to discriminatory practices to which minorities are exposed, the Commission observed:

> Lacking both incentive and opportunity, the probabilities are very great that, however, superior one's gifts may be, he will rarely live a life of high achievement. Follow-up studies of highly gifted young Negroes, for instance, reveal a shocking waste of talent—a waste that adds an incalculable amount to the price of prejudice in this country. (p. 33)

Two decades later, the *Marland Report* (1971) commented on the low priority that the federal, state, and local government assigned to the education of the gifted: "Existing services to the gifted and talented do not reach large and significant subpopulations (e.g., minorities and disadvantaged) and serve a very small percentage of the gifted and talented population generally" (p. xi). That report asserted that "the problems of screening and identification are complicated by assumptions that talents cannot be found as abundantly in certain groups as in others—with the emphasis heavily in favor of the affluent" and speculated that this may account for the meager research and identification among minority and disadvantaged groups (p. II-8).

The *Marland Report* flatly declared that: "Since the full range of human talents is represented in all races of man and in all socioeconomic levels, it is unjust and unproductive to allow social or racial background to affect the treatment of an individual" (pp. II-9 and II-10). Almost two decades later when passing the Jacob K. Javits Gifted and Talented Students Education Act of 1988 (P.L. 100-297), Congress reasserted the conviction that youngsters with talent potential are found in all cultural groups, across all economic strata, and in all areas of human endeavor.

The under-inclusion of economically disadvantaged and minority children in programs for the gifted has been so well documented over the years that it hardly needs recounting. Simply put, the significant and constant increases in both the number and proportion of racial/ethnic minority and economically disadvantaged children in the public school population are not reflected in programs for the gifted and talented.

IMPROVING THE IDENTIFICATION OF THE GIFTED IN MINORITY AND DISADVANTAGED POPULATIONS

The 1993 Department of Education report, *National Excellence: A Case for Developing America's Talent*, argues that: "Schools must eliminate barriers to participation of economically disadvantaged and minority students with outstanding talents" and "must develop strategies to serve students from underrepresented groups" (p. 28). To do this, the report asserted, identification of students with talent potential and their inclusion in programs for developing their potential, must be given a high priority for schools and communities.

The most widely accepted explanation for underrepresentation of disadvantaged students in programs for the gifted is the ineffectiveness and inappropriateness of the identification and selection procedures that have traditionally been and continue to be used. Youngsters who are not selected for programs are seldom provided with the needed opportunities to nurture and develop their talent potential.

This monograph (a) reviews traditional identification practices, (b) examines the environmental and value differences among several cultural subgroups, (c) describes the results of an exploratory study of the characteristics of disadvantaged and limited English proficient gifted students, (d) explores gifted behaviors as they relate to specific populations, (e) synthesizes insights emerging from the Javits Gifted and Talented Students Education Act, and (f) presents elements which can be used to construct a new paradigm of giftedness.

Assumptions Underlying Traditional Identification Procedures

Twelve postulates or assumptions underlie the critique of the traditional programs and processes that have guided identification procedures and guide thinking about new models or paradigms:

1. There exists no single accepted "theory of giftedness."
2. Academic achievement is an important indicator of giftedness, but cannot be the sole determinant in identification procedures.
3. Cultures may differ in terms of those talents recognized and rewarded; no culture or population has a monopoly on any talent potential, whatever its nature.
4. The aptitudes, attributes, and characteristics that are associated with talent potential are culturally imbedded.
5. The talents of minority and economically disadvantaged students are not of a different order nor of a lower standard.
6. The purpose of identification is to locate students who can then be provided with appropriately differentiated educational opportunities.
7. Screening, identification, and the consequent cultivation of talent potential can only be improved and enhanced if insights into the nature of talent potential and the contexts in which it is nurtured are understood.
8. The concept of "disadvantaged" has meaning only if it is understood, not in terms of deficiencies, but rather as differences.

9. The problems of underrepresentation of minority and economically disadvantaged gifted students are intrinsically related to the more general problems of education and schooling of these populations—the fact that these students are more likely to be in schools and classes that are segregated or racially imbalanced and that have poorer facilities, fewer instructional resources, larger classes, fewer programs for the gifted, more inexperienced teachers, and other factors that contribute to limited or unequal educational opportunities.
10. Since decisions about giftedness in children are never more than predictions, wide nets should be thrown in the early stages of selection to increase the power of those predictions.
11. The concept that talent potential is culturally imbedded and impacted by environmental factors applies to all populations. Focusing on improving talent identification and development in a particular target population could well lead to better insights about talent identification and its nature more generally.
12. Valid assessment procedures and strategies that would more effectively identify talent potential of minority disadvantaged populations must deal with both the actual and perceived problems of traditional methods. They must encourage and support the efforts of various minority groups to examine the concept of giftedness within their own cultural and environmental contexts and provide the basis for recognizing talents, without apologies for differences, where these exist, in their expression and performance.

A Review and Critique of Traditional Identification Approaches

Since Terman's "Genetic Studies of Genius" was begun in 1925, a narrow definition of giftedness—limited to intelligence, academic aptitude, and academic achievement—has guided identification procedures. Standardized tests of intelligence, aptitude, and achievement were widely, often exclusively, employed with pre-set cut-off points or percentages determining which children were to be included in programs for the gifted. Psychometric constructs of giftedness have traditionally guided identification and programming.

Through the years, there have been advocates for definitions of giftedness that go beyond high intellectual or academic ability. In 1971, the *Marland Report* broadened the definition, defining gifted children as those with demonstrated achievement and/or potential ability in general intellectual ability, specific academic aptitude, creative or productive thinking, leadership ability, visual and performing arts, and psychomotor ability. The report urged casting wider nets to identify children with a broader spectrum of talent potential.

Although the definition of giftedness has broadened in the past two decades, intellectual ability and academic aptitude still dominate identification processes as well as programming. Psychometric identification models are widely used despite research findings that lead to characterizing giftedness as a complex, multifaceted phenomenon, requiring the use of a variety of objective and subjective techniques and procedures if it is to be effectively assessed. A survey by Coleman and Gallagher (1992) found that "all 49 of the states which have state level policies related to gifted education use some form of standardized IQ and achievement test in their identification process. However, a variety of other sources are often included" (p. 16).

While this psychometric approach to identification of giftedness may have succeeded in identifying children who are good test takers, high academic achievers, and members of the dominant or majority population, it is widely acknowledged that the approach has not worked effectively in identifying talent potential among students from economically disadvantaged families and communities, those from racial or ethnic minority groups, and those with limited English proficiency. Moreover, the psychometric approach has not proved useful in relating identification assessment information to programs, curricula, counseling activities, and evaluation with most populations, but especially with underrepresented populations. There are other populations—e.g., children with dyslexia, attention disorder, or learning disability—who do not perform well on tests and whose talent potential may go unrecognized as well.

Concern with the limitations of the psychometric construct of giftedness has led to two distinct but related developments:

- There has been the ongoing search for better means to identify minority and disadvantaged students within the psychometric concept of giftedness—i.e., recognition of the under inclusion and under selection of disadvantaged populations using the customary instruments and procedures and of the need to search for more effective techniques and procedures. Three thrusts are aimed at enlarging the pool of intellectually able minority students: (a) Modifying or adapting traditional criteria or standards for participation in programs for the gifted; (b) Using alternative procedures with target populations such as culturally specific checklists, aggregation of data from varied sources, and quotas; and (c) Employing "dynamic assessment" procedures in which learning potential is assessed by measuring cognitive learning modifiability during active learning tasks.
- There has been a shift from psychometric constructs of giftedness to psychological constructs, a shift from test-driven models to ones that focus on traits, aptitudes, and behaviors as defining giftedness.

A number of concerns have been raised regarding assessment procedures and techniques used in the traditional identification paradigms. Two aspects of the identification process—limited nominations and referrals and test bias and inappropriateness—are the focus of much of the questioning and criticisms of the traditional paradigms.

Limited Nominations and Referrals

Referrals usually constitute the first step in an identification process and studies show consistent limitations on nominations and referrals of disadvantaged populations. Two factors contribute to underreferral: teacher attitudes toward minority students and the type of schools such students are likely to attend.

Minority and other disadvantaged students are less likely to be nominated for or included in an identification or screening process because of the low expectations educational professionals have for culturally and linguistically diverse students, their low levels of awareness of cultural and linguistic behaviors of potentially gifted minority students, their insensitivity to the differences within and among groups, and their inability to recognize "gifted behaviors" that minority students exhibit.

Minorities and economically disadvantaged children are found in disproportionately large concentrations in school environments that are often described as "impoverished educational environments"—poorly equipped, often overcrowded, segregated, or racially imbalanced. Such schools and classrooms tend to provide fewer higher learning opportunities, chances to engage in enriched experiences, and fewer occasions to exhibit gifted behaviors. Since such schools have fewer provisions for identifying and nurturing talent potential, nominations and referrals are limited.

The concentration on the perceived or alleged deficiencies of disadvantaged populations has diverted attention from understanding the characteristics, behaviors, and attributes of minority students who have achieved, such as their positive self-esteem, attitudes toward school and school-related experiences, positive motivation, identify with healthy role models, and family relationships.

Three actions seem to hold promise for increasing nominations and referrals from minority and disadvantaged groups:

- ❖ Develop greater understanding of cultural differences in the ways gifted characteristics, traits, and attributes are manifested or exhibited in diverse settings so that they will be recognized more readily by teachers and other staff members.
- ❖ Expand the numbers and types of persons involved in the process to include self-and peer-nominations as well as referrals by parents and community leaders.

❖ Provide a rich educational environment that will stimulate students and enable them to demonstrate the kinds of behaviors and performances that will facilitate the recognition of their talent potential.

TEST BIAS AND INAPPROPRIATENESS

The limitations of standardized tests, particularly tests of intelligence and academic aptitude which constitute the linchpins of most identification programs, have long been cited. The content, construct, and predictive or criterion-related validity of tests of mental ability have long been questioned. It has been argued that standardized tests discriminate against minority and economically disadvantaged students and those whose linguistic and perceptual orientation, cognitive styles, learning and response styles, economic status, and cultural or social background differ from the dominant groups used to norm such tests—i.e., White, middle-class populations.

In addition to numerous technical criticisms of standardized testing—their validity, design, development, norming, and interpretation—there is a serious charge of bias attributed to institutionalized racism. Cummins (1989), for example, asserts that the structure for classrooms has been "legitimized by the assumption that IQ tests were valid indicators of minority students' academic abilities, and that their school failure was an inevitable consequence of mental inferiority due to . . . genetic inferiority, bilingualism, linguistic deficiency or cultural deprivation" (p. 96).

The issues regarding the value and validity, bias, and appropriateness have been debated for a good many years, but only recently have a variety of actions have been taken to deal with the many concerns and problems attributed to the centrality of standardized testing in the identification process. Actions include the modification or adaptation of traditional standards and the use of alternative procedures and strategies. Examples of such actions include:

❖ Some schools have banned the use of standardized group intelligence tests, sometimes substituting surrogate tests, such as reading tests.
❖ Most commercial test makers now review test items for bias, norm their tests using more diverse populations and, in a few instances, provide separate norms for various sub-populations.
❖ Test makers have designed or promoted the use of already existing nonverbal tests (touted as "culture-free") on the presumption that such measures are less biased and more fair for minority and disadvantaged populations.
❖ Test makers have designed a number of multimodal assessment indices.
❖ The administration, scoring, and interpretation of results of some standardized tests have been modified to isolate patterns of strength among subgroups.

- ❖ A few tests—e.g., the *Black Intelligence Test for Children*—have been designed selecting items that are biased toward the knowledge and information a minority population is more likely to have acquired.
- ❖ Some school districts have set special cut-off scores for target populations even though this procedure often raises problems for identified minority students by stigmatizing them as being included on the basis of lower standards.
- ❖ Multiple criteria and non-traditional measures—i.e., instruments other than or in addition to IQ tests—are being used to enhance the opportunities for minority students to be considered in the identification procedures.
- ❖ Matrices, inventories, and rating scales have been developed, some of which aggregate data from several sources in order to deal with the perceived inadequacies of standardized tests alone.

Harris and Ford (1991) have contended that:

> The difficulty of defining, identifying, and nurturing gifted Black Americans lies in the current overreliance upon standardized tests, the reification of intelligence and the IQ, and the use of unidimensional instruments to assess the multidimensional construct called intelligence. This overreliance on, misuse of, and perhaps even abuse of standardized tests is confounded by the *inadequate attention paid to the influence of context—namely, environment and culture—upon the development and manifestation of giftedness in different racial groups.* (p. 4) [Emphasis added]

The task educators of the gifted face is twofold—with both tasks calling for greater understanding of which cultural differences make a difference with respect to talent potential and its development and how these can be behaviorally observed:

- ❖ To improve the traditional identification approaches by designing, adapting, modifying, and extending strategies and procedures to take into account the influence of race, culture, caste, and socioeconomic status.
- ❖ To shift to other constructs of giftedness that focus on "gifted behaviors" and respond more vigorously to cultural and environmental differences as influences on the display of talent potential.

Understanding and Attending to Cultural Influences Affecting Talent Identification and Development

The concern with underrepresentation of minorities and disadvantaged in programs for the gifted is with inadequate selection for and participation in those areas of talent that society recognizes and rewards. There are not talent areas that are especially reserved for or allotted to African Americans or Hispanics or any other minority group. Minority gifted students often bring unique strengths to particular contexts as a consequence of their cultural experiences in the family, the community, and the school.

The goal for gifted culturally diverse students is not unlike that for gifted in general—it is to enable them to enter and participate fully in mainstream society; to succeed at a high level academically; to enter and succeed in college where they can acquire high-level specialized training; and to become leaders, mathematicians, scientists, historians, medical researchers, lawyers, writers, performing artists, and every other area of specialized talent.

Although there is consensus that cultural variables affect talent identification and its development, a number of issues need be considered in designing new approaches.

Conflict in Values

One issue raised is the conflict between the cultural and sub-cultural values on the one hand and the mainstream (i.e., White middle class) values on the other—a conflict that is particularly significant in that academic success and achievement in most recognized areas of specialized talent are usually the means for entering the mainstream. The challenge for minority gifted is one of maintaining the values of one's culture while acquiring or developing the values of the dominant culture that affect performance in an area of talent.

Gifted children from all groups, especially adolescents, confront values-driven attitude problems with their peers as represented by a number of pejorative terms—e.g., *nerd*, *egghead*, *brain*, to cite a few. As a consequence, "some adolescent peer groups within a culture may reject school achievement in a reaction to negative stereotyping by classmates and perceived inaccessibility to the American dream" (Kitano, 1991, p. 8). In the case of gifted minority and disadvantaged youth, there is considerable risk of being ostracized and isolated by their peers if they achieve. Such youth may choose to underachieve rather than hazard being accused of "acting white," or of being "raceless," or of rejecting their own culture.

WITHIN-GROUP CULTURAL DIVERSITY

Within-group cultural differences are often as great or greater than the differences among the four major "minorities"—African Americans, Hispanics/Latinos, Asian Americans, Native Americans/American Indians. These difference include socioeconomic status, especially poverty levels; first language or mother tongue and English proficiency; residency in an urban/suburban/rural or inner-city environment; recency of immigration or migration; and a variety of other factors. Still, within groups that one would expect to be at risk, "there are many well-adjusted, well-cared for children even in inner city environments who are reinforced in their intellectual pursuits" (Frasier, 1989, p. 222).

In addition to the within-group diversity within minority populations, many changes in the demographics of American society affect all groups, including majority groups. Among these are the deterioration of urban centers in which minorities are often concentrated; the changing nature and stability of family structures affected by, among other factors, single-parent families and one or both parents working outside the home; increased number of families living below the poverty level; concentrations of communities in which a language other than English is the first language; growth in schools and classes segregated by race, ethnic background, or socioeconomic status, to name a few. All of these affect the cultural experiences with which children come to school and affect the climate of the school as well.

DIFFERENTIAL CULTURAL AND ENVIRONMENTAL INFLUENCES ON GIFTEDNESS

Knowledge and insights regarding cultural differences are emerging from the search for talent potential among groups who have been traditionally underrepresented. Cultural differences studies deal with such topics as the group's perception of giftedness, family structure and child-rearing patterns, cognitive functioning and information processing strategies, family and community values, and peer responses to achievement.

Two kinds of research have been helpful for understanding cognitive strength—studies on characteristics of achievers and underachievers and comparisons of achievers from different cultural groups. Attention needs to be given to gifted females on two levels—as gifted women in the general population and as a subgroup within a racial or ethnic minority group. Different cultures treat gifted female achievers distinctively, and those variations are usually part of the overall pattern of that culture's perception of females.

In sum, family structure, child-rearing patterns, values, socialization patterns, and resources together with community values, relationships, and resources, exercise powerful influences on the behaviors of children and youth. As Passow (1986) has asserted:

When students are black, red, or brown, are culturally different, are non- or limited-English speaking, have non-standard dialects, or are poor, those who are gifted or talented among them are especially disadvantaged because of the attitudes and expectations toward the population of which they are a part. We must first discard group stereotypes and view each child in terms of his or her individuality as part of a cultural group. We need to understand how cultural differences impact both positively and negatively on the cognitive and affective development of individuals. (p. 155)

GIFTED ATTRIBUTES AND GIFTED BEHAVIORS

Over the years, researchers have identified characteristics—traits, aptitudes, and behaviors—that appear to be common to all gifted students and that distinguish them from students not considered gifted. Typically, lists of characteristics include references to such traits, aptitudes, and behaviors as the gifted child's: (a) facility in manipulating abstract symbol systems, (b) early language interest and development, (c) unusually well developed memory, (d) ability to generate original ideas, (e) precocious language and thought, (f) superior humor, (g) high moral thinking, (h) independence in thinking, (i) emotional intensity, (j) high levels of energy, (k) early reading and advanced comprehension, (l) logical thinking abilities, (m) high levels of motivation, (n) insights, and (o) advanced interests.

Many writers suggest that such traits, aptitudes, or behaviors can be considered *general/common attributes of giftedness*. Leung (1981) calls such characteristics "*absolute attributes of giftedness*" since they appear to be "universal and cross-cultural" in contrast to "*specific behaviors*" or manifestations of those attributes in particular contexts or settings. Clearly such traits, attributes, and behaviors are not absolute in the sense that every gifted individual always exhibits or manifests every one of them. Rather, they are attributes that seem to be ascribed to children who have been identified as being gifted. An apparent implication that can be drawn from this distinction is that *the search for better identification procedures for gifted economically disadvantaged and culturally diverse students should focus on ways of recognizing the specific behaviors or manifestations of these attributes in various cultural, contextual, and environmental settings.*

The task for educators is to understand how these characteristics are manifested in the specific behaviors of individuals from diverse cultural and economic backgrounds. For example, do economically disadvantaged Hispanic or African American children "manipulate abstract symbol systems" differently from middle-class White students, the populations on whom most studies of behavioral characteristics have been done? If so, in what ways. The specific behavioral differences need to be observed, recognized, and acted upon within a specific context or environment.

Examples are provided of how behavioral differences might ensue from the interaction of cultural values with attributes of giftedness. These examples call attention to how some absolute attributes of giftedness might be displayed by individuals with particular cultural backgrounds, recognizing that there will be diversity and variations within each group and subgroup. Some of the efforts to develop culture-specific checklists and rating scales based on the particular behaviors of gifted minority students are reviewed. Each of these rating scales, checklists, and observation forms is aimed at directing attention to gifted behaviors as exhibited by minority and/or economically disadvantaged gifted students.

EMERGING INSIGHTS FROM THE JAVITS GIFTED AND TALENTED STUDENTS EDUCATION ACT

The purpose of the Jacob K. Javits Gifted and Talented Students Education Act of 1988 "is to provide national leadership for efforts to identify and serve gifted and talented students, especially those who are economically disadvantaged, are limited English proficient, or have disabilities." Under the provisions of the act, dozens of programs have been funded focused on identifying and nurturing the talents of economically disadvantaged and LEP students. Many of these programs represent efforts to deal with the inadequacies of the traditional paradigms in identifying talent potential.

Callahan, Tomlinson, and Pizzat (n.d.) identified 11 programs that have attempted to deal with the question of equity and the issues relating to the identification of economically disadvantaged and limited English proficient students using innovative approaches. Their review led them to identify some "commonalities and themes" that were displayed to different degrees and clarity:

❖ Acceptance of intelligence as multi-faceted.
❖ Recognition of multiple manifestations of giftedness.
❖ Emphasis on authentic assessment tools and assessment over time.
❖ Development of a philosophy of inclusiveness rather than exclusiveness.
❖ Strong links between the identification process and instruction.
❖ Use of identification to enhance understanding.
❖ Early and on-going plans and procedures to evaluate the process.

Toward a New Paradigm for Identifying Talent Potential Amongst Culturally Diverse Populations

The models and paradigms that have dominated the search for talent potential, primarily psychometric and test-driven, have been justly criticized because of the drastic and unconscionable underrepresentation of culturally different, economically disadvantaged and limited English proficient gifted students. Although the traditional paradigms seemed to have worked somewhat better with the non-minority middle-class groups, even with that population they have neither adequately nor satisfactorily identified the range and variety of talent potential.

The search for new paradigms that would enhance the search for talent potential has been ongoing, one that has intensified over recent years as educators and others have become increasingly concerned with underrepresentation of economically disadvantaged and minority students in programs for the gifted.

This review of the issues and the efforts regarding the assessment of talent potential of children from diverse cultures makes clear the fact that the problems of identifying and nurturing talent potential are not resolved by formulating constructs of giftedness solely for minority and economically disadvantaged students that differ from those for the majority populations, or by watering down criteria or standards for excellence or outstanding performance, or by seeking different areas of talent in various populations. On the other hand, the review makes clear that cultural and environmental contexts have a significant impact on behavior and performance and must be attended to if the search for talent potential is to succeed.

The challenge is one of creating paradigms that take culture and context into account in order to enhance the possibilities for identifying talent potential of many kinds in all populations so that appropriate opportunities and conditions can be provided for nurturing potential to talented performance. New paradigms will consider the following elements differently from the traditional psychometric models:

1. **New Constructs of Giftedness.** Giftedness is being reconceptualized and redefined to encompass a broad range of cognitive and affective traits and qualities that are dynamically displayed as potential to be nurtured and developed. New constructs of giftedness reflect multifaceted, multicultural, multidimensional perspective and are defined by traits, aptitudes, and behaviors to be nurtured rather than by static test performance.

    Although certain talent areas may have greater value and relevance in some cultures than others, the basic elements of the gifted construct are similar across cultures. Culturally diverse, economically disadvantaged, and limited English proficient groups do not value broadly defined concepts of intelligence and aptitude any less than a middle-class group, although they may not give the same value to a standardized test score that conveys a narrow view of intelligence. By defining giftedness dynamically, the possibilities from demonstrating potential by individuals from all groups are markedly increased.

2. **Absolute Attributes and Specific Behaviors**. Although it has long been understood that culture and environmental contexts play a significant role in the display of talent potential, educators have been slow in implementing and applying those understandings. There is consensus that there are *absolute attributes of giftedness*—traits, aptitudes, and behaviors that are universally associated with talent potential and performance—and *specific behaviors* that represent different manifestations of gifted potential and performance as a consequence of the social and cultural contexts in which they occur. Dynamic assessment focuses on the specific behaviors, the ways the absolute attributes are displayed in a particular context.

    In various settings, traits or aptitudes might be displayed differently. It is the specific behaviors that must be assessed as manifestations of attributes of giftedness. The identification process must facilitate the display of these specific gifted behaviors.

3. **Cultural and Contextual Variability**. To acknowledge that cultural variables significantly affect behavior both positively and negatively is only a first step toward improved identification processes. Generalizations can be made about a particular culture's child-rearing patterns, family structure and relationships, community values, educational aspirations, cognitive functioning and information processing strategies, peer relationships, socializing mechanisms, and other aspects of a group's social and psychological functioning. However, their application to specific individuals in particular contexts can vary considerably.

    Specific knowledge about every cultural or ethnolinguistic group cannot possibly be acquired. Nevertheless, educators must increase their sensitivity to and understanding of culturally determined and environmentally affected behaviors and to recognize and interpret such behaviors in the context in which they are displayed. Behavioral and performance indicators of talent potential, self-perceptions of ability, teacher attitudes and insights, familial characteristics, environmental features of people or services that hinder the development of potential—all of these are relatively focused when considered in a particular setting. That is, there are overall understandings and insights regarding cultures and there are knowledge and insights regarding the specific populations within which talent potential is being sought and nurtured.

4. **More Varied and More Authentic Assessment**. The use of multiple criteria and non-traditional measures—instruments and assessment tools other

than intelligence and achievement—is now widely advocated. Authentic assessment involves data collection that is derived, in part, from observing the interaction of students with learning opportunities. For example, many of the checklists and observation forms developed for Javits programs use such techniques to guide the teacher's search for gifted behaviors.
5. **Identification Through Learning Opportunities**. Economically disadvantaged and limited English proficient students are more likely to be in schools and classrooms where they have fewer opportunities for the display of gifted behaviors. The concept of self-identification takes on considerable meaning and importance for this population. It involves the creation of environments that will make it possible for students to engage in rich learning opportunities as a means of displaying gifted behaviors and talent potential.

Conclusion

New paradigms are needed that reconceptualize the giftedness construct, focus on gifted behaviors, design dynamic approaches to assessing gifted and talented behaviors within the students' sociocultural context, and integrate identification processes with learning opportunities. In forging new paradigms, strategies need to be employed that consider a variety of factors that impact on the behaviors of gifted economically disadvantaged and limited English proficient students, looking at these factors within and across various cultural groups and diverse environmental contexts.

In coming to grips with more effective approaches to the identification and development of talents among minorities, the promise is that *educators will better understand how to identify and nurture talent potential among all learners.*

References

Callahan, C. M., Tomlinson, C. A., & Pizzat, P. M. (n.d.). *Contexts for promise: Noteworthy practices and innovations in the identification of gifted students.* Charlottesville, VA: University of Virginia.

Coleman, M. R., & Gallagher, J. J. (1992). *Report on state policies related to identification of gifted students.* Chapel Hill, NC: Gifted Education Policy Studies Program, University of North Carolina-Chapel Hill.

Cummins, J. (1989). Institutional racism and the assessment of minority children. In R. J. Samuda & S. L. Konga (Eds.). *Assessment and placement of minority students* (pp. 95–198). Toronto, Ont.: C. J. Jogrefe.

Department of Education (1993). *National excellence: A case for developing America's talents.* Washington, DC: U.S. Government Printing Office.

Educational Policies Commission (1950). *Education of the gifted.* Washington, DC: National Education Association and American Association of School Administrators.

Frasier, M. M. (1989). Identification of gifted black students: Developing new perspectives. In C. J. Maker & S. S. Schiever (Eds.), *Critical issues in gifted education: Defensible programs for cultural and ethnic minorities* (pp. 213–225). Austin, TX: Pro-Ed.

Harris, J. J., III, & Ford, D. Y. (1991). Identifying and nurturing the promise of gifted black American children. *Journal of Negro Education, 60*(1), 3–18.

Kitano, M. K. (1991). A multicultural education perspective of serving the culturally diverse gifted. *Journal of the Education of the Gifted, 15*(1), 4–19.

Leung, E. K. (1981, February). *The identification and social problems of the gifted bilingual-bicultural children.* Paper presented at The Council for Exceptional Children Conference on the Exceptional Bilingual Child, New Orleans, LA.

Marland, S. P., Jr. (1971). *Education of the gifted and talented.* Volume 1: Report to the Congress of the United States by the Commissioner of Education. Washington, DC: U.S. Government Printing Office.

Passow, A. H. (1986). Educational programs for minority/disadvantaged gifted students. In L. Kanevsky (Ed.), *Issues in gifted education* (pp. 147–172). San Diego, CA: San Diego City Schools GATE Program.

Terman, L. M. (1925). *Genetic studies of genius* (Vol. 1). Stanford, CA: Stanford University Press.

CHAPTER 12

Core Attributes of Giftedness: A Foundation for Recognizing the Gifted Potential of Minority and Economically Disadvantaged Students

Mary M. Frasier
Scott L. Hunsaker
Jongyeun Lee
Sandra Mitchell
Bonnie Cramond
Sally Krisel
Jaime H. Garcia
Darlene Martin
Elaine Frank
Vernon S. Finley

The University of Georgia
Athens, Georgia

Reprinted from Frasier, M. M., Hunsaker, S. L., Lee, J., Mitchell, S., Cramond, B., Krisel, S., . . . Finley, V. S. (1995). *Core attributes of giftedness: A foundation for recognizing the gifted potential of minority and economically disadvantaged students* (Research Monograph No. 95210). Storrs: University of Connecticut, The National Research Center for the Gifted and Talented. Reprinted with permission of The National Research Center on the Gifted and Talented.

Executive Summary

Introduction

An ultimate goal of gifted educators is to recognize, as early as possible, those children who show potential for exceptional performance as adults and to provide them with the special instruction they need to develop that potential. A common assertion is that children who show this potential for exceptional performance are present in every segment of society (Baldwin, 1991; Clark, 1992; Davis & Rimm, 1994; Gallagher, 1994b; Kitano & Kirby, 1986; Maker, 1983; Marland, 1972; Pendarvis, Howley, & Howley, 1990). However, it is consistently observed that gifted and talented children who are members of minority populations, who have limited proficiency in the English language (LEP), or who come from economically disadvantaged families and areas are underrepresented in programs for the gifted (Ford & Harris, 1990; Frasier, in press; Gallagher, 1991; Gallagher & Courtright, 1988).

One of the reasons given to explain the underrepresentation of these students in gifted programs relates to the ability of educators to recognize their display of "gifted behaviors" (Baca & Chinn, 1982; Bermudez & Rakow, 1990; Bernal, 1980; Dabney, 1988; Leung, 1981; Pendarvis, Howley, & Howley, 1990; Whitmore, 1982). These authors suggest that the low socioeconomic status (SES), minority group membership, or limited competence in the use of the English language of these children may negatively affect the identification of these children as gifted. As Gallagher (1994b) notes, for example, difficulties in trying to sort out the unique characteristics of minority gifted students may be related to the fact that many of them come from poverty homes. Clark (1992) maintains that "A major problem encountered in providing for gifted students among the low SES population is the attitude, shared by teachers and parents alike, that giftedness could not exist in this population" (p. 428). According to Callahan and McIntire (1994), the emphasis on remediation rather than development of talent may account for the low recognition of gifted Native American and Alaska Native students. Others have made similar observations about the emphasis on remediation rather than on the development of talent in minority groups (Baldwin, 1991; Cummins, 1989; Ford & Harris, 1990; Hilliard, 1991; Samuda, Kong, Cummins, Pascual-Leone, & Lewis, 1989). The purpose of this paper is to explore a different perspective for observing and assessing characteristics of giftedness in minority, LEP, and economically disadvantaged student populations.

First, a summary of what we know about the attributes of gifted and high achieving students from minority or economically disadvantaged families and areas is presented. Second, a proposal for focusing on core attributes that underlie the giftedness construct as a more viable basis for observing and identifying giftedness in minority or economically disadvantaged student groups is presented. A description of how a set of core attributes of giftedness was derived is also provided. Finally, implications for using these core attributes as the basis for a paradigm that better addresses the identification and education of gifted students from underrepresented populations are presented.

TARGET POPULATIONS

Race, ethnicity, culture, minority group status, low socioeconomic status, handicapped status, preschool and primary aged children, and gender have all been used to label students who are underrepresented or underserved in programs for gifted children (Gallagher, 1994a; Passow, 1982; Richert, 1991; VanTassel-Baska, Patton, & Prillaman, 1991; Whitmore & Maker, 1985). It is beyond the scope of this paper to address each one of these groups. Because African American, Native American, and Hispanic students have been and continue to be the most prominent subjects when underrepresentation in gifted programs is discussed, it is these gifted students who are the focus in this paper. For the most part, these students will be referred to as the target population. Labels such as minority, culturally different, and economically disadvantaged are frequently used interchangeably in the literature and in practice to refer to the students who are the target population in this paper. Therefore, anyone of these terms will be used in this paper as appropriate.

SCOPE OF THE LITERATURE REVIEW

The literature chosen for review in this paper was selected if it contained primary descriptions of the cognitive and affective characteristics of target population students. Causes for any of these descriptions are included only if they are an integral part of the discussion of their characteristics. However, the primary concern is not the cause but the characteristics of these students that have emerged over the years.

Because of the limited base of empirical research investigating the attributes of gifted target students, some of the descriptions have evolved from speculative opinions and conclusions derived from practice or experience. However, as Ogawa and Malen (1991) have observed, such literature can still provide important insights because of the meanings people attach to the phenomenon of interest, in this case the gifted potential in students from target populations.

Many of the studies and other reports explicitly describing the characteristics of target students were carried out from 1960 through the 1980s. One of the reasons may be that the objectives of researchers and practitioners during this period were primarily focused on developing theories to account for cultural deficiencies or cultural differences. More recently, studies and reports have focused on developing identification strategies and programs to address the educational and environmental deficiencies that impede the identification of gifted target students.

What We Know About Attributes of Giftedness in Target Student Populations

Findings from several research studies and reports have recounted the attributes of gifted or high achieving target population students. The reports and studies reviewed here are concerned with comparisons within and between groups and descriptions based on studies of specific cultural and disadvantaged groups. The themes of these studies and reports are concerned with personality variables, motivation to achieve, cognitive attributes, and other behavioral descriptions.

Between-Group and Within-Group Comparison Studies and Reports

Frierson (1965) was interested in the effects of cultural deprivation on the development of talent. He undertook a study to determine any significant differences between upper and lower status students who were divided into four groups: (a) upper status gifted students, (b) lower socioeconomic status gifted students, (c) upper status average students, and (d) lower socioeconomic status average students. Frierson concluded that differences between the two groups of gifted children were clearly associated with differences in their socioeconomic status.

Other studies comparing target population students were concerned with differences in self-concept, personality variables, and other factors attributing to their success. Tidwell (1981) conducted a study of the characteristics that distinguished gifted minority and low socioeconomic status children from their nongifted peers. Children in this study were selected for gifted program participation by criteria that did not rely on intelligence test scores as the primary criterion. She found that they had significantly higher self-concepts than nonselected students. Davidson and Greenberg (1967) compared differences in personality variables between high and low achievers from lower class backgrounds. Attributes that distinguished between the two lower class groups were found to be very similar to those that distinguish between middle class achievers and underachievers. Glaser and Ross (1970) retroactively investigated factors that contributed to the differential success rates of individuals growing up in disadvantaged environments. Fourteen factors were found to distinguish between successful Mexican American and African American males and those who were successful. Successful subjects were described as (a) having a strong sense of self, pride, and worth; (b) being able to free themselves from the negative conditions of their environment; (c) having a strong belief that hard work or study would pay off, and (d) being effective in their ability to channel any rage they felt over being disadvantaged into strategic actions. Further, successful subjects were attracted by goals such as creativity and self-determination, and had high risk-taking capacities especially when experimenting.

While results of studies comparing personality or nonintellective traits of gifted advantaged and disadvantaged children appear to reveal many similarities across cultural and economic boundaries, significant but more negative differences in cognitive functioning have been reported in other studies. Tannenbaum (1983) suggested that these differences are most evident in cognitive organizing as is demonstrated by the lowered performance of disadvantaged gifted children on tests of mental ability. Sisk (1973) concurred when she describes the deficiencies in cognitive functioning of disadvantaged gifted students as evidenced by their limited vocabularies, use of nonstandard grammar, inability to observe and state sequences of events, inability to perceive cause and effect relationships, and inability to categorize.

A different view of the cognitive competencies of African American individuals, including children, is presented by Shade (1991). Drawing from several sources, she concluded that African Americans appear to have high motoric capabilities and use visual perception as a way of protecting and orienting themselves in the environment rather than for gathering information. African American children are also largely trained to concentrate more on people rather than non-people type information, thus being more people than object oriented. Shade also pointed to a preference among African Americans for affective materials and a high level of social interaction in their learning environments. Whereas Tannenbaum (1983) and Sisk (1973) saw cognitive differences as deficiencies that underlie the low test performance of African American children and their weak performances in the classroom, Shade noted that the differences really reflected cognitive strengths that are expressed in distinct ways due to differences in information processing preferences and differences in information analysis and organization.

Bruch (1971) isolated patterns of cognitive strengths among southeastern African American students using an abbreviated version of the Stanford-Binet Intelligence Test. She concluded that these students evidenced strengths in visual, auditory, and figural content (e.g., art and music); memory; convergent production in practical problem-solving situations; awareness of details of descriptions; fluency of ideas; spontaneous categorization and classification of spatial items; and awareness of natural relationships or systems. Similarly, Meeker (1978) used the Structure of Intellect (SOI) to determine that the pattern of gifted strengths among Navajo children included auditory memory and figural ability.

Finally, Baldwin (1978) described the common characteristics of students whose achievement might be negatively affected by cultural diversity, socioeconomically deprived status, and geographic isolation. Her list of characteristics included descriptions of their communication and learning styles as characterized by a language that is rich in imagery and is persuasive, a sensitiveness and alertness to movement, and an intuitive grasp of situations. She also described these children as (a) having strong group affiliations; (b) being skilled in dealing with their environment; (c) being adept at logical reasoning, planning, and pragmatic problem solving; (d) having a high tolerance for ambiguities; (e) having the ability to produce inventive and revolutionary ideas; and (f) being flexible and fluent thinkers.

Descriptions Specifically Related to Giftedness in Specific Minority Groups and Gifted Economically Disadvantaged Students

Hispanics. Bernal (1974) conducted a study to determine behavioral descriptors of gifted Mexican American students. Attributes or characteristics with the highest discriminant power were found to be related to these children's leadership behaviors, acceptance of adult authority, self-control, and above-average school performance. Zappia (1989) provided a similar description of Hispanic children when she describes their language preference, proficiency, and use patterns (in both languages) in the home, school, and community. Other attributes include their being able to successfully function in two cultures and to communicate fluently, even if the English used is non-standard (Maker & Schiever, 1989).

Native Americans. Tonemah and Brittan (1985) noted the strong tribal perspective associated with the concept of giftedness in their description of gifted attributes of Native American students. They delineated characteristics of gifted potential in four areas: (a) acquired skills in language, learning, and technological skills; (b) tribal/cultural understanding referring to their exceptional knowledge of ceremonies, tribal traditions, and other tribes; (c) personal/human/qualities such as high intelligence, visionary/inquisitive/intuitive, respectful of elders, and creative skills; and (d) aesthetic abilities, referring to unusual talents in the visual and performing arts, and arts based in the Indian culture. Garrison (1989) described gifted Native American individuals as tending to be less dependent on language to communicate ideas, to learn by observation and to teach by modeling, and to consider the group more important than the individual.

African Americans. Hilliard (1976) concluded that gifted African American children demonstrate a synthetic-personal style. That is, they tend to approach the world in a way that allows them to bring together divergent experiences and to distill them to discover the essence of a matter without undue concern for all the small pieces which go to make up a given experience. This is in contrast to the atomistic-objective style wherein the habitual pattern for approaching an experience involves an attempt to break down that experience into components which can be understood.

Lee (1984, 1989) concluded from his study of successful rural African American adolescents, that they have positive self-concepts linked to their extended view of themselves as members of collective family and community systems, possess traditional values associated with their religious faith, and have good interpersonal relationships. They are also successful in school and active in a variety of extra-curricular activities. In addition these successful youth are keenly aware of future occupational opportunities and understand the education they must acquire to be prepared for such opportunities. Shade (1981) concluded from her study of educationally successful African American middle class students that the males are more introverted, emotionally stable, and more shrewd, though less expressive than males in the standardized sample of the *Coan-Cattell Early School Personality Questionnaire (ESPQ)*. Females were found to be more introverted and less expressive, more independent and less in need of protection, and displayed a tendency to be less placid, conforming, and tranquil than females in the standardized sample. Both males and females were very aware that to achieve their goals they must learn how to operate within the framework of certain expectations of their school and community, while also maintaining their concept of self-determination.

Economically disadvantaged children. As a result of observations made during a series of summer workshops conducted with disadvantaged children, Torrance (1971, 1977) developed a checklist to help guide the search for giftedness in culturally different groups. He named this checklist *The Checklist of Creative Positives*. Attributes included on the checklist are concerned with (a) problem solving skills (e.g., originality of ideas in problem solving, fluency and flexibility in figural media); (b) communication styles (e.g., use of expressive speech, use of colorful language rich with imagery); and (c) learning styles (e.g., enjoyment of skills in group activities). It also includes descriptions of (a) interests and activities enjoyed by culturally different children (e.g., enjoyment of and ability in music, rhythm, creative movement, dance, dramatics); and (b) descriptions of the typical methods these children use to respond to various stimuli (e.g., high emotional responsiveness, exceptional ability to express feelings and emotions).

A Summary of Themes

The literature reflects a strong tendency to focus on (a) similarities and differences in personality traits between gifted minority and majority students, (b) unique learning and communication styles presumed to be characteristics of specific cultural groups, and (c) the exceptional abilities that gifted target students demonstrate as they negotiate between their culture and the majority culture. Different issues shape the approach to the research and other writings developed to describe the characteristics of gifted target students. One approach was to focus on deficiencies. The emphasis is on economic disadvantage and its effects on cognitive functioning, performance in academic areas, and on general educational background and experiences. Another approach focused on these children's cognitive and creative strengths as revealed through testing and observing. Yet another approach was shaped by comparing the characteristics of disadvantaged students with advantaged students. Finally, an approach was developed out of a perceived need to base characteristics of gifted target students on results from investigations carried out within a specific cultural group.

These different approaches may well be the result of the continuous search that has been conducted to find effective ways to resolve the difficulties that minority students face in gaining recognition of their gifts and talents. They may also represent the many factors that must go far beyond descriptions of relevant characteristics of giftedness when describing gifted minority children. More than for any other group, these more extended discussions must include concerns with (a) discrimination in American society, (b) the value of efforts to establish the concept of giftedness within the boundaries of a specific cultural group, (c) the need to distinguish the meaning of giftedness within a minority group from the meaning of giftedness in the Euro-American culture, (d) the inadequacies of traditional assessment measures and procedures to identify gifted minority students, and (e) the effort that must be put forth to reconcile the concept of individual recognition for excellence with cultural concepts that emphasize group solidarity as a unique cultural feature.

Attributes Underlying the Giftedness Construct

As noted earlier, one of the problems felt to impact the representation of target population students in programs for the gifted is related to the inability of educators to recognize these students' display of gifted behaviors in the classroom. Plans to address this concern by describing giftedness in economically disadvantaged and limited English proficient populations were an integral part of a project at The University of Georgia (Frasier, 1990). The overall goal of this project was to develop a more effective way to facilitate the recognition of gifted children from these groups. A proposal to focus on the core attributes underlying the giftedness construct as a more viable basis for characterizing giftedness in these students is presented in this section. The method by which these attributes were developed is summarized along with suggestions for using the core attributes as the foundation for developing observation and identification programs to better recognize the gifted potential in target population student groups.

In the initial phase of our project, educators were asked to provide a prototypical description of a target population child they felt was bright. These educators were asked to focus on describing intellectual and specific academic aptitudes because school programs most often address exceptional abilities in these two areas.

A guide to assist them in developing their descriptions was created using (a) two of the intelligences proposed by Gardner (1983)—linguistic and logical-mathematical, (b) the five generic characteristics proposed by Gallagher and Kinney (1974) to describe gifted advantaged and disadvantaged children, and (c) examples of items from culture-specific checklists that reflected behaviors that were associated with displays of logical-mathematical and linguistic intelligences.

A review of this guide revealed a number of similarities. For example, the checklist items also appeared to reflect the underlying meanings of the gifted abilities proposed by Gallagher and Kinney and appeared to articulate behaviors that students would exhibit when showing ability in either of the two intelligences proposed by Gardner. Based on these observations, a decision was made to explore these connections more fully. The next section discusses the method by which this investigation took place and the rationale for making the core attributes associated with the giftedness construct central to this investigation.

The Rationale for Focusing on Attributes Underlying the Giftedness Construct

A construct is a set of hypothesized traits, abilities, or characteristics abstracted from a variety of behaviors to have educational or psychological meaning (Sax, 1980). Giftedness is a psychological construct, according to Hagen (1980). As such, she contends that it is not a directly observable trait of an individual. She also maintains that accurate inferences about the giftedness construct depend on the choices of characteristics and behaviors that we choose to observe and appraise. This approach to giftedness is reflected in current thinking where the giftedness construct is described as incorporating a broad range of cognitive, motivational, and personality characteristics (Hoge, 1989; Passow & Rudnitski, 1993). Further, the appropriateness of focusing on core attributes of giftedness is reflected in recommendations by Hoge (1988, 1989) to base assessments of giftedness on a clear statement specifying the traits, aptitudes, and behaviors that underlie the construct. This need to reach consensus on a clear statement of the traits, aptitudes, and behaviors that underlie the giftedness construct is reflected in the research findings and discussions of writers such as the following.

Bernal (1980) was an early advocate of the value of basing the identification of gifted students on an evaluation of their exhibition of behaviors associated with the giftedness construct. He was particularly assertive that such a move would provide less reason for educators to be bound to the cognitive preferences of the dominant ethnic group and greater reason to seek a valid and operationally useful identification and selection process for all gifted children. Culross (1989) noted that seeking consensus regarding what constitutes giftedness would reduce the pitfalls in screening and selecting students for gifted programs. Leung (1981) suggested that absolute characteristics of giftedness provide an effective way for educators to consider attributes of giftedness in different cultural and economic groups. Finally, Shaklee et al. (1994) felt that the best way to identify young gifted and talented minority or economically disadvantaged gifted students was to base observation and assessment procedures on universal identifiers of intellectual potential.

Each of these researchers and writers speaks to the importance of clarifying the attributes underlying the giftedness construct as the basis for observing gifted potential in the target population. The development of a common language to describe these core attributes of giftedness may provide a more viable foundation on which to build observation and identification methods to discover gifted potential as it is expressed within and across groups, regardless of cultural, physical, geographical, or socioeconomic differences.

Method

A qualitative content analysis method was chosen to carry out this analysis of the gifted literature to determine common features that characterize gifted children from the target population and the gifted population in general. Our goal was to achieve "semantic validity" by sorting data units which had similar meanings or connotations into the same category.

A brief statement of the parameters that structured the search for core attributes follows:

1. The basic attributes defined as underlying the giftedness construct would be referred to as traits, aptitudes, and behaviors according to Sax's (1980) and Hagen's (1980) definitions and interpretations of a construct.
2. Dynamic rather than static descriptions would be used to define the basic attributes associated with the giftedness construct.
3. When selecting categories, the broadest and most flexible concepts would be sought to encompass the core traits, aptitudes, and behaviors that reflect the essence or core of giftedness, within and across different cultures and contexts.

The steps that were followed in carrying out this analysis are briefly outlined:

Step 1 Locate data sources.

> The University of Georgia Libraries' catalog was used to develop data on the general attributes of gifted children as found in books and other reports, published from approximately 1957 to the present.

The literature was searched for checklists or rating scales that had been specifically developed to observe the characteristics of gifted African American, Hispanic, and Native American students.

Step 2 Define the recording unit; locate units of information.

Recording units are defined as a phrase or sentence that described the characteristics of a gifted child.

The information in each data source was thoroughly read to locate phrases or sentences that were used to describe the characteristics of gifted children. Books, book chapters, and other reports yielded 306 data entries; 120 data entries were generated from culture specific checklists and rating scales. Each entry was coded by author, year, page number, and category (i.e., gifted, talented, creative, or genius) and placed on a separate card.

Step 3 Develop categories for coding.

Sixteen broad categories in which to place results of independent coding of data were developed: (a) learning style, (b) memory, (c) inquiry, (d) ethical/moral, (e) reasoning, (f) problem solving ability, (g) insight, (h) imagination/creativity, (i) interests, (j) motivation, (k) humor, (l) communication skills, (m) leadership, (n) critical evaluation of self/others, (0) relationship with people and ideas, and (p) altruism.

Step 4 Sort data units into the static or dynamic pile.

Based on the parameters established earlier, 44 data units derived from books, book chapters, or other reports, and 25 data units derived from checklists were eliminated because it was agreed by the researchers that they represented static descriptions of gifted attributes. In the first data pool 260 data units remained and 95 data units remained in the second.

Step 5 Sort data units into categories.

Researchers independently read and sorted the data units into one of the 16 initial categories or they created a new category. Five additional categories were created: (a) sensorial/ emotional sensitiveness, (b) aesthetic sensitivity, (c) mental maturity, (d) precocity, and (e) physical characteristics.

Data units were reviewed three times before the researchers reached 95% agreement regarding the placement of the phrases or sentences into one of the 21 categories.

Step 6 Determine core categories.

If one or more of the following criteria suggested by Weber (1990) could be applied to a category, the category was eliminated:
- Reflects characteristics that may be interpreted as being more related to specific cultural values and beliefs (e.g., ethical and moral behaviors; aesthetic sensitivities).
- Is debatable as a category in which the level of performance could be described as gifted or not gifted (e.g., critical evaluation of self and others, altruism, interpersonal relationships).
- Includes data units that are in the culture-specific literature but not in the general literature.

Using these criteria, 10 categories were retained as the core attribute categories. The definitions and general descriptions of these 10 categories are presented in Table 1.

CONCLUSIONS

SUMMARY OF FINDINGS

Of the 262 descriptive units of information generated from the general literature 167 (64%) were related to one of the core attribute categories. Eighty-two (86%) of the 95 descriptive units of information generated from the culture-specific checklists were related to one of the core attribute categories. Well over half of the descriptive units of information in both information pools were considered to reflect the same or similar characteristics associated with gifted students.

IMPLICATIONS

It was proposed that identifying the core attributes associated with the giftedness construct would provide a better basis for establishing procedures to recognize, identify, and plan educational experiences for gifted students from minority or economically disadvantaged families and areas. Ten core attributes were identified: communication skills, imagination/creativity, humor, inquiry, insight, inter-

Table 1

Definitions and General Descriptions of the 10 Core Attributes of Giftedness (Traits, Aptitudes, and Behaviors)

Core Attribute	General Description
Motivation: Evidence of desire to learn	Forces that initiate, direct and sustain individual or group behavior in order to satisfy a need or attained goal
Communication skills: Highly expressive and effective use of words, numbers, symbols, etc.	Transmission and reception of signals or meanings through a system of symbols (codes, gestures, language, numbers)
Interest: Intense (sometimes unusual) interests	Activities, avocations, objects, etc. that have special worth or significance and are given special attention
Problem-solving ability: Effective (often inventive) strategies for recognizing and solving problems	Process of determining a correct sequence of alternatives leading to a desired goal or to successful completion or performance of a task
Imagination/Creativity: Produces many ideas; Highly original	Process of forming mental images of objects, qualities, situations, or relationships, which are not immediately apparent to the senses; solve problems by pursuing nontraditional patterns of thinking
Memory: Large storehouse of information on school or non-school topics	Exceptional ability to retain and retrieve information
Inquiry: Questions, experiments, explores	Method or process of seeking knowledge, understanding, or information
Insight: Quickly grasps new concepts and makes connections; senses deeper meanings	Sudden discovery of the correct solution following incorrect attempts based primarily on trial and error
Reasoning: Logical approaches to figuring out solutions	Highly conscious, directed, controlled, active, intentional, forward-looking, goal oriented thought
Humor: Conveys and picks up on humor well	Ability to synthesize key ideas or problems in complex situations in a humorous way; Exceptional sense of timing in words and gestures

ests, memory, motivation, problem-solving, and reasoning. Implications for using these core attributes (a) to facilitate educators' recognition of gifted abilities in student populations from minority or economically disadvantaged families and areas, and (b) to guide educators in the selection of measures for identification minority or economically disadvantaged families and areas follow:

1. Students from minority and economically disadvantaged families and areas are likely to fare better in the identification procedures for gifted programs when a variety of test and nontest measures are used to assess potential across the wide range of traits, behaviors, and aptitudes associated with the giftedness construct.
2. The use of a wide variety of test and nontest measures make it less likely that students who are underrepresented in gifted programs will be handicapped by identification systems that rely on one or two measures to determine eligibility for gifted program services.
3. The interpretation of performances on this variety of measures would require the use of standards that accommodated the differences in the expression of gifted student characteristics as exhibited by students who come from diverse cultural, ethnic, economic, and environmental backgrounds. The core attributes of giftedness provide a common framework within which to make these interpretations.
4. The core attributes of giftedness provides an important way to assist educators working with minority or economically disadvantaged students in the establishment of links between specific gifted characteristics and the manner in which they may be displayed in their classrooms.

Arriving at a single conception of giftedness is difficult, given the abundance of competing conceptions of giftedness in the literature and the variety in the rules and regulations used by different states and local programs to determine who is eligible for services. This paper has provided a way to consider achieving consensus about the core attributes of giftedness, regardless of the words used to define the concept or the influences of culture and environment on gifted abilities. Findings from this study of the characteristics of gifted individuals as they are described in the general literature and in the culture-specific literature, suggest that gifted individuals are most consistently recognized by their motivation, interests, problem-solving ability, imagination/creativity, memory abilities, inquiry skills, insight, reasoning capacities, and sense of humor. It is suggested that these core attributes be the basis for referring, observing, and identifying children for gifted program services and for designing programs to address their needs.

REFERENCES

Baca, L., & Chinn, P. C. (1982). Coming to grips with cultural diversity. *Exceptional Education Quarterly, 2*(4), 33–45.

Baldwin, A. Y. (1978). Introduction. In A. Y. Baldwin, G. H. Gear, & L. J. Lucito (Eds.), *Educational planning for the gifted: Overcoming cultural, geographic, and socioeconomic barriers* (pp. 1–5). Reston, VA: The Council for Exceptional Children.

Baldwin, A. Y. (1991). Ethnic and cultural issues. In N. Colangelo & G. A. Davis (Eds.), *Handbook of gifted education* (pp. 416–427). Boston: Allyn & Bacon.

Bermudez, A. B., & Rakow, S. J. (1990). Analyzing teachers' perceptions of identification procedures for gifted and talented Hispanic limited English proficient students at-risk. *Journal of Educational Issues of Language Minority Students, 7,* 21–33.

Bernal, E. M. (1974). Gifted Mexican American children: An ethno-scientific perspective. *California Journal of Educational Research, 25,* 261–273.

Bernal, E. M. (1980). *Methods of identifying gifted minority students.* Princeton, NJ: Educational Testing Service. (ERIC Document Reproduction Service No. ED 204 418)

Bruch, C. B. (1971). Modification of procedures for identification of the disadvantaged gifted. *Gifted Child Quarterly, 15,* 267–272.

Callahan, C. M., & McIntire, J. A. (1994). *Identifying outstanding talent in American Indian and Alaska Native students.* Washington, DC: U.S. Department of Education.

Clark, B. (1992). *Growing up gifted: Developing the potential of children at home and at school* (4th ed.). New York: Merrill.

Culross, R. (1989). Measurement issues in the screening and selection of the gifted. *Roeper Review, 12*(2), 76–78.

Cummins, J. (1989). Institutionalized racism and the assessment of minority children: A comparison of policies and programs in the United States and Canada. In R. J. Samuda, S. L. Kong, J. Cummins, J. Pascual-Leone, & J. Lewis (Eds.), *Assessment and placement of minority students* (pp. 95–107). Toronto: C. J. Hogrefe.

Dabney, M. G. (1988). An alternative model for identification of potentially gifted students: A case study. In R. L. Jones (Ed.), *Psychoeducational assessment of minority group children: A casebook* (pp. 273–304). Berkeley, CA: Cobb & Henry.

Davidson, H. H., & Greenberg, J. W. (1967). *Traits of school achievers from a deprived background* (Project No. 2805 No. Contract No. OE-5-1O-132). New York: The City College of the City University of New York.

Davis, G. A., & Rimm, S. B. (1994). *Education of the gifted and talented* (3rd ed.). Englewood Cliffs, NJ: Prentice-Hall.

Ford, D. Y., & Harris, J. J. (1990). On discovering the hidden treasure of gifted and talented African American children. *Roeper Review, 13*(1), 27–32.

Frasier, M. M. (1990). *An investigation of giftedness in economically disadvantaged and limited English proficient populations* (The National Research Center on the Gifted and Talented Proposal). Athens, GA: The University of Georgia.

Frasier, M. M. (in press). Gifted minority students: Reframing approaches to their identification and education. In N. Colangelo & G. A. Davis (Eds.), *Handbook of gifted education* (2nd ed.). Boston: Allyn and Bacon.

Frierson, E. C. (1965). Upper and lower status gifted children: A study of differences. *Exceptional Children, 32*(2), 83–90.

Gallagher, J. J. (1991). Issues in the education of gifted students. In N. Colangelo & G. A. Davis (Eds.), *Handbook of gifted education* (pp. 14–23). Boston: Allyn and Bacon.

Gallagher, J. J. (1994a). Current and historical thinking on education for gifted and talented students. In P. O'Connell-Ross (Ed.), *National excellence: A case for developing America's talent, an anthology of readings* (pp. 83–107). Washington, DC: Office of Educational Research and Improvement, U.S. Department of Education.

Gallagher, J. J. (1994b). *Teaching the gifted child* (4th ed.). Boston: Allyn and Bacon.

Gallagher, J. J., & Courtright, R. D. (1988). The educational definition of giftedness and its policy implications. In R. J. Sternberg & J. E. Davidson (Eds.), *Conceptions of giftedness* (pp. 93–111). New York: Cambridge University Press.

Gallagher, J. J., & Kinney, L. (1974). Talent delayed-talent denied: The culturally different gifted child. In *Quail Roost Conference*. Reston, VA: The Foundation for Exceptional Children.

Gardner, H. (1983). *Frames of mind: The theory of multiple intelligences*. New York: Basic Books.

Garrison, L. (1989). Programming for the gifted American Indian student. In C. J. Maker & S. W. Schiever (Eds.), *Critical issues in gifted education: Defensible programs for cultural and ethnic minorities* (pp. 116–127). Austin, TX: Pro-Ed.

Glaser, E. M., & Ross, H. L. (1970). *A study of successful persons from seriously disadvantaged backgrounds* (Final Report Contract No. 82-05-68-03). Washington, DC: Department of Labor, Office of Special Manpower Programs.

Hagen, E. (1980). *Identification of the gifted*. New York: Teachers College Press.

Hilliard, A. (1976). *Alternatives to I. Q. testing: An approach to the identification of gifted "minority" children*. Sacramento, CA: California State Department of Education, Sacramento Division of Special Education. (ERIC Document Reproduction Service No. ED 147009)

Hilliard, A. G. (1991). The ideology of intelligence and I.Q. magic in education. In A. G. Hilliard (Ed.), *Testing African American students: Special re-issue of The Negro Educational Review* (pp. 136–145). Morristown, NJ: Aaron Press.

Hoge, R. D. (1988). Issues in the definition and measurement of the giftedness construct. *Educational Researcher, 17*(7), 12–16, 22.

Hoge, R. D. (1989). An examination of the giftedness construct. *Canadian Journal of Education, 14*(1), 6–17.

Kitano, M. K., & Kirby, D. F. (1986). *Gifted education: A comprehensive view*. Boston: Little, Brown.

Lee, C. C. (1984). Successful rural black adolescents: A psychosocial profile. *Adolescence, 20*(77), 129–142.

Lee, C. C. (1989). Rural Black adolescents: Psychosocial development in a changing environment. In R. L. Jones (Ed.), *Black adolescents* (pp. 79–95). Berkeley, CA: Cobb & Henry.

Leung, E. K. (1981). *The identification and social problem of the gifted bilingual-bicultural children*. Paper presented at The Council for Exceptional Children Conference on the Exceptional Bilingual Child, New Orleans, LA. (ERIC Document Reproduction Service No. ED 203653)

Maker, C. J. (1983). Quality education for gifted minority students. *Journal for the Education of the Gifted, 6*(3), 140–153.

Maker, C. J., & Schiever, S. W. (Eds.). (1989). *Critical issues in gifted education: Defensible programs for cultural and ethnic minorities*. Austin, TX: Pro-Ed.

Marland, S. P., Jr. (1972). *Education of the gifted and talented* (Report to the Congress of the United States by the U.S. Commissioner of Education). Washington, DC: U.S. Government Printing Office.

Meeker, M. (1978). Nondiscriminatory testing procedures to assess giftedness in Black, Chicano, Navajo, and Anglo children. In A. Baldwin, G. Gear, & L. Lucito (Eds.), *Educational planning for the gifted: Overcoming cultural, geographic, and socioeconomic barriers* (pp. 17–26). Reston, VA: Council for Exceptional Children.

Ogawa, R. T., & Malen, B. (1991). Towards rigor in reviews of multivocal literatures: Applying the exploratory case study method. *Review of Educational Research, 61*(3), 265–286.

Passow, A. H. (1982). The gifted disadvantaged: Some reflections. In *Fifth National Conference on Disadvantaged Gifted/Talented* (pp. 19–27). Ventura, CA: Ventura County Superintendent of Schools Office.

Passow, A. H., & Rudnitski, R. A. (1993). *State policies regarding education of the gifted as reflected in legislation and regulation* (CRS93302). Storrs, CT: University of Connecticut, The National Research Center on the Gifted and Talented.

Pendarvis, E. D., Howley, A. A., & Howley, C. B. (1990). *The abilities of gifted children*. Englewood Cliffs, NJ: Prentice Hall.

Richert, E. S. (1991). Rampant problems and promising practices in identification. In N. Colangelo & G. A. Davis (Eds.), *Handbook of gifted education* (pp. 81–96). Boston: Allyn and Bacon.

Samuda, R. J., Kong, S. L., Cummins, J., Pascual-Leone, J., & Lewis, J. (1989). *Assessment and placement of minority students*. Toronto: C. J. Hogrefe.

Sax, G. (1980). *Principles of educational and psychological measurement and evaluation*. (2nd ed.). Belmont, CA: Wadsworth.

Shade, B. J. (1981). Racial variations in perceptual differentiation. *Perceptual and Motor Skills, 52*, 243–248.

Shade, B. J. (1991). African American patterns of cognition. In R. L. Jones (Ed.), *Black Psychology* (pp. 231–247). Berkeley, CA: Cobb & Henry.

Sisk, D. (1973). Developing teacher mediators/teacher training for disadvantaged gifted. In *First National Conference on the Disadvantaged Gifted*. Ventura, CA: National/State Leadership Institute on the Gifted and Talented.

Tannenbaum, A. J. (1983). *Gifted children: Psychological and educational perspectives*. New York: Macmillan.

Tidwell, R. (1981). A psycho-educational profile of gifted minority group students identified without reliance on aptitude tests. *Journal of Non-White Concerns, 9*, 77–86.

Tonemah, S. A., & Brittan, M. A. (1985). *American Indian gifted and talented assessment model* (Grant from the U.S. Education Department, Indian Education Programs No. G008420046). Norman, OK: American Indian Research and Development.

Torrance, E. P. (1971). Are the Torrance tests of creative thinking biased against or in favor of disadvantaged groups? *Gifted Child Quarterly, 15*, 75–80.

Torrance, E. P. (1977). *Discovery and nurturance of giftedness in the culturally different*. Reston, VA: The Council for Exceptional Children.

VanTassel-Baska, J., Patton, J. J., & Prillaman, D. (1991). *Gifted youth at risk: A report of a national study*. Reston, VA: Council for Exceptional Children.

Weber, R. P. (1990). *Basic content analysis*. Beverly Hills, CA: Sage.

Whitmore, J. R. (1982). Recognizing and developing hidden giftedness. *The Elementary School Journal, 82*(3), 274–283.

Whitmore, J. R., & Maker, C. J. (1985). *Intellectual giftedness in disabled persons.* Rockville, MD: Aspen.

Zappia, I. A. (1989). Identification of gifted Hispanic students: A multidimensional view. In C. J. Maker & S. W. Schiever (Eds.), *Critical issues in gifted education: Defensible programs for cultural and ethnic minorities* (pp. 19–26). Austin, TX: Pro-Ed.

SECTION IV

Highly Gifted Black Students

Malik S. Henfield

Defining and measuring intelligence is no easy task, and efforts to do so have a long, contentious history, specifically when focused on Black students or populations. At the time of this anthology—2011—professionals and laypersons still hold entrenched, polemic views about definitions of intelligence, measures of intelligence, correlates or the origins (nature vs. nurture) of intelligence, and how to equitably measure this construct. Thus, we are pleased to include a section on Martin D. Jenkins, who presents what we believe to be the only *consistent* work on Blacks who score in the superior range on intelligence/IQ tests.

We encourage readers to study Jenkins and those he references as highly intelligent "negroes"—the now outdated term used at the time of his writing. To state the obvious, we beseech readers to use contemporary means (e.g., Internet, online journals) and other professional outlets to gather additional readings by Jenkins and other scholars interested in and dedicated to this ignored population and topic.

As we are, readers should be both surprised and appalled that such scholarship remains limited in focus and quantity in this century. Too few studies and too few scholars have focused consistently on Black students with high IQ scores. Terminology and wording—definitions and how we say things—matter and mean a great deal in both historical and contemporary ways. Jenkins' scholarship *challenged and challenges* myths, biases, and stereotypes; his lifelong scholarship reminded readers—supporters and nonsupporters—of where we were or have been, where we are, and where we need to go for the better good of *all* citizens.

Accordingly, as readers focus their efforts on underrepresentation, be mindful that gifts and talents are evident and prevalent in *all* racial groups. We can do and must do better at recruiting and retaining these students for gifted education identification and assessment, as well as services. We extol readers from all disciplines and walks of life to focus, in concerted ways, on highly intelligent Black students—a long-neglected population—a population who, during the Jim Crow Era, had still defied myths and stereotypes about Blacks relative to their intellect and potential. If we do not recognize, honor, and study them now, then when will we?

CHAPTER 13

A Socio-Psychological Study of Negro Children of Superior Intelligence*

Martin D. Jenkins

The gifted child has been the subject of extended research during the past fifteen years. Numerous studies, notably those of Terman,[1] Witty,[2] and Hollingsworth[3] have revealed much of psychological and educational significance concerning the incidence and characteristics of American children of superior intelligence. The Negro child of superior intelligence, however, has been almost altogether neglected; little is known about the incidence and characteristics of such children. The study herein reported was undertaken to remedy this hiatus in psychological knowledge.

---

*This article is based on the writer's doctoral dissertation. The research was done under the direction of Professor Paul A. Witty of Northwestern University. Professor Witty and the writer have collaborated in the publication of two phases of the study. Cf. "The educational achievement of a group of gifted Negro children." *Journal of Educational Psychology*, 25: 585–97, N 1934; and, The case of "B"—a gifted Negro girl. *Journal of Social Psychology*, 6: 117–24, F 1935. See also Martin Jenkins, "A Socio-Psychological Study of Negro Children of Superior Intelligence." Unpublished Doctor's Dissertation. Evanston: Northwestern University, 1935.

The term intelligence is used throughout to denote *test-intelligence*.

[1] L. Terman, *Genetic studies of Genius*—(Mental and Physical Traits of a Thousand Gifted Children.) Palo Alto: Stanford University Press, 1925.
[2] Paul A. Witty, "A Study of one hundred Gifted Children," *Bulletin, University of Kansas*, Vol. II, No 7, 1930.
[3] Leta S. Hollingsworth, *Gifted Children*, New York: Macmillan & Co., 1929.

Reprinted from Jenkins, M. D. (1936). A socio-psychological study of Negro children of superior intelligence. *The Journal of Negro Education*, 5, 175–190. Reprinted with permission from *The Journal of Negro Education*.

Problem

The research was designed to answer the following questions:
1. What is the incidence of Negro children of superior intelligence in a segment of the school population of Chicago, Illinois?
2. At what age and grade-level are Negro children of superior intelligence found?
3. In what respects do superior Negro children conform to the general pattern of superior children studied by pervious investigators in matters such as home background, educational achievement, interests and developmental history?
4. What is the racial composition of Negro children of superior intelligence?

Procedure

Selection of Subjects

The subjects of this study were identified in a systematic search for superior Negro children in grades 3–8 of seven public schools of Chicago. In these schools there are approximately eight thousand Negro children. The method of selection was similar to that used by Terman.[4] Classroom teachers nominated the following children: (1) the child thought most intelligent, (2) the child doing the best classroom work and (3) children one or more half-years underage for grade.

Five hundred and thirty-nine children, who constituted approximately 6.5 per cent of their school population, were nominated by teachers. The McCall Multi-Mental Scale, a group test of mental ability, was administered to 512 of the nominees and the Stanford-Binet examination (abbreviated form), an individual test of mental ability, was then given to every child who had been credited with an I.Q. of 120 or more on the McCall Scale. One hundred three children of Stanford-Binet I.Q. 120 or above were identified; these children constitute the subjects of the study.

Tests and Instruments Used

The following tests and instruments were administered: The New Stanford Achievement Test, Advanced Examination, Form W; The Personal Index (a battery of four character and personality tests); The Pupil Report (a questionnaire concerning pupil interests and activities); and The Sims Score Card for Socio-Economic Status. In addition, each subject was rated by one teacher on traits such as *leadership, originality, et cetera;* and information relative to the heredity and envi-

---

[4] L. M. Terman. *op. cit.* Ch. 2.

ronmental background, developmental history, school progress, interests and aptitudes of subject of I.Q. 125 or above was secured by interviews with parents.

The Community Background

Objective test scores reflect cultural as well as innate factors. Essential to a valid interpretation of test data is an understanding of the socio-economic milieu of the individual or groups whose test performance is being evaluated. The superior children discussed in this paper all live in Chicago's South Side between 45th and 68th Streets. This section is populated almost exclusively with Negroes. The community affords opportunity for educational and cultural development—standard schools providing instruction from the kindergarten through the university, libraries, museums, parks, *et cetera*, are available to all persons. The community contains a large number of professional and well-to-do persons, but there is a large number of indigent persons in the area. (Approximately 20 to 25 per cent of the total population of the area are on the relief rolls.) The areas in which the seven schools included in the survey are located, are, in general, of somewhat higher socio-economic level than the average Negro residential area in Chicago.

Related Studies

The considerable body of literature relating to children of superior intelligence has recently has been summarized by Terman and Burks[5] and the studies concerned with the intelligence test performance of Negro children have been revived and analyzed by a number of writers.[6] Consequently, it will be necessary here only to comment upon those studies which bear directly upon Negro children of superior intelligence.

Bond's[7] article in 1926 was the first published work dealing with Negro children of superior intelligence. He reports that eight of the thirty-three children tested by him scored at or above 130 I.Q. on the Stanford-Binet examination. The chief value of this study lies in the author's recognition of the importance of the study of Negro deviates in the upper I.Q. levels.

Proctor's[8] unpublished study of high I.Q. Negro children of Washington, D.C., represents the first thorough study of Negro children of superior intelligence.

---

[5] L. M. Terman and B. S. Burks, "The Gifted Child." In Murchison, Carl (Ed.) *The Handbook of Child Psychology* (Second revised edition.) Worchester: Clarke University, 1933. pp. 773–801.
[6] Cf. T. R. Garth, *Race Psychology*. New York; McGraw-Hill, 1932; J. St. Clair Price, Negro-White Differences in General Intelligence. JOURNAL OF NEGRO EDUCATION, 3: 424–52, Jl 1934; P. A. Witty and H. C. Lehman, "Racial Differences; The Dogma of Superiority." *Journal of Social Psychology*. 1930; D. Yoder, "The Present Status of the Question of Racial Differences." *Journal of Educational Psychology*, 19: 463–70, 1928.
[7] H. M. Bond, Some Exceptional Negro Children. *Crisis*, 34: 257–59, 1927.
[8] Lillian S. Proctor. "A Case Study of Thirty Superior Colored Children of Washington D.C.," Unpublished Master's Thesis. Chicago: University of Chicago, 1929.

Proctor presents case studies of thirty children whose I.Q.'s (Stanford-Binet) range from 129–175. The group of superior Negro children conforms to the general pattern of superior children at most points. This study affords cogent evidence that the superior Negro child is not an anomaly in the elementary school population.

Terwillinger's[9] unpublished master's thesis represents an attempt to identify Negro children of 125 I.Q. or above in certain public schools in New York City. This investigator reports that her subjects were drawn from a total population of more than seven thousand. In fact, however, the ten subjects reported by her were all drawn from two schools in which the combined enrollment was 3,581. Long[10] devotes a section of his study of the test intelligence of third grade children selected on the basis of socio-economic status to a superior group. (120 I.Q. and above). Long's finding will be cited later.

Other studies of Negro children neglect the upper deviates. Analysis of published studies, however, reveals that many Negro children of high I.Q. have been found. Fifteen studies of Negro children which report subjects above 120 I.Q. are listed in Table I. The studies cited were made in various localities and under varying conditions. Consequently, one may not justifiably generalize concerning the incidence of Negro children of high I.Q. from a composite of the studies. It is not without significance, however, that in some instances, the proportion of high I.Q. children approaches or exceeds the normal proportion of such children in the white population.[11]

Analysis of the literature leads to two conclusions: (1) the Negro child of high I.Q. is not an anomaly in the school population, (2) Superior Negro children manifest, in general, the same characteristics as do other children of superior intelligence.

THE FINDINGS

INCIDENCE OF NEGRO CHILDREN OF SUPERIOR INTELLIGENCE

The McCall Multi-Mental Scale Data. Limitation of time prevented the writer from administering an individual examination to all of the pupils nominated by teachers. A group test, the McCall Multi-Mental Scale[12] was utilized as a means of selecting nominees for individual examination. This test was administered to 512 pupils nominated by teachers. This test was administered by teachers. The pupils nominated constitute 6.3 percent of the total enrollment of 8,145 pupils.

---

[9] Janet Terwillinger, "A Study of Negro Children of I.Q. Above 125." Unpublished Master's Thesis. New York: Teachers College, Columbia University, 1934.

[10] H. H. Long, "Test Results of Third-Grade Children Selected on the Basis of Socio-Economic Status." I, JOURNAL OF NEGRO EDUCATION 4: 192–212, Ap 1935.

[11] The commonly accepted figures for the distribution of I.Q.'s of unselected American school children is as follows: Six per cent score at or above 120 I.Q. One per cent score at or above 130 I.Q. Four tenths percent score at or above 140 I.Q.

[12] Cf. William McCall, Manual, *Manual of Directions for the McCall Multi-Mental Scale*. New York. Teachers College Bureau of Publications, 1925.

Table I
Studies Which Include Negro Children of 120 I.Q. and Above

Investigator	Date	Locality	Test	N	Cases in I.Q. Intervals		
					120–29	130–39	140–
Clark[7]	1923	Calif.	National	500	177*†	.....	12
Long[8]	1934	D.C.	Kuhlman-Anderson	4,864	177	50	10
Bond[9]	926	Okla.	Stanford-Binet	33	......	7	1
Strachen[10]	1926	Mo.	Stanford-Binet	609	14*§	5*‖	1*○
Hewitt[11]	1930	Va.	Illinois	90	4	2	1
Schwegler and Winn[12]	1920	Kansas	Stanford-Binet	58	1	1	......
Goodenough[13]	1926	Tenn., La.	Goodenough	613	8	1	1
		Calif.	Goodenough	69	3	......	1
Lacy[14]	1926	Okla.	Stanford-Binet	817	14	2	1
Hirsch[15]	1926	Tenn.	Dearborn	449	7	1	......
Garth and Whatley[16]	1925	Texas	National	1,272	9	......	......
Beckham[17]	1339	Md., D.C., N.Y.	Stanford-Binet	1,100	18	5	......
Terwilliger[18]	1934	N.Y.	Stanford-Binet	3,681	4	4	2
Proctor[19]	1929	D.C.	Stanford-Binet	††	1	16	13
Long[20]	1935	D.C.	Stanford-Binet	††	25	4	5
Jenkins[21]	1935	Ill.	McCall.	8,145	82	54	36
			Stanford-Binet	8,145	45	39	29

* Number of cases computed from percentages.
† I.Q. 110–139.
§ I.Q. 116–125.
‖ I.Q. 126–135.
○ I.Q. 136 and above.
†† Not given.
[7] W. W. Clark, *Los Angeles Negro Children*, Educ. Res. Bull., Los Angeles Public Schools. Vol. 3. No. 2. 1923.
[8] H. H. Long "The Intelligence of Colored Elementary Pupils. JOURNAL NEGRO EDUCATION, 3:205–222. 1934.
[9] H. M. Bond. *op. cit.*
[10] Lexie Strachen, "Distribution of Intelligence Quotients of Twenty-Two Thousand Primary School Children," *Journal Educational Educational Research*, 16:169–174. 1926.
[11] A. Hewitt. "A Comparative Study of the Intelligence of White and Colored Children," *Elementary School Journal*, 31:111–119. 1930.
[12] R. A. Schwegler and M. A. Winn, "A Comparative Study of the Intelligence of White and Colored Children," *Journal Educational Research*, 2:838–848. 1920.
[13] Florence Goodenough. "Racial Differences in the Intelligence of School Children," *Journal Experimental Psychology*, 9:388–397. 1926.
[14] L. D. Lacy. "Relative Intelligence of White and Colored Children. *Elementary School Journal*, 26:542–546. 1926.
[15] M. D. Hirsch. *A Study of Natio-Racial Differences*. Genetic Psychology Monographs, Vol. I. No. 3. 1926.
[16] T. R. Garth and G. A. Whatley. "The Intelligence of Southern Negro Children, *School and Society*, 22:501–505. 1925.
[17] A. S. Beckham. "A Study of the Intelligence of Colored Adolescents of Different Socio-Economic Status in Typical Metropolitan Areas. *Journal Social and Abnormal Psychology*, 4:70–91, 1933.
[18] Janet Terwilliger, *op. cit.*
[19] Lillian S. Proctor, *op. cit.*
[20] H. H. Long. "Test Results of Third Grade Negro Children Selected on the Basis of Socio-Economic Status. I. JOURNAL NEGRO EDUCATION 4:192–212. 1935.
[21] Present study.

The mean McCall I.Q. of the group of nominees is 115.3 (S.D. = 15.7). Seven per cent of the group score at or above 140 I.Q., and 33.5 per cent of the group score at or above 120 I.Q. The estimated percentages of high I.Q.'s (McCall) in the total population of 8,145 pupils is given in Table II. Of the total population 2.11 per cent score at or above 120 I.Q., 1.11 per cent score at or above 130 I.Q. and 0.44 per cent score at or above 140 I.Q.

The Stanford-Binet Examination Data. One hundred-three children attained a Stanford-Binet I.Q. of 120 or more.[13] The I.Q.'s range from 120, the arbitrarily selected lower limit, to 200. The distribution of I.Q.'s is as follows:

I.Q.	N
200–209	1
190–199	0
180–189	0
170–179	0
160–169	1
150–159	9
140–149	18
130–139	29
120–129	45
Total	103

The mean I.Q. is 134.2 (S.D. = 12.3). Twenty-seven subjects test at or above 140 I.Q. and fifty-five subjects attain at or above 130 I.Q. No children are found within the I.Q. range 170–190.

Table III shows the estimated percentages of high I.Q.'s, (Stanford-Binet) in each of the seven schools and in the total population.[14] Of the total population of 8,145 children, 1.23 per cent score at or above 120 I.Q., 0.66 per cent score at or above 130 I.Q. and 0.33 per cent score at or above 140 I.Q. Disparate proportions of high I.Q.'s are found in the various schools. The percentage of gifted children

---

[13] I.Q.'s were "corrected" in accordance with Terman's procedure: The method is described in *Genetic Studies in Genius*. Vol. I. as follows:
"An attempt has been made to correct the I.Q.'s to correspond to what they would have been had the scale been more nearly adequate in the upper range.... The correction used involved the following addition of months to the mental age score for those passing various numbers of test out of the total twelve tests in year groups 16 and 18.
Tests passed in 16 and 18.   5   6   7   8   9   10   11   12
Number of months added.   3   6   9   12   15   18   21   24"
The validity of the method was checked by comparing the number of very high I.Q. children at various age levels. When the correction was used the frequency children scoring above I.Q. 170 showed little tendency to increase in the total age range covered. (pp. 42–43.)

[14] The proportion of superior children varies with the nature of the population. Terman, for example, found the following percentages of gifted children (140 I.Q. and above) to school population in four California cities:
Los Angeles   0.30 per cent
San Francisco   0.43 per cent
Oakland   0.44 per cent
Berkeley and Almeda   1.00 per cent
Cf. L. M. Terman, *op cit.* p. 29.

Table II
Estimated Percentage of High I.Q.'s (McCall) of Children in a Population of 8,145 Negro Pupils (Based on the Test Performance of 512 Highly Selected Subjects)

McCall I.Q.	N	Per cent of total population of 8,145 pupils equaling or exceeding
Above 149	14	.17
Above 139	36	.44
Above 129	90	1.11
Above 119	127	2.11

Table III
Estimated Percentage of High I.Q.'s (Stanford-Binet) for Each of Seven Schools and for the Total Population of 8,145 Negro Pupils Based on the Test Performance of 100 Highly Selected Subjects

I.Q.	A	B	C	D	E	F	G	Per cent of total Population
Above 139	.80	.83	.57	.41	.18	.16	.0	.33
Above 129	1.43	1.57	1.14	.50	.50	.47	.21	.66
Above 119	2.53	2.31	2.00	1.25	.86	.71	.57	1.23

(140 I.Q. or above), for example, ranges from 0.80 per cent in school A to .00 per cent in school G.

Sex differences. No significant sex difference in I.Q. was found (D/Sigma Diff. = .38. The mean I.Q. of boys is 134.6 (S.D. = 10.8) and of girls 133.9 (S.D. = 13.0). The highest I.Q. was earned by a girl.

There are seventy-two girls and only thirty-one boys in this group of superior Negro children. The greater frequency of girls obtains at each I.Q. interval and was observed in all but one of the schools surveyed. The sex ratio is 232:100 on the basis of the McCall I.Q. (512 subjects) and 233:100 on the basis of the Stanford-Binet I.Q. (103 subjects). Proctor's[15] group of superior Negro children displayed a similar distributional pattern, the ratio of her group being, girls to boys, 131:100. The finding, however, is strikingly dissimilar to the findings of other studies of superior children in the elementary schools. Terman[16] reports a preponderance of boys in his gifted group, the ratio, boys to girls, being 121.100. Witty's[17] gifted group is about equally divided consisting of fifty-one boys and forty-nine girls; and the sex ratio in Long's[18] group of superior Negro children (34 cases) is 113:100 in favor of boys.

Distribution in terms of age- and grade-levels. At no age is there found an unusually large number of subjects. The model age is eight years, there being twenty-three children of this age. The ten-year-olds contribute the next largest

---
[15] L. S. Proctor, *op. cit.*
[16] L. M. Terman, *op. cit.* p. 49.
[17] P. A. Witty, *op. cit.* p. 29.
[18] H. H. Long, *op. cit.* The sex distribution, which does not appear in the article, was furnished the writer by Dr. Long.

Table IV
Age-Grade Placement of 103 Negro Children of Superior Intelligence

Age	\multicolumn{8}{c}{Grade Placement}	Total
	2	3	4	5	6	7	8	9	Total
6-6-11		3							3
7-7-11	2	10	2						14
8-8-11		11	10	1	1				23
9-9-11			4	7	1	1			13
10-10-11				6	9	3	2		20
11-11-11					1	8	4		13
12-12-11						3	10	1	14
13-13-11							3		3
Total	2	24	16	14	12	15	19	1	103
Mean grade				5.3		Mean age			9 yrs., 7 mos.
S.D.				1.6		S.D.			20 months

number of subjects, twenty children being in this age category; seventeen children are below age eight. The mean age is 9 years, 7 months, (S.D. = 1.6). Table IV shows the age-grade distribution.

HEREDITY AND ENVIRONMENTAL BACKGROUND

Data relative to the heredity and environmental background of the subjects were secured by means of interviews with the parents of sixty-four children of 125 I.Q. and above and by administration of the Sims Score Card for Socio-Economic Status to the superior group and to a control group.

Birthplace of children and of parents. The superior group is predominantly a Chicago-born group, 73.4 per cent of the children were born in Chicago, while 15.6 per cent were born in a Southern state. (It is perhaps significant that not a single member of the superior group has ever attended school in a Southern state.) The parents and grandparents of these children, on the other hand, were chiefly Southern born, 67.4 per cent of the parents and 85.6 percent of the grandparents being natives of a Southern state.

Education of parents. The parents constitute a well-educated group. The median father has had 13.9 years of schooling and the median mother has had

12.8 years of schooling. The findings here are similar to those of other investigators, Terman[19] found the median amount of schooling for parents of his gifted group to be 12.1 years; and for Witty's[20] group the median amount of schooling was 13 years for the fathers, and 12 years for the mothers. Approximately 60 per cent of the fathers and 70 per cent of the mothers of Proctor's[21] group of superior Negro children had had training above the high school level.

Occupational status of parents. The percentage of fathers falling in the various categories of the Taussig Scale[22] is as follows:

	Classification	N	Percent
V	Professional and large business	21	33.4
IV	Clerical or semi-intellectual	23	36.6
III	Skilled occupations	10	15.9
II	Semi-skilled occupations	5	8.0
I	Unskilled occupations	4	6.3
	Total	65	100.2

More than two-thirds of the fathers fall in the upper occupational levels (33.4 per cent in Group V and 36.6 per cent in Group IV). Less than 15 per cent of the fathers fall in the two lower occupational levels.[23]

Table V[24] shows the classification according to occupation of fathers of the superior group compared with similar data present by Terman[25] (gifted children) and by Goddard[26] (superior children).

A comparatively small percentage of the Negro fathers are engaged in commercial occupations while a relatively large percentage are in public service occupations. The public service group is composed predominantly of postal workers.

The finding that children of superior intelligence are the progeny of fathers in upper occupational strata is similar to the finding of Terman, Witty and Proctor. Long's group of thirty-four Negro children of 120 I.Q. and above, however, is composed predominantly of children of relatively low socioeconomic status. "The fathers of 17.6 per cent of these pupils are professional, 23.5 per cent are skilled,

[19] L. M. Terman, op. cit.
[20] P. A. Witty, op. cit, p. 10
[21] L. S. Proctor, op. cit. p. 49
[22] F. W. Taussig, *Principles of Economics* Vol. II. New York: Macmillan, 1916. pp. 134–147.
[23] The limitations of the Taussig Scale and other measures of socio-economic status, when applied to Negro groups, should be recognized. The hierarchy of occupations is not the same for Negroes and whites in the United States, consequently, a given occupation may represent a different socio-economic level in the two groups. The classification of postal workers is a case in point. Taussig places "mailmen" in Group II of his scale, along with semi-skilled workers and the like. The Negro postal worker, however, certainly enjoys a higher relative status than this within the Negro group; the writer, therefore, feels justified in placing postal workers in Group IV. Cf. in this connection J. St. Clair Price. Op. cit. p. 431–432.
[24] These data were secured from the subjects at the time the Stanford-Binet Examination was administered.
[25] L. M. Terman, op. cit. p. 63.
[26] H. H. Goddard, *School Training of Gifted Children*. Yonkers-on-Hudson, New York: World Book Co. 1928. p. 132.

Table V
Classification of Fathers of Eighty Four Subjects According to Occupation Compared With Terman's and Goddard's Findings

Classification	Present Study Per cent	Terman Per cent	Goddard Per cent
Professional	35	29	21
Commercial	13	46	37
Industrial	19	20	39
Public service	22	5	3
Personal service	10		

35.3 per cent are semi-skilled, 11.8 per cent are unskilled and 11.8 per cent are of unknown occupations."[27]

Socio-economic status. The Sims Score Card for Socio-Economic Status[28] was administered to the superior group and to a randomly selected control group. Table VI[29] gives the distribution of the scores of the superior and control groups. The mean score of the superior group is 18.7 (S.D. = 6.1). Based on the norms for a group of New Haven, Connecticut school children (Sims' original data) this score represents a "high" level of socio-economic status. The mean score of the control group is 15.6 (S.D. = 5.7). This score represents above a "medium high" level of socio-economic status. The difference in favor of the superior group is statistically significant (D/Sigma Diff. = 3.0). In view of the great amount of overlapping, however, it is clear that whatever is measured by the Sims Scale is not the *crucial* factor in the superiority of the superior group.

Racial Composition

The racial composition of sixty-three subjects of 125 I.Q. and above was determined from genealogical data provided by parents. The weaknesses inherent in this approach are recognized. In some instances individuals are unable to determine their own degree of racial mixture. The data are further subject to the weakness of all genealogical material: deliberate inaccuracy of report and failure to account for the totality of ancestry. That the method is essentially a satisfactory one, however, is attested by Herskovits who checked the genealogical reports of Howard University students, concerning their racial composition, against a number of anthropological criteria. Herskovits, commenting on the validity of the method observes:

---

[27] H. H. Long. Test results of third grade Negro children selected on the basis of socio-economic status I. JOURNAL OF NEGRO EDUCATION 4:20, 1935.
[28] *Cf.* V. S. Sims. *The measurement of Socio-Economic Status*. Bloomington (Illinois): Public School Publishing Co. 1927.
[29] The score of the third grade children were not used. The control groups was selected as follows: Teachers of each of the superior subjects were instructed to, "Select that pupil of the same sex whose name immediately follows that of the superior pupil on your class roll; Sibling and relatives excepted." Thus, the control group is similar to the superior group in sex and grade status.

Table VI

Distribution of Scores on the SIM's Score Card for Socioeconomic Status, Superior and Control Groups

	Number of cases	
Score	Superior	Control
31–34	1	1
28–30	6	1
25–27	5	3
22–24	9	5
19–21	10	10
16–18	13	9
13–15	10	13
10–12	7	15
7–9	1	4
4–6	2	6
Total	64	67
Mean score	18.7	15.6
S.D.	6.1	5.7

This is of particular methodological interest for it indicates that more use can be made of Negro genealogical material than has been thought possible. . . . (I believe) that for a given group for which genealogies are taken, such use can be made of their statements as to ancestry as can be made of statements from any other element of our population that lacks written record of ancestry.[30]

The following procedure was utilized in determining the racial composition of the children. Parents were asked to state to the best of their ability, their racial composition, *i.e.*, approximate proportions of Negro, white, Indian, or other racial ancestry. The racial composition of each child was then computed from that of his parents. The subjects were divided into four groups: (1) **N** (those having no white ancestry), (2) **NNW** (those having more Negro ancestry than white), (3) **NW** (those having about an equal amount of Negro and white ancestry), (4) **NWW** (those having more white ancestry than Negro). Gross classifications of this character tend to eliminate minor errors in final estimates.

Tables VII shows the number and percentage of subjects in each of the four classifications. Presented also in Table VII are Herskovits' data based on anthropometrical and genealogical data secured from samplings of the populations of five different rural and urban communities.[31] Almost one-half of the superior group (46.1 per cent) are found in the NNW category and slightly less than one-quarter are in the N classification. Thus more than two-thirds of the group are of Negro

---
[30] M. J. Herskovits, *The Anthropometry of the American Negro*. New Work: Columbia University Press, 1930. p. 266.
[31] *Ibid.* p. 15

Table VII
The Racial Composition of Sixty-Three Negro Children of Superior Intelligence Compared With the Racial Composition of 1,551 Cases Reported by Herskovits

Classification	Number	Percent	Herskovit's Populations Percent
N	14	22.2	28.3
NNW	29	46.1	31.7
NW	10	15.9	25.2
NWW	10	15.9	14.8
Total	63	100.1	100.0

or predominantly Negro ancestry. The NW and NWW classifications each include 15.9 per cent of the cases.

These percentages are strikingly similar to those of Herskovits for the general Negro population. Comparing Herskovits data with our own we find about the same percentages included in the N and NWW classifications, while a larger proportion of the superior group occurs in the NNW category than in Herskovits population. (46.1 per cent and 31.7 per cent respectively). These superior Negro children are not atypical in racial composition.

Educational Achievement

It is well established that in general, above-average performance on mental tests is indicative of superior ability to succeed in the school situation. All investigators of gifted and superior children have found that these children, as a group, are accelerated in school and that their educational achievement, as measured by standardized tests, is far in advance of both their chronological age- and grade-placement expectancy.[32]

Data relative to the school progress of the children here under consideration were obtained from the school records and from parents. The New Stanford Achievement Test,[33] Advanced Examination, Form W, was used to measure educational attainment.

Progress through the grades.[34] The subjects constitute an accelerated group (See Table I). No subject is over-age for this grade and 81 per cent of the groups are under-age for grade. Only 10.6 per cent of the total school population from which the superior group was selected are under-age for grade. Thus this group of superior Negro children manifests eight times the "normal" amount of underageness. Sixty-seven per cent of the group have skipped at least one half-grade, the mean number

---

[32] *Cf.* L. M. Terman and Barbara Burks, *loc. cit.*
[33] *Cf.* T. L. Kelley, et al., *The New Stanford Achievement Test: Guide for Interpreting.* Yonkers-on-Hudson, New York: World Book Co. 1929
[34] Based on the record of 65 subjects of 125 I.Q. or above.

of half-grades skipped being 1.2. None of the children has repeated a grade. The mean progress quotient (P.Q.) is 119 (S.D. = 7.7).[35]

These superior Negro children constitute an accelerated group. That our subjects conform in this respect to the general pattern for children of superior intelligence may be seen by a comparison of their school progress with that of groups of superior children studied by other investigators. Terman[36] found that 84.9 per cent of this group had skipped a grade and that 4 per cent had repeated a grade; the mean PQ of his group was 114. Witty[37] reports the PQ of his group was 116. Of Proctor's[38] group of thirty Negro children of superior intelligence, twenty-six were under age for grade, none was retarded and twenty-three had skipped at least on half-grade.

The New Stanford Achievement Test Data[39]

Grade and age status. In general the subjects have mastered educational subject matter (as measured by the test) in excess of their present grade placement. The mean group member has mastered educational subject matter 1.1 grades above his present grade status; the range is from -.6 to +3.6 grades. Five subjects tested below the norm for their present grade placement.

The subjects, without exception, exceed the test norms for their chronological age. The main subject has attained an educational development of 2.7 grades in excess of the average child of his chronological age. This is an arresting fact when one considers that the average subject has been in school somewhat less than five years. Two of the children have mastered educational subject-matter more than five grades in excess of that which is their normal (for age) grade placement.

Educational, subject, and accomplishment quotients. The mean educational quotient[40] is 127.2 (S.D. = 10.2). The E.Q.'s range form 106 to 169; the distribution is as follows:

E.Q.	Frequency
160–169	1
150–159	1
140–149	8
130–139	22
120–129	38
110–119	22

---

[35] The progress quotient (PQ) of a given child is obtained by dividing the standard age for the child's grade by the child's age as of the beginning of the semester. Here, the standard age for grade is based on age-grade data for the population of six of the schools included in the study.
[36] L. M. Terman, *Genetic Studies in Genius*, Vol. I pp. 257, 273.
[37] P. A. Witty, *A Study of One Hundred Gifted Children*, p. 19.
[38] L. S. Proctor. "A Case Study of Thirty Superior Colored Children of Washington, D.C.," p. 43.
[39] Based on ninety-three cases.
[40] $E.Q. = \dfrac{\text{Educational age}}{\text{Chronological age}}$

Table VIII

Mean Subject Quotients, Educational Quotients, Accomplishment Quotients, and Intelligence Quotients of 64 Girls and 29 Boys, and of the Total Group

Subject	Boys	S.D.	Girls	S.D.	Total	S.D.
Paragraph Meaning	135.7	16.6	135.2	12.0	135.3	13.6
Word Meaning	136.0	13.7	135.0	11.5	135.3	12.2
Total Reading	136.0	14.2	135.3	10.4	135.5	11.8
Dictation (Spelling)	126.4	15.0	129.1	13.8	128.2	14.6
Language Usage	133.3	22.1	134.1	18.8	133.8	19.9
Literature	125.0	19.6	123.3	15.6	123.8	16.9
History and Civics	132.3	19.6	119.8	15.2	123.7	17.6
Geography	127.7	16.2	123.6	15.6	125.2	16.0
Physiology and Hygiene	131.9	15.8	123.6	14.0	125.9	14.6
Arithmetic Reasoning	124.0	14.8	120.9	12.6	121.9	13.3
Arithmetic Computation	123.6	17.7	121.9	13.2	122.4	14.7
Total Arithmetic	124.0	14.8	121.1	11.7	122.0	12.8
Educational Quotient	129.8	11.6	125.9	9.8	127.2	10.2
Accomplishment Quotient	97.9	9.1	95.8	7.2	95.4	6.9
Accomplishment Q Read	102.7	6.4	102.6	6.7	102.5	8.2
Intelligence Q (Binet)	134.6	10.8	133.9	13.0	134.2	12.3

100–109   1

Table VIII shows the mean educational quotients, subject quotients, and accomplishments quotients of the superior group. The highest quotients are in reading and in language usage (the means are 135.5 and 133.8, respectively), subjects which apparently are least dependent on classroom instruction for their development. The mean reading quotient of the group (135.5) is slightly higher than the mean I.Q. (134.3). The lowest subject quotient is that in arithmetic (mean = 122.0).

The accomplishment quotient[41] is an approximation or crude measure of the extent to which pupils are achieving in terms of their mental abilities. Almost without exception investigators have reported a negative correlation between intelligence quotients and educational quotients. The accomplishment quotient technique apparently sets an expected measure of attainment which is too high for the bright to hope to attain in the traditional school.

The A.Q.'s of the group range from 79 to 114; the mean A.Q. is 95.4 (S.D. = 6.9). Most of the high A.Q.'s were earned by subjects of relatively low I.Q. This inverse relationship between the A.Q. and the I.Q. is revealed by the accomplishment of subjects within various I.Q. intervals. Table IX gives the mean I.Q., E.Q., and A.Q. of children in the I.Q. intervals 140 and above, 130–139 and 120–129.

---

[41] $A.Q. = \dfrac{E.Q.}{I.Q.}$

Table IX
The Mean E.Q. and A.Q. for Various I.Q. Levels

Interval	No.	Mean I.Q.	Mean E.Q.	Mean A.Q.
146 and above	26	148.9	133.7	91
130–139	26	134.0	126.4	95.2
120–29	41	123.0	122.0	99.2
Total group	93	134.2	127.2	95.4

The mean E.Q. varies directly with the intelligence level while the A.Q. varies inversely.

Sex differences in achievement. In general, the boys manifest superiority in subject-matter attainment. The girls are superior to boys in only two sub-tests, those of spelling and language usage, and in neither case is the superiority statistically significant. The boys are superior to the girls in each of the other sub-tests, but in only one, that of history and civics, is the difference statistically significant (D/Sigma Diff. = 3.05).

Findings of other investigators.[42] Comparison of the educational achievement of superior Negro children with that of other groups of superior children reveals, in general, a striking similarity. Terman's[43] gifted children earned a mean E.Q. of 135 and a mean A.Q. of approximately 90. Witty[44] reports a mean E.Q. of 136 and a mean A.Q. of approximately 90 for his gifted subjects. In both of these studies the highest attainment is in reading and language usage and the lowest attainment is in arithmetic. It is to be noted, however, that our superior Negro children fall somewhat below other groups in achievement in arithmetic. Proctor's[45] group of superior Negro children also made a relatively poor record in arithmetic.

INTERESTS, CHARACTER AND PERSONALITY TRAITS

An appraisal of the total personality of the child leads to a consideration of factors other than intelligence and educational attainment. Non-intellectual phases of personality such as sociability, ambition, character and interests are unquestionably of crucial importance in determining the adjustment of the individual to both school and life situations.

Information concerning the interests of the subjects was obtained from the subjects and from their parents, and data relative to certain character and personality traits were secured by teacher ratings and by the administration of the *Personal Inventory*.[46] A randomly selected control group, similar to the superior group in sex

---

[42] See for a more extended discussion: P. A. Witty and M. D. Jenkins, "The Educational Achievement of a group of Gifted Negro children," *Journal Educational Psychology* 25: 585–597, 1934.
[43] L. M. Terman, *op. cit.* p. 291.
[44] P.A. Witty, *op. cit.* p. 19.
[45] L.S. Proctor, *op. cit.*
[46] Cf. G. C. Loofbourow, "A group Test of Problem Behavior Tendencies in Junior High School Boys. *Journal Educational Psychology,,* 24: 641–653, 1933.

and grade was used for comparative purposes. The findings may be briefly summarized as follows:

Preferred school subjects. Arithmetic is the most popular school subject, being liked by 58 per cent of the superior group and by 70 per cent of the control group. Interesting is this fact in view of the relatively low achievement of the superior group in the arithmetic tests.

Preferred activities. Both groups express about the same degree of preference for various activities such as playing, reading, *et cetera*. Seventy per cent of the superior group report participation in some group activity not directly connected with the school. These data suggest that superior children are not less well-adjusted than are average children.

Special aptitudes. Parents were asked to indicate (on a check list) any special aptitudes shown by the subjects; aptitudes were to be checked only if the child had revealed exceptional ability. According to parents, 78.2 per cent of the subjects have given evidence of brightness, 57.8 per cent have special aptitude along mechanical lines. All this, of course, is merely suggestive, parental reports concerning the precocity of their children must always be discounted.

Ratings on character and personality traits. Subjects were rated, each by one teacher, on a rating scale which included nine traits: "Self-confidence," "industry," "leadership," "cooperativeness," "originality," "perseverance," "dependability," "ambition," "desire to excel," "personal attractiveness." The mean subject was rated above average in each of the nine traits, being most superior in "ambition," "desire to excel," and least superior in "leadership."

Performance on the Personal Index. In each of the four parts of the "Personal Index" the superior group made a more satisfactory record.[47]

CONCLUSIONS

INCIDENCE OF NEGRO CHILDREN OF SUPERIOR INTELLIGENCE

Superior Negro children are not anomalous in the elementary school population. In view of the relatively large numbers of very superior Negro children reported by Clark, Long, Strachen, Hewitt, Proctor, and the writer, it is singular that there still persists the idea that the Negro child of high I.Q. is found but rarely. This point of view, which should be emended, has arisen from an uncritical analysis of test data. Most of the studies concerned with the mental test performance of Negro children have been conducted in localities which provide meager opportunities for educational and cultural development. In such localities the potentialities of Negro children cannot be realized. Given opportunity for development, however, the gifted Negro child will emerge.

---

[47] Due to lack of satisfactory statistical control the test data will not be given here.

Girls are found with greater frequency than are boys in the superior group, the ratio being 233:100 (on the basis of the Stanford-Binet I.Q.). The preponderance of girls is observable at every I.Q. level, and was found in all but one of the seven school canvassed. The finding here is similar to that of Proctor[48] whose groups of superior Negro children includes more girls than boys, but dissimilar to that of Long[49] whose superior group includes more boys than girls. The available evidence, however, supports the tentative conclusion that, in the Negro elementary school population, more girls than boys are to be found in the high I.Q. levels.

Superior Negro children are spread rather evenly throughout the various age and grade levels, no age or grade having preponderance of subjects. The findings here are at variance with the frequently-expressed opinion that Negro children tend toward mediocrity above the primary-school level. A definite conclusion relative to this questions however, must await a follow-up study of the group.

The Effect of Racial Composition

The finding indicated that intelligence-test performance of elementary school-children is not a function of "race". The discovery of a Negro child who scores in the very highest range of the Stanford-Binet constitutes one of the most significant findings of this study. The I.Q. of this girl (I.Q. 200) has been equaled or excelled by fewer than ten of the hundreds of thousands of children to whom intelligence tests have been administered. This one case, which is well authenticated, shows that Negro children are to be found in the very highest range of test-intelligence.

That Negro ancestry is not a limiting factor in intelligence-test performance is suggested further by the racial composition an American "Negro" may range from practically pure white to "pure" Negro. Now, if whites are superior to Negroes in intelligence-test performance *because of a racial factor*, a group of Negro children of superior intelligence, however, constitutes a typical cross-section, in racial composition, of the American Negro population. The findings of this study suggest that the differences in the test performance of white and Negro children found by so many investigators are not due to inherent racial factors.

Superior Negro Children Not Different From Other Superior Children

One may note a well-marked tendency in educational circles to set up a dichotomy based on assumed Negro-white differences. There is evidence, however, that Negro children are not inherently different from other American children. Certainly sufficient facts have been adduced here to indicate that superior Negro children exhibit the same characteristics that typify other "racial" groups of superior

---

[48] L. S. Proctor, *op. cit.*
[49] H. H. Long, *op. cit.*

children. In home-background, in developmental history, in physical development, in school progress, in educational achievement, in interests, in activities, and in social and personal characteristics Negro children of superior intelligence resemble other American children of superior intelligence. The data presented here concerning Negro children of superior intelligence add weight to the already abundant evidence that intelligence and educability are matters of individual differences.

CHAPTER 14

Case Studies of Negro Children of Binet IQ 160 and Above

Martin D. Jenkins

IDENTIFICATION*

The study herein reported has its origin in an experience of the writer in connection with an earlier study of gifted Negro children carried on in Chicago, Illinois. In that study two children of extremely high IQ were identified—one of IQ 200[1] and one of IQ 163. In view of the significance of children of this high IQ level, and since the writer had no reason for believing that he had chanced upon the two brightest Negro children in America, he has for the past few years sought out cases of Negro children of extremely high IQ.

In the present study a number of a number of cases of Negro children of Binet IQ 160 and above are assembled in order (1) to ascertain the existence of such children in diverse populations; (2) to examine the origin and characteristics of the children; and (3) to follow the development of the subjects over a period of years. The present discussion is concerned almost altogether with the first two of these purposes. Report of the development of the subjects must, obviously, be deferred until an appreciable number of them have reached maturity.

It is to be observed that the cases are assembled from a number of different sources and that they are restricted to children tested with the Binet examination

---

*This article is adapted from a paper originally prepared for presentation at the cancelled 1942 meeting of the American Psychological Association.

[1] *Cf.* Paul A. Witty and Martin D. Jenkins, "The Case of 'B' -a Gifted Negro Girl," *Journal of Social Psychology*, 6:117–124, 1935.

Reprinted from Jenkins, M. D. (1943). Case studies of Negro children of Binet IQ 160 and above. *The Journal of Negro Education, 12*, 159–166. Reprinted with permission from *The Journal of Negro Education*.

=by reputable psychologists. Since no systematic survey has been conducted, this paper is not concerned with the frequency of occurrence of gifted Negro children.

Binet IQ 160 was arbitrarily adopted as the lower limit for inclusion in the study. For the group of children used for standardizing the original Stanford-Binet, IQ 160 is approximately 7.5 P.E. above the median. The larger sampling of subjects tested for the 1937 revision places IQ 160 approximately 5.5 P.E.[2] above the median and assigns it a standard score equivalent of 3.75. At the time the original Stanford-Binet was standardized Terman reported a case of IQ 160 as being "the highest one in the Stanford University records."[3] In his survey of gifted children in the state of California Terman[4] found 113 who tested at or above IQ 160 (corrected S-B). On the basis of Terman's findings it may be estimated that fewer than 1/10 of 1 per cent of school children are to be found at or above Binet IQ 160. In many school populations, of course, no child tests at this high level.

As the IQ rises above 160 the frequency of occurrence, of course, decreases. Five of the subjects of the present study have tested at or above IQ 180. Statistically cases at this level should occur about once in a million times. Actually they occur with somewhat greater frequency. In his California study Terman found only 15 children testing at this level and Hollingworth reports that "In twenty-three years seeking in New York City and the local metropolitan area. . . . I have found only twelve children who test at or above 180 IQ (S-B)."[5]

It is apparent, then, that the subjects of this study are extreme deviates in psychometric intelligence.

The real significance of the IQ at the level being considered here is not surely known. Children who test at this level are characterized by precocity of thinking and by surpassing ability to accomplish the tasks of the school. Certain it is however that they are not "geniuses" in the accepted sense of the term. Perhaps it is safe to say that it is from among the ranks of these extreme deviates in IQ that genius is recruited.

Source of the Cases

The cases included were secured as follows: two were subjects of the writer's study of gifted Negro children in Chicago;[6] four were reported by Lillian Porter, a member of the Research Department of the Washington, D.C., Public Schools, in her unpublished study of gifted Negro children in Washington;[7] and three addi-

---

[2] The P.E. Values are given in Leta Hollingworth, *Children Above 180 I.Q.* Yonkers-on-Hudson, New York: World Book, 1942, p. xii.
[3] Lewis M. Terman, *Measuring Intelligence*, Boston: Houghton Mifflin Co., 1916, p. 102.
[4] Lewis M. Terman, *Mental and Physical Traits of a Thousand Gifted Children,* Genetic Studies of Genius, vol. I Stanford University: Stanford University Press, 1925. p. 45.
[5] Leta S. Hollingworth, *op. cit.,* p. xiii.
[6] Martin D. Jenkins, "A Socio-Psychological Study of Negro Children of Superior Intelligence." *Journal of Negro Education*, 5:175–190, 1936.
[7] Lillian S. Porter "A Case Study of Thirty Superior Colored Children of Washington, D.C." Unpublished Master's Thesis. Chicago: University of Chicago, 1929.

tional cases were found in the files of this Research Department (Dr. Howard H. Long, Director, Divisions 10-13, Washington Public Schools). Five cases were reported to the writer in personal communications: two cases by Professor Harvey Zorbough of the New York University Clinic for the Social Adjustment of the gifted; one case by Dr. Albert S. Beckham, psychologist in the child study Department of the Chicago Public Schools; one case by Dr. M. G. Reiman of Catholic University; and one case by Professor Arthur G. Bills of the University of Cincinnati.

These are, altogether, 14 cases for whom data have been assembled. Two additional cases, one "who tests at about 180 IQ (S-B)," and another "who tests at about 160 IQ (S-B)" were reported to the writer by the late Leta S. Hollingworth, whose death prevented the securing of detailed information concerning the subjects mentioned by her.

A word may be inserted here concerning the difficulty of securing verified cases of Negro children of exceptionally high Binet IQ. In general the high IQ child (without regard to race) is identified either (1) in surveys of gifted children, (2) in psycho-educational clinics, usually those connected with universities, or (3) in schools or school systems which provide for the individual examination of exceptional children. A relatively small proportion of the Negro population is covered by any of these. For example, so far as the writer has been able to ascertain, not a single Negro child who scores as high as 160 IQ on the Binet has been identified in any of the Southern states, probably because there are extremely few places where such a child might be identified.

It should be understood further, that the highly gifted child must be identified at a relatively early age. On the original Stanford-Binet an IQ of 160 cannot be earned by an individual whose CA exceeds 12-1 (using uncorrected MA), and on the 1937 revision the highest CA at which IQ 160 is possible is 14-11.

There is the further difficulty of securing data concerning high IQ children who have been identified. The assembling of information for another investigator takes time that the busy psychologist does not always feel warranted in giving. For example one psychologist reported to the writer that "we have 700 pages of material on _____. I would like to make a summary of it available to you but preparing the summary would be a long job and no one on the staff has the time to do it."

The Cases

To present a series of case studies in a brief article is particularly unsatisfactory since the value of the case study lies in its exhaustive analysis of the individual subject. All that can be attempted here is a summary of the characteristics of this group of exceptionally bright children at the time of their identification (Cf. Table I).

Table I

Characteristics of 16 Negro Children of Binet IQ 150 and Above

Case	Sex	Location	CA[a]	Binet IQ	EQ	School Grade	Racial Composition[b]	Occupation Father	Occupation Mother	Education Father	Education Mother
1	F	Chicago	9-5	200[c]	158	5	N	Electrical Engineer	Teacher	College graduate	Normal School
2	M	Chicago	10-6	163[c]	169	8	NWW	Attorney	Teacher	College and Professional Graduate	Graduate School (M.A.)
3	M	Cincinnati	6-9	173[d]	—	6	N	Pharmacist	Teacher	College Graduate	Graduate School (M.A.)
4	M	Washington	8-5	175	164	6	NNW	College Teacher	Housewife	College Graduate (M.A.)	Normal School
5	M	Washington	9-11	163	147	6	NWW	Machinist	Housewife	2nd High school	Normal School
6	F	Washington	5-8	162	159	1	NWW	Attorney	Housewife	College and Professional Graduate	Normal School
7	M	Washington	8-7	162	134	4	NW	Government Clerk	Housewife	High School Graduate	Normal School
8	F	New York	—	180–185	approx. 200	—	NW	Journalist and Author	Housewife	—	—
9	M	New York	10-8	184[e]	144[f]	7	NNW	—	Psychiatrist's aid	College Graduate	2nd yr. college
10	M	Chicago	8-6	174[g]	—	6	NW	Social Work Executive	Housewife	College and Professional Graduate	College Graduate
11	M	Washington	5-2	161	—	Nursery School		College Teacher	Housewife	College Graduate (M.A.)	—
12	M	Washington	6-9	163	167[f]	1	NWW	College Teacher	Government Clerk	College Graduate (M.A.)	—
13	M	Washington	7-8	169	—	3	NNW	Physician	Teacher	College and Professional Graduate	Normal School
14	F	Washington	5-7	164	2a level[f]	Kindergarten	NNW	Porter	Housewife	High School	Normal School
15	F	New York	—	180 (approx.)[h]	—	—	—	—	—	—	—
16	M	New York	—	180 (approx.)[h]	—	—	—	—	—	—	—

[a] Chronological age at time of identification.
[b] Obtained either by genealogy or by observation.
[c] "Corrected I.Q."
[d] An earlier Binet test at CA 2 yielded an IQ of 180.
[e] There is a history of prior Binet testing yielding an even higher IQ.
[f] Reading test only.
[g] A subsequent examination, about a year later, yielded a Binet IQ of 198.
[h] Cases reported by Leta S. Hollingworth. No further data available.

Mental Test Performances

The IQ's, eight of which were derived by the Stanford-Binet and five by the Merrill-Terman revision (one undetermined), range from 162–200. The Test performance of these children reveals qualitative as well as quantitative excellence. This characteristic is perhaps revealed most clearly on the vocabulary test. For example, a nine year old child who passed the vocabulary test on the XVI level, defined *Mars* as "the god of war in Roman mythology"; *mosaic*, as "a number of brightly colored stones—no tiles—put together to form a design"; and *treasury*, as "a place where a cooperating group keeps the money." Similarly, a 10 year old child who passed the vocabulary test on the XVIII year level defined *Mars* as "the planet 4th in distance away from the sun; also the god of war in Greek mythology"; *bewail*, as "to moan disconsolately"; and *flaunt* as "to show disdain for somebody." Numerous examples of a similar nature might readily be cited.

Achievement Test Performance

Achievement test data (of tests administered at the time of identification) are available for 10 cases. Characteristically the educational test performance of these children is not so high as their mental test performance. This condition is generally found among the highly gifted. The EQ exceeds the IQ in only two cases: That of case 2, IQ 163, EQ (New Stanford) 169, and that of case 8, IQ 185, EQ "in vicinity of 200." It is worth noting that both of these children developed in an extremely stimulating home environment, and that both are the few of the cases here presented whose careers subsequent to identification suggest authentic genius.

In some of the other cases there is a marked discrepancy between the IQ and EQ: Case 1, IQ 200, EQ (New Stanford) 158; Case 7, IQ 162, EQ (New Stanford) 134; Case 9, IQ 184, EQ (New Stanford Reading) 144. In no instance, however, does the educational quotient fall below the level attained (theoretically) by the best one per cent of school children (i.e. EQ 130).

School Progress

Of the 10 subjects who were at or above the first grade level at the time of their identification and for whom information is available concerning school progress, 8 were accelerated in school, some to an extreme degree. Cases 4 and 10 were in the 6th grade at age 8; case 3 was in the 6th grade at age 6; and case 2 was in the 8th grade at age 10. It is to be observed that in spite of this drastic acceleration these children are fully capable of doing the work of the grades in which they are placed. Each of them tested above grade in achievement. It is apparent, however, that this extreme acceleration imposes a handicap to making a satisfactory social and emotional adjustment.

With one exception these children attended traditionally organized schools. Recognition appears to have been given to the superiority of these children, in most instances, by either acceleration or enrichment. In some cases, however, teachers of these children were unaware of the extent of their deviation. The teacher who nominated child 1 as the "best student" in her 5th grade class named as the "most intelligent" a 12 year old girl of 90 IQ!

With two (or possibly three) exceptions these children attended segregated (on the basis of race) schools.

Occupation and Education of Parents

These exceptional children typically come from homes of high socio-economic status. Their fathers are found predominantly in occupations which require a high order of ability. Thus, three are college teachers, two are attorneys, and one each is a physician, pharmacist, social work executive, journalist and electrical engineer. Not all of the fathers, however, rank so high on the occupational scale. Thus, one is a government clerk, one is machinist and one is a porter. In terms of the Taussig scale classification, ten are in class V (professional); one in class IV (clerical or semi-intellectual occupation); one in Class III (skilled labor); and one is in class I (unskilled occupation).

Among the mothers who are employed, four are teachers, one a government clerk and one a psychiatrist's aide. Interestingly enough, of the eight mothers who are now housewives, five are former teachers. Thus, altogether nine of the mothers either are, or have been, school teachers.

The educational level of the parents is of course consonant with their occupational status. Of the fathers, ten are college graduates and eight of these hold either graduate or professional degrees. The lowest level of training reported for any one of the fathers is second year high school. Of the mothers, three are college graduates, two of these holding graduate degrees, and six have the equivalent of two years of college training. The lowest level of training reported for any one of the mothers is at the high school level.

In view of the fact that the writer has not personally visited the homes of all the subjects, the material level of the home environments cannot here be described with certainty. In general, however, these children come from middle-class homes. None of the parents is wealthy, but most are sufficiently well-to-do to afford their children advantages superior to those of the average American home. In several instances, however, families are characterized by economic insecurity; in three cases parents have been WPA employees, and in another case the father is employed as a porter.

Familial Background

The familial background of the subjects has not, in most cases, been fully explored. There is evidence in some cases, however, of individuals of exceptional ability in the family lines. The father of case ___ was the first Negro to be awarded Phi Beta Kappa at the University of Illinois; the grandfather of case ___ was an eminent biologist and the first Negro to be awarded the Ph.D. degree by the University of Chicago; the grandfather of case ___ was an inventor; the grandfather of case ___ was a composer and the first person to collect and publish Negro spirituals. There are, in addition, numerous individuals in the families of these children who have been highly successful physicians, teachers, attorneys, and the like, in their own communities.

It is possible that further search will reveal a larger incidence of eminent ancestry. But it must be understood that even the most exceptional members of the racial group of which these subjects are members have a much more restricted opportunity for attaining eminence than do members of the dominant racial group in this country.

Racial Composition

There is no valid method for determining the degree of racial mixture; indeed, there is no really valid method for determining race. Nevertheless an attempt is made here to present a rough picture of the racial composition of the subjects. Based on a combination of the genealogical report of the parents and observation of the subject, the cases are classified in the following categories: (1) no apparent white ancestry (N); (2) more Negro than white ancestry (NNW); (3) approximately equal amounts of Negro and white ancestry (NW); (4) more white than Negro ancestry (NWW). Under this classification the subjects are distributed as follows:

N-2; NNW-4; NW-3; NWW-4. It is to be seen that each category of racial mixture is represented among the subjects.[8] It is of some interest to note that three of the subjects are the progeny of Negro fathers and white mothers.

Other Characteristics

Many additional details about these subjects—their social adjustment, their health histories, their emotional maturity, and their developmental histories will not be presented here because full data concerning these characteristics have not yet been assembled. On the basis of information now at hand, however, the generalization may be made that the Negro child of extremely high IQ manifests

---

[8] Competent anthropologists estimate that approximately 80 per cent of the Negro population in the United States has some amount of white ancestry. It is probable that in the urban communities from which these subjects come the percentage is even higher.

essentially the same characteristics as the white child of extremely high IQ, at least during the early years of his development.

Conclusions

The case study as a method is valuable in revealing factors that contribute to individual development. It has the disadvantage, however, of usually requiring a very large number of cases to provide a basis for reliable generalizations. Certainly the cases presented in this study do not constitute an adequate or complete description of the highly gifted Negro child. Nevertheless, the data are sufficiently extensive to permit the derivation of several general conclusions.

Perhaps the most important fact revealed by this study is that an appreciable number of Negro children of extremely high IQ are to be found. These extreme deviates are of the greatest significance as they indicate that Negroes are as variable as other racial groups and that Negro ancestry is not a limiting factor, *per se*, in psychometric intelligence. These cases give emphasis to the fact that it is individual differences rather than so-called racial differences which are important. The late Havelock Ellis, in discussing the subject presented here as Case 1, gave expressions to this point of view as follows: "Little B is thus a significant and instructive figure. She exemplifies Dr. Buhler's doctrine of the predominance of individuality over race. . . . And further, while we have to recognize the deep-rooted prejudice of the white man where the black man is concerned, we see that there is no ground for the commonly proclaimed limiting influence of Negro blood on intelligence."[9]

The second major generalization to be derived from these cases is that they demonstrate that we may discover extreme deviates in psychometric intelligence in our schools unrecognized and denied the type of educational experiences which are necessary for their best development. The fact that this study includes only children identified in large urban communities (New York, Chicago, Washington, and Cincinnati) gives added weight to this conclusion. There is no reason to believe that Negro children of the IQ level being considered here are concentrated in the cities represented by the cases studied. It may be concluded, or at least hypothesized, that similar children, unidentified and unrecognized, are to be found in other communities throughout the country, their potential usefulness to society, partly or wholly lost.

Finally, these cases bring into sharp focus the limitations which our society places on the development of the highly gifted Negro. These children are nurtured in a culture in which racial inferiority of the Negro is a basic assumption. Consequently, they will experience throughout their lives, educational, social and occupational restrictions which must inevitably affect achievement and motivation. Wide individual differences, of course, are to be anticipated in reaction to this con-

---

[9] Havelock Ellis, "Precocious Children," *Chicago Herald and Examiner*, Je 8, 1935, p. 7.

dition. Some of these individuals will meet frustration and draw away; others will go on to careers of high usefulness and accomplishment.

The abstract mental tests that contribute to the IQ do not measure the factors of personality and motivation that largely determine success in life. The findings of studies of gifted children, especially those of Terman and of Hollingworth, indicate that the highly gifted children identified in the elementary school does, in high school, college and early adulthood, usually fulfill his early promise. But not always is this true; failure among the gifted is frequent. The present article is concerned only with the characteristics of the subjects at the time of their identification. It is to be expected that study of the future development of these and similar cases will provide a test not only of the hypothesis that the dysgenic environment in which the highly gifted Negro finds himself inhibits accomplishment, but also of other hypotheses concerning the constancy of high psychometric ratings, the likelihood of satisfactory personal and social adjustment of the highly gifted, and the effect of factors, as material environment and drive, upon achievement.[10]

---

[10] The present study is one of a number of studies concerning superior Negro children and adults now being carried on in the Department of Education at Howard University. The writer solicits information from any reliable source concerning such individuals.

CHAPTER 15

The Upper Limit of Ability Among American Negroes

Martin D. Jenkins

Professor Jenkins (Ph.D., Northwestern, 1935) has taught at Virginia State College, North Carolina Agricultural and Technological College, and Cheyney Training School for Teachers; since 1938 he has been teaching at Howard University. A specialist in educational psychology, Dr. Jenkins became interested in gifted children while studying for his doctorate.

More than three decades of psychometric investigation among American Negroes has yielded a rich fund of information concerning this population group. Perhaps the most generally known finding, and certainly the most emphasized, is that when "comparable" groups of whites and Negroes are tested, the Negro group is almost invariably inferior to the white in psychometric intelligence (intelligence as measured by psychological tests). Preoccupation with the significance of the low *average* performance of Negro groups has served to divert attention from an equally important phenomenon—the variability of the group and especially the upper limit reached by its really superior members.

The question of the upper limit of ability among Negroes has both theoretical and practical significance. Psychologists generally attribute the low average performance of Negro groups on intelligence tests to cultural factors. It is well known that Negroes generally experience an inferior environment; and there is certainly no question but that an inferior environment tends to depress the psychometric intelligence. There are, however, many Negro children who are nurtured in an environment that is equal or superior to that of the average white child. Thus, we may hypothesize that *if race in itself is not a limiting factor in intelligence, then, among Negroes whose total environment compares favorably with that of the average American*

Reprinted from Jenkins, M. D. (1948). The upper limit of ability among American Negroes. *The Scientific Monthly, 66*, 399–401. Reprinted with permission of AAAS.

white, there should be found a "normal" proportion of very superior cases, and the upper limit of ability should coincide with that of the white population. This hypothesis is especially attractive from a negative aspect; thus, if very superior individuals are not to be found in the Negro population, the environmental explanation would clearly be inadequate to account for the phenomenon. The existence of such individuals, on the other hand, would afford additional evidence, but not absolute proof, of course, of the validity of the environmental explanation of "racial differences" in psychometric intelligence.

The practical significance of the question is apparent. If Negroes are to be found at the highest levels of psychometric intelligence, then we may anticipate that members of this racial group have the ability to participate in the culture at the highest level. In these days of reconsideration of the role of the dark races throughout the world, this question has more than mere national significance.

Analysis of the literature relating to the intelligence-test performance of Negro children reveals that a considerable number of these children have been found within the range that reaches the best 1 percent of white children (I.Q. 130 and above) and at the level of "gifted" children (I.Q. 140 and above). There are at least sixteen published studies that give an account of Negro children possessing I.Q.'s above 130; twelve of these report cases above I.Q. 140. These investigations were made by different psychologists in various localities and under varying conditions; moreover, the I.Q.'s were derived by a number of different tests. Further, the populations studied were located almost exclusively in Northern urban communities. Consequently, one may not justifiably generalize, from a composite of these studies, concerning the incidence of Negro deviates. It is of significance, however, that of the 22,301 subjects included in the thirteen studies for which N's are reported, 0.3 percent scored at I.Q. 140 and above, and fully 1 percent scored at I.Q. 130 and above. These percentages are similar to those obtained from a "normal" I.Q. distribution of American school children.

Of especial significance are the cases of very bright children of Binet I.Q. 160 and above. It may be estimated that fewer than 0.1 percent of school children are found to be at or above this level. As the I.Q. rises above 160 the frequency occurrence, of course, decreases. Statistically, cases at or above I.Q. 180 should occur about once in a million times, although they actually occur with somewhat greater frequency. In his classic California study of the gifted, Terman found only 15 children testing as high as I.Q. 180; and Hollingworth reports: "In twenty-three years seeking in New York City and the local metropolitan area I found only twelve children who test at or above 180 I.Q. (S-B)." It is apparent then, that children who test upwards of Binet I.Q. 160 are extreme deviates in psychometric intelligence and representative of the very brightest children in America.

I have assembled from various scores the case records of 18 Negro children who test above I.Q. 160 on the Stanford-Binet examination. Seven of these cases test above I.Q. 170, 4 above I.Q. 180 and 1 at I.Q. 200. Two of these cases were tested initially by me; the other 16 were reported by psychologists in university centers and public school systems. Analysis of the case records indicates that these children during the early years of their development, at least, manifest the same characteristics as do other very high I.Q. children: originality of expression, creative ability, and surpassing performance in school subjects. Some of these children, but not all, are greatly accelerated in school progress. Two, for example, had completed their high-school course and were regularly enrolled university students at age thirteen; both of these subjects were elected to Phi Beta Kappa and earned the baccalaureate degree at age sixteen.

It is of some significance that all these children were found in Northern or border state cities (New York, Chicago, Washington, and Cincinnati). No Southern Negro child, so far as I have been able to ascertain, has been identified as testing at or above Binet I.Q. 160. It is certain that among the 80 percent of the total Negro population that lives in the Southern states, children with potentiality for such development exist. Whether the fact that no children with this development have been discovered is due to lack of environmental opportunity and stimulation, or merely to lack of identification, is not surely known.

I am not attempting here to show that approximately as many Negro children as white are to be found at the higher levels of psychometric intelligence. There appears little doubt that the number of very bright Negro children is relatively smaller than the number of bright white children in the total American population. Nevertheless, it is apparent that children of very superior psychometric intelligence may be found in many Negro populations, and that the upper limit of the range attained by the extreme deviates is higher than is generally believed.

The performance of extreme deviates at the college and adult levels has not yet been extensively studied. Such evidence as is available, however, indicates that at maturity, as in childhood, some Negroes are to be found at the highest level of psychometric intelligence. In a recent unpublished study conducted at Howard University, it was found that of approximately 3,500 Negro freshmen entering the College of Liberal Arts over a period of seven years, 101 scored in the upper decile, and 8 in the upper centile (national norms) on the American Council on Education Psychological Examination. In a more extensive study, the National Survey of Higher Education of Negroes, there were, among 3,684 students in twenty-seven Negro institutions of higher education located chiefly in the Southern states, 23 cases in the upper decile and 4 in the upper centile on the A.C.E. Psychological Examination. It is of some significance that in the same study 12 upper decile cases are reported among the 105 Negro students in two Northern universities (almost half as many as were found altogether among the 3,684 students in the twenty-seven Negro colleges). This contrast is in accord with the general but undocumented opinion that among Negro college students there are proportionately fewer extreme deviates in psychometric intelligence in the Southern segregated colleges than in the Northern nonsegregated institutions.

The Army General Classification Test data assembled during World War II have not yet become fully available. One may predict with a fair degree of confidence, however, that these data will reveal some Negro cases at the very highest levels of performance. In view of the fact, however, that the Negro selectees were predominantly from communities that provide inadequate provision for the educational and cultural development of Negroes, we may expect that a very small proportion of the total population will be found at the higher levels of performance. Subgroups which have had a normal cultural opportunity should, in accordance with our hypothesis, yield an appreciable proportion of superior deviates.

The findings of the studies cited in this article support the hypothesis formulated at the outset. In some population groups there is to be found a "normal" proportion of Negro subjects of very superior psychometric intelligence, and the extreme deviates reach the upper limits attained by white subjects. Although the incidence of superior cases is much lower among Negroes than whites, a phenomenon which might well be accounted for by differential environmental factors, we may conclude that race per se (at least as it is represented in the American Negro) is not a limiting factor in psychometric intelligence.

The abstract mental tests that contribute to psychometric intelligence do not measure the factors of personality and motivation that largely determine success in life. The findings of studies of gifted children, especially those of Terman, Hollingworth, and Witty, indicate that the highly gifted child usually fulfills his early promise. But not always. Failure among the gifted is also frequent.

The data of this article bring into sharp focus the limitations that our society places on the developmental of the highly gifted Negro. These superior deviates are nurtured in a culture in which racial inferiority of the Negro is a basic assumption. Consequently, they will typically experience throughout their lives educational, social, and occupational restrictions that must inevitably affect motivation and achievement. The unanswered question relative to the influence of this factor on the adult achievement of superior Negroes is a problem for future investigators to solve.

CHAPTER 16

Intellectually Superior Negro Youth: Problems and Needs

Martin D. Jenkins
President, Morgan State College

INTRODUCTION

This chapter is concerned with the problems and needs of intellectually superior Negro children and adolescents. For present purposes the term, intellectually superior youth, is arbitrarily defined to include those children and adolescents who rank in approximately the upper five per cent of their local population in psychometric intelligence or school achievement. This percentage is not, however, to be regarded as unduly rigid. Superiority is a relative term, and whether the upper ten percent or the upper one per cent of youth are regarded as superior, the generalizations developed in this discussion apply with equal force. It is important to observe, further, that concern here is with the youth who are superior in their local group; not merely those who are superior in terms of national norms.

The present discussion is based on the thesis that the conservation of intellectual capital is one of the major obligations of education—that this responsibility is particularly encumbent upon schools serving Negro youth. Beset as we are, racially, by almost insuperable handicaps, we can ill-afford to squander our intellectual capital by neglecting the development of those highly endowed individuals who are best fitted to assume positions of leadership.

The Factual Background[1]

Analysis of the literature relating to the intelligence-test performance of Negro children reveals that a considerable number of these children have been found within the range that reaches the best 1 per cent of white children (IQ 130 and above) and at the level of "gifted" children (IQ 140 and above). There are at least sixteen published studies that give an account of Negro children possessing IQ's above 130; twelve of these report cases above IQ 140. These investigations were made by different psychologists in various localities and under varying conditions; moreover, the IQ's were derived by a number of different tests. Further, the populations studied were located almost exclusively in Northern urban communities. Consequently, one may not justifiably generalize, from a composite of these studies, concerning the incidence of Negro deviates. It is of significance, however, that the 22,301 subjects included in the thirteen studies for which N's are reported. 0.3 per cent scored at IQ 140 and above, and fully 1 per cent scored at IQ 130 above. These percentages are similar to those obtained from a "normal" IQ distribution of American school children.

Of especial significance are the cases of very bright children of Binet IQ 160 and above. It may be estimated that fewer than 0.1 per cent of American school children are to be found at or above this level. The writer has assembled from various sources the case records of 18 Negro children who test above IQ 160 on the Stanford-Binet examination.[2] Seven of these cases test above IQ 170, 4 above IQ 180, and 1 at IQ 200. Analysis of the case records indicates that these children during their early years of their development, at least, manifest the same characteristics as do other very high IQ children: originality of expression, creative ability, and surpassing performance in school subjects. Some of these children, but not all, are greatly accelerated in school progress. Two, for example, had completed their high-school course and were regularly enrolled university students at age thirteen; both of these subjects were elected to Phi Beta Kappa and earned the baccalaureate degree at age sixteen.

The performance of extreme deviates at the college and adult levels has not yet been extensively studied. Available evidence, however, indicates that at maturity, as in childhood, some Negroes are to be found at the highest level of psychometric intelligence. In an unpublished study conducted at a leading university for Negro youth, it was found that of approximately 3,500 Negro freshmen entering the college over a period of seven years, 101 scored in the upper decile, and 8 in the upper centile (national norms) on the American Council on Education Psychological Examination. In a more extensive study, the National Survey of Higher Education

---

[1] This section, drawn largely from the writer's article, "The Upper Limit of Ability Among American Negroes," *Scientific Monthly*, 66: 399 – 401, My 1948, summarizes studies of superior Negro youth in the upper 1 per cent American youth in psychometric intelligence.
[2] Martin D. Jenkins, "Case Studies of Negro Children of Binet IQ 160 and Above," *Journal of Negro Education*, 13:159–66, Spring, 1943.

of Negroes,[3] there were, among 3,684 students in twenty-seven Negro institutions of higher education, located chiefly in the Southern states, 23 cases in the upper decile and 4 in the upper centile on the American Council on Education Psychological Examination. It is of some significance that in the same study 12 upper decile cases are reported among the 105 Negro students in two Northern universities, almost half as many as were found altogether among the 3,684 students in the twenty-seven Negro colleges. This contrast is in accord with the general but undocumented opinion that among Negro college students there are proportionately fewer extreme deviates in psychometric intelligence in the Southern segregated colleges than in the Northern non-segregated institutions.

It is not the attempt here to show that approximately as many Negro youth as white are to be found at the higher levels of psychometric intelligence. There appears little doubt that the number of very bright Negro youth as measured by current intelligence tests is relatively smaller than the number of bright white youth in the total American populations. Nevertheless, it is apparent that subjects of very superior psychometric intelligence may be found in many Negro populations, and that the upper limit of the range attained by the extreme deviates is higher than is generally believed.

SPECIAL PROBLEMS OF SUPERIOR NEGRO YOUTH

The problems of superior Negro youth are similar to those of superior youth generally; the racial factor, however, accentuates these problems in varying degrees. The superior Negro youth, as a consequence, typically has special social and educational needs different in degree, and in some instances almost different in kind, from those of the youth population as a whole.

Discussed briefly below are six special problems of the typical superior Negro youth; *i.e.*, problem areas in which the Negro youth is more likely than his white counterpart to encounter difficulty or neglect. It is to be held in mind that the discussion deals with the *typical* superior Negro child. There is always the danger, when dealing with averages, that the wide range of social and educational experiences of individual children will be obscured. The problems presented here do not apply with equal force to every youth. It is to be recognized that the impact of varying environmental experience creates for every individual child a unique problem pattern and a unique needs pattern.

1. *The superior Negro youth is less likely than his white counterpart in the general population to be identified as superior.* This problem has two phases, the first being in the area of *expectation*. It is a curious fact that many school people simply do not expect to find highly superior Negro children. On numer-

---
[3] *General Studies of College for Negroes.* (Vol. II of the *National Survey of the Higher Education of Negroes),* Washington: U.S. Government Printing Office, 1942. Ch. 5.

ous occasions, teachers from elementary level through college have been heard to express discouragement at not having any bright youngsters in their classes. During the writer's search for gifted Negro children in the Chicago public schools a number of years ago, doubt was expressed by a number of teachers, and even some college professors, that the population to be studied would yield an appreciable number of such cases. Interviews with Negro college students who rank in the upper tenth of American college students in psychometric intelligence have frequently yielded responses from subjects who had attended racially-mixed high schools to the effect that may administrators, teachers, and counselors discount the superiority of any Negro child.

These are, of course, fragmentary and impressionistic data. It is not to be concluded that school people, generally, are unaware of the existence of the superior Negro youth. The attitude described is sufficiently general, however, as to increase the difficulty of identification of the superior Negro youth.[4]

The second phase of this problem is that of identification. The superior child is identified most readily and most accurately by the use of standardized tests. The typical Negro youth is likely to be in a school where these psychometric devices are not used. A large number, perhaps a majority, of superior children are outstanding in their academic performance, but many are not. It is the members of this latter group who are likely to remain undetected and whose true abilities may never be recognized.

2. *The superior Negro child is less likely to be in a school which gives special attention to his needs.* Although educational authorities are not in agreement as to the best method of organizing the curricular experiences for superior children, there is full agreement that some special adaptation is required. Progressive schools and teachers have utilized a number of approaches, including special classes and enrichment at the elementary and secondary levels; and special sections, honors, plans and enrichment at the college level. The typical Negro youth is likely to be in a school which does not utilize any of these procedures. As an inescapable result many superior youth never have their abilities really challenged and are not encouraged to realize their highest potentialities.

3. *The superior Negro child is less likely to have adequate educational and vocational guidance.* One of the differentiating characteristics of good and poor schools is the quality and extent of the guidance services rendered their children. The superior school, by means of its competent guidance person-

---

[4] The view that Negroes are not found at the upper ability levels is a pervasive one which is sometimes held in very important quarters. For example, E. W. Kenworthy in an article in the New York Times Magazine for June 11, 1950, quotes the conclusions of official War College studies made as late as 1940 that, "the Negro is far below the whites in capacity to absorb instruction" and that Negroes are, "incapable of mastering the more technical military jobs."

nel, its testing program, its curricular organization and its library and other resources makes a planned and deliberate attempt to encourage pupils to make educational and vocational choices consistent with their abilities and interests. The typical Negro youth finds himself in an inferior school in which this type of program is virtually absent, and in which he receives little assistance in making crucial educational and vocational decisions.

The superior Negro youth in non-segregated schools, even those with an excellent guidance program, face a peculiar handicap. Time and again, the writer has had products of such schools report that their white teachers and counselors appeared to be completely unaware of the expanding occupational opportunities available to Negro youth, particular those of superior ability. In this unawareness, such teacher and counselors sometimes channel superior Negro youth into low-level trade and industrial occupations rather than into the higher-level occupations for which their abilities fit them.

4. *The superior Negro youth is less likely to have an intellectually stimulating environment and is, therefore, less likely to achieve near the upper level of his potentiality.* The typical Negro youth attends a school which is quantitatively and qualitatively substandard. It is unnecessary here to adduce statistical evidence of the overcrowding, poor physical facilities, inadequate laboratories and libraries, insufficient teaching and guidance personnel which characterize the schools attended by a majority of Negro youth. Whatever their intellectual level Negro youth, generally, have been crippled by their schools.

A concomitant of substandard school which the superior Negro youth typically attends is the low-average achievement level of the school population of which he is a member. This phenomenon has a two-fold effect upon the superior Negro youth: he learns to accept and be satisfied with low standards of performance, and he lacks sufficient competition among his fellows to make him extend himself intellectually.

The superior Negro youth experiences an equally inferior out-of-school environment: on the physical side, the typically poor home and poverty stricken community; the absence of adequate libraries, art galleries, museums, theaters, and other cultural institutions. On the psychic side, the absence of parental and community example and stimulation to intellectual achievement; the essential anti-intellectualism achievement; the essential anti-intellectualism of his peers (and frequently his community leaders and teachers); and the feeling of frustration engendered by our biracial social order.

The effect of the school and community environment in which the typical Negro youth develops is perhaps the most serious and significant handicap of the superior Negro youth.

5. *The superior youth is more likely to be of low social economic level, and is therefore less likely to persist and achieve at high level in school.* Examination of the statistics of enrollment in any public school system in the country will reveal the great academic mortality of the Negro school population. A much smaller proportion of the Negro youth compared to the whites enter and finish the work of secondary and college levels. Although many factors contribute to this attrition, the economic factor is an important contributing cause. The factor of poverty weighs much more heavily upon Negro youth than white and it is reasonable to assume that a larger proportion of superior Negro youth than white fail to continue their formal education for financial reasons.

   The economic factor plays an important part too in the achievement of many of these youth who do persist in school. The youth who must work his way through high school and college, often at a bare subsistence level, seldom has the time and energy to do full justice to his intellectual development.

6. *The superior Negro youth is likely to become preoccupied with racial matters to the detriment of achievement in other areas.* Race is the most important single fact in the life of any American Negro. Wherever he lives and whatever he does for a living he is every conscious of the restrictions placed upon him and his fellows by their racial identity. It is almost inevitable that the superior Negro youth will become more sensitive to and more preoccupied with racial problems than Negro youth generally. It is almost inescapable that he will spend a considerable portion of this time studying problems of race and participating in protest movements.

   The most superior cases bring into sharp focus the limitations which our society places on the development of the highly gifted Negro. These youth are nurtured in a culture in which racial inferiority of the Negro is a basic assumption. Consequently, they will experience throughout their lives educational, social, and occupational restrictions which must inevitably affect achievement and motivations. Wide individual differences, of course, are to be anticipated in reaction to this condition. Some of these individuals will meet frustration and draw away; others will go to careers of high usefulness and accomplishment.

Remedial Measures

It is always easier, of course, to discern problems than to define solutions. Some of the problems mentioned above arise out of deep-seated maladjustments of our social order and are subject to no ready solution; others may be immediately and successfully attacked by our schools and other agencies. Adequate provision for the conservation of intellectual talent among Negro children and adolescents will entail re-orientation with respect to the problem of individual differences, and reorganization of established educational and social practices. The needs and remedial measures suggested by the problems of the superior Negro youth may now be considered.

Our failure to recognize superior Negro youth is, without doubt, due in part to the fact that our thinking has been conditioned too much by the low-average performance of students in our schools and colleges. So concerned have we been with the needs of remedying, in part, the meager educational backgrounds of substandard students, with the need of raising the general average level of achievements, that we have neglected almost entirely the very existence of those individuals who constitute the most valuable intellectual material we have. Every administrator and teacher in our schools must recognize the existence and potential value of these individuals to society and to the race. Writers of books and articles dealing with the Negro should, where appropriate, give especial attention to the dissemination of information about the existence and performance of superior individuals.

1. *The need for the identification of youth of superior ability.* In a well organized school system the superior child is identified through periodic testing at the elementary and secondary levels. At the college level the superior youth is discovered by the means of intelligence and achievement tests, particularly those administered in the freshman year. An appreciable proportion of the schools attended by Negro youth do attempt some objective measurement of ability. In many instances, however, the test results are either not used, or emphasis is placed upon the identification and treatment of the below average rather than the superior youth; thus, the program often does not function in the identification of first-rate minds.

    Testing, although important, is alone not sufficient. Due to the fact that Negro youth so often are found in a substandard environment many have not had an opportunity to gain the experiences presupposed by the standardized test technique. We may find, consequently, students who test relatively low but who achieve high; these youth who manifest surpassing educational performances must be included as members of the superior group.

    The identification of talent is an essential prerequisite to the conservation of talent. Schools and colleges need to develop functional testing programs which have as a major objective the identification of superior students. Classroom teachers from elementary school through college should be ever on the alert to discover the most talented of their pupils.

2. *The need for curricular provision for superior students.* The crux of the problem of conservation lies at the point of adaptation of the curriculum to meet the needs of the superior youth. All too often one hears the statement, "The good student needs no special provision, he will take care of himself." The tragic waste which inheres in such a point of view cannot be too greatly overstressed. If educators of Negro youth are to make it possible for superior individuals to realize their own high potentialities, it must be recognized that the superior student does not "adequately take care of himself" under the traditional school organization. Especially designed educational experiences must be provided superior youth.

    Special provision for superior youth at the elementary, secondary, and college levels may take the form of (1) special classes, of which homogeneous grouping, sectioning, and at the college level, honors courses, are variants; (2) acceleration, which may also be accomplished by permitting the pupils to carry extra subjects; and (3) curriculum enrichment. Descriptions of the various plans used by school and colleges may be found in any textbook on exceptional children. [5]

    Moderate acceleration, plus the type of enrichment which provides wide experiences for the pupil, which stimulates him to do independent and creative work, and which prepares him for his role as a leader, is in the writer's opinion, the most fruitful method of providing for the needs of superior youth. This type of enrichment involves recognition of pupils' interests, larger individual freedom, encouragement of creative and research-type work projects, and independent reading. Ideally, the curriculum should conform to this pattern for all children. If, however, complete individualization of instruction cannot be achieved in large and unwieldy classes, certainly the planning of work for the relatively few superior children in each classroom should not be beyond the ingenuity of teachers and administrators. The conservation of talent places upon schools and colleges serving Negro youth an urgent responsibility for adaptation of the curriculum to meet the needs of superior individuals.

3. *The need of adequate education and vocational guidance of superior youth.* The school should, of course, provide guidance for all; certainly all school people accept the view that guidance is an integral part of the educative process. The need for guidance is particularly acute in the case of the highly endowed individual. If we accept the same premise that the superior youth constitute our greatest social asset, then it becomes apparent that ineffective guidance of these youth results in a type of dissipation of resources which we can least afford. Adequately conceived personnel procedures, sufficiently well oriented with respect to the problem of the superior stu-

---

[5] For a recent brief discussion *cf.*, Merle R. Sumption, Dorothy Norris and Lewis M. Terman, "Special Education for the Gifted Child," *49th Yearbook, National Society for the Study of Education,* 1950. Part II, pp. 259–80.

dent, will help assure that that this type of individual will not make an attempt at educational and occupational adjustment on a level below that which he is capable of attaining.

Through guidance procedures the superior Negro youth should come to have a clear understanding of his occupational opportunities and of his possible role as an occupational pioneer. Every Negro youth, and this applies with special force to the superior youth, must understand that although his racial identity constitutes a severe handicap, he can aspire in this county to fill any position for which he has the requisite ability. As our social order becomes increasingly democratic, Negro youth have increasing opportunities to occupy jobs and positions not formerly held by Negroes. As these new opportunities develop it is highly important that the initial occupant be able to fulfill his role as a pilot. He must, of course, be highly capable in a job sense. But equally important, he must be adaptable, willing to stand the slurs and ostracism of his coworkers, without developing feelings of frustration and bitterness. This is an important guidance and educational task which is being largely neglected.

4. *The need for financial aid for students of superior ability.* The problem of providing financial aid to students of limited means is met with largely on the college level although the problem is by no means absent at the secondary level. It is unnecessary here to review the generally low economic status of Negro college students. Several investigations of the incomes of parents of students in Negro colleges afford cogent evidence that the typical student is supported by very meager financial resources. Without doubt, many students of high potential either are unable, because of inadequate finance, to enter college at all, or find it necessary to discontinue, for this reason, their collegiate training. There is an obvious need here for financial aid for these individuals, aid which, at the present time, must be provided largely by the colleges themselves.

Although all colleges provide varying amounts of scholarship assistance, in almost none of these institutions is this type of aid adequate. Particularly is this true among institutions for Negro youth. This is quite understandable, of course, when we consider the fact that all Negro institutions of higher learning are underfinanced; there is not enough money for building and equipment, for instructional purposes, for operating expenses. But somehow our colleges must facilitate the financial adjustment of students of high potential. This may be done in part by internal budgetary adjustment. It may be done in part by securing outside assistance. At Morgan State College, for example, the General Assembly of Maryland, at the request of college officials, provided twenty-nine scholarships, carrying full room, board, and tuition, to be awarded to outstanding graduates of the high schools of the State. It may be done in part by establishing and subsidizing a special search for superior youth as was done in the new regrettably-abandoned National Competition at Howard University. It may be done in part by encouraging individuals and organizations to provide financial assistance to students of high ability. This can be done in part at both the secondary and college levels, by helping students of high ability over critical financial emergencies by means of part-time jobs, loans, and other types of assistance.

The schools and colleges alone, however, cannot by themselves solve the problem of financial aid to students. It is to be hoped that, in the not-too-distant future, the Federal government will provide scholarships and loans for superior youth in order that their talents may, to a larger degree than at present, be conserved and utilized for the benefit of society.[6]

5. *The need for research concerning superior Negro youth.* Aside from the writer's fragmentary studies, practically no research has been devoted to the problem of superior Negro youth. This fertile field, which has remained unrecognized and uncultivated, fairly bristles with question marks. What is the incidence of superior Negroes in our schools and colleges? Is academic achievement highly correlated with mental level among the superior? What sex differences appear? What personality characteristics do these superior individuals manifest? What vocations do they enter and what factors contribute to their occupational success or failures? To what extent is our present leadership recruited from the ranks of the superior? How shall we define the superior youth in a population of low average IQ level? What kinds of curricular adaptations and teaching methods are most appropriate to meet the needs of superior youth? Certainly here is an area of sufficient sociological and psychological importance to merit the attention and to challenge the interest of able students.

6. *The need for a social order in which superior Negro youth will have full opportunity to participate in the occupational world during their adult years.* What will it profit us if we identify superior Negro youth and provide for all their needs in their early years and deny them opportunity to achieve in their adult years? Despite increasing opportunities, Negroes of superior abilities

---

[6] That the problem of providing for the needs of superior youth in this country is a serious and important one is suggested by the fact that the Educational Policies Commission has just issued a report, based upon a two-year study, calling upon the nation to make more adequate provision for its gifted young men and women. The Commission estimates, "that less than half the talents of gifted Americans are now being used because they fail to finish high school and college." It insists that, "The American people must invest a larger portion of their economic resources in the education of individuals of superior talent." See: *Baltimore Sun,* June 5, 1950, p. 1.

still face a tremendous handicap in the occupational world. Certainly the experience of a number of businesses and industries, the Federal government, school systems, and recently, the armed services, should allay the shibboleths that white persons will not work with or under the supervision of Negroes who occupy high level positions. Fair employment practices, which recognize ability and proficiency rather than race as qualifications for employment are an absolute essential if the nation is to realize the values inherent in the abilities of superior Negro youth.

The conservation of intellectual talent should be one of the major goals of modern education. To identify exceptional individuals, to provide opportunity for their development, to stimulate them to their highest achievement, to assure that their potentialities become actualities, are both an obligation of and an opportunity for teachers of Negro youth.

SECTION V

Assessment of Black Students

Donna Y. Ford, Malik S. Henfield, and Tarek C. Grantham

INTELLIGENCE

One of the most problematic and controversial topics in all of education is how to equitably design and execute assessment policies, practices, and procedures, including selecting and using tests and other instrumentation to measure intelligence. Assessment of intelligence of Black students, be it for gifted education, special education, college admissions, employment, or some other experience and opportunity, has a long history of bias that results in marginalizing the intellectual abilities of Blacks. Traditional paper-and-pencil standardized testing has played a detrimental role in Black students' underidentification and underrepresentation.

The relatively long history of inequities in standardized testing—test bias, test unfairness, misinterpretation of results, misuse of results, and more—has been given a substantial amount of attention in psychology (e.g., educational psychology, psychology of giftedness, Black psychology, counseling psychology) and education (e.g., teacher education, gifted education, special education, school counselor education) for centuries. Historically, no past or current era has been as contentious, entrenched, polemic, and full of abuse as the testing of slaves, Blacks, and immigrants and how to interpret and use their test results. As authors in this section tell us, we have much to learn about the assessment of Black intelligence and a long way to go.

Approaches to assessment that aim to equitably identify gifted Black students have received far too little attention in the field of gifted education. This section includes an extensive introduction and review of useful screening measures, psychometric assessment measures (tests), and assessment models. A call for nondiscriminatory assessment of Black intelligence encourages readers to focus on the macro and micro levels of the process to measure ability, focusing specifically on bias in testing.

Test bias scholarship has focused on demographic variables such as race, gender, language, income, region, and disability, to name a few. Whether the topic is test bias or test fairness, comparatively speaking, Black students have borne the weight of deficit thinking regarding their intelligence and potential. A comprehensive discussion of test bias is shared by The National Center for Fair and Open Testing (see http://fairtest.org/mission-statement for more information).

Terminology aside, the terms *fair* and *unbiased* are related but not synonymous. Having said this, the myriad issues and problems regarding test bias cannot and must not be considered without regard to the impact both have on equitable identification and eventual access.

This section explains many bias concerns related to the content of tests, as well as validity issues. For example, the reader is encouraged to consider the extent to which: (a) there are systematic differences in the meaning of test scores associated with (racial) group membership, (b) people from two groups who have the same observed score do not have the same standing on the trait of interest, and (c) a test predicts some criterion of interest in the systematic over- or underprediction based on group membership. Several statistical measures of test bias are described by the authors in this section as well.

Section V offers a discussion of test fairness, which concerns *how* a test is used and depends extensively on judgment or subjectivity. As with teacher referral, for example, subjectivity—even among researchers—is nearly impossible to achieve. It is an ideal but not real in a number of ways. Specifically, paper-and-pencil standardized tests are viewed by many gifted education and assessment professionals as neutral, objective measures, tools, or instruments. Authors in this section have challenged this view. The reader is asked to consider how items and responses (e.g., correct answers, wording, focus, content) determined by humans are truly neutral. To assume neutrality is naïve, colorblind, and a serious disservice to psychometrics and education! No test or instrument will ever be totally free of bias, so we must work in an equitable way to increase fairness in interpretation and use, particularly with the assessment of intelligence in Black people. As a result, educators and schools benefit, communities benefit, and gifted Black students themselves benefit. We believe this is a reasonable request!

CHAPTER 17

On Black Intelligence

Robert L. Williams
Department of Psychology
Washington University (St. Louis)

> *If a tree is to be judged by its fruit, if the intelligence of a race bears any relation to its accomplishment, it seems difficult to draw any conclusion other than that the Black and Brown races are inferior to the white race [R. S. Ellis, 1928: 284].*

The dispute over the intellectual inferiority of Black people and the corresponding problem of measuring Black intelligence have generated a great deal of heat during the past two decades. Because of the political, social, economic, educational, ethical, and legal considerations involved, discussions of racial differences in intelligence have created more controversy than any other single issue in the field of psychology. Some of the central disputants have compromised on occasion, but essentially there has been a sharp cleavage of opinion about the intelligence of Black people and intelligence testing. In a word, opinion is split over whether lower scores by Blacks on traditional ability tests are attributed primarily to genetic heritage or to such environmental factors as discrimination, poor diet, bad living conditions, inferior schools, or the bias of intelligence tests. It is seriously questioned today whether traditional ability tests may serve as valid measures of Black intelligence. In spite of the vast array of research accomplished during the past twenty years with regard to cultural bias in ability-testing, no satisfactory, culture-fair tests were developed.

The meaning of intelligence is rather diverse and, although considerable attention has been given this concept, it is still ill-used and poorly understood. The ambiguity and senselessness of the nature of intelligence is exceeded only by the research on ESP. Definitions of intelligence are so diverse that it would be impractical to list them here. A few examples are given as representative.

1. Intelligence is what the intelligence tests measure.
2. Intelligence is defined by a consensus among psychologists. It is the repertoire of the intellectual skills and knowledge available to a person at any one period of time (Humphreys, 1970).
3. Intelligence is the summation of the learning experiences of the individual (Wesman, 1968).
4. Intelligence is the aggregate or global capacity of the individual to act purposefully, to think rationally, and to deal effectively with his environment (Wechsler, 1944).

It is clear from the preceding examples that, not only is there lacking a consensus among psychologists regarding the definition of intelligence, but there is no absolute definition as well. From a Black perspective, the real concern is not merely that of defining intelligence, but one which challenges the basic scientific considerations of validity, reliability, and standardization of intelligence tests.

Validity

Validity pertains to the extent to which a test measures what it is intended to measure. Does the traditional ability test measure the intelligence of Black children? It is doubtful that current ability tests measure a Black child's "global capacity . . . to deal effectively with his environment." It is obvious enough that a Black child engages in many intelligent behaviors which are not validated in white, middle-class society. For example, a Black child might respond with, "My mother told me to hit 'em back if anybody hits me," to one of the standard IQ test questions. That answer actually represents "a summation of the learning experiences" for that particular Black child in his Black culture. It would be less than intelligent for the child to exhibit responses contrary to his teachings and to the dictates of his cultural norms. If one child is taught not to hit back and another is taught to hit back, it is a value judgment as to which is more intelligent teaching. Most tests take the philosophic frame of reference that white, middle-class standards are the correct ones.

Reliability and Objectivity

The reliability of a test refers to the extent to which a person earns the same score or rank each time he is measured. One of the most common causes of unreliability of a test is the inclusion of items which are scored on the basis of subjective judgment. For example, persons from different cultural backgrounds will respond differently to the question, "What is the thing to do if you find a purse with ten dollars in it?" One child might say, "Try to find the owner"; another might respond, "Keep it." Such items lack objectivity in scoring as they fail to take cultural differences into consideration. A Black perspective is penalized and, therefore, the reliability of such tests is low for measuring the intelligence of Black children.

STANDARDIZATION

A test must be representative of the group for whom it was intended. Two of the major ability tests—the Stanford-Binet and the Wechsler Scale for Children—excluded Blacks, Mexican Americans, and Puerto Ricans from the representative sample. If the purpose of standardizing a test is to make it useful for certain reference groups, then the WISC and Stanford-Binet are invalid for use with Blacks, Mexican Americans, and Puerto Ricans.

With regard to Black and white differences in intelligence, two main schools of thought have emerged: the deficit model and the cultural difference model.

The deficit model assumes that Black people are deficient when compared to whites in some measurable trait called intelligence, and that this deficiency is due to genetic or cultural factors or both. To support this notion, such terms as "heritability of IQ," "cultural deprivation," and "the disadvantaged" have been employed. Proponents of this school of thought assume that the intellectual and educational "deficit" suffered by the so-called culturally deprived is clearly revealed by such psychological tests as the Stanford-Binet, the Wechsler, Scholastic Aptitude Test, Stanford Achievement, Iowa Basic Skills, Graduate Record Examination, Miller Analogies, and others. These tests are devised to measure one's capacity to learn or, more specifically, what one has learned. The test items are supposedly selected on the basis that individuals of the same age have had the same opportunity to become familiar with the content of the items. Two five-year-old children, one Black and one white, from different cultural backgrounds, will answer quite differently such a question as, "What is the thing to do if another child hits you?" The deficit model assumes a set of acceptable, standard responses. If the Black child gives a response that is not validated as acceptable by the norm—e.g., "Hit 'em back"—he is declared deficient in his "ability to comprehend and size up certain social situations."

One's intelligence, according to this school of thought, is based on the solution of brief problems of various kinds and on the quality of one's response to a wide range of questions. The final, standardization score, which is called the Intelligence Quotient, or IQ, is usually computed so that it is given a scale score for which the average of the reference population is about 100. Jensen (1969) and Humphreys (1970), two proponents of the deficit model, claim that in the general population Blacks are about 15 IQ points, or one standard deviation, below whites.

It is important here to make a clear distinction between IQ and intelligence. They are not the same, although many researchers use the two interchangeably. IQ is a symbol which refers to a set of scores earned on a test, nothing more. An IQ per se cannot be inherited. Most of the research on intellectual differences between Blacks and whites is based on differences in test scores, or IQ. Since the tests are biased in favor of middle-class whites, all previous research comparing the intellectual abilities of Blacks and whites should be rejected completely. If Black children score lower on ability tests than white children, the difference does not mean that Black children are actually inferior in intelligence; all it means is that the Black children performed differently on the tests than whites. Test inferiority is not to be equated with actual inferiority. For too many years, American educators and psychologists have embraced the myth that low scores on ability tests are sufficient indicators of a weakness or deficit in the individuals' mental ability.

The deficit model therefore engages in faulty reasoning: if a child scores low on a test, he is classified as lacking the ability of those who scored higher. The model assumes that the low scorers and high scorers had similar or equal opportunities to learn the knowledge required by the tests. This assumption is not true. Another deficit model proponent states:

> Full-blooded Negroes are rarely met with in our graduate schools. Those classed as Negroes are usually Mulattoes. Even disregarding this fact, it is undeniable that the work of the Negroes is much inferior to that of the whites. They have not demonstrated the capacity to do the grade of scientific work done by the whites [Ellis, 1928: 289].

It is assumed in the above paragraph that the reason Blacks are not in graduate schools is because of their inferiority. The model does not consider the discriminatory practices used in preventing Blacks from being admitted to graduate schools.

Briefly stated, the cultural difference model asserts that the differences noted by psychologists in intelligence testing in family and social organizations and in the studies of the Black community are not the result of pathology, faulty learning, or genetic inferiority. These differences are manifestations of a viable and structured culture of the Black American. The difference model also acknowledges that Blacks and whites come from different cultural backgrounds which emphasize different learning experiences necessary for survival. To say that the Black American is different from the white American is not to say that he is inferior, deficient, or deprived. One can be unique and different without being inferior. The model therefore recognizes the difference between equality and sameness. Two pieces of fruit—e.g., an apple and an orange—may be equal in weight, in quality of goodness, and in marketability, but they are not the same. An apple cannot become an orange, and vice versa. Each must express its respective characteristics of "appleness" and "orangeness," yet both are fruit. Whereas the deficit model espouses a "get like me" response, the difference model endeavors to increase the number of options as to what constitutes acceptable and nonacceptable responses. Instead of being confined by an egalitarian doctrine that confuses equality with sameness, the cultural difference model recognizes that this society is pluralistic in nature where cultural differences abound.

Because of the vast cultural differences in Black and white societies, significant language differences are present. Differences in language and dialect may produce differences in cognitive learning styles, but a difference is not a deficiency. Linguists do not limit themselves to defining dialect as the way words are pronounced. "Dialect refers to the linguistic structure of a people. The dialect is a fully developed linguistic system" (Baratz and Baratz, 1968). Instead of calling Black language wrong, improper, or deficient in nature, one must realize that the Black child is speaking a well-developed language commonly referred to as nonstandard English.

Intelligence is frequently based quite heavily on language factors. It is a common observation that Black and white children do not speak alike. The differences in linguistic system favor white children since standard English is the lingua franca of the tests and public schools.

Take, for example, the Scholastic Aptitude Test (SAT) which contains a verbal and numerical factor. Those students who do not show high verbal or numerical ability score low on the SAT and are typically excluded from entering college. If this is true, then Blacks have been routinely excluded due to the different dialect and language system. It does not mean that Black people do not have the intellectual ability to compete in college. For example, Blacks typically are not inferior in verbal ability. The average Black adolescent will know how to "play the Dozens," and play them well. He will know from memory the "Signifying Monkey," "Shine," "Mr. Boon," and many other indicators of verbal ability, but these do not get measured in the typical classroom. In fact, many Black children can state bits of poetry and prose in iambic pentameters. A case in point is revealed in the following revision of a Mother Goose rhyme made by a bright, Black eight-year-old child:

> Baa Baa Black Sheep, have you any wool?
> Yes sir, yes sir, two bags full.
> One for the Black man, one for the Jew
> Sorry, Mr. Charlie, but none for you.

A special Commission on Tests appointed by the College Entrance Examination Board indicated that the Board Examinations taken by about 2,000,000 high school students a year failed to recognize and assess a wide variety of talents, skills, and mental attributes. Over the years many students, particularly Black ones, have been grossly penalized. Basically, the Commission on Tests found the SAT, which measures fluency in English and ability to deal with mathematical and spatial concepts, to be discriminatory against certain minority groups. Although high verbal and numerical abilities are generally those required in traditional academic liberal arts and scientific education, the commission found these indicators to be too narrow for application to all who might benefit from college. The commission recommended that the tests gradually be replaced by a flexible assortment of other tests, measuring not only verbal and mathematical ability, but many other dimensions of excellence. These dimensions included musical and artistic talents, sensitivity and commitment to social responsibility, political and social leadership, athletic, political, and mechanical skills, styles of analysis and synthesis, ability to express oneself through artistic, oral, nonverbal, or graphic means, ability to organize and manage information, ability to adapt to new situations, characteristics of temperature, and so on.

In a recent memo directed to school counselors, the Washington University Director of Admissions had these points to make:

> We believe that this university has a great deal to offer to a wide variety of students—the scholar and the singer, the debater and the dancer, the athlete, the artist and the actor, the editor and the engineer. Accordingly, we urge you to recommend capable, interesting students, even if there is some slight "lopsidedness" in their records. Where there is need for compensating strength for lower SAT scores, for instance, we will trust you to point this out to us. It is impossible to overemphasize how highly we regard your evaluation as we search for an ever-widening array of talents and abilities.

It is clear from this discussion that traditional ability tests play a major role in current educational procedures and consequently in determining what doors in life will be opened to a Black child. Tests are used to determine admission, grouping, selection, assignment to special classes, and educational tracts. If the tests are unfair (biased), then it is clear that they place (misplace) or label (mislabel) a certain portion of the population in general and the Black population in particular. Throughout the country, disproportionately large numbers of Black children are being misplaced in special education classes. Many states legally define the educable mentally retarded as those children obtaining an IQ below 80.

In St. Louis, during the academic year 1968–1969 Blacks comprised approximately 63.6% of the school population, whereas whites comprised 36.4%. Of 4,020 children in Special Education, 2,975 (76%) were Black; only 1,045 (24%) were white. Thus, there were three times as many Black children as white in classes for

the mentally retarded. Again, children are placed in these classes primarily on the basis of scores earned on biased intelligence tests. At its annual meeting in 1969 the Association of Black Psychologists called for a moratorium on the administration of IQ tests to Black children. The association charged that tests:
1. label Black children as uneducable;
2. place Black children in special classes;
3. potentiate inferior education;
4. assign Black children to lower educational tracks than whites;
5. deny Black children higher education opportunities; and
6. destroy position growth and development of Black children.

It is clear that the continued administration of traditional ability tests to Black children without correcting for the cultural bias is a violation of the child's Constitutional rights under the provisions of the Fourteenth Amendment for equal protection under the law. The Skelly-Wright decision in the case of Hobson v. Hansen in Washington, D.C., set an early precedent. In that decision, the Court ordered that the tract system be abolished, since unfair ability tests were used in sorting the children into tracts. Another case, Diana et al. v. the California State Board of Education, led to a decision in favor of a Mexican-American child and her parents. In Boston, the case of Pearl Stewart v. Agnes Phillips and the Massachusetts Board of Education charges that children are being placed in special classes irrationally and unfairly. Other court cases will follow in the near future.

While Jensen (1969) and Humphreys (1970) declare that Black people are inferior to white people in intelligence, the courts are reaching decisions which negate their allegations. Thus, it becomes merely an academic exercise to continue this straw man debate. Black professionals must be about the business of developing appropriate measuring instruments and educational models for Black children.

References

BARATZ, S. S. and J. C. BARATZ (1968) "Negro children and urban education: a cultural solution." Bull. of Minnesota Council for the Social Studies (Fall).
ELLIS, R. S. (1928) The Psychology of the Individual Differences. New York: D. Appleton.
HUMPHREYS, L. (1970) A personal communication.
JENSEN, A. R. (1969) "How much can we boost I.Q. and scholastic achievement?" Harvard Educ. Rev. 39: 1-123.
Commission on Tests (1970a) I. Righting the Balance. New York: College Entrance Examination Board.
---(1970b) II. Briefs. New York: College Entrance Examination Board.
WECHSLER, D. (1944) The Measurement of Adult Intelligence. Baltimore: Williams & Wilkins.
WESMAN, A. G. (1968) "Intelligence testing." Amer. Psychologist 23 (April): 267-274.

CHAPTER 18

Assessment and Identification of African-American Learners With Gifts and Talents

James M. Patton
The College of William & Mary

ABSTRACT: This article presents a schema designed to guide the development of theory, methodology, and research related to the psychoeducational assessment of African-American learners with gifts and talents. The relationships among African-American worldviews, needed psychoeducational assessment theory and methodology, and desirable assessment and identification instruments and practices are explored. Assessment paradigms, instruments, and practices most reliable and valid for identifying gifts and talents among African-American learners are offered.

Several researchers (e.g. Richert, 1987; VanTassel-Baska, Patton, & Prillaman, 1989) have observed that those whose gifts and talents are masked because they are racially and culturally different or socioeconomically at risk are often neglected within programs for gifted and talented students. Educators' philosophies, definitions, and identification processes related to these students are often contradictory, ineffective, and insufficient (Patton, Prillaman, & VanTassel-Baska, 1990). This observation is not new. More than a half-century ago, Jenkins (1936) observed:

> The gifted child has been the subject of extended research during the past fifteen years. Numerous studies, notably those of Terman, Witty, and Hollingworth have revealed much of psychological and educational significance concerning the incidence and character-

istics of American children of superior intelligence. The Negro child of superior intelligence, however, has been almost altogether neglected; little is known about the incidence and characteristics of such children. (p. 175)

One problem is that there is no systematic, well-defined logic of inquiry for assessing and identifying gifts and talents among African-American learners. Instead, attempts to identify gifts and talents among African Americans have frequently relied on assessment approaches that are not grounded in African-American worldviews, ethos, and culture and do not consider the types of intelligences African Americans have developed consonant with tasks viewed important by this group of individuals.

The purpose of this article is to offer a schema designed to guide theory and the development of assessment methodology and tests that should enhance our capacities to identify gifts and talents among African-American learners.

Philosophical and Theoretical Roots of Psychoeducational Testing

Theory, methodology, and practice in the social sciences emanate partially from one's set of philosophical premises or worldviews. This worldview shapes a specific logic of inquiry, modes of knowing, and ways of organizing and verifying knowledge, all of which are culture bound (Gordon, 1985). The seminal works of Gould (1977, 1981), Hilliard (1984), Nobles (1983), and Kamin (1974, 1975) have provided a thorough analysis of the shared cultural, philosophical, and political worldviews of the early European and Euro-American developers of intelligence tests. These Europeans shared a particular worldview and a perspective on the constructs of intelligence and giftedness that were reflected in their assessment theories and methodologies and are fundamental to the tenets of contemporary norm-referenced testing. These early test developers had a tradition of positivism and a penchant for valuing knowledge well adapted for deductive scientific analysis, knowledge that could be reduced to discrete measurement (Dixon, 1976). This orientation assumed not only hierarchical levels of abilities within limited constructs of intelligence, but also notions that IQ tests accurately measured intelligence and tapped universal mental aptitudes and abilities. Nobles (1987), Hilliard (1984), Guthrie (1976), Ogbu (1988), and others (e.g., Cole & Scribner, 1973; Sattler, Hilliard, Lambert, Albee, & Jensen, 1981; Vernon, 1969) have argued, however, that IQ tests more closely sample discrete, cognitive behavior valued by middle-class, Western-oriented societies, *not* universal cognitive capacities or processes.

According to Ogbu (1988), IQ tests measure distinct, Euro-centric cognitive skills, specific to Western culture. Because these tests are grounded on samplings of cognition and behavior valued by "the middle class in Western societies, they inevitably discriminate against members of other cultures" (p. 29) and cannot adequately measure intelligence of African Americans.

Despite abundant evidence of the shortcomings of traditional assessment and identification procedures, the practice of using unidimensional IQ tests and other norm-referenced tests continues unabated. In fact, VanTassel-Baska et al. (1989) found that 88.5% of the states responding to a national survey indicated use of traditional, norm-referenced tests in the identification of at-risk, gifted learners. Judge Peckham's ban on the use of IQ tests in assessing African-American learners in California is clearly the exception (Jensen, 1980).

Although African Americans compose approximately 16.2% of all students enrolled in America's public schools, they make up only 8.4% of those enrolled in programs for the gifted (Alamprese & Erlanger, 1988). Creating definitions of giftedness and psychoeducational assessment theory, methodology, practice, and tests that consider philosophical worldviews and cultural systems of African Americans should contribute to increasing the numbers of African Americans identified as gifted.

Developing a Theory of Assessment

Theory has been defined as a symbolic representation of experience (Kaplan, 1964). Theory serves as a medium through which experiences can be constructed and subsequently analyzed, synthesized, measured, interpreted, and criticized. Psychoeducational assessment is guided, shaped, and influenced by theory. Use of a particular test or method presupposes some implicit or explicit theory about the construct or attribute being measured and the inquiry method being employed (Kaplan, 1964). The selection of theory and method not only flows from one's culturally based philosophical worldviews but also influences the results of tests (Dixon, 1976).

Table 1 identifies aspects of a "pure" African-American philosophical system that could guide theory development related to the identification and development of constructs of intelligence and giftedness as well as subsequent selection of psychoeducational assessment methodologies and practices. The orientation in Table I is defined as "pure" because it reflects historical, classical, African-oriented, philosophical worldviews and ethos that provide the foundation for the deep structure unifying cultural themes of African Americans (Dixon, 1976).

As noted in the first column, African Americans embrace a holistic view of reality, or metaphysics, and incorporate a concern for contextual factors in all interpretations of knowledge. This view recognizes the functional connectedness of

Table 1
Some Fundamental Dimensions of Classical African-American-Oriented Philosophical Worldviews and Theoretical Orientations

Metaphysics	Axiology	Epistemology
Use of a Holistic View of Reality	Importance of Person-to-Person Interaction	Affective Orientation
The individual tends to engage in synthetical and contextual thinking. Emphasis is placed on viewing the "whole" field and then understanding the interconnectedness of what might seem to be disparate parts of the field.	The individual is committed to developing strong social bonds that often transcend individual privileges. Communal existence is paramount to individual reality. Interpersonal relations and leadership skills are valued parts of this belief system.	The individual places emphasis on emotions and feelings and is sensitive to emotional cues. The tendency for emotional expressiveness is usually apparent. Connecting the affective with cognitive and psychomotor ways of knowing is important.

Note: The information obtained in the metaphysics and axiology sections of this table are drawn from the philosophical and conceptual works of Dixon (1976), Nichols (1976), Maurier (1979), and Nobles (1991). Information in the epistemology section is drawn from these same authors and the theoretical work of Boykin (1983).

the whole and its parts and the importance placed on the unity of ideas and the unity of people in African-American culture. Knowledge is advanced through a union of seemingly opposite realities; the unknown is revealed by a logic of inquiry that pulls together what appears to be contradictions. Distinctions are not made between beliefs and actions and intelligence and doing. Accordingly, intelligence must be mediated in "doing" something; it must be applied for some purpose. Also, this holistic metaphysical orientation coexists with a complementary belief system consistent with this view of ultimate reality.

According to the axiological and epistemological orientations offered in Table 1, interpersonal relationships have ultimate value. Relationships with people are valued over all interactions. The ability to use skills in interpersonal relations in the development of leadership gifts and talents is strongly valued in this belief system. Further, knowledge is gained through affective as well as cognitive processes; in fact, this schema presumes that a false dichotomy exists between the two.

Certainly, all African Americans do not embrace this "pure" philosophical system. Nevertheless, many young African-American learners relate strongly to the conceptual framework outlined in Table 1 and reconstruct life experiences through lenses affected by the worldviews incorporated in that table. For example, many perceive often contradictory elements as part of a total picture existing within various contexts, and often combine seemingly disparate experiences into insightful "wholes." Sternberg (1991) referred to this type of intelligence as *synthetic giftedness*. Hilliard (1976) and Anderson (1988) inform us that many of these students do best in response to oral tasks when the communicator is perceived to "be all right." Many young African Americans learn information better when it has human social content and is characterized by fantasy and humor. Their performance is influenced often by authorizing figures' expression of confidence or doubt, invitation or rejection.

The preceding philosophical worldviews, values, and behaviors of African Americans auger for the development of assessment and identification systems that are grounded in pluralistic definitions and theories of the giftedness construct and that include cognition skills other than analytical abilities. Other forms of giftedness such as creativity, personality dispositions, and motivational states (Harris & Ford, 1991; Sternberg, 1991) are recognized as well. Ogbu (1988) informs us that African Americans, like other cultural groups, have formed and developed a set of intelligences suited for their cultural tasks. As such, the disparate manifestations of intelligences as expressed through the worldviews, values, and behaviors of African Americans must be included in definitions and theories of giftedness and subsequent assessment and identification systems.

The recent works of Gardner (1983) and Sternberg (1985, 1991), as well as the earlier works of Renzulli (1973), Torrance (1977), and Hilliard (1976), represent examples of pluralistic views of intelligence and giftedness that recognize giftedness within the context of one's own culture and allow for a variety of ways of expressing giftedness. Harris and Ford (1991) reminded us that Sternberg's triarchic view of intelligence (i.e., analytic, synthetic, and practical) and Gardner's theory of multiple intelligences (i.e., linguistic, musical, logical-mathematical, spatial, bodily-kinesthetic, and personal [interpersonal and intrapersonal]) are more culturally sensitive and represent definitions of intelligence that recognize the interrelationship of the culture, language, worldview, values, and behaviors of African Americans. Surely, it would follow that employing a multidimensional definition of giftedness, incorporating the previously mentioned cultural and contextual norms into assessment and identification systems, and using multimodal assessment systems reflective of the multidimensional nature of giftedness, should result in the increase in the number and kinds of African-American children and youth identified as gifted.

By defining the giftedness construct broadly, one acknowledges the many possible blends of giftedness and the multiple forms this construct may take. For example, a person could be gifted if he or she were superior in breaking problems down into little pieces and understanding all of their parts. Another person could have a superior ability in "reading" his or her environment, figuring out the norms and conventions of that environment, and engaging in certain behavior patterns to succeed in that environment. And yet, a third person may have superior musical or spatial intelligence and be considered gifted. The first person mentioned generally does well on conventional intelligence and achievement tests. The other two people, however, manifest forms of giftedness not easily measured by traditional tests. Assessment and identification systems based on a unidimensional construct of intelligence may identify the first person as being gifted and miss the remaining ones. In reality, all these people may be gifted with respect to a multidimensional view of giftedness. We need to investigate the use of identification procedures that include standardized and nonstandardized quantitative (i.e., aptitude, achievement, creativity, and personality measures) and qualitative (i.e., home, peer, and community nominations; observational checklists; interview techniques; and student products and portfolio assessments) measures. Such measures might accommodate multiple and contextual definitions of intelligence and the various expressions of intelligence inherent in African-American worldviews, values, and customs. I suggest that a culturally sensitive, multimodal assessment and identification approach be used to identify gifted, African-American learners.

Imperatives for Appropriate Assessment

Within the past 15 years, researchers have made advances toward appropriate assessment and identification of gifted African-American learners. In fact, a 1981 National Identification Conference (Richert, Alvino, & McDonnel, 1982) attempted to identify a comprehensive listing of promising practices in the identification of "disadvantaged" gifted. A body of literature based on theory, research, and experiences suggests the use of certain instruments and procedures for assessing and identifying young, gifted African-American learners. A sample of those identified in the literature as effective in assessing and identifying gifted African Americans follows. Table 2 lists selected tests and approaches most consistent with African-American cultural norms and conventions.

Screening

Hilliard (1976) and Torrance (1977) have developed checklists and rating scales for assessing the distinct social and psychological indicators of giftedness and creativity within a context of African-American culture. Inclusion of these rating scales and checklists in the initial screening of potentially gifted and talented learners has been purported to increase the number of African Americans thereby identified (Frasier, 1989).

The Hilliard checklists were developed at the request of the San Francisco Unified School District. The task was to devise prescreening devices that would recognize the "basic African-American cultural contributions to patterns of human behavior" (1976, p. 14). Hilliard's resulting checklists, the "Who" and "O" are based on the uniqueness and commonalities of the deep structure culture of African Americans. These checklists emphasize synthetic-personal stylistic characteristics of African-American learners and place value on behavior that charac-

Table 2
Selective Assessment Approaches, Tests, and Checklists Potentially Useful in Screening, Assessing, and Identifying Gifts and Talents of Young African-American Learners

Screening measures that attempt to incorporate knowledge and understanding of African-American culture: • The "Who" and "O" Checklists (Hilliard, 1976) • Checklist of Creative Positives (CCP) (Torrance, 1977)
Assessment measures with psychometric designs and practices that recognize culturally relevant norms: • The Colored, Standard, and Advanced Progressive Matrices (Raven, 1930, 1947a, 1947b) • The Matrix Analogies Test-Expanded and Short Form (MAT-EF and MAT-SF) (Naglieri, 1985a, 1985b; Naglieri & Prewett, 1990) • The Kaufman Assessment Battery for Children (K-ABC) (Kaufman & Kaufman, 1983) • Torrance Test for Creative Thinking (TTCT) (Torrance, 1987)
Assessment models useful in intervention and program planning: • The Baldwin Identification Matrix (Baldwin, 1984) • The Frasier Talent Assessment Profile (F-TAP) (Frasier, 1990) • The Program of Assessment Diagnosis and Instruction (PADI) (Johnson, Starnes, Gregory, & Blaylock, 1985) • The Potentially Gifted Minority Student Project (Alamprese & Erlanger, 1988)

terizes divergent experimentation, improvisation, inferential reasoning, and harmonious interaction with the environment (Hilliard, 1976). The checklists include items that reflect behavioral styles of African Americans, such as "seems to notice everything"; "always asks the best questions"; "seems to know how people feel)"; and "is really hard to con."

The "Who" and "O" scales provide an excellent opportunity to gain subjective, culturally relevant information useful in the identification process. The scales were designed as prescreening devices only; when they have been used in concert with traditional prescreening procedures, previously overlooked gifted African-American learners have been identified (Frasier, 1989; Hilliard, 1976).

Torrance (1977) identified a set of behaviors of African Americans that provided the basis for the development of his Checklist of Creative Positives (CCP). He identified a "set of characteristics that helped to guide the search for strengths of culturally different students for giftedness among such students" (p. 25). These 18 characteristics were called "creative positives." Torrance argued that indicators of these creative positives, such as articulateness in role playing, sociodrama, storytelling, use of expressive speech, responsiveness to the kinesthetic, originality of ideas in problem solving, and humor, could best be assessed through observational techniques with results recorded on a checklist. The CCP enjoys wide use as a prescreening instrument for those wishing to predict and identify a gifted-and-talented candidate pool of African-American learners.

IDENTIFICATION

This use of traditional, norm-referenced, intelligence tests has not resulted in the proportionate identification of African-American learners with gifts and talents. However, some intelligence tests, as a result of their attempts to be less culturally and class biased, show promise (Baska, 1986a, 1986b; Frasier, 1989; VanTassel-Baska et al., 1989). For example, the Coloured, Standard, and Advanced Progressive Matrices (Raven, 1938; 1947a, 1947b) are frequently used by school systems to identify learners for gifted programs and were selected by a panel of experts in 1981 (Richert et al.,1982) as useful in the identification of potentially gifted African Americans. Though the heavy reliance on these tests is not sufficient grounds to recommend their use, their high-to-moderate positive correlations with other intelligence and achievement tests and their high concurrent validity of use with African Americans (Court & Raven, 1982; Sattler, 1982; Valencia, 1979) are strong arguments for their use with African-American learners. Other attractive features of these tests are their quick and simple, untimed administration and the option of individual or group administration.

Another test, the Matrix Analogies Test-Expanded and Short Form (MAT-EF and MAT-SF), has been normed on a large, representative sample in the United States with regard to gender, race, ethnicity, geographic region, and socioeconomic status. The test has a high degree of internal reliability and evidence of validity. It measures nonverbal ability through the use of figural matrices and is useful with people whose scores may be influenced by speed (Naglieri & Prewett, 1990). A recent study by Ward, Ward, and Patton (1992) showed that the MAT-EF correlated with the Wechsler Intelligence Scale for Children-Revised (WISC-R) and the Peabody Individual Achievement Test-Revised (PIAT-R) in a pattern that validated the test as a nonverbal measure of general intellectual ability. Results indicate that the MAT-EF was the highest estimate of general intellectual ability for a large portion of African Americans tested as a part of a federally funded program, entitled Project Mandala. The newness of the MAT instruments and the use of updated norms, however, may result in students' obtaining lower scores than they would on other aptitude measures.

Frasier (1989) reported that considerable evidence has been accumulated that the Kaufman Assessment Battery for Children (K-ABC) (Kaufman & Kaufman, 1983) "is fair to minorities" (p. 281); African Americans, as a group, have scored higher on the K-ABC than on more traditional intelligence tests. The developers attribute these higher scores to the test's emphasis on a multidimensional concept of intelligence and "de-emphasis of applied skills and verbal expression" (Kaufman & Harrison, 1986, p. 157). However, the K-ABC has been faulted for its low ceiling for gifted populations (Sattler, 1982); and there is little evidence of the test's validity (Salvia & Ysseldyke, 1988).

The Torrance Test of Creative Thinking (TTCT) is frequently used to identify gifted African-American learners (Torrance, 1987). Not only does this test measure an important dimension of giftedness, creativity, but it has also been found to do so in a culture-fair way. This test enjoys moderate levels of reliability based on recent data obtained from longitudinal studies of its ability to "predict quantity and quality of public personal creative achievements" (Torrance, in press). And, although scoring is time consuming and complex, the test is quick and easy to administer; and it may be used with individuals or groups and in grades K through graduate school. These features make the TTCT appealing, especially in light of the paucity of other tests of creativity.

Matrix and Profile Approaches

Several assessment models take a more comprehensive or holistic approach to identifying gifted African-American learners. As previously stated, a holistic approach closely fits the worldview and cultural manifestations of African-American cultures. The Baldwin Identification Matrix (BIM) (Baldwin, 1984) and its modifications (Dabney, 1983, 1988) have been reported as effective approaches to identifying high numbers and different types of gifted African-American learners. These matrix approaches were designed to allow the results of objective and subjective data sources to be juxtaposed with data from multiple sources and collected, reviewed, and interpreted before making a decision about the selection of individuals for inclusion in programs for the gifted.

More recently, Frasier's work on the development of assessment "profiles" holds promise for enhancing our capacity to identify more and diverse kinds of gifted and talented African-American learners. The Frasier Talent Assessment Profile (F-TAP) (Frasier, 1990) requires the collection of quantitative and qualitative data from multiple sources (e.g., aptitude, achievement, performance, creativity, and psychosocial attributes). From these data, the user develops an individual profile, from which further data can be collected, reviewed, and interpreted. Identification and selection decisions are based on multiple, broad indicators of potential giftedness. As a result, completed profiles demonstrate the often disparate and unequal performance in the various domains of intelligence of gifted African-American learners and result in these individuals being considered superior in one area (e.g.. creativity) and maybe average in another area (e.g., achievement).

A recent study designed to determine the reliability of this profile-identification process has been successful in establishing its reliability (Ward, Ward, Landrum, & Patton, 1992). Further, this research, conducted as a part of Project Mandala (Patton, Prillaman, Laycock, & VanTassel-Baska, 1989), also found that this profile approach was not influenced by race or culture. Its use resulted in the identification of large numbers of young (children in the 4–8 and 11–14 age ranges), gifted,

African Americans who exhibited disparate gifts and talents across the previously cited domains of intelligence.

Intervention Planning

Several curriculum-based assessment models have been documented as being useful in increasing the inclusion of African-American learners in programs for the gifted and talented. Based on "dynamic assessment" models advocated by Haywood (1988) and popularized previously by Feuerstein (1968, 1977), an "identification through teaching" approach (test, teach, retest) is used as the basis for assessment, identification, and instruction. The procedure allows students to exhibit their skills over extended periods of time, enabling the students to further refine these skills while project staff refines their judgments about the abilities and talents of students to meet the demands of a gifted program (Johnson, Starnes, Gregory, & Blaylock, 1985). Responsiveness to differentiated classroom curricula, then, becomes a part of the gifted-program selection paradigm.

The Program of Assessment, Diagnosis, and Instruction (PADI) reported by Johnson et al. (1985) and the Potentially Gifted Minority Student Project, recently described by Alamprese and Erlanger (1988), are sterling examples of the effectiveness of an ongoing-activity approach to increasing the number of identified gifted and talented African Americans. Both use the identification-through-teaching approach and employ several additional strategies that have resulted in increased numbers of African Americans being identified as gifted and talented. First, both programs use assessment instruments that are known to tap the reasoning and creativity potential of African-American learners (Johnson et al., 1985). Second, both programs employ multidimensional, diagnostic batteries. These batteries include assessment instruments and procedures that yield objective and subjective information from multiple data sources and are reflective of an expanded vision of the giftedness construct. Last, the curriculum-based-measurement (CBM) emphasis of both programs allows teachers to use assessment data to *teach* students, not just rank them.

Although the tests, assessment models, and procedures of these two programs are not in every case consonant with African-American worldviews and culture, they represent less culturally biased approaches and attempts to address the cultural norms, conventions, ethos, and behaviors of African Americans. We need more study of such programs, guided by sound and appropriate philosophical and theoretical principles and research, consistent with African-American worldviews.

Emerging Alternative-Assessment Approaches

As previously mentioned, despite the recommendations made in the past 15 years to change the way school systems identify young, gifted or potentially gifted

African Americans, heavy reliance on the use of norm-referenced intelligence tests and teacher nominations continues (VanTassel-Baska et al., 1989). Other measures are required. We must bridge the dissonance between the culture of African Americans and that of school practices and assessment practices. We need to continually modify traditional measures of general aptitude by removing tasks unsuitable for African-American children and by adding standardized tasks based on the previously discussed ethos and deep-structure culture of African Americans. We must continue to explore alternative-assessment approaches to the identification of gifted and talented African-American children, approaches that employ techniques other than pencil-and-paper tests and multiple-choice formats. Some promising research emphasizes the use of alternative forms of performance and portfolio assessment, asking students "to perform tasks that closely emulate the mental tasks of life" (Archambault, 1992, p. 5). In addition, the involvement of parents in these alternative-assessment approaches has been advocated by Howard (1990).

Additional Research Directions

Tests are not neutral. They reflect in their content, style, administration, and interpretation the predominant culture of their developers. This fact has led to the political use of psychoeducational assessment and testing, to the disservice of African Americans as a collective body. There are ways to overcome this problem. Research and development is needed to advance test development and gifted education in several ways:

1. New and expanded visions about the constructs of intelligence and giftedness have emerged (Asante, 1988; Gardner, 1983; Ogbu, 1988; Sternberg, 1985, 1991) and should provide a solid foundation for future research.
2. Pluralistic procedures for identifying gifted African Americans, which use multiple, qualitative and quantitative measures, are available and should be used.
3. CBM approaches, which purport to improve the correspondence between testing and teaching the school's curriculum (i.e., curricular validity, Fuchs & Fuchs, 1986) and enhance the communication of assessment data (Deno & Fuchs, 1987) have been incorporated into new pluralistic assessment approaches.
4. Research guided by the principles of alternative, qualitative assessment approaches must be increased and expanded and must address reliability and validity issues.
5. All assessment efforts should focus on the identification of strengths of African Americans, as manifested in diverse ways, and should recognize the unique traits and psychosocial characteristics of achieving African

Americans. Shade's (1978) research related to psychosocial traits of gifted African-American learners points the way to appropriate indicators of giftedness among African Americans.

6. Though the deep-structure culture of African Americans is unique and common to people of African descent, there exists some diversity in its sociopsychological manifestations. Recognition and understanding of both of these factors should lead to the development of psychoeducational assessment theory, methodology, instruments, and practice based on intragroup research and study. More work needs to be undertaken to uncover intragroup differences in cognition, behavior, and motivation before comparisons can be made between two different cultural groups (Gordon, 1985).

The identification of gifts and talents of African-American learners continues to loom as a challenge. New theories, paradigms, methodology, tests, and practices are begging for special educators' attention. A reconceptualization of theory and methodology related to assessment, testing, and the construct of giftedness in which Afro-centric worldviews guide and serve as a foundation represents an essential first step in the process. Until this is undertaken, neither psychometry nor the field of gifted education will enjoy the liberating qualities needed for progress in social sciences.

References

Alamprese, J. A., & Erlanger, W. J. (1988). *No gift wasted: Effective strategies for educating highly able disadvantaged students in mathematics and science. Vol. I: Findings.* Washington, DC: Cosmos Corporation.

Anderson, J. A. (1988). Cognitive styles and multicultural populations. *Journal of Teacher Education, 39*(1), 2–9.

Archambault, F. X. (1992). *Alternative assessment and the evaluation of programs for the gifted and talented.* Unpublished manuscript. University of Connecticut, National Research Center on the Gifted and Talented, Storrs.

Asante, M. K. (1988). *Afrocentricity.* Trenton, NJ: African World Press.

Baldwin, A. Y. (1984). *The Baldwin Identification Matrix 2 for the Identification of the Gifted and Talented: A handbook for its use.* New York: Trillium Press.

Baska, L. (1986a). Alternatives to traditional testing. *Roeper Review, 8*(3), 181–184.

Baska, L. (1986b). The use of the Raven advanced progressive matrices for the selection of magnet junior high school students. *Roeper Review, 8*(3), 181–184.

Boykin, A. W. (1983). The academic performance of Afro-American children. In J. Spence (Ed.), *Achievement and achievement motives* (pp. 321–371). San Francisco: W. H. Freeman.

Cole, M., & Scribner, S. (1973). Cognitive consequences of formal and informal education. *Science Education, 182,* 553–559.

Court, J. H., & Raven, J. (1982). *Research and references: 1982 update.* London: H. K. Lewis.

Dabney, M. (1983, July). *Perspectives and directions in assessment of the black child.* Paper presented at the meeting of the Council for Exceptional Children, Atlanta.

Dabney, M. (1988). An alternative model for identification of potentially gifted students: A case study. In R. L. Jones (Ed.), *Psychoeducational assessment of minority group children: A casebook* (pp. 273–294). Berkeley, CA: Cobb & Henry.

Deno, S. L., & Fuchs, L. S. (1987). Developing curriculum-based measurement systems for data-based special education problem solving. *Focus on Exceptional Children, 19*(8), 1–16.

Dixon, V. J. (1976). World views and research methodology. In L. M. King, V. J. Dixon, & W. W. Nobles (Eds.), *African philosophy: Assumptions and paradigms for research on black persons* (pp. 51–102). Los Angeles: Fanon Center Publication.

Feuerstein, R. (1968). *The learning potential assessment device: A new method for assessing modifiability of the cognitive functioning of socioculturally disadvantaged adolescents.* Unpublished manuscript, Israel Foundation Trustees, Tel Aviv.

Feuerstein, R. (1977). Mediated learning experience: A theoretical basis for cognitive human modifiability during adolescence. *Research to practice in mental retardation: Proceedings of the 4th Congress of IASMD. Vol. 2. Education and training* (pp. 105–116). Baltimore: University Park Press.

Frasier, M. (1989). A perspective on identifying black students for gifted programs. In C. J. Maker & S. W. Schiever (Eds.), *Critical issues in gifted education: Defensible programs for cultural and ethnic minorities, Vol. II* (pp. 213–255). Austin, TX: Pro-Ed.

Frasier, M. (1990, April). *The equitable identification of gifted and talented children.* Paper presented at the annual meeting of the American Educational Research Association, Boston.

Fuchs, L. S., & Fuchs, D. (1986). Curriculum-based assessment of progress toward long- and short-term goals. *Journal of Special Education, 20,* 69–82.

Gardner, H. (1983). *Frames of mind.* New York: Basic Books.

Gordon, E. W. (1985). Social science knowledge production and minority experiences. *The Journal of Negro Education, 54*(2), 117–133.

Gould, S. J. (1977). *Ever since Darwin.* New York: Norton.

Gould, S. J. (1981). *The mismeasure of man.* New York: Norton.

Guthrie, R. V. (1976). *Even the rat was white.* New York: Harper & Row.

Harris, J. J., & Ford, D. Y. (1991). Identifying and nurturing the promise of gifted Black American children. *Journal of Negro Education, 60*(1), 3–18.

Haywood, H. C. (1988). Dynamic assessment: The learning potential assessment device. In R. L. Jones (Ed.), *Psychoeducational assessment of minority group children: A casebook* (pp. 39–63). Berkeley, CA: Cobb & Henry.

Hilliard, A. G. (1976). *Alternatives to I.Q. testing: An approach to the identification of "gifted" minority children.* Final Report, Sacramento Division of Special Education, California State Department of Education. (ERIC Document: Reproduction Service No. ED 147009)

Hilliard, A. G. (1984). I.Q. thinking as the emperor's new clothes: A critique of Jensen's bias in mental testing. In C. R. Reynolds & R. T. Brown (Eds.), *Perspectives in mental testing* (pp. 139–169). New York: Plenum Press.

Howard, K. (1990). Making the portfolio read. *Quarterly of the National Writing Project and the Center for the Study of Writing, 12*(2), 4–8.

Jenkins, M. D. (1936). A socio-psychological study of Negro children of superior intelligence. *Journal of Negro Education, 5*(2), 175–190.

Jensen, A. R. (1980). *Bias in mental testing.* New York: Free Press.

Johnson, S. T., Starnes, W. T., Gregory, D., & Blaylock, A. (1985). Program of assessment, diagnosis, and instruction (PADI): Identifying and nurturing potentially gifted and talented minority students. *The Journal of Negro Education, 54*(3), 416–430.

Kamin, L. J. (1974). *The science and politics of I.Q.* Potomac, MD: Lawrence Erlbaum.

Kamin, L. J. (1975). Social and legal consequences of I.Q. tests as classification instruments: Some warnings from our past. *Journal of School Psychology, 13*(4), 317–323.

Kaplan, A. (1964). *The conduct of inquiry.* San Francisco: Chandler.

Kaufman, A. S., & Harrison, P. L. (1986). Intelligence tests and gifted assessment: What are the positives? *Roeper Review, 8*(3), 154–159.

Kaufman, A. S., & Kaufman, N. L. (1983). *Kaufman Assessment Battery for Children (K-ABC).* Circle Pines, MN: American Guidance Service.

Maurier, H. (1979). Do we have an African philosophy? In R. A. Wright (Ed.), *African philosophy: An introduction* (pp. 1–17), (M. McDevitt, Trans.). Washington, DC: University of America Press.

Naglieri, J. A. (1985a). *Matrix Analogies Test-Short Form.* New York: Psychological Corporation.

Naglieri, J. A. (1985b). *Matrix Analogies Test-Expanded Form.* New York: Psychological Corporation.

Naglieri, J. A., & Prewett, P. N. (1990). Nonverbal intelligence measure: A selected review of instruments and their use. In C. R. Reynolds & R. W. Kamphaus (Eds.), *Handbook of psychological and educational assessment of children: Intelligence and achievement* (pp. 348–370). New York: Guilford Press.

Nichols, E. J. (1976). *The philosophical aspects of cultural difference.* Unpublished table, University of Ibadan, Nigeria.

Nobles, W. W. (1983). *Critical analysis of scholarship on black family life.* Final Report, United Church of Christ Commission for Racial Justice, Washington, DC.

Nobles, W. W. (1987). Psychometrics and African-American reality: A question of cultural antimony. *The Negro Educational Review, 38,* 45–55.

Nobles, W. W. (1991). African philosophy: Foundations for Black psychology. In R. L. Jones (Ed.), *Black psychology* (pp. 47–63). Berkeley, CA: Cobb & Henry.

Ogbu, J. (1988). Human intelligence testing: A cultural-ecological perspective. *National Forum, 68*(2), 23–29.

Patton, J. M., Prillaman, D., Laycock, V., & VanTassel-Baska (1989). *A research and demonstration project for culturally diverse, low income, and handicapped gifted and talented learners.* Washington, DC: Office of Educational Research and Improvement, U.S. Department of Education.

Patton, J. M., Prillaman, D., & VanTassel-Baska, J. (1990). The nature and extent of programs for the disadvantaged gifted in the United States and territories. *Gifted Child Quarterly, 34*(3), 94–96.

Raven, J. C. (1938). *Standard progressive matrices.* London: H. K. Lewis.

Raven, J. C. (1947a). *Colored progressive matrices.* London: H. K. Lewis.

Raven, J. C. (1947b). *Advanced progressive matrices.* London: H. K. Lewis.

Renzulli, J. S. (1973). Talent potential in minority group students. *Exceptional Children, 39,* 437–444.

Richert, E. S. (1987). Rampant problems and promising practices in the identification of disadvantaged gifted students. *Gifted Child Quarterly, 31*(4), 149–154.

Richert, E. S., Alvino, J., & McDonnel, R. (1982). *The national report on identification: Assessment and recommendations for comprehensive identification of gifted and talented youth.* Sewell, NJ: Educational Improvement Center-South.

Salvia, J., & Ysseldyke, J. E. (1988). *Assessment in special and remedial education.* Boston: Houghton and Mifflin.

Sattler, J. M. (1982). *Assessment of children's intelligence and special abilities.* Boston: Allyn & Bacon.

Sattler, J. M., Hilliard, A., Lambert, N., Albee, G., & Jensen, A. (1981, August). *Intelligence tests on trial: Larry P. and PASE.* Paper presented at the annual meeting of the American Psychological Association, Los Angeles.

Shade, B. J. (1978). Social-psychological characteristics of achieving black children. *The Negro Educational Review, 29*(2), 80–86.

Sternberg, R. (1985). *Beyond I.Q.* Cambridge, MA: Cambridge University Press.

Sternberg, R. (1991). Giftedness according to the triarchic theory of human intelligence. In N. Colangelo & G. A. Davis (Eds.), *Handbook of gifted education* (pp. 45–53). Boston: Allyn & Bacon.

Torrance, E. P. (1977). *Discovery and nurturance of giftedness in the culturally different.* Reston, VA: Council for Exceptional Children.

Torrance, E. P. (1987). *Using tests of creative thinking to guide the teaching of creative behavior.* Bensenville, IL: Scholastic Testing Service.

Torrance, E. P. (in press). *The blazing drive: The creative personality.* Buffalo, NY: Bearly.

Valencia, R. R. (1979). Comparison of intellectual performance of Chicano and Anglo third grade boys on the Raven's colored progressive matrices. *Psychology in the Schools, 16*(3), 448–453.

VanTassel-Baska, J., Patton, J., & Prillaman. D. (1989). Disadvantaged gifted learners at-risk for educational attention. *Focus on Exceptional Children, 22*(3), 1–16.

Vernon, P. E. (1969). *Intelligence and cultural environment.* London: Methuen.

Ward, T., Ward, S., & Patton, J. (1992). *An analysis of the utility of the matrix analogies test with at-risk gifted learners.* Paper presented at the annual meeting of the American Educational Research Association, San Francisco.

Ward, T., Ward, S., Landrum, M., & Patton, J. (1992). *Examination of a new protocol for the identification of at-risk gifted learners.* Paper presented at the annual meeting of the American Educational Research Association, San Francisco.

About the Author

JAMES M. PATTON (CEC VA Federation) is an Associate Professor of Education and Associate Dean of the School of Education at The College of William & Mary, Williamsburg, Virginia.

CHAPTER 19

What Good Is This Thing Called Intelligence and Why Bother to Measure It?

Asa G. Hilliard
Georgia State University

This article contains a review of issues and documentation concerning the possibility of "measuring" the intelligence of students. The construct validity of "intelligence," the role of cultural context as a modifier of the meaning of test results, and the lack of meaningful predictive validity of IQ tests are discussed. A discussion of the utility *of the intelligence construct and IQ measures, and their relationship to the design of beneficial pedagogy follows. Based on reviews of empirical evidence, it is concluded that the measurement of intelligence as practical, at present, makes no contribution to the design of instruction that is beneficial to students, as far as academic achievement is concerned. The main effects of the present popular intelligence measures are found to be negative.*

Our ultimate message is a strikingly simple one. The purpose of the entire process—from referral for assessment to eventual placement in special education—is to improve instruction for children. The focus of educational benefits for children became our unifying theme, cutting across disciplinary boundaries and sharply divergent points of view.

These two things—the validity of assessment and the quality of instruction—are the subject of this report. Valid assessment, in our view, is marked by its relevance to and usefulness for instruction. (Holtzman, 1982, pp. x, xi).

Reprinted from Hilliard, A. G. (1994). What good is this thing called intelligence and why bother to measure it? *Journal of Black Psychology, 20*, 430–444. Reprinted with permission of Sage Publications.

> While academic failures are often attributed to characteristics of learners, current achievement also reflects the opportunities available to learn in school. If such opportunities have been lacking or if the quality of instruction offered varies across subgroups of the school-age population, then school failure and subsequent E.M.R. referral and placement may represent a lack of exposure to quality instruction for disadvantaged or minority children. (Heller, Holtzman, & Messick, 1982, p. 15)
>
> The IQ test's claim to validity rests heavily on its predictive power. We find that prediction alone, however, is insufficient evidence of the test's educational utility. What is needed is evidence that children with scores in the E.M.R. range, learn more effectively in a special program or placement. As argued in more detail in Chapter 4, we doubt that such evidence exists, although we are not prepared as a panel to advocate the discontinuation of IQ tests, we feel that the burden of justification lies with its proponents to show that in particular cases the tests have been used in a manner that contributes to the effectiveness of instruction for the children in question. (Heller et al, 1982, p. 61)

I must state at the onset that I come to the discussion of the *utility* of "intelligence" testing and the utility of the intelligence construct from the point of view of an educational psychologist interested in the improvement of education. I recognize that there can be many reasons for interest in the human mind and how it functions, and that some psychologists and others will be interested in "measuring" whatever is possible to be measured, perhaps just for its own sake.

Of course, the question of the utility of mental measurement can easily be divorced from the question of whether intelligence can be measured simply for the sake of doing it. It is also clear that, in a free society, scientists ought to be able to pursue any interesting question for which they can find support, or which they can do on their own, so long as they do no harm. So research to determine if such a thing as intelligence exists and, if it does, what its nature is, is likely to continue, and I have no quarrel with that.

However, major concerns arise when psychometricians and others move beyond inquiries about human intellect to the application of their science to the area of human problem solving. It is at this point that we must be concerned about the validity of *connection*s between mental measurement and success in problem solving in teaching and learning.

For many reasons, some of them obvious, the primary focus of my critique is on the use of mental measurement in education. Using IQ tests for predicting recidivism in the criminal justice system, studying the impact of nutrition on cognitive development, and other such interests will continue to preoccupy those involved in mental measurement. Of course, any use of mental measurement should be justified on the basis of its contribution to improving the human condition.

By looking at education, certain principles can be illuminated, some of which can be applied to many other areas of use of mental measurement.

The Illusion of Measurement: The Quality of the Database

Although it is not my intention here to go into great detail about the nature of the phenomenon: intelligence, how it is organized, and what it does, I cannot help but make a couple of passing observations. I do this to indicate my strong belief that psychological scientists have not yet measured intelligence, and that whatever the results of IQ testing are, they should not be treated as if they validate a scientific description of intelligence.

Some years ago, I recall having a conversation with Jerrold Zacharias and Judith Schwartz at MIT. The conversation was about mental measurement. I will never forget the expression of disdain that Zacharias had for the efforts of psychologists who attempt to measure intelligence. He insisted that the word *measurement* in science had a very precise meaning and that the instruments and quantification procedures of IQ psychometrists could not meet the scientific criteria that would allow us to say that they were indeed measuring devices.

His criticism was not about cultural bias, fairness, or other popular points; he raised the scientific point about the nature of the phenomenon being measured and, in particular, whether an interval scale for quantification could be constructed to measure the phenomenon. Of course, if an interval scale cannot be constructed, then measurement does not occur.

> The main defect in both sides, or either side, of this argument is that the protagonist pays so little attention to the *quality of the data base*. They revert to saying that the data are not very good, but let's use them anyway because they are all we have.
>
> The worst error in the whole business lies in attempting to put people, of whatever age or station, into a single, ordered line of "intelligence" or "achievement" like numbers along a measuring tape: eighty-six comes after eighty-five and before ninety-three. Everyone knows that people are complex—talented in some ways, clumsy in others; educated in some ways, ignorant in others; calm, careful, persistent, and patient in some ways; impulsive, careless, or lazy in others. Not only are these characteristics different in different people, they also vary in any one person from time to time.

To further complicate the problem there is variety in the *types* of descriptions, the traits *tall*, *handsome*, and *rich* are not along the same sets of scales as *affectionate*, *impetuous*, or *bossy*.

As an old professional measurer (by virtue of being an experimental physicist), I can say categorically that it *makes no sense to try to represent a multi-dimensional space with an array of numbers ranged along one line*. This does not mean it's impossible to cook up a scheme that tries to do it; it's just that the scheme won't make any sense. It is possible to strike an average of a column of figures in a telephone directory, but one would never try to dial it. Telephone numbers at least represent some *kind* of idea: they are all addressed like codes for the central office to respond to. . . . Implicit in the process of averaging is the process of adding. To obtain an average, first add a number of quantitative measures, then divide by however many there are. This [all very simple] *provided the quantities can be added*, but for the most part with disparate subjects, they cannot be. (Zacharias, 1977, pp. 69, 70, italics added)

One of the interesting things to me is that these types of issues seldom if ever receive serious attention in published work in psychometrics. Rather, the professional conversation is usually confined to safe ground, that is, to the mathematics of statistical procedures or to the formal properties of a research design. But Zacharias and others raise the fundamental issue about the *nature and quality of the data* purportedly being measured. Psychometric "science" *assumes* but does not demonstrate the quality of the database that is being processed.

As with the case of Zacharias, opinions of linguists such as Roger Shuy (1977) get little or no response from the psychometric community. Yet he, like Zacharias, deals scientifically with the fundamentals of the nature of the phenomenon being measured, the quality of the database. In his classic article, Shuy makes the point, the profound point, that the most important part of language is its deep structure or deep meaning, its functional semantics. Its surface structure, that is, its phonology and vocabulary, can be quantified very easily. However, Shuy argues that the part that interests the psychologist most, the semantics, are from the point of view of a linguist, least susceptible to measurement by traditional tests.

I suspect that the views of the physicist and the linguist are too hot to handle for the psychometrists who attempt to measure the mind. I am unaware of any recognition of these difficulties in the applied mental measurement literature. I might add that it is in precisely these two areas of concern that we find the source of what some refer to as cultural bias in the IQ test. But it is really a *validity* problem, not mainly a bias or fairness problem.

In 1989, a summit conference was held on the construct of intelligence and its measurement in Melbourne, Australia. A set of selected papers from that conference was published in 1991 (Rowe, 1991). Helga Rowe was principal research officer for the Australian Council for Educational Research. To the best of my knowledge, this was the most recent summit to attempt to make a state-of-the-art statement about the measurement of intelligence. Psychologists from 14 countries were represented at the seminar, and the conference was used as a satellite conference preceding the 24th International Congress of Psychology, which took place in Sydney, Australia.

Several important points appear in the conference papers. First, the importance of *context* in mental measurement was recognized:

> Erickson's (1984) overview of research from an anthropological view shows, for example, that mental abilities (including language and mathematical abilities) that were once thought to be relatively or even totally (as presumed by classical learning theory and Piagetan developmental theory) independent of context, are much more sensitive to context than traditionally thought. Cognitive processes such as reasoning and understanding develop in the context of personal use and purpose. The demand characteristics of a learning task can be changed by altering the context within which it is presented. (Rowe, 1991, p. 6)

This fundamental matter of context makes measurement matters messy. It raises the number of variables to be considered exponentially. To recognize context is to complicate the task of the psychometrist astronomically. It is time for measurement scientists to stop sweeping such difficulties under the rug. Rowe (1991) goes on:

> As pointed out by Erickson (1984), differences in performance as described earlier, cannot be explained merely in relation to abstract versus concrete thinking, as has been quite generally assumed. Rather, the differences in performance are very much related to differences in problem definition by self and others. When a person has made the problem his own, i.e., when he/she has formulated a task or question, he/she goes through a series of cognitive processes including decision-making points, each involving personal abilities, knowledge, and skills, as well as processes of social interaction that do not come into play when, for example, he/she is engaged in completing a worksheet or doing an IQ test. It is not just that learning tests are often "out of context" as Erickson . . .

notes, but they are *in a context* in which the power relationships and processes of social interaction are such that the students has no influence on problem formulation and the tasks offer no context of personal use and purpose.

A full appreciation of the role of context, personal purpose and use, and of processes of social interaction would fundamentally reshape our conceptualizations of and approaches to assessment, as well as to teaching and learning. (p. 7, italics added)

Like the measurement perspective of the physicist Zacharias and the linguistic perspectives of the linguist Shuy, this issue of context raises another point that psychometric scientists have yet to address. The points are not trivial, but the responses to them have been, if we look at applied mental measurement in education today.

A second interesting point that came out of the Melbourne conference was that psychologists have no common definition of or theory of intelligence.

Although scientific psychologists have been studying intelligence for a century, they do not seem to have come closer to a widely acceptable, consistent general theory of intelligence. On the contrary, they offer an array of limited, although usually sophisticated subtheories, addressing specific issues, with little concern for integration with other views. (Richele, 1991)

Finally, the Melbourne seminar on intelligence revealed several places where researchers failed to find the expected correlation between IQ and achievement in complex problem solving.

As can be seen in table 13.1, the overall results failed to fulfill the expectation of a close positive relationship of intelligence tests scores and performance scores derived from system control. The reported correlation coefficients are remarkably low; in most cases they are close to zero. Few coefficients reach values of .4–.5. Only in four studies ... can correlation coefficients of this size be found. Thus the reported results from these studies do not support the general assumption that intelligence tests are good predictors of an individual's performance when operating a complex system... . In addition, most studies agree with respect to the interpretation of the results in two important ways. One, it is argued that the tasks (i.e., simulated systems) have higher ecological validity and are closer to reality than problem situations, such as intelligence tests' items, or the Tower of Hanoi ... which have traditionally been studied by cognitive psychologists. Two, the low correlation coefficients allow us to infer that intelligence tests scores cannot be regarded as valid predictors for problem solving and decision making in complex, real-life environments. (Kluwe, Misiak, & Haider, 1991, pp. 228, 232)

Once again, these are not trivial issues, but the response to them has been trivial if we look at common practice in the schools.

To summarize, there are several nontrivial, interrelated, and overlapping measurement issues and problems that bear on the construct validity and the measurement validity of intelligence.

1. The poor quality of the database.
2. The inability to construct an interval scale.
3. Performing addition on unlike quantities.
4. The loss of meaning from the responses of clients due to ignoring the context of responses which give them meaning.
5. The failure to consider the sciences of cultural linguistics (Hoover, Politzer, & Taylor, 1991; Smith, 1978, 1979) and cultural anthropology (Cole, Gay, Glick, Sharp, et al., 1971; Hall, 1977; Helms, 1992) and their meaning for the psychometric use of language as a measurement medium.

To fail to deal aggressively with these issues is to reduce the measurement of intelligence activities to little more than a meaningless ritual.

APPLYING INTELLIGENCE AND ITS MEASUREMENT IN SCHOOLS

When it comes to the schools, the debate over the technical and scientific issues in mental measurement are of peripheral interest. However, when mental measurement is *applied* in the schools, then the value of that activity for school improvement must be examined. It can be seen from the quotations at the beginning of this article, quotations that come from the National Academy of Science panel report on placing children in special education, that *the school use of tests calls for tests that assist in the design of instruction that results in benefits to students*. By linking the activities in mental measurement to school treatment strategies and by linking both of those to student outcomes, and in particular *beneficial* outcomes, the traditional task and goal of mental measurement must be transformed. Initially, traditionally, and presently in the United States, the goal of mental measurement was and is merely ranking and classification to *predict* achievement (Hilliard, 1990).

So the matter of requiring that professional activity be beneficial to students is the most important conceptual or paradigmatic change in American education as far as the use of intellectual assessment is concerned.

By requiring the benefits criterion, a whole new range of research studies is called for: true validity studies, *instructional* validity studies. How can validity studies that ignore variation in school treatment, failing to control for it, be considered scientifically valid (Kozol, 1991)? If mental measurement, on the other hand, is to be used for diagnosis and remediation, how can validity be determined in ignorance of the reliability, validity, and quality control of the instructional practices, regular and "special"? Do children benefit from the uses of psychological services, especially the measurement of IQ? At the same time, do children benefit from special teaching services that are dictated by the results of tests? Are the services to which students are sentenced special pedagogically? The answers to each of these questions seem to be a resounding "no" (Glass, 1983; Heir & Latus, 1993; Heller et al., 1982; Skyrtic, 1991). In other words, the record on instructional benefits to students as a consequence of the use of mental measurement is abysmal.

Two points have not yet been considered in looking at the benefits question. First, we find that when good teaching is offered to children, many of whom fall into traditionally low-performing categories, their "intellectual disabilities" appear to disappear (Backler & Eakin, 1993; Edmonds, 1979; Sizemore, 1988). In other words, there are children in schools whose grades *and IQ test scores* have been low, traditionally, who live in impoverished and even violent neighborhoods with all the things that are supposed to make learning difficult, but who are some of the highest academic performers in their school districts or even in their states. Perhaps IQ predicts the quality of school treatment that children are likely to receive.

If a school such as the Vann School in Pittsburgh, the Madison school in Pittsburgh, or the Martinez school in Dallas is serving a population of students that would be expected to fall in the lower academic achievement quartile, but their actual performance places them in the highest academic quartile, *then the IQ correlation is a failure;* IQ did not predict such achievement. Yet we find precisely that in many cases. But we really only need to find it in one case to show that the IQ tests predict future achievement *if* teaching service quality is not equalized as a part of the context within which children operate. Mental measurement and intelligence theorists have yet to do the types of validity studies to prove or disprove this. A rare exception may be found (Fuller, 1977).

Second, we must ask the question, *is mental measurement in the schools a prerequisite to the production of successful achievement with children?* I have been seeking out high-performing schools and teachers for the better part of three decades now. One of the things that is striking to me is that in excellent schools there are almost no cases where the use of IQ or other means of making estimates of the mental capacities of students is an important part of the considerations for the design of instruction in these excellent schools, nor does IQ inform instructional design for successful teachers! *The highest performing educators work without the IQ net!* Conversely, IQ teachers and IQ schools have nothing to brag about.

It ought to be clear to virtually anyone who looks at this problem that the current IQ ritual is irrelevant to the design of powerful, successful instruction for students, or that if mental measurement or assessment is to become useful in the school experience, then a paradigm shift is needed.

Fortunately, such a paradigm shift has already occurred among many psychologists and educators who are attempting to apply the work of cognitive change psychologists (Dent, 1991; Feuerstein, 1979, 1980; Feuerstein, Klein, & Tannenbaum, 1991; Hehir & Latus, 1993; Hilliard, 1987a, 1987b; M. R. Jensen, 1992; Lidz, 1991).

To summarize, at the moment, psychology has yet to demonstrate its ability to measure the capacity of any children, let alone the capacity of children who are situated in different cultural and low socioeconomic contexts, using the medium of a standard language and cultural material in a set of pluralistic cultural contexts. Second, psychometrics cannot be developed by *quantifying things that are not quantifiable*. Third, IQ psychometry cannot validate the treatment categories to which mental measurement sentences schoolchildren, for example, the "educable mentally retarded" category and the "learning disabilities" category. Moreover, even if it could, educators have no unique, validated differentiated pedagogy for such categories. Fourth, there is a large database on effective schools that makes no reference whatsoever to mental measurement of intelligence, and there is a smaller database on *highly* effective schools, also without mental measurements. Therefore, the mental measurement of intelligence is in no way a prerequisite for present success in school. No body of data shows that any use of traditional IQ or mental measurement is tied to valid teaching and learning. Therefore, IQ measurement is a professionally meaningless *ritual*, a ritual with unnecessarily harmful consequences, that shapes professional thought and action in a negative way, causing professionals to overlook successful strategies and approaches in education. It is a ritual that shapes student self-image in a negative way.

The Consequences of Invalid Theory and Practice

It is almost scandalous that professionals in psychology today who serve the children of all the people have bought into the IQ myth. Unhappily, Arthur Jensen (1969, 1980) is not alone among psychologists, for example, who believe in the genetic inferiority of people of African descent when compared to Europeans. Snyderman and Rothman (1990) report on their survey of psychologists and researchers, many of whom are diplomats in their respective professional associations, such as some of the members of the American Psychological Association:

> In this case, a plurality of experts (forty-five percent) and a majority of respondents, believed the black-white IQ difference to be the product of both genetic and environmental variation, compared to only fifteen percent who feel the difference is entirely due to environmental variation. Twenty-four percent of experts do not believe there are sufficient data to support any reasonable opinion, and fourteen percent did not respond to the question. Eight of the experts (one percent) indicate a belief in an entirely genetic determination. That a majority of experts who respond to this question believe genetic determinants to be important in the black-white IQ difference is remarkable in light of the overwhelmingly negative reaction from both the academic and public spheres that met Jensen's statement of the same hypothesis. Either expert opinion has changed dramatically since 1969, or the psychological and educational communities are not making their opinions known to the general public. (pp. 128–129)

Clearly, there is a need to explore the impact of such beliefs on the helping behavior of professionals, which parallel very closely the beliefs of the general public (Duke, 1991). A well-documented, clear history of gross abuse exists here (Gould, 1981; Guthrie, 1976: Kamin, 1974). Where we can see that there is no database to support the idea that mental measurement is helpful, such opinions raise the question of whether mental measurement is harmful. That is a question to which serious attention of researchers must be turned. The only justification for using IQ routinely, or for employing a system dependent on IQ, is that clear and substantial benefits (academic achievement benefits) accrue to students. It is not a good argument to say that testing helps to get resources, when neither the IQ test nor the help that the resources bring are beneficial.

The poverty of psychometric science is revealed when we note that there is no scientific definition of the variable "race" (Fairchild, 1991; Montagu, 1974; Yee, 1983). There is no scientific accounting for the intervening variable of school "treatment." There is no scientific accounting for linguistic and cultural diversity in the design of measuring instruments (Helms, 1992). But psychometricians are supremely confident of their measurement and of the predictive validity of their instruments.

The Promise of Intelligence Thinking

Research in mental measurement can continue. Research in the utility of mental measurement can continue. But what good is intelligence if it does not help us to change instruction? Like thousands of others, I am deeply impressed with some of the advances in the study of the human mind and how it works. I am impressed with Jean Piaget, Milton Budoff, Robert Sternberg, Reuven Feuerstein, and Mogens Jensen (1992). I am impressed with the work of Howard Gardner (1983). They and others have given us a language that clarifies the workings of the human mind, that highlights its dynamism, its growth as an open system, and the variety of ways in which the human mind can express itself, sometimes referred to as "multiple intelligences." But all of these advances in thinking will come to naught if the fundamental paradigm that brought us here is not revised.

I see people take the work of psychologists like Feuerstein, whose interest is in cognitive functions and structures, and instead of looking at the power of the approach to produce changes in learners, become interested in how to score the assessment system and how to compare students to each other in a system that does not have ranking as its goal. I am interested too in the treatment of Gardner's (1983) work, where many people who come to it with the old paradigm bring with them an interest in scoring multiple intelligences so that individuals may be ranked in multiple ways rather than one, losing, in my opinion, the potential of the construct change. Gardner's construct change enlarges the vision of educators about the variety in intellectual processes. It implies the need to address a broader range of curriculum goals. But the construct change is not accompanied by a paradigm shift. We may wind up with seven ways to hurt children rather than one. The essence of the paradigm shift is that we view the human intelligence as modifiable, as growing. That is just as true of the "seven intelligences" as it is of the one (Suzuki, 1984). Sorting people into the new categories and ranking them within the categories will be as meaningless pedagogically as using one dimensional intelligence. On the other hand, the multiple intelligence map opens up the mind of the teachers to targets for mediation, to enhance potential and to enrich curriculum.

I want to make it clear that I do not oppose research and the attempt to define intelligence and to measure it systematically. What I do oppose is acting as if those tasks have already been completed. I do not oppose attempting to use what is learned from the study of how the human mind functions to improve the education process. What I do oppose is acting as if nonpedagogically trained psychologists and noninstructionally related mental measurement devices have a meaningful and beneficial application to the design of effective instruction for students. I believe that the inertia in traditional practice prevents psychologists from putting their best foot forward.

I have often said that there is another paradigm for conceptualizing and assessing mental functions, a paradigm which has already been shown to be useful in improving the instructional process. This means that there is a meaningful function for psychologists in the educational process, a function which includes assessment, if not measurement, at this time, but a function which requires a fundamental change in the role of psychologists. In fact, to be prepared to perform a meaningful assessment, psychologists must become master teachers (Feuerstein, 1980; M. R. Jensen, 1992). It is through the application of teaching, of somewhat known validity, that learners can be provoked to reveal the patterns of thinking and learning that can be used to construct educational dialogue that can result in cognitive, affective, and content benefits for students.

I am willing to leave the door open; perhaps the future will yield a traditional test or assessment of intelligence and a consensus on the construct to benefit students. Should the benefits be clear and unmistakable, I shall be the first to embrace such an approach. However, my experience as a teacher, and my understanding of the goals of psychometrics, leaves me pessimistic about these possibilities, the fundamental issue being whether the mind is fixed and limited or modifiable and susceptible to growth through nurturing. Depending on our beliefs on this issue and our beliefs about the efficacy of instruction, we embark on one of two paradigmatic paths that diverge at an ever-growing rate.

Models of mental functioning, such as those proposed by the cognitive modifiability psychologists and by the multiple intelligence psychologists, are useful less because they answer the question of how to measure intelligence, but by conceiving of intelligence in the way that they do, they imply a pedagogical map that has vast implications for teacher training, assessment approaches, and approaches to the evaluation of achievement outcomes. For example, Gardner's (1983) map of multiple intelligences is less interesting to me as a device for classifying people among the intelligences than it is to establish the rich domain of human functioning toward which educational facilitation can be directed for all learners.

I believe that we have been stuck in the old paradigm because of politics, not because of professionalism. The activity of psychologists in ranking and classifying ethnic populations, who are deemed "racial" populations, is a blot on the history of the profession, with a stain that clouds professional perception even to the present day. Psychology is, or ought to be, a healing discipline; if not, then not only does the construct of intelligence and the measurement of intelligence become irrelevant, but psychology itself perhaps ought not exist. Happily, the model of what we could become and what we ought to become already exists. The kind of intelligence in the healing paradigm may someday be fully articulated and, yes, even measured.

Certainly, we want to assess the mind in valid and appropriate ways and to use the information from that assessment to create a better life for the people. But the beneficial aspects will not come about automatically, and until such time as they do come about, why bother to apply what we know about intelligence? Just stay in the laboratory until there is something beneficial to offer.

REFERENCES

Backler, A., & Eakin, S. (Eds.). (1993). *Every child can succeed: Readings for school improvement.* Bloomington, IN: Agency for Instructional Technology.

Cole, M., Gay, J., Glick, J. A., Sharp, D. W., et al. (1971). *The cultural context of learning and thinking: An exploration in experimental anthropology.* New York: Basic Books.

Dent, H. E. (1991). The San Francisco Public Schools experience with alternatives to IQ testing: A model for non-biased assessment. In A. G. Hilliard III (Ed.), *Testing African American students* (pp. 146–162). Morristown, NJ: Aaron.

Duke, L. (1991, January 9). Whites racial stereotyping persists: Most retain negative beliefs about minorities, survey finds. *The Washington Post,* p. A1.

Edmonds, R. R. (1979, March/April). Some schools work and more can. *Social Policy,* pp. 28–32.

Fairchild, H. H. (1991). Scientific racism: The cloak of objectivity. *Journal of Social Issues, 47*(3), 101–115.

Feuerstein, R. (1979). *The dynamic assessment of retarded performers: The learning potential assessment device.* Baltimore, MD: University Park.

Feuerstein, R. (1980). *Instrumental enrichment.* Baltimore, MD: University Park.

Feuerstein, R., Klein, P. S., & Tannenbaum, A. J. (1991). *Mediated learning experience (MLE) theoretical, psychological and learning implications.* London: Freund.

Fuller, R. (1977). *In search of the IQ correlation: A scientific whodunit.* Stony Brook, NY: Ball-Stick-Bird.

Gardner, H. (1983). *Frames of mind: The theory of multiple intelligences.* London: Paladin.

Glass, G. V. (1983, January). Effectiveness of special education. *Policy Studies Review, 2*(1). (University of Kansas)

Gould, S. (1981). *The mismeasure of man.* New York: Norton.

Guthrie, R. (1976). *Even the rat was white.* New York: Harper & Row.

Hall, E. T. (1977). *Beyond culture.* New York: Anchor.

Hehir, T., & Latus, T. (Eds.). (1993*). Special education at the century's end: Evolution of theory and practice since 1970* (Reprint Series No. 23). Cambridge, MA: Harvard Educational Review.

Heller, K. A., Holtzman, W. H., & Messick, S. (Eds.). (1982). *Placing children in special education: A strategy for equity.* Washington, DC: National Academy Press.

Helms, J. E. (1992). Why is there no study of cultural equivalence in standardized cognitive ability testing? *American Psychologist, 47*(9), 1083–1101.

Hilliard, A. G., III. (1987a, April-July). The learning potential assessment device and instrumental enrichment as a paradigm shift. *Negro Educational Review, 38*(2–3), 200–208.

Hilliard, A. G., III. (Ed). (1987b, April-July). *Testing African American students [Special issue]. Negro Educational Review, 38*(2–3).

Hilliard, A. G., III. (1990). Back to Binet: The case against the use of IQ tests in the schools. *Contemporary Education, 61*(4), 184–189.

Holtzman, W. H. (1982). Preface. In K. A. Heller, W. H. Holtzman, & S. Messick (Eds.), *Placing children in special education: A strategy for equity.* Washington, DC: Nations Press.

Hoover, M. R., Politzer, R. L., & Taylor, O. (1991). Bias in reading tests for Black language speakers: A sociolinguistic perspective. In A. G. Hilliard III (Ed.), *Testing African American students* (pp. 81–98). Morristown, NJ: Aaron.

Jensen, A. (1969). How much can we boost IQ? *Harvard Educational Review.*

Jensen, A. (1980). *Bias in mental testing.* New York: Free Press.

Jensen, M. R. (1992). Principles of change models in schools psychology and education. In *Advances in cognition and educational practice* (Vol. 1B, pp. 47–72). Greenwich, CT: JAI.

Kamin, L. (1974). *The science and politics of IQ.* New York: Wiley.

Kluwe, R. H., Misiak, C., & Haider, H. (1991). The control of complex systems and performance in intelligence tests. In H. A. H. Rowe (Ed.), *Intelligence, reconceptualization and measurement.* Australian Council for Educational Research. Hillsdale, NJ: Lawrence Erlbaum.

Kozol, J. (1991). *Savage inequalities: Children in America's schools.* New York: Crown.

Lidz, C. S. (1991). *Practitioner's guide to dynamic assessment.* New York: Guilford.

Montagu, A. (1974). *Man's most dangerous myth: The fallacy of race.* New York.

Richele, M. N. (1991). Reconciling views on intelligence. In H. A. H. Rowe (Ed.), *Intelligence, reconceptualization and measurement.* Australian Council for Educational Research. Hillsdale, NJ: Lawrence Erlbaum.

Rowe, H. A. H. (Ed.). (1991). *Intelligence, reconceptualization and measurement.* Australian Council for Educational Research. Hillsdale, NJ: Lawrence Erlbaum.

Shuy, R. W. (1977). Quantitative linguistic analysis: A case for and some warnings against. *Anthropology and Education Quarterly, 1*(2), 78–82.

Sizemore, B. (1988, August). The algebra of African-American achievement. *Effective Schools: Critical Issues in the Education of Black Children*, pp. 123–149. (Washington, DC: National Alliance of Black School Educators).

Skyrtic, T. M. (1991). The special education paradox: Equity as the way to excellence. *Harvard Educational Review, 61*(2), 148–206.

Smith, E. A. (1978). *The retention of the phonological, phonemic, and morphophonemic features of Africa in Afro-American ebonics* (Seminar Series Paper No. 40). Fullerton: California State University at Fullerton, Department of Linguistics.

Smith, E. A. (1979). *A diagnostic instrument for assessing the phonological competence and performance of the inner-city Afro-American child* (Seminar Series Paper No. 41). Fullerton: California State University at Fullerton, Department of Linguistics.

Snyderman, M., & Rothman, S. (1990). *The I.Q. controversy: The media and public policy.* New Brunswick, NJ: Transaction.

Suzuki, S. (1984). *Nurtured by love: The classic approach to talent education.* Smithtown, NY: Exposition.

Yee, A. H. (1983). Ethnicity and race: Psychological perspectives. *Educational Psychologist, 18*(1), 14–24.

Zacharias, J. R. (1977). The trouble with tests. In P. L. Houts (Ed.), *The myth of measurability.* New York: Hart.

Additional Reading

Bailer, W. R., Charles, D. C, & Miller, E. L. (1967). Mid-life attainment of the mentally retarded: A longitudinal study. *Genetic Psychology Monographs, 75,* 235–329.

Bower, B. (1992). Infants signal the birth of knowledge. *Science News, 142*(20), 325.

Bruer, J. T. (1993, Summer). The mind's journey from novice to expert: If we know the route, we can help students negotiate their way. *American Educator*, pp. 6–46.

Chase, A. (1977). *The legacy of Malthus: The social cost of scientific racism*. New York: Alfred A. Knopf.

Chomsky, N. (1971). Deep structure, surface structure, and semantic interpretation. In D. Steinberg & L. Jakobovitz (Eds.), *Semantics*. New York: Cambridge University Press.

Cohen, R. (1969). Conceptual styles, culture conflict, and non-verbal tests of intelligence. *American Anthropologist, 71*(5), 828–857.

Cohen, R. (1971). The influence of conceptual rule sets on measures of learning ability. In *Race and Intelligence*. Anthropological Association.

Dillon, R., & Steinberg, R. J. (1986). *Cognition and instruction*. New York: Academic Press.

Donaldson, M. (1978). *Children's minds*. New York: Norton.

Ginsburg, H. (1972). *The myth of the deprived child: Poor children's intellect*. Englewood Cliffs, NJ: Prentice-Hall.

Hilliard, A. G., III. (1976). *Alternatives to IQ testing: An approach to the identification of "gifted" minority children*. Final report to the California State Department of Education, Special Education Support Unit. (ERIC Clearinghouse on Early Childhood Education. ED 146-009).

Hilliard, A. G., III. (1979). The pedagogy of success. In *The most enabling environment*. Washington, DC: Association for Early Childhood International.

Hilliard, A. G., III. (1981). IQ thinking as catechism: Ethnic and cultural bias or invalid science. *Black Books Bulletin, 7*(2), 99–112.

Hilliard, A. G., III. (1983, Winter). Psychological factors associated with language in the education of the African-American child. *Journal of Negro Education, 52*(1), 24–34.

Hilliard, A. G., III. (1984). IQ thinking as the emperor's new clothes. In C. Reynolds & R. T. Brown (Eds.), *Perspectives on bias in mental testing* (pp. 139–169). New York: Plenum.

Hilliard, A. G., III (1990). Misunderstanding and testing intelligence. In J. Goodlad & P. Keating (Eds.), *Access to knowledge: An agenda for our nation's schools*. New York: College Board.

Hilliard, A. G., III (1994). Thinking skills and students placed at greatest risk in the educational system. In *Restructuring learning: 1990 Summer Institute Papers and Recommendations* (pp. 147–156). Washington, DC: Council of Chief State School Officers.

Jacobs, P. (1977). *Up the IQ*. New York: Wyden.

Labov, W. (1970). The logic of non-standard English. In F. Williams (Ed.), *Language and poverty*. Chicago: Markham.

Lidz, C. S. (Ed.). (1987). *Dynamic assessment: An interractional approach to evaluating learning potential*. New York: Guilford.

Lipsky, D. K., & Gartner, A. (1989). *Beyond separate education: Quality education for all*. Baltimore: Paul H. Brookes.

Oakes, J. (1985). *Keeping track: How schools structure inequality*. New Haven, CT: Yale University Press.

Slack, W. V., & Porter, D. (1980). The Scholastic Aptitude Test: A critical appraisal. *Harvard Educational Review, 50*(2), 154–175.

Spitz, H. H. (1986). *The raising of intelligence: A selected history of attempts to raise retarded intelligence*. Hillsdale, NJ: Lawrence Erlbaum.

Wigdor, A. K., & Garner, W. K. (Eds.). (1982). *Ability testing: Uses, consequences, and controversy*. Washington, DC: National Academy Press.

Wiggins, G. P. (1993). *Assessing student performance: Exploring the purpose and limits of testing*. San Francisco: Jossey-Bass.

CHAPTER 20

Addressing Underrepresentation of Gifted Minority Children Using the Naglieri Nonverbal Ability Test (NNAT)

Jack A. Naglieri
George Mason University

Donna Y. Ford
The Ohio State University

Abstract

A persistent problem in education is the underrepresentation of diverse students in gifted education programs. Many educators attribute the poor participation of diverse students in gifted programs to the ineffectiveness of standardized tests in capturing the ability of these students. Thus, a primary agenda of school selection committees is to find more culturally sensitive measures. This study examined the effectiveness of the Naglieri Nonverbal Ability Test (NNAT) in identifying gifted Black and Hispanic students in comparison to White students. The sample was comprised of 20,270 students in grades K–12 who were similar to the U.S. population on several demographic variables. The distributions of NNAT standard scores were studied separately for White, Black, and Hispanic groups. Results indicate that similar percentages of White (5.6%), Black (5.1%), and Hispanic (4.4%) children earned an NNAT standard score of 125 (95th percentile rank). These findings suggest that the NNAT may be useful as part of a procedure to identify diverse students for gifted education services.

Reprinted from Naglieri, J. A., & Ford, D. Y. (2003). Addressing underrepresentation of gifted minority children using the Naglieri Nonverbal Ability Test (NNAT). *Gifted Child Quarterly, 47,* 155–160. Reprinted with permission of Sage Publications.

> **PUTTING THE RESEARCH TO USE**
>
> There are many smart minority children in our country who may not be considered gifted because they lack the reading, writing, and arithmetic skills typically seen in gifted children and they are identified, in part, by tests of ability that demand school-related knowledge and skills. School ability tests that have verbal and quantitative sections put at a disadvantage minority children with limited educational skills, and, therefore, these children are more likely to earn lower IQ scores. This problem has led some educators to suggest the use of alternative means of assessment that may have limited validity or reliability. In this study, we have shown that a nonverbal test of ability that does not require children to answer verbal and quantitative questions to earn a high IQ can help find more gifted children from minority groups. Those children who demonstrate high performance on a nonverbal test of general ability, but lack academic skills should be served in classes for the gifted. Because there has historically been a reliance on traditional intelligence test scores, rather than nonverbal rests, we have little data on how children who are identified with nonverbal tests might perform in gifted programs. Exactly how they can be served is a question for researchers and policy makers to ponder.

The underrepresentation of minority children in classes for the gifted has been and continues to be one of the most important problems facing educators of gifted students (Ford, 1998). As of 1993, the U.S. Department of Education reported that Black, Hispanic, and Native American students were underrepresented by 50–70% in gifted education programs. Ford reported that, despite recent efforts to redress this problem, the underrepresentation of minority students in gifted programs has been persistent and, for some groups, has increased. School personnel and researchers have sought to resolve this problem by examining the ability tests used and procedures followed (de Bernard, 1985; Sternberg, 1985). Many reports attribute the problem to standardized tests, contending that these tests fail to assess the strengths and abilities of culturally, ethnically, and linguistically diverse populations (e.g., Frazier et al., 1995). Support for this assertion comes from reports showing that Black, Hispanic, and Native American students consistently score lower than White students on traditional standardized tests (Brody, 1992; Sattler, 1988).

Despite the fact that intelligence tests such as the Wechsler Intelligence Scale for Children–Third Edition (Wechsler, 1991) and the Stanford-Binet IV (Thorndike, Hagen, & Sattler, 1986) yield lower scores for minority children (see Kaufman, 1994, for a discussion of the WISC-III), they have been widely used for gifted identification. Wasserman and Becker (2000) have provided a summary of recent research on the WISC-III (Wechsler, 1991), Stanford-Binet Intelligence Scale, Fourth Edition (Thorndike, Hagen, & Sattler), and Woodcock-Johnson Tests of Cognitive Ability (WJ-R; Woodcock & Johnson, 1989) that used samples matched on key demographic variables. They found that the average differences in favor of Whites between standard scores for matched samples of Black and White groups were as follows: WISC-III = 11.0; Stanford-Binet IV = 8.1; and Woodcock-Johnson Tests of Cognitive Ability = 11.7. These sizable mean score differences suggest that fewer minority children might be identified when such tests are used for determination of giftedness.

Other reports contend that policies and procedures have a disparate impact on the participation of diverse students in gifted programs, especially the common procedure used by schools: teacher referral. Some researchers (e.g., Ford, 1998) have suggested that teachers often under-refer diverse students for gifted education screening and placement. An additional policy used in some school systems is that students must be assessed in English, which has a profound impact on linguistically diverse or limited English proficient students (de Bernard, 1985).

Given the widespread concerns about testing and assessing diverse students with traditional measures, it is important that school administrators closely examine tests considered culturally fair. Many of these tests fall under the label of "nonverbal tests." Nonverbal tests like the Raven's Progressive Matrices (Raven, 1947) and the Naglieri Nonverbal Ability Test (NNAT; Naglieri, 1997a) have been used to evaluate diverse populations of children. Raven's Progressive Matrices and the NNAT are comprised of nonverbal, geometric designs arranged in a 2 x 2 or 3 x 3 matrix. These items can be considered to have content that is culturally reduced because they do not contain items that require the child, for example, to define words or solve oral (English) arithmetic problems. The tests seem especially useful for identification of gifted minority children because the nonverbal content is more appropriate for a wide variety of children (Jensen, 1980; Naglieri & Prewett, 1990; Sattler, 1988).

Researchers have found that the nonverbal measures are less influenced by limited English language skills and, therefore, are more appropriate for bilingual children (Hayes, 1999; Naglieri & Yazzie, 1983). Verbal test scores can be adversely influenced when children have poor language skills and live in poverty (Kaufman, 1994; Naglieri, 1999). The use of nonverbal tests helps reduce problems associated with measuring ability through the use of language tests like vocabulary, for example. For these reasons, nonverbal tests of ability are considered appropriate for a wide variety of persons, especially those with limited English language skills and academic failure (Bracken & McCallum, 1998; Zurcher, 1998).

Raven's Progressive Matrices (Raven, 1947) is the oldest and most widely used nonverbal test. This test has been studied in many countries around the world and with a substantial variety of individuals. Despite its widespread use in the United States, the test has been consistently criticized for its poor psychometric qualities, including the lack of a well-constructed norm group, uneven gradients of item difficulty, inadequate numbers of items, and the need for better documentation of psychometric qualities in the test manual (Jensen, 1980; Nicholson, 1989). Most importantly, however, the difficulty with Raven's Progressive Matrices most relevant to this discussion is findings of higher mean score differences between White and minority children (see Mills & Tissot, 1995; Vincent, 1991). The purpose of this study, therefore, was to examine the question of identification of minority children as gifted using a different nonverbal test: the NNAT.

The Naglieri Nonverbal Ability Test uses the same progressive matrix format as Raven's tests, but there are some important differences. First, the NNAT, like its original versions, the Matrix Analogies Test-Short Form (MAT-SF; Naglieri, 1985a) and Matrix Analogies Test-Expanded Form (MAT-EF; Naglieri, 1985b), was constructed using items that are least influenced by color-impaired vision (only the colors white, black, blue, and yellow are used). Second the NNAT is well standardized on a sample of more than 89,000 students in grades K–12. Third, the psychometric properties of the test are amply documented (Naglieri, 1997b). Finally, there is a research base on the NNAT and its earlier versions (the MAT-EF and MAT-SF) that support its use for diverse populations of children.

Naglieri's progressive matrices tests have a history of yielding small differences between White and minority groups. Naglieri (1985b) summarized the results of two studies involving minority children conducted using the original versions of the NNAT, the MAT-SF and MATEF standardization sample. White (n = 336) and Black (n = 336) children matched on school, gender, and age in years performed similarly (effect size= 0.17 or about 2.6 standard score points) on the MAT-SF. Results for the MAT-EF were similar; matched samples of White (n = 55) and Black (n = 55) children earned standard scores (mean of 100, SD of 15) of 90.6 and 90.0, respectively. In other research, the MAT correlated significantly with the Wechsler Intelligence Scale for Children-Revised (WISC-R; Wechsler,1974) Performance IQ Scale (r = .43, p <.001) and Raven's Progressive Matrices (r = .64, p < .001) for a sample of 114 Native American students (Naglieri, 1985b).

In addition to these initial studies conducted on the first editions of progressive matrices tests by Naglieri (1985a, 1985b), there has been one published study that examined differences between matched samples of White with Black, Hispanic, and Asian American children on the second edition (NNAT; Naglieri, 1997a). In this study, Naglieri and Ronning (2000a) examined differences between three matched samples of White (n = 2,306) and Black (n = 2,306); White (n = 1,176) and Hispanic (n = 1,176); and White (n = 466) and Asian (n = 466) children on the NNAT. They found only small differences between the NNAT mean scores for the White and Black samples (d-ratio = .25 or about 4 standard score points) and minimal differences between the White and Hispanic (d-ratio = .17 or about 2.5 standard score points), as well as White and Asian groups (d-ratio = .02 or less than one standard score point). Additionally, Naglieri and Ronning (2000b) found that the NNAT correlated similarly with achievement as measured by the Stanford Achievement Test (Ninth Edition) for the White and minority groups. This implies that children's performance on the NNAT is predictive of their scores on a test of academic achievement (SAT). The results also suggested that the NNAT scores had utility for assessment of White and minority children and that, should the NNAT be used for identification of gifted children, similar numbers of each population might be identified. The present study was conducted to examine the question of identification based upon an ability score and to meet the need for more research on the second edition of this nonverbal test of ability.

Method

Participants

The sample included 20,270 children from the NNAT standardization sample tested during the fall of 1995. These students are representative of the national school population according to socioeconomic status (SES), urbanicity, and ethnicity (see Table 1). The data provided in Table 1 show that the characteristics of the separate Black, Hispanic, and White groups are similar in composition. There were comparable percentages of children from the four regions except for West, which had more Black and Hispanic children. The groups differed slightly on urban, suburban, rural community settings. Most of the Black and White children were from suburban and rural settings, while the Hispanic children were fairly evenly dispersed from each setting. Socioeconomic data for the groups showed that the White and Black samples were similar except that there were more Whites at the middle SES level. The Hispanic sample had a large percentage at the low and low middle levels of SES.

Instrument

The Naglieri Nonverbal Ability Test (Naglieri, 1997a) is a brief nonverbal measure of ability that does not require the child to read, write, or speak (Naglieri, 1997b). The test is a nonverbal measure of general ability comprised of progressive matrix items that utilize shapes and geometric designs interrelated through spatial or logical organization. All of the NNAT items require the child to examine the relationships among the parts of the matrix and determine which response is the correct one based only on the information provided in the matrix. The NNAT items are organized into seven levels, each containing 38 items selected to be most appropriate for children at the grade or grades for which that level is intended. Each level contains items that overlap with adjacent higher and lower levels, as well as unique items. Shared items were used to develop a continuous scaled score across the entire standardization sample. The seven levels and corresponding grades for which they are appropriate are as follows: A / K; B / 1; C / 2; D / 3 & 4; E / 5 & 6; F / 7–9; G / 10–12.

NNAT raw scores are converted to Nonverbal Ability Index (NAI) standard scores set at a mean of 100 and SD of 15 through an intermediate Rasch value called a scaled score. Level D of the NNAT was used as the base level to which all other levels were equated. The appropriate equating constant was then added to the spring standardization Rasch item difficulties of each level to produce a continuous Rasch ability scale across all levels of the tests (for more information, see Naglieri, 1997b). The internal reliability coefficients for the NNAT by grade range from .83 to .93 with a median internal reliability across all levels of .87 (Naglieri, 1997b).

Data Analyses

The following question was addressed in this study: Are the percentages of children who earned NNAT standard scores from 120 to 140 comparable by racial and ethnic groups? This question is essential given the underrepresentation of minority children in gifted education programs. Frequency distributions of standard scores were computed by race or ethnic group to answer this question. Comparison of these frequency distributions allowed for determination of the percentage of each group that would meet the intellectual ability criteria based upon a standard score and corresponding percentile cut-off point. In summary, the numbers and percentages of children who earned standard scores of 120, as well as 125, 130, 135, and 140 or above (corresponding to the 91st, 95th, 98th, 99th, and 99.6th percentile ranks) on the NNAT, were computed for each group.

Results

The sample of 14,141 White children earned a mean NNAT score of 99.3 (SD = 16.7), which was similar to the mean scores earned by the Black (n = 2,863; mean = 96.1; SD = 17.5) and Hispanic (n = 1,991; mean = 97.3; SD = 16.8) children. The percentages of children who earned NNAT standard scores of 120 or higher, 125 or higher, through 140 or higher are provided in Table 2. These values show that there was similarity in the relative proportions of students from the three groups. That is, 2.5% of White, 2.6% of Black, and 2.3% of Hispanic children earned NNAT standard scores at the 98th percentile (a standard score of 130). The NNAT standard score of 125 (95th percentile) resulted in 5.6, 5.1, and 4.4% of the White, Black, and Hispanic samples, respectively. These data imply that, if the

Table 1
Demographic Characteristics of the NNAT Samples

	White		Black		Hispanic	
Variable	n	%	n	%	n	%
Total n	14,141		2,863		1,991	
Gender						
Male	7,090	50.0	1,519	53.0	1,058	53.0
Female	7,088	50.0	1,346	47.0	939	47.0
Region						
Northeast	2,220	15.7	678	23.7	192	9.6
Midwest	4,629	32.6	484	16.9	137	6.8
Southeast	3,459	24.4	556	19.4	229	11.4
West	3,872	27.3	1,147	40.0	1,444	72.1
Urbanicity						
Urban	411	3.3	302	11.0	604	31.2
Suburban	5,476	44.6	1,536	56.1	827	42.8
Rural	6,392	52.1	899	32.8	503	26.0
SES status						
Low	2,353	19.2	568	20.8	813	42.0
Low middle	2,464	20.1	716	26.2	567	29.3
Middle	2,510	20.4	231	8.4	58	3.0
High-middle	2,910	23.7	533	19.5	119	6.2
High	2,042	16.6	689	25.2	377	19.5

NNAT were used as one of the criteria in a system of identification of gifted children, similar percentages of White, Black, and Hispanic children would be selected using the cut-offs of 125 or 130.

Discussion

The results of this investigation are consistent with previous research on the NNAT, which has shown that samples of White and minority children perform similarly on this nonverbal measure of ability. The findings, however, go beyond the examination of mean score differences and correlations to achievement provided by Naglieri and Ronning (2000a, 2000b) to include an important examination of the differential rates of identification for diverse groups. These results are similar to previous studies of the NNAT and its earlier version, the MAT (Naglieri, 1985a, 1985b), which demonstrated that the instrument yielded small differences between majority and minority groups (Naglieri, 1985b; Naglieri & Ronning, 2000a). More importantly, however, the similar percentages of White, Black, and Hispanic children who earned NNAT standard scores of 125, for example, illustrated the potential utility of this instrument for the identification of gifted minority children. With the exception of the Cognitive Assessment System (Naglieri &

Table 2
NNAT Scores

	White		Black		Hispanic		Expected
	n	%	n	%	n	%	%
120 & above	1,571	10.3	269	9.4	190	9.5	9.0
125 & above	906	5.6	145	5.1	88	4.4	5.0
130 & above	467	2.5	75	2.6	46	2.3	2.0
135 & above	190	1.1	42	1.5	18	0.9	1.0
140 & above	90	0.6	19	0.6	9	0.4	0.4
Total Sample n	14,141		2,863		1,991		

Note. Expected percentage values are those associated with normal curve probabilities.

Das, 1997) and Kaufman Assessment Battery for Children (Kaufman & Kaufman, 1983) other measures of intelligence have not produced similar findings.

The underrepresentation of Black and Hispanic children in classes for the gifted has been and continues to be of interest to many educators and psychologists. While there is ample evidence that traditional intelligence tests yield differences between groups that do not favor minority populations (e.g., Brody, 1992), they continue to be used. The small mean score differences for the NNAT previously reported by Naglieri and Ronning (2000a), in combination with the data presented in this study, imply that ability can be assessed for these minority populations in a manner that may not lead to underrepresentation. Additionally, because the NNAT can be administered in a group setting (or individually using the NNAT-Individual [Naglieri, 2002]), the information can be obtained in considerably less time per student.

The importance of this study and those that preceded it illustrate how a nonverbal test can be used to evaluate fairly minority children's cognitive ability and, subsequently, provide access to gifted education services. The primary difference between the NNAT and other group ability tests is that the latter typically include verbal, quantitative, as well as nonverbal tests. Some researchers have argued that a general ability test with verbal and quantitative items is limited in utility because it demands English language skills and knowledge directly taught in school (Naglieri, 1999; Naglieri & Prewett, 1990). This study showed that the NNAT found similar percentages of White, Black, and Hispanic children to be intellectually gifted. These results further support Naglieri and Ronning's (2000a) suggestion that a nonverbal measure can be a more appropriate measure of general ability for minority children than a measure of general ability that contains both verbal and nonverbal content.

The most important finding of this study (and previous ones) is that, when the NNAT was used, the mean score differences and percentages of children with high standard scores between White and minority groups were small. These results suggest that, when this approach is used as part of the identification process, it could help diverse students gain access to gifted education services.

The next step in the study of the utility of this approach is to examine what classroom modifications and interventions, if any, are necessary when children are identified and placed in gifted programs partially on the basis of nonverbal measures. When children with high NNAT scores and low achievement (because of language differences or limited exposure to academic content) are identified, a curriculum that meets their particular educational needs will be necessary. These children will be different from those who have high NNAT and high verbal and quantitative scores (e.g., they may have poor basic skills), and some type of differentiated instruction will be needed. Researchers should carefully study the implications of such a potential change in the results of identification and how to teach children who score very well on nonverbal tests of ability, but have lower levels of achievement. They should also examine issues like how long it will take for these students to obtain high levels of achievement. These and other issues should be examined so that we can more fully address the problem of underrepresentation of minority children in classes for the gifted. In the mean time, we must remember that a significant segment of our student population—culturally and linguistically diverse students—have been consistently and significantly underrepresented in our gifted programs; thus, new answers to this persistent problem must be pursued. Nonverbal intelligence tests show promise for increasing the opportunity for diverse students to participate in gifted education programs.

References

Bracken, B. A., & McCallum, R. S. (1998). *Universal nonverbal intelligence test.* Itasca, IL: Riverside.

Brody, N. (1992). *Intelligence.* San Diego: Academic Press.

de Bernard. A. E. (1985). Why Jose can't get into the gifted class: The bilingual child and standardized reading tests. *Roeper Review, 8,* 80–82.

Ford, D. Y. (1998). The underrepresentation of minority students in gifted education: Problems and promises in recruitment and retention. *Journal of Special Education, 32,* 4–14.

Frazier, M. M., Martin, D., Garcia, J., Finley, V. S., Frank, E., Krisel, S., et al. (1995). *A new window for looking at gifted children.* Storrs: National Research Center on the Gifted and Talented, University of Connecticut.

Hayes, S. C. (1999). Comparison of the Kaufman Brief Intelligence Test and the Matrix Analogies Test-Short Form in an adolescent forensic population. *Psychological Assessment, 11,* 108–110.

Jensen, A. R. (1980). *Bias in mental testing.* New York: Free Press.

Kaufman, A. S. (1994) *Intelligent testing with the WISC-III.* New York: Wiley.

Kaufman, A. S., & Kaufman, N. L. (1983). *Kaufman assessment battery for children.* Circle Pines, MN: American Guidance Service.

Mills, C. J., & Tissot, S. L. (1995). Identifying academic potential in students from underrepresented populations: Is using the Ravens Progressive Matrices a good idea? *Gifted Child Quarterly, 39,* 209–217.

Naglieri, J. A. (1985a). *Matrix analogies test–Short form.* San Antonio, TX: The Psychological Corporation.

Naglieri, J. A. (1985b). *Matrix analogies test–Expanded form.* San Antonio, TX: The Psychological Corporation.

Naglieri, J. A. (1997a). *Naglieri nonverbal ability test.* San Antonio, TX: The Psychological Corporation.

Naglieri, J. A. (1997b). *NNAT multilevel technical manual.* San Antonio, TX: The Psychological Corporation.

Naglieri, J. A. (1999). *Essentials of CAS assessment.* New York: Wiley.

Naglieri, J. A., & Das, J. P. (1997). *Cognitive assessment system.* Itasca, IL: Riverside

Naglieri, J. A., & Prewett, P. N. (1990). Nonverbal intelligence: A selected review of instruments and their use. In R. W. Kamphaus & C. R. Reynolds (Eds.), *Handbook of psychological and educational assessment: Volume I: Intelligence and achievement* (pp. 348–370). New York: Guilford Press.

Naglieri, J. A., & Ronning, M. E. (2000a). Comparison of White, African-American, Hispanic, and Asian children on the Naglieri Nonverbal Ability Test. *Psychological Assessment, 12,* 328–334.

Naglieri, J. A., & Ronning, M. E. (2000b). The relationships between general ability using the NNAT and SAT reading achievement. *Journal of Psychoeducational Assessment, 18,* 230–239.

Naglieri, J. A., & Yazzie, C. (1983). Comparison of the WISCR and PPVT-R with Navajo children. *Journal of Clinical Psychology, 39,* 598–600.

Nicholson, C. L. (1989). Matrix Analogies Test (MAT). *Diagnostique, 15,* 115–123.

Raven, J. C. (1947). *Coloured progressive matrices.* London: H. K. Lewis.

Sattler, J. M. (1988). *Assessment of children* (3rd ed.). San Diego, CA: Sattler.

Sternberg, R. J. (1985). *Beyond IQ: A triarchic theory of human intelligence.* New York: Cambridge University Press.

Thorndike, R. I., Hagen, E. P., & Sattler, J. M. (1986). *Stanford-Binet intelligence scale: Fourth edition.* Itasca, IL: Riverside.

Vincent, K. R. (1991). Black/White IQ differences: Does age make the difference? *Journal of Clinical Psychology, 47,* 266–270.

Wasserman, J. D., & Becker, K. A. (2000). *Racial and ethnic group mean score differences on intelligence tests.* Paper presented at the annual meeting of the American Psychological Association, Washington, DC.

Wechsler, D. (1974). *Wechsler intelligence scale for children-Revised.* San Antonio, TX: The Psychological Corporation.

Wechsler, D. (1991). *Wechsler intelligence scale for children-Third edition.* San Antonio, TX: The Psychological Corporation.

Woodcock, R. W., & Johnson, M. B. (1989). *Woodcock-Johnson revised tests of achievement: Standard and supplemental batteries.* Itasca, IL: Riverside.

Zurcher, R. (1998). Issues and trends in culture-fair assessment. *Intervention in School and Clinic, 34,* 103–106.

Author Note

This research was supported in part by grant R215K010121 from the U.S. Department of Education.

CHAPTER 21

Nondiscriminatory Assessment: Considerations for Gifted Education

Laurice M. Joseph
Ohio State University

Donna Y. Ford
Vanderbilt University

Abstract

Nondiscriminatory assessment practices have been proposed as a model of assessment for individuals of diverse cultures who are suspected as having a disability. This paper presents the use of nondiscriminatory assessment practices in evaluating students of diverse cultures who may be identified as gifted. Principles and guidelines for nondiscriminatory ways of assessing students of diverse cultures who may be gifted are presented. Implications for putting nondiscriminatory assessment procedures into practice are provided.

There is a legacy of research, as well as theories and opinions that are critical of the practice of applying standardized tests to linguistically, ethnically, and culturally diverse populations. The central focus in the debates, particularly of those who oppose the use of standardized tests with diverse groups, is on the issue of fairness and the discriminatory impact of standardized tests. It has been consistently argued that such tests contribute to the underrepresentation of diverse students in gifted education and their overrepresentation in special education placements. Standardized tests are used extensively, and sometimes exclusively, to

> ## PUTTING THE RESEARCH TO USE
>
> First and foremost, educators need to be strongly encouraged to identify or refer students from diverse cultures or ethnic groups who may potentially be eligible for gifted and talented programming. Once students have been referred for assessment, nondiscriminatory assessment practices should be implemented. Nondiscriminatory assessment models have been considered to be best practice for assessing children who are culturally or ethnically diverse and have suspected learning problems. However, nondiscriminatory assessment has not been used to identify children who are culturally or ethnically diverse and who may be potentially gifted. The model that is presented here provides processes by which assessment and identification for gifted and talented programs can be provided for children who are culturally or ethnically diverse in a manner that minimizes bias. This means that professionals who are a part of the assessment process need to gather data from a variety of sources and individuals within cultural contexts so that assessment is multifactored, multidisciplinary, and culturally sensitive. Assessment team members need to select assessment instruments carefully so these tools are culturally sensitive and fair and will yield data that is comprehensive for making the best possible program decisions. The assessment team should include professionals that are knowledgeable about the ethnicity and culture of the student being evaluated. Data gathered from assessments should lead to designing appropriate enriched programs that embrace diverse cultures and ethnicity for students.

screen, identify, and place students in gifted education classes and services (Council of State Directors of Programs for the Gifted and the National Association for Gifted Children, 2003). And despite cautions against the exclusive use of such tests for identifying gifted students (e.g., National Association for Gifted Children [NAGC], 2001), many districts continue to use a single test and strict cutoff scores to identify gifted students, according to data collected from state departments of education (Council of State Directors). The implications of using a single test, strict cutoff scores, and tests alone (without other means of assessment) for identification and placement is indefensible. For instance, gifted children have often been identified through the use of a cutoff score on an intelligence test such as the Wechsler or Binet, or through a group intelligence test such as the Slosson or OLSAT (Sparrow & Gurland, 1998). However, ceiling effects make cutoff scores problematic (Kaufmann, 1993), and cultural bias can also occur from the use of cutoff scores (Tyerman, 1986). While Black students comprised 17% of the U.S.

school population in 1998, they comprised only 7.4% of the students in gifted education programs. Likewise, while Hispanic Americans represented 14.3% of the school population, they comprised only 8.63% of students in gifted education programs (U.S. Department of Education, 1998).

Although used extensively in school settings, there has been a great deal of controversy surrounding the use and usefulness of intelligence tests for making decisions about students. Major criticisms have been made with regard to the use of intelligence tests, and these criticisms include the following: (a) Intelligence tests have an inherent bias toward emphasizing convergent, analytical, and scientific modes of thought; (b) intelligence tests measure a limited range of cognitive abilities and do not (cannot) measure the entire range of abilities that make up intelligence (Groth-Marnat, 2003; Sternberg, 2000); (c) intelligence tests do not adequately measure many cognitive abilities that contemporary theories and research specify as important in understanding, learning, and problem solving (Flanagan & Ortiz, 2001); (d) intelligence tests are limited in their ability to make long-term predictions (Groth-Marnat); (e) intelligence tests are not measures of innate fixed ability, and their use in classifying students is questionable; (f) intelligence tests may not be appropriate to use with culturally diverse students; and (g) intelligence tests may not be appropriate to use with linguistically diverse students. Interestingly, many test developers today attempt to attend to the potential cultural nuances within their respective instruments, but allocate a small section in their test manuals to discuss the challenges in using their instrument for assessing individuals of diverse cultures (Esters, Ittenback, & Han, 1997). Thus, those administering, interpreting, and using tests may not be adequately prepared to understand and address cultural nuances.

Criticisms Regarding Using Tests With Diverse Groups

Three questions seem to capture the attention of educators when administering tests to diverse groups. (1) Is the test biased against diverse groups? (2) Is the test culturally loaded? (3) Is it fair to use tests with diverse groups?

In their review of tests, Flanagan and Ortiz (2001) categorized tests based on their degree of cultural loading and degree of linguistic demand. Tests can vary significantly on each dimension: For example, a test can be high in linguistic demand but low or moderate in degree of cultural loading. Degree of cultural loading represents the extent to which a given test requires specific knowledge of or experience with mainstream U.S. culture. Degree of linguistic demand reflects the extent to which individuals must be English proficient and otherwise familiar with how language (vocabulary, definitions, homographs, homonyms, similarities, clichés, proverbs, etc.) is used in the U.S. Therefore, tests can be linguistically biased, not because of any inherent structural defect, but because of the expectations and assumptions regarding the comparability of language proficiency among individuals taking the test. A student who is more proficient in the English language is likely to score higher on a test than someone who is less proficient. Further, the higher the linguistic demands of the test, the more likely students with limited English proficiency are to score low. In essence, Flanagan and Ortiz maintain that:

1. Tests of intelligence are constructed in ways that presume that a given level of language proficiency is present in the average individual who has the ability to comprehend the instructions, formulate and verbalize responses, or otherwise use language ability in completing the expected task.
2. Bias results in cases in which individuals are limited in English proficiency or for whatever reasons are not developmentally equivalent in language proficiency in comparison to a norm group.

Personal Biases

While educators may recognize the limits of intelligence tests in general, but particularly with diverse individuals, they seldom have formal training in understanding their own personal and professional biases. Educators who hold stereotypes about diverse individuals will impact the performance of diverse students, as well as how they interpret test results. Confirmatory bias exists when educators consciously or unconsciously administer and interpret tests with stereotypes or preconceived ideas about diverse individuals. Ortiz (2002) notes that confirmatory bias can occur in both the type of data collected and the manner in which the data are interpreted (Matsumoto, 1994). For example, confirmatory bias can occur if standardized test data is only supplemented with rating scale results completed by the teacher who made the referral on the student. Chances are, the referring teacher will likely reflect her same concerns about the student on a rating scale she is asked to complete as part of an evaluation to determine if the student has a disability or is gifted. Collecting subjective data or insufficient data contributes to misinterpretation of assessment results. Bias at the interpretation level can also occur when the evaluator(s) fails to note the significant strengths or weaknesses in students' performance on assessment measures. Additionally, bias in interpreting results can occur if not all assessment data that was gathered is interpreted and reported.

"Educators can reduce this form of bias by avoiding attempts to confirm presumptions or pre-existing deficits and, instead, testing hypotheses" (Ortiz, 2002, p. 1323). The process of assessment should begin with the hypothesis that the individual's performance, particularly if low, is not intrinsic in nature, but a function of his or her environment and external factors (e.g., unequal opportunity to learn, poor educational experiences, lack of access to reading, etc.). Stated another way, the assumption of normality should guide the assessment process; when the process of assessment or evaluation is guided with the presumption of normality, it reduces the tendency to search for data or "see" patterns of dysfunction where none may exist" (Ortiz, p. 1323). In essence, educators who lack formal preparation to work with and evaluate diverse students might need to seek such training. This may help to reduce stereotypes and other preconceived notions about diverse individuals and, in turn, may increase the validity of interpretations and the overall assessment process. This process has been referred to as nondiscriminatory assessment practices (Ortiz).

Nondiscriminatory Assessment

Nondiscriminatory assessment is much more than considering which instruments should be used and which should not be used. It is more than simply eliminating tests that may contain bias (Ortiz, 2002). Although educators must aim for conducting completely nondiscriminatory or nonbiased assessment, some scholars contend that "completely unbiased assessment is an illusion, because it is impossible to eliminate every single instance of bias or every potentially discriminatory aspect of assessment" (Ortiz, p. 1321). Nondiscriminatory assessment is concerned with fairness in all aspects of evaluating individuals. It includes selecting the least biased instruments, seeking to avoid confirmatory biases (having preconceived notions or stereotypes about diverse individuals), and ensuring that policies and procedures are fair or nondiscriminatory. "Nondiscriminatory assessment is a collection of approaches, each designed to systematically reduce bias with the broader framework" (Ortiz, p. 1324).

Nondiscriminatory Assessment Procedures and Recommendations

Ortiz (2002) developed one possible framework for nondiscriminatory assessment. It is guided by 10 promising procedures and recommendations:
1. Assess and evaluate the learning ecology.
2. Assess and evaluate language proficiency.
3. Assess and evaluate opportunity for learning, as well as whether limited, inappropriate, or lack of instruction occurred.
4. Assess and evaluate educationally relevant cultural and linguistic factors.
5. Evaluate, revise, and retest hypotheses.
6. Determine the need for and language of assessment.
7. Reduce bias in traditional testing practices.

8. Utilize authentic and alternative assessment procedures.
9. Evaluate and interpret all data within the context of the learning ecology.
10. Link assessment data to selecting or designing instruction.
11. Intervene by providing opportunities for learning and appropriate instruction.
12. Assess and evaluate the effectiveness of interventions.

Each of these is described in more detail below.
1. *Assess and evaluate the learning ecology.* Nondiscriminatory assessment begins with exploring extrinsic causes that might be related to performance. Within the context of the learning environment, hypotheses should be developed around a student's unique experiential background and, therefore, factors associated with culture and experiences that can (adversely) affect test performance. Given various opportunities within the context of the learning environment, one should seek to evaluate how a student who may be potentially gifted responds to cognitive and academic tasks.
2. *Assess and evaluate language proficiency.* An evaluation of a student's language proficiency is crucial to nondiscriminatory assessment. Poor test scores (and academic performance) associated with language proficiency levels can be properly evaluated, which leads to the development of instructional interventions that are linguistically appropriate for a student from a diverse culture who is potentially gifted.
3. *Assess and evaluate opportunity for learning.* As noted by Ortiz (2002), the curriculum, personnel, policies, and instructional setting must be evaluated to determine whether diverse students have been provided with an adequate "opportunity to learn." Data can be collected from evaluations of the classroom environment and teaching methods; direct observation of students' academic performance; review of educational records, progress reports, and attendance records; review of the content and level of the curriculum; analysis of the match between the students' needs and the curriculum, and between students' language and language of instruction; assessment of the cultural relevance of the curriculum, teaching strategies and styles, and teacher attitudes and expectations; interviews with students and their families; determination of peer relationships and pressures; and more. In other words, it may be difficult to determine potential giftedness if students of diverse cultures are not provided with appropriate opportunities to demonstrate advanced abilities.
4. *Assess and evaluate educationally relevant cultural and linguistic factors.* Learning takes place not only in school, but also in the broader scope of a student's social and cultural milieu. With diverse individuals, including individuals of diverse cultures who may be gifted, it is important to assess

and evaluate these milieu and their influences on school learning, language development, and educational process. Language assessments, observations of the individual, home visits, and interviews with family members can shed light on these factors.

5. *Evaluate, revise, and retest hypotheses.* All reasonable and viable factors that could be related to an individual's test performance should be evaluated and ruled out. Data to test hypotheses should be collected and used to revise original hypotheses. Relevant data to collect appear in the previous recommendations (e.g., learning opportunities, etc.). All efforts must be made to reduce or eliminate potentially discriminatory attributions regarding students' test performance.

6. *Determine the need for and language of assessments.* When a student is not proficient in English, test performance may be significantly affected. To address this issue, these individuals should be assessed in their primary language or native mode of communication by an assessor who possesses knowledge regarding the factors relevant to the student's unique experiences and how they may affect learning and development.

7. *Reduce bias in traditional testing practices.* This may be accomplished by administering tests in a nondiscriminatory manner or modifying the testing process in a way that is less discriminatory initially. Some suggestions include bilingual administration of tests, extending or eliminating time constraints when appropriate, and accepting alternative response formats (e.g., gestures, in a different language, additional probing and querying of incorrect responses, etc.). Like Ortiz (2002), we recognize that these changes and others should not compromise the standardization of the tests.

8. *Utilize authentic and alternative assessment procedures.* Nonstandardized assessment instruments and strategies can provide valuable information about students. Curriculum-based assessments, performance-based assessments, portfolio assessments, nonverbal reasoning tests, and metacognitive awareness inventories (e.g., Mokhtari & Reichard, 2002) should be included in the assessment process. Additionally, observing the strategies that students are using while completing items on tests may provide insights as to how they are reasoning about information. The data derived from these types of assessment procedures provide the evaluator with an opportunity to view performance through a qualitative lens. Every effort must be made to avoid using single scores, interpreting only results from quantitative sources of data, and unduly favoring certain data over other data, as these can lead to discriminatory inferences and outcomes (Ortiz, 2002). Moreover, evaluators should keep in mind that direct, curriculum-based, and performance-based assessments offer a more direct link to

intervention than cognitive ability tests (Canter, 1997). While these types of alternative measures have been used in the identification of children with suspected disabilities, they have not been used as often in the identification of individuals who may be gifted.

9. *Evaluate and interpret all data within the context of the learning ecology.* "All data collected over the course of nondiscriminatory assessment should be evaluated in an integrated manner, utilizing information obtained about student's unique experiences and background as the appropriate context" (Ortiz, 2002, p. 1332).

10. *Link assessment to instruction.* Assessment, even the most comprehensive assessment and the most nondiscriminatory assessment, is of little value unless it can be used to target or develop instruction. Students who may be gifted need targeted enriched instruction rather than a "one-size-fits-all" enriched instruction. This will help them maximize and apply their exceptional talents. It should be noted that there is inadequate data to suggest that many standardized intelligence tests used as part of comprehensive assessment processes have treatment utility (Braden, 1997; Sternberg, 2000), and this is a consideration that must be addressed as it contributes, in part, to the overall validity of an instrument (American Educational Research Association, American Psychological Association, and National Council on Measurement in Education, 1999).

11. *Intervene by providing opportunities for learning and appropriate instruction.* Vygotsky (1978) defined intelligence as the zone of proximal development, which is considered to be what a student can accomplish if provided appropriate mediational or "cultural" tools. Many educators today use the term *scaffolding* when they refer to providing appropriate types of assistance to students. When diverse students score low, it may be necessary to scaffold their learning by modifying instructional programs and providing students with test-taking skills, language-based skills, opportunities to receive corrective feedback and practice, and other relevant interventions. These students may not have been provided with opportunities to perform cognitive/academic tasks, such as inductive and deductive reasoning tasks. They may need opportunities to be exposed to tasks that demand these ways of thinking and to have particular ways of thinking modeled for them (e.g., teacher vocalizations of thought processes while solving problems). For instance, most of us learned to solve verbal analogies by being provided with demonstrations of solving these types of analogies. Before many of us learned to apply the scientific method to science fair projects, scientific inquiry procedures were demonstrated to us with opportunities to practice through in-class simulations or lab experiments. Thus, providing insufficient opportunities to learn and providing inappropriate instruction can

be considered biased educational practices (Canter, 1997), and one creates bias when he or she excludes individuals from receiving opportunities.
12. *Assess the effectiveness of instruction.* The effectiveness of targeted instruction should be assessed to determine if instruction is truly targeted to meet individual enrichment needs or if modifications to existing instruction need to be made. The assessment to instruction link is not linear but rather circular and continuous. As children acquire skills observed through assessment data, instruction on more advanced skills are provided and assessed, and so forth.

OTHER CONSIDERATIONS FOR NONDISCRIMINATORY ASSESSMENT

The following are presented as additional methods for decreasing biases and disparate impact when assessing students from diverse backgrounds. Flanagan and Ortiz (2001) provided several recommendations for promoting nondiscriminatory assessment: (a) Develop culturally based and linguistically based hypotheses regarding test performance of diverse individuals; (b) apply cultural-linguistic contexts to all data, and assess all information within the cultural background of the individual; (c) assess students' language history, development, and proficiency; (d) assess the effects of cultural and linguistic differences on students when comparing data across groups; (e) assess environmental and community factors and their impact on students' test performance (including socioeconomic status, parents' educational level, etc.); and (f) utilize authentic and alternative assessment practices (Flanagan & Ortiz; Ortiz, 2002).

Assessment evaluators should be encouraged to establish rapport with the student outside the testing situation in order to help increase the validity of the assessment instrument and process. Evaluators should also learn about the student's culture before comparisons are made with the normative sample of the testing instrument. This task may be difficult if educators have not received formal preparation in cross-cultural communication and assessment. Along these lines, Ortiz (2002) noted three shortcomings in the preparation of school psychologists. First, few school psychologists are provided sufficient training to become competent in conducting assessments with diverse individuals. Secondly, they are seldom taught to consider how their use of biased or discriminatory instruments might impact students. Finally, few are taught how to make testing and assessment less biased or discriminatory. Ortiz further acknowledged that some educators may have stereotypes about diverse individuals that can contribute to biased interpretations of their test scores. Preconceived notions affect the questions asked during interviews, the behaviors observed, instruments selected, and the work samples selected. Specifically, Ortiz raises issues about confirmatory bias whereby "personal and professional bias often leads to idiosyncratic interpretations of the same data, particularly when assessment was begun with preconceived ideas" (p. 1323). Likewise, hypotheses about test performance that are made on the basis of stereotyped or preconceived notions can often steer assessment away from the real cause of low test scores among diverse individuals. Thus, it is recommended that nondiscriminatory assessment incorporate the notion of hypothesis generation and testing. It is also recommended that the process of assessment begin with the hypothesis that the individual's difficulties are not intrinsic in nature, but rather that they are more likely attributable to external or environmental factors. A professional who acquires the knowledge and skills to be culturally competent is much better equipped to conduct assessments that are far less discriminatory than an individual who possesses none of these skills, even if he or she matches the child in terms of language or culture (Ortiz).

Miller-Jones (1989) suggests two additional recommendations: first, that professionals develop assessment procedures that permit and direct examiners to probe for the reasoning behind the child's response to an item; and, second, that professionals use multiple tasks with a variety of different materials such that the tasks are appropriate for the culture in question. Along these lines, Helms (1992) recommended that educators assess the level of acculturation of diverse individuals, as well as the level of acculturation required by the test items; modify existing test content to include test items that reflect a diversity of cultural content; explore and probe the meaning of "incorrect" responses; and make greater and more consistent use of separate racial group norms. This latter recommendation allows one to go beyond age-based comparisons and gather information on individuals from similar and different cultural groups. Skiba, Knesting, & Bush (2002) noted that nondiscriminatory assessment should not stop at cultural and linguistic considerations. Assessment must also consider the extent to which students have not had an equal opportunity to learn because of inadequate schooling or poor instruction and learning experiences.

The above recommendations reinforce the importance of educators going beyond tests (or testing) to consider all components of the assessment process. However, within the context of testing, one component that is often overlooked, and perhaps not very well emphasized in training programs that offer assessment courses, is being keen observers of the strategies students use while attempting to solve test items (e.g., Kaufmann, 1994). Some alternative intelligence measures, for instance, include a checklist for the evaluator to complete on a range of possible observed strategies that students applied while solving problems (e.g., Das-Naglieri Cognitive Assessment System, Naglieri & Das, 1997). Most importantly, the overall recommendation is that the performance of diverse individuals must include considerations of culture, including language proficiency, cultural background, communication and values, social exposure, and level of acculturation.

Nondiscriminatory Assessment Principles

In addition to the proposed framework by Ortiz (2002), nondiscriminatory assessment is guided by culturally responsive principles, a few of which are described below. The overall goal of nondiscriminatory assessment, as we see it, is to eliminate or reduce as much as possible biases in instruments, policies, and procedures. When interpreting the test scores of diverse students, educators must gather two important and interrelated pieces of information: (a) the individual's level of acculturation and (b) the degree to which performance on any given test is contingent upon culture-specific knowledge.

Principle 1.

> Intelligence tests measure a limited range of abilities, and a large number of variables considered "intelligent" are beyond the scope of most intelligence tests; no test or battery of tests can ever give a complete picture; they can only assess certain areas of present functioning. (Groth-Marnat, 2003, p. 140)

Even though tests proclaiming to measure intelligence are limited, it is well known that interindividual differences exist regarding the construct of intellectual abilities (Braden, 1997; Sternberg, 2000). Some children learn at faster rates and generalize knowledge across various context more readily than other children, despite similar types and amounts of instruction. Thus, intelligence test scores should never be used rigidly as part of any decision-making process (Gregory, 1999; NAGC, 2001).

Principle 2. All tests have some degree of cultural and linguistic loading. Probably no test can be created that will entirely eliminate the influence of learning and cultural experiences. "The test and materials, the language in which the questions are phrased, the test directions, the categories for classifying the responses, the scoring criteria, and the validity criteria are all culture bound" (Sattler, 1992, p. 579). Thus, practitioners must search for and use instruments containing the least amount of cultural loadings, as well as collect information from multiple sources in various ways.

Principle 3. Whenever standardized, norm-referenced tests are used with individuals from diverse backgrounds, the possibility exists that what is actually being measured is acculturation or English proficiency, rather than ability.

> The structure and design of intelligence tests and the construction of representative norm groups are based on the notion of equiva-

> lency in levels of acculturation for both the individuals on whom the test is standardized and on whom the test will be used. (Ortiz, 2002, p. 1326)

Thus an in-depth analysis of the individual's level of acculturation (e.g., language proficiency, cultural values and styles, etc.) should be conducted and used when administering tests and interpreting results.

Principle 4. "When cultural differences are limited to examining linguistic differences, this leads to neglect of factors that are extremely important in understanding the nature of test results" (Flanagan & Ortiz, 2001, p. 213). Such factors may include conceptions of time, competitiveness, field-dependence, and field-independence, and so forth. Thus, educators must have an understanding of the concept of *culture*, including values, beliefs, customs, traditions, communication styles, and more, and an understanding of how these dimensions of culture affect test performance (see Helms, 1992). It may also be important to have at least one member of the assessment team who has formal training in cross-cultural assessment and/or is from the same culture as the diverse individual being assessed.

Principle 5. The cultural and linguistic demands of a test can differentially affect the performance of diverse individuals. "Namely, the more cultural and linguistic demands of the test, the more adverse the impact on the test scores of diverse students" (Flanagan & Ortiz, 2001, p. 260). Practitioners, therefore, must strive to adopt tests that have the least amount of linguistic demands and interpret the test scores of diverse individuals with knowledge of their language skills (Ortiz, 2002).

Principle 6. Cultural and linguistic differences serve to artificially depress the scores of diverse individuals. Thus, the less acculturated the individual, the lower the test score is likely to be. Further, the greater the cultural and linguistic demands of the test, the greater the probability that diverse individuals will have lower test scores than mainstream individuals. It is necessary, therefore, when making group comparisons, to consider the differences in the groups relative to cultural background and language skills. Hypotheses regarding the nature and extent of group differences should include considerations of culture and language (Ortiz, 2002). Moreover, diverse individuals must not be penalized for their cultural and linguistic differences by being denied access to challenging curriculum and gifted education programs.

Principle 7.

> The greater the difference between an individual's cultural or linguistic background and the cultural or linguistic background of individuals comprising the norm group, the more likely the test will measure lower performance as a function of this experien-

tial difference as opposed to being due to actual lower ability. (Flanagan & Ortiz, 2001, p. 259)

The very purpose of assessment should be to enhance learning rather than simply to diagnose the causes of poor performance (Ortiz, 2002). Thus, to close the performance gap between diverse and mainstream groups and to improve the test performance of diverse individuals, educators will need to improve the quality of the schooling and educational experiences. Such experiences include, for example, providing students assistance in test-taking skills, study skills, listening skills, and language- or literacy-based instruction.

Principle 8.

Test scores from different cultural groups may reflect the impact of different experiences and "social inequality" in the face of inadequate cultural and educational opportunity. Unbiased tests provide an accurate estimate not only of individual capability, but also of the inhospitable conditions that depress that capability. (Skiba et al., 2002, p. 61)

As discussed in the previous principle, test performance is influenced by the nature and quality of one's experiences. To interpret the test scores of individuals without considering this reality is to contribute to a biased assessment that renders the information collected unusable. Every effort must be made to interpret results with the effects of social injustices as a fundamental consideration.

Principle 9. A test that is considered nonbiased technically or statistically can still contain low to high degrees of cultural and linguistic demands (Flanagan & Ortiz, 2001). Thus, all instruments, including those considered technically sound, should be evaluated for their degree of cultural and linguistic demands. When the linguistic demands of a test are low or reduced, the linguistic demands must still be considered. Essentially, if cultural and educational considerations to the depressed scores of diverse individuals are overlooked, those scores will become biased estimates of individual potential by misattributing the effects of inadequate educational opportunity to a lack of individual aptitude or ability (Skiba et al., 2002).

Principle 10. "Proper and systematic consideration of the relevant cultural and linguistic characteristics of tests provides a framework for interpretation that is more valid and reliable than what is ordinarily obtained using traditional methods" (Flanagan & Ortiz, 2001, p. 255). Appropriate assessment must involve a determination of how well any particular assessment situation matches the practices that individuals experience as part of their cultural context (Miller-Jones, 1989). In this regard, practitioners must consider ways to accommodate differences (e.g., translated tests, language interpreter, nonverbal tests, authentic assessments, etc.).

Principle 11. No matter how much a test developer might want to emphasize the fairness of a given test by demonstrating the inclusion of racially or ethnically diverse individuals, claims about equity can be highly misleading and inaccurate (Valdes & Figueroa, 1994). "Practitioners should, thus, be careful not to fall prey to the assumption that stratification in the norm sample on the basis of race is equivalent to stratification on the basis of culture" (Valdes & Figueroa, p. 227). If different groups have different group norms on intelligence tests, then those subgroup norms should be considered when making decisions (e.g., placement).

Principle 12. "The assumption of normality should guide the assessment process; when the process of assessment or evaluation is guided with the presumption of normality, it reduces the tendency to search for data or 'see' patterns of dysfunction where none may exist" (Ortiz, 2002, p. 1323)

Principle 13. "Nondiscriminatory assessment should be multi-faceted, collaborative, and guided by a comprehensive framework that integrates efforts to reduce bias in a cohesive and systematic manner" (Ortiz, 2002, p. 1327).

Taken together, these principles suggest that practitioners must consider that research that overwhelmingly supports the notion that intelligence tests are not biased is based on definitions of bias that are either untenable or inaccurate. Bias is not simply a function of item content, factor structure, or racial differences. Bias is more a function of differences in experience that are due to factors involving many variables, including culture and language (Flanagan & Ortiz, 2001). Thus, the absence of technical bias in intelligence tests in no way absolves those who administer and make decisions based on those tests from socially responsible decision making (Skiba et al., 2002). In the final analysis, culturally competent assessment is much more than ensuring that tests are unbiased. Rather, "culturally competent assessment represents a commitment to data collection . . . [and] assists in identifying and eliminating sources of bias throughout the educational process." (Skiba et al., p. 62).

IMPLICATIONS FOR EDUCATORS

Nonbiased assessment, as described herein, holds much promise for increasing the representation of diverse students in gifted education. To address the issue of diverse students being underrepresented in gifted education, educators may consider implementing to the greatest extent possible, several aspects of nondiscriminatory assessment practices, including the careful selection of tests and instruments. Several other recommendations are in order. First, educators must develop hypotheses to study and explain group differences on the test performance of gifted diverse students. Second, tests, other instruments (e.g., checklists, nomination forms, referral, referral forms), policies, and procedures (e.g., teacher referrals) must be examined for possible disparate impact. How do they contribute to minority student underrepresentation? For instance, if teachers tend not to refer diverse students for gifted education screening, what is the efficacy of continuing this practice (Ford, 1996; Ford, Harris, Tyson, & Frazier Trotman, 2002)?

Third, the notion of "assessment" consisting of being comprehensive in collecting information must replace the notion of "testing" consisting of using information from only one instrument. We caution educators against making identification decisions (e.g., labeling) and placement decisions based on a single test score. This practice, we believe, is indefensible. Information gleaned from a single test is too limited (Dent, 1996; Sternberg, 2000), as already discussed.

Fourth, we believe that the concept of fairness and access should be at the forefront of discussions regarding diverse gifted students. Every effort must be made to help or support diverse students (all students) in testing and assessment situations. For linguistically diverse students, such support or advocacy can come in the form of bilingual test administrators, using interpreters, as well as adopting tests and instruments translated in their language.

Fifth, professionals administering, interpreting, and using tests must be trained to do so with considerations of cultural diversity in mind. Testing and assessment, we believe, cannot be conducted in a decontextualized, culture-blind fashion. The test results are only as good as the testing situation (Kaufmann, 1994), which includes the examiner acknowledging and considering the examinee's cultural and linguistic background, as well as level of acculturation (Sattler, 1992). This understanding goes a long way in helping educators to interpret test scores and use the results for the benefit of the child. Stated another way, tests should benefit, not harm, students (Ford, 1996; Ford & Frazier Trotman, 2000; Kaufmann, 1994; Sattler).

Sixth, we recommend that school districts examine the demographics of their gifted programs relative to economic, racial, and linguistic diversity. These data should then be used to conduct studies on variables that contribute to underrepresentation. For instance, diverse current and former students and families can be interviewed about their experiences in gifted education. This information can be used to improve, where necessary, gifted education services. Other areas of study might consist of the following: (a) exploring the number or percentage of diverse students referred for gifted education screening compared to mainstream students; (b) exploring the number or percentage of diverse students referred for gifted education screening but who failed to meet criteria; (c) examining the profiles of diverse students who score high on achievement indices (grades and achievement tests) but low on intelligence tests, and vice versa; and (d) examining if high-SES diverse students are being identified as gifted compared to low-SES diverse students.

Decisions regarding the extent to which a nondiscriminatory model of assessment practices can be implemented, as well as some of the other suggestions provided here for increasing the underrepresentation of students of diverse cultures, depend upon allocation of resources within individual school districts. However, every effort must be made to ensure that belief systems, tests, policies, and procedures do not serve as gatekeepers that close the doors of opportunity for diverse students.

REFERENCES

American Educational Research Association (AERA), American Psychological Association (APA), and National Council on Measurement in Education (NCME). (1999). *Standards for educational and psychological testing.* Washington, DC: American Psychological Association.

Braden, J. (1997). The practical impact of intellectual assessment issues. *School Psychology Review, 26,* 242–248.

Canter, A. (1997). The future of intelligence testing in the schools. *School Psychology Review, 26,* 255–261.

Council of State Directors of Programs for the Gifted and the National Association for Gifted Children. (2003). *State of the states gifted and talented education report, 2001–2002.* Washington, DC: Author.

Dent, H. (1996). Nonbiased assessment or realistic assessment? In R. L. Jones (Ed.), *Handbook of tests and measurements for Black populations* (Vol. 2, pp. 103–122). Hampton, VA: Cobb & Henry.

Esters, I. G., Ittenback, R. F., & Han, K. (1997). Today's IQ tests: Are they really better than their historical predecessors? *School Psychology Review, 26,* 211–223.

Flanagan, D. P., & Ortiz, S. (2001). *Essentials of cross-battery assessment.* New York: Wiley.

Ford, D. Y. (1996) *Reversing underachievement among gifted Black students: Promising practices and programs.* New York: Teachers College Press.

Ford, D. Y. & Frazier Trotman, M. (2000). The Office for Civil Rights and non-discriminatory testing, policies, and procedures: Implications for gifted education. *Roeper Review, 23,* 109–112.

Ford, D. Y., Harris, J. J., III, Tyson, C. A., & Frazier Trotman, M. (2002). Beyond deficit thinking: Providing access for gifted African American students. *Roeper Review, 24,* 52–58.

Gregory, R. J. (1999). *Foundations of intellectual assessment: The WAIS-III and other tests in clinical practice.* Boston: Allyn & Bacon.

Groth-Marnat, G. (2003). *Handbook of psychological assessment* (4th ed.). New York: Wiley.

Helms, J. E. (1992). Why is there no study of cultural equivalence in standardized cognitive ability testing? *American Psychologist, 47,* 1083–1101.

Kaufmann, A. S. (1993). King WISC assumes the throne. *Journal of School Psychology, 31,* 345–354.

Kaufmann, A. S. (1994). *Intelligence testing with the WISC-III.* New York: Wiley.

Matsumoto, D. (1994). *Cultural influences on research methods and statistics.* Pacific Grove, CA: Brooks/Cole.

Miller-Jones, D. (1989). Culture and testing. *American Psychologist, 44,* 360–366.

Mokhtari, K., & Reichard, C. A. (2002). Assessing students' metacognitive awareness of reading strategies. *Journal of Educational Psychology, 94,* 249–259.

Naglieri, J. A., & Das, J. P. (1997). *Das-Naglieri Cognitive Assessment System.* Chicago: Riverside Publishing Company.

National Association for Gifted Children. (2001). *Position paper: Using tests to identify gifted students.* Washington, DC: Author.

Ortiz, S. O. (2002). Best practices in nondiscriminatory assessment. In A. Thomas & J. Grimes (Eds.), *Best Practices in School Psychology IV* (pp. 1321–1336). Bethesda, MD: National Association of School Psychologists.

Sattler, J. (1992). *Assessment of children* (Rev. 3rd ed.). San Diego, CA: Author.

Skiba, R. J., Knesting, K., & Bush, L. D. (2002). Culturally competent assessment: More than nonbiased tests. *Journal of Child and Family Studies, 11,* 61–78.

Sparrow, S., & Gurland, S. T. (1998). Assessment of gifted children with the WISC-III. In A. Prifitera & D. Saklofske (Eds.), *WISC-III clinical use and interpretation* (pp. 59–72). San Diego, CA: Academic Press.

Sternberg, R. J. (2000). The concept of intelligence. In R. J. Sternberg (Ed.), *Handbook of intelligence* (pp. 3–15). Cambridge: Cambridge University Press.

Tyerman, M. J. (1986). Gifted children and their identification: Learning ability not intelligence. *Gifted Education International, 4,* 81–84.

U.S. Department of Education (1998). *Elementary and Secondary School Civil Rights Survey (1998).* Retrieved January 10, 2004, from http://www.demo.beyond2020.com/ocrpublic/en

Valdes, G., & Figueroa, R. A. (1994). *Bilingualism and testing: A special case of bias.* Norwood, NJ: Ablex.

Vygotsky, L. S. (1978). *Mind in society: The development of higher psychological processes.* Cambridge, MA: Harvard University Press.

SECTION VI

Recruitment and Retention of Black Students in Gifted Education

Donna Y. Ford, Tarek C. Grantham, and Malik S. Henfield

In other publications, the coeditors of this book have individually and collectively urged professionals in gifted education to think, take risks, and read and act outside of the box by adopting an interdisciplinary, and thus comprehensive, approach to their work in general but particularly with Black students. For years and in many venues, we have advised and urged educators to do all that is possible and equitable to increase the representation of Black students in gifted education. In addition to complaining, we and the authors in this section have offered solutions and compromises. Our goal has been to ensure that students, families, and educators are all in a win-win situation when the focus is on both how to (and how we must) recruit *and* retain Black students in gifted education.

The concept and reality of recruitment and retention has a fundamental goal: to ensure that Black students achieve success—social and emotional, psychological, academic, and more—in the short and long run.

In this anthology, as well as in our individual and collective works, our message has been clear and consistent: effectively and equitably reversing Black students' underrepresentation is a serious and unnegotiable matter of recruitment *and* retention—not one or the other! We need more systemic commitment to gifted Black students.

The concept of recruitment and retention is not new to higher education, thanks to the scholarship of Tinto and Sedlacek, for example, beginning in the 1970s. However, to disciplines such as gifted education, the concept and reality of recruitment and retention is in its infancy. The larger field of education, especially gifted education, has a long way to go to achieve progress and to meet the spirit of Black student recruitment and retention that *Brown v. Board of Education* in 1954, the Civil Rights Acts of 1964, the Javits Act of 1988, and other relevant legislation called for.

Under the advocacy and vision of Ford, this concept was introduced to gifted education in the early 1990s. Thankfully, many educators and decision makers have latched on to this notion and promised to change the horizon for Black students in gifted programs.

All of us who are concerned about equity and social justice in education must find ways to recruit and then retain Black students in gifted education. This need focuses on prevention first and foremost, followed by intervention. The overarching questions and concerns about recruitment and retention focus on culture-bound notions, models and theories of intelligence and giftedness, characteristics, testing and assessment, and eventual placement and services.

References

Brown v. Board of Education of Topeka, 347 U.S. 483 (1954).
Civil Rights Act of 1964, Pub. Law 88-352 (July 2, 1964).
Title V, Part D. [Jacob K. Javits Gifted and Talented Students Education Act of 1988], Elementary and Secondary Education Act of 1988 (2002), 20 U.S.C. sec. 7253 et seq.

CHAPTER 22

The Underrepresentation of Minority Students in Gifted Education: Problems and Promises in Recruitment and Retention

Donna Y. Ford, The Ohio State University

Concerns over recruiting and retaining minority students in gifted education programs have persisted for several decades, and, although many educators, policymakers, and researchers have deliberated about the underrepresentation of minority students in gifted education, few articles, reports, or studies exist on this topic. This article seeks to fill this void, describing factors that inhibit the recruitment and retention of minority students in gifted education programs. These factors include screening and identification issues (e.g., definitions and instrumentation); educational issues (e.g., quality of students' education); and personnel issues (e.g., lack of teacher training in gifted and urban education, low teacher referral). Also discussed are retention issues, namely, factors that may affect the decision of minority students to remain in gifted education programs. Finally, recommendations for recruiting and retaining minority students are offered.

Reprinted from Ford, D.Y. (1998). The underrepresentation of minority students in gifted education: Problems and promises in recruitment and retention. *The Journal of Special Education, 32,* 4–14. Reprinted with permission of Sage Publications.

One of the most persistent, troubling, and controversial issues in education is the disproportionate representation of minority students in special education, including gifted education. The concerns over recruiting and retaining minority students in gifted education programs have persisted for several decades. One of the earliest articles to address the underidentification of minority students (specifically, African American students) as gifted was written by Jenkins (1936). Since that time, other authors have focused on the underrepresentation of African American, Hispanic American, and American Indian students in gifted education, primarily addressing assessment issues. Because Asian American students have been over-represented in gifted education programs, most articles have focused on improving the representation of other minority students in gifted education.

Although many educators, policymakers, and researchers have been concerned about the underrepresentation of minority students in gifted education, few articles, reports, or studies exist on this topic. There has been limited attention to the impact of practices, procedures, and policies. This article seeks to fill this void, describing factors that inhibit the recruitment and retention of minority students in gifted education programs. These factors include screening and identification issues (e.g., definitions and instrumentation), educational issues (e.g., quality of students' education), and personnel issues (e.g., lack of teacher training in gifted and urban education, low teacher referral). Also discussed are retention issues—that is, factors that may affect the decision of minority students to remain in gifted education programs. Finally, recommendations for recruiting and retaining minority students are offered. These recommendations focus on promising practices, procedures, and policies. This article begins by describing the nature and extent of articles published on gifted students and gifted minority students in special education and gifted education journals and reports. Trends in the participation of minority students in gifted education are also described.

Although concerns about the underrepresentation of gifted minority students have proliferated in recent years, relatively few articles and studies have addressed this topic. An ERIC database search revealed that between 1966 and 1996, a total of 9,801 articles focused on gifted students, with 795 of them focusing on gifted minority students (see Note 1). Thus, only 8% of the articles on gifted students found in the ERIC database during the past three decades focused on gifted minority students. A breakdown of those articles indicates that 1.1% focused on Hispanic American students ($n = 110$), 1.3% on American Indian students ($n = 132$), 5% on African American students ($n = 491$), and 6% on Asian American students ($n = 62$).

Table 1 summarizes the number of articles published on gifted students ($n = 2,816$) and gifted minority students ($n = 60$) in five selected journals specializing in gifted education during the same three decades. These five journals accounted for 29% of the total articles on gifted students in the ERIC database. Most of these

Table 1
ERIC Search of Articles on Racially and Culturally Diverse Students in Selected Gifted Education Journals (1966 to 1996)

Journal	Total number of articles	Asian American students	Hispanic American students	American Indian students	African American students
Gifted Child Quarterly	781	1	2	2	4
Gifted Child Today	553	1	1	2	3
Journal for the Education of the Gifted	335	2	4	2	7
Roeper Review	876	2	2	3	16
Gifted Education International	271	0	0	0	6
Total	2,816	6	9	9	36

Note. The searches were conducted using key words *gifted, gifted and minority, gifted and Black or African American, gifted and Hispanic American, gifted and American Indian,* and *gifted and Asian American*

Table 2
ERIC Search of Articles on Gifted Students in Selected Special Education Journals (1966 to 1996)

Journal	Total number of articles	Gifted	Gifted Asian American	Gifted Hispanic American	Gifted American Indian	Gifted African American
Teaching Exceptional Children	1,037	60 (5.8%)	0	0	0	0
The Journal of Special Education	923	18 (1.1%)	0	0	0	1
Exceptional Children	1,557	82 (5.3%)	0	1	0	1
Remedial and Special	485	6 (1.2%)	0	1	0	1
Teacher Education and Special Education	476	4 (.8%)	0	0	0	1
Total	4,478	170 (3.8%)	0	2 (0%)	0	4 (0%)

Note. The searches were conducted using key words *gifted, gifted and minority, gifted and Black or African American, gifted and Hispanic American, gifted and Indian American,* and *gifted and Asian American.*

journal articles (n = 36) focused on African American students. Six articles focused on Asian American students, nine on Hispanic American students, and nine on American Indian students. In essence, 2.1% of the articles in these five gifted education journals focused on minority students.

Relatively few articles in special education journals have focused on gifted students (see Note 2). Table 2 presents figures for five special education journals. Of 4,478 articles published in these selected journals, only 170 articles (3.8%) focused on gifted students between 1966 and 1996. Further, even fewer articles focused on gifted minority students (n = 5). The small number of articles published on gifted students in special education journals has significant implications given that 21 states (42%) house gifted education coordinators in special education (Coleman, Gallagher, & Foster, 1994).

In many ways, gifted education is in a precarious position; almost one third of states have no mandate for gifted education programs (Coleman et al., 1994). Further, only 27 states (54%) have clear policies on due process for gifted students (Coleman & Gallagher, 1992). This lack of mandate suggests that gifted students are not viewed as a population in need of special services, yet underachievement is a major problem for many gifted students (Ford, 1996; National Commission on Excellence in Education, 1983). Obviously, holding states accountable for gifted minority student underrepresentation and associated inequities is difficult when states neither mandate gifted education nor house gifted education under special education. Nonetheless, the U.S. Office of Civil Rights (OCR) is reviewing more than 50 high schools nationally regarding the underrepresentation of minority students in gifted education programs and higher ability groups (Tinsley, 1997).

Further, the limited number of publications and studies makes it difficult for educators and policymakers to develop solutions to this persistent and pervasive problem. The present ERIC search—even if not exhaustive—suggests that information on this student population is severely limited. As Artiles, Trent, and Kuan (1997) noted, this lack of data on minority students can have serious consequences for researchers and practitioners. Of course, the most serious consequences are for minority students: Such limited information on gifted minority students makes reversing their underrepresentation difficult.

Minority Underrepresentation Trends, 1966 to 1996

Few articles identified in the present ERIC search described in detail the extent and nature of minority student underrepresentation in gifted education. Most reports presented the general statement that minority students are underrepresented in gifted education, and most focused on assessment issues. Few of the identified studies and reports discussed sociocultural and sociopolitical factors that might be contributing to or exacerbating the underrepresentation of minority students in gifted education. Scant data exist on the ways in which practices, procedures, and policies contribute to minority student underrepresentation.

At the time of the 1992 OCR report, schools reported that 25,077,421 students were enrolled in the nation's public schools. One percent of these students were American Indian, 4% were Asian American, 13.7% were Hispanic American, 21.1% were African American, and 60% were White. Thus, as recently as 1992, students of color constituted some 40% of the school population nationally.

Further analysis indicates that 1,412,011 students were identified as gifted (5.7%) at the time of the 1992 OCR report. Of those students identified as gifted, .5% were American Indian, 7% were Asian American, 7.9% were Hispanic

Table 3

Trends in the Representation of Minority Students in Gifted Education Programs from 1978 to 1992

Student population	1978	1980	1982	1984	1992
Hispanic American	6.8	9.0	8.6	13.2	13.7
	5.15	5.4	4.0	7.2	7.9
	(u = 25%)	(u = 40%)	(u = 53%)	(u = 45%)	(u = 42%)
American Indian	.8	.7	.5	.8	1.0
	.3	.3	.3	.3	.5
	(u = 62%)	(u = 57%)	(u = 40%)	(62%)	(u = 50%)
Asian American	1.4	2.2	2.6	3.7	4.0
	3.4	4.4	4.7	6.8	7.0
	(o = 59%)	(o = 50%)	(o = 45%)	(o = 46%)	(o = 43%)
African American	15.7	20.1	25.8	24.5	21.1
	10.3	11.1	11.0	12.9	12.0
	(u = 33%)	(u = 45%)	(u = 57%)	(u = 47)	(u = 41%)

Note: Percentages are rounded; top number indicates percentage of student population, and middle number represents percentage of gifted education, "o" indicates overrepresentation; "u" indicates underrepresentation. Percentage of underrepresentation was calculated using the following formula: 1 − (percentage of gifted education program divided by percentage of school district). Source for 1978 to 1984 data: Chinn & Hughes (1987). Source for 1992 data: OCR Elementary and Secondary School Civil Rights Compliance Report (1992).

American, 12.1% were African American, and 72.4% were White. Table 3 shows trends in minority representation from 1978 to 1992 and reflects the underrepresentation of students of color in gifted education programs nationally. In 1992, African American students represented 21.1% of the school population but 12% of gifted education—an underrepresentation of 41%. Further, Hispanic American students were underrepresented by 42%, and American Indians were underrepresented by 50%. Conversely, Asian American students were overrepresented by 43% and White students were overrepresented by 17%.

National concerns about the persistent underrepresentation of minority students in gifted education programs were partly responsible for the Jacob K. Javits Gifted and Talented Students Education Act of 1988. Its goal is "to provide financial assistance to State and local educational agencies . . . to initiate a coordinated program of research . . . designed to build a nationwide capability in elementary and secondary schools to meet the special educational needs of gifted and talented students" (Sec. 3062(b)). Equally important, the Javits Act gives "highest priority" to students who are economically disadvantaged, limited English proficient, or have disabilities or handicapping conditions (Sec. 3063 (a)(1)). Similarly, in 1993, the U.S. Department of Education set forth its most culturally inclusive definition of giftedness to date:

> Children and youth with outstanding talent perform or show the potential for performing at remarkably high levels of accomplishment when compared with others of their age, experience, or environment. These children and youth exhibit high performance capacity in intellectual, creative, and/or artistic areas, and unusual leadership capacity, or excel in specific academic fields. They require services or activities not ordinarily provided by the schools. Outstanding talents are present in children and youth from all cultural groups, across all economic strata, and in all areas of human endeavor.

Prior to this definition, most states adopted the 1978 federal definition or some version of it (Cassidy & Hossler, 1992), which did not mention, directly or indirectly, issues of diversity and equity. The number of states that have adopted (or will adopt) the 1993 definition or a version of it has yet to been seen. We do know, however, that as of 1994, most states ($n = 40$) mention in their policies the need to better identify and serve gifted minority students, and 41 states report using different criteria procedures for special populations (Coleman et al., 1994). For example, 7 states use some form of a quota system, and 15 states allow trial placement or preplacement experiences. Forty-three states encourage schools to serve students with potential who do not meet the standard or traditional criteria (Coleman et al., 1994).

Thus, it is clear that minority students (with the exception of Asian Americans) are poorly represented in gifted education programs, but the nature and extent of this underrepresentation are unclear. The majority of studies and reports identified failed to analyze data by gifted education categories—intellectual ability, academic ability, creativity, visual and performing arts, and leadership. Only three reports examined the representation of students by gifted education categories (Coleman & Gallagher, 1992; Coleman et al., 1994; O'Connell, 1986). Coleman et al. (1994) surveyed state directors of gifted education and found that 49 states identify intellectually gifted and academically gifted students, 41 states identify creatively gifted students, 35 states identify artistically gifted students, and 30 states identify students gifted in leadership. Further, 15 states identify gifted students in critical thinking, 11 identify psychometrically gifted students, 9 identify psychosocially gifted, and 5 identify gifted students who have an understanding of their cultural heritage.

A recurring recommendation for increasing the representation of minority students in gifted education programs is to use multiple identification criteria and sources (e.g., Ford, 1994; Frasier & Passow, 1994). Most states ($n = 44$) have policies related to the screening process, and most states report using more than one criterion and source of information to screen and identify gifted students. Many

Javits projects have also reported promising results when multiple information is used (U.S. Department of Education, 1994); particularly noted is an increase in the percentage of minority students identified (e.g., Borland & Wright, 1994; Saccuzzo, Johnson, & Guertin, 1994).

However, national efforts to redress the underrepresentation of minority students are not necessarily reflected in significant increases in minority students' representation in gifted education programs. As Table 3 shows, despite changes in gifted education definitions, procedures, practices, and policies, African American, Hispanic American, and American Indian students continue to be underrepresented in gifted education programs nationally. In some instances, the gap is widening, with more minority students being underrepresented today than several decades ago. The years 1978 and 1992 will serve as cases in point. In 1978, African American students were underrepresented in gifted education programs by 34%; that figure increased to 43% in 1992. In 1978, Hispanic American students were underrepresented by 25%; in 1992, the figure increased to 42%. In 1978, American Indians were underrepresented by 62%; in 1992, the figure decreased to 50%. Regardless of the year, Asian American students have been overrepresented in gifted education; however, the percentage of overrepresentation decreased between 1978 and 1992.

EXPLANATIONS FOR MINORITY STUDENT UNDERREPRESENTATION

Many explanations have been offered for the underrepresentation of African American, Hispanic American, and American Indian students in gifted education programs. The majority of explanations can be categorized as (a) recruitment issues/screening and identification (e.g., definitions, instrumentation, policies, procedures); (b) personnel issues (e.g., teacher training, teacher expectations); and (c) retention issues (e.g., student-teacher relations, peer relations, learning environment).

RECRUITMENT ISSUES: SCREENING AND IDENTIFICATION

Definitions. Five federal definitions of giftedness have existed since 1972. Unlike stipulations placed on states and school districts in special education, each state and school district can define giftedness as it sees fit. A student can receive services as creatively gifted in one school district or state that serves this gifted category, but not be served in another school district that does not serve this gifted category. Most states have adopted the 1978 federal definition of gifted (or a version of it). Some states do not use federal definition(s); instead, they adopt Gardner's (1985) or Renzulli's (1986) definition.

Even in states that mandate gifted education, school districts do not have to identify and/or serve creatively gifted students, artistically gifted students, or students gifted in leadership. Most states serve intellectually and academically gifted students. Thus, many gifted students, regardless of racial background, are neither identified nor served.

Regardless of the definition of giftedness adopted, many states have designated arbitrary cutoff scores on achievement and intelligence tests. For example, in some states, gifted students must have an IQ of 130 or higher; some states require achievement test scores at the 95th percentile or higher; in other states, students must score at or above the 98th percentile. Further, some states identify the highest 3% of the student population; other states identify 5%. Some states require schools to use four sources or types of information during the decision-making process; others require five sources or types of information. Thus, a student can be identified as gifted in one state (or even neighboring school district), but not in another based upon the definition adopted. Further, when and how that student is screened, identified, and served varies from one school district to another.

Standardized achievement and aptitude tests. Forty-five states use an achievement and/or aptitude test in the screening and identification process. The heavy or exclusive reliance on tests poses major problems for African American, American Indian, and Hispanic American students, all of whom have a history of performing poorly on these tests. Debates persist in explaining the poor performance of minority students on standardized tests. Some educators have argued that minority students are intellectually inferior to White students; others have contended that minority students have cultural deficits that contribute to their poor performance (see Steinberg et al., 1996). More recently, educators have begun to question and reconsider the validity and reliability of the tests themselves (e.g., Jones, 1996). Arguments against using standardized tests with minority students have proliferated in recent years on the grounds that these tests are culturally biased (Samuda, Kong, Cummins, Lewis, & Pascual-Leone, 1991). That is, tests normed on a sample of all or predominantly White students are less valid and reliable for minority students.

Regardless of the view one holds when explaining minority students' test performance, few educators and researchers would disagree that the most important aspect of any test or assessment instrument is the degree to which it is valid and reliable. Factors affecting test reliability include trait instability; sampling error; administrator error; scoring error; and the test takers' health, motivation, degree of fatigue, and luck in guessing.

Samuda et al. (1991) also reported that the emphasis placed on the definition of abstract words, sentence completion, analogies, and so forth in the Stanford-Binet Intelligence Scale (Thorndike, Hagen, & Sattler, 1986) and other standardized intelligence tests presupposes a certain mastery of standard English comprehension and usage. Perhaps the most obvious example is that we continue to give students tests in English when their primary language is not English; or we test students on their command of standard English when they communicate best in other dialects (e.g., Black Vernacular English).

Other tests lack cultural sensitivity in terms of format and presentation. For example, how valid are the results if a minority student takes a pictorial test in which none of the people on the test is of color? What impact does the race of the examiner have on minority students' test performance? How important is the rapport between the student and test administrator? How important is minority students' familiarity with the test format? How important are the quality and presentation of instructions (e.g., oral, written, both)? How do students' test-taking skills affect their test performance and attitudes toward evaluation?

A final variable worth discussing is cognitive and learning style. Decades of research demonstrate that many minority students tend to learn differently from White students. For example, African American students are likely to be field dependent learners (relational, social, holistic, global learners) who approach learning situations intuitively rather than logically (Boykin, 1994; Hale-Benson, 1986; Shade, 1994). These styles of learning influence both school and test performance (Eighteenth Annual Report to Congress, 1996).

In essence, issues affecting the reliability and validity of tests can result in biases against minority students. An examination of standardized test reveals that (a) language differences exist between the test (or test maker) and the students; (b) the test questions center on the experiences and facts of the dominant culture, and the answers support middle class values, which are often rewarded with more points; (c) the tests favor highly verbal students (e.g., they require a great deal of reading, word recognition, vocabulary, sentence completion, and verbal responses); and (d) the tests do not consider the extent to which some students may not be oriented toward achievement. Consequently, minority students may not perform well on traditional tests of achievement and ability.

EDUCATIONAL ISSUES AND CONSIDERATIONS

Products and work samples are used by 44 states; outside school achievement is also used by 44 states to screen and identify gifted students (Coleman et al., 1994). What are the implications for students who are at an educational disadvantage? Quality of instruction and educational experience have a powerful influence on students' achievement. Darling, Hammond (1995), Irvine (1991), and Kozal (1992) have found persistent and considerable inequities in the education received by minority students. These inequities relate to funding, staffing, and resources. In most urban school districts and in districts with a large minority population, there are teacher shortages, an overreliance on untrained (e.g., uncertified) and substitute teachers, and inadequate per-pupil expenditures.

Minority students are also likely to be placed in low-ability groups and non-college preparatory tracks, which decreases the likelihood that these students will be identified as gifted. Oakes and Guiton (1995) found that schools with a large percentage of minority students are less likely than other schools to offer academically rigorous curricula, high-ability groups, and academic tracks (e.g., advanced placement, honors courses).

Relatedly, and always a function of quality of education, several studies have found high percentages of underachievement among gifted African American students (e.g., Ford, 1992, 1995). More likely than not, underachievement will decrease the likelihood that the potential of minority students will be realized and recognized. Poor educational experiences and underachievement will affect minority students' performance when they are completing products and work samples used to screen and identify gifted students. Thus, given the poor quality of their educational experiences, numerous negative educational outcomes, and high percentages of underachievement, minority students may be placed at further disadvantage during the screening and identification process.

Personnel Considerations and Issues

Thus, numerous psychometric and educational issues must be examined to better understand minority students' low representation in gifted education programs. Further, we must examine the human dimension of screening and identification. How do referrals and nominations by teachers, parents, peers, and students themselves influence minority students' representation in gifted education?

Teacher referrals/nominations. Forty-six states use teacher nominations in the screening process and 42 use teacher input in placement decisions (Coleman et al., 1994). The fact that 86% of teachers are White (Darling-Hammond, 1995) is of concern. In addition, the lack of teacher training in gifted education poses many problems. Several studies indicate that teachers are less effective and less accurate than parents in recognizing students who require gifted education services. Specifically, 61% of the teachers surveyed by Archambault et al. (1993) had received no staff development in the area of gifted education. Similarly, Kames and Whorton (1991) found that half the states require no certification or endorsement in gifted education, 3 states make this training optional, 5 states have statements of competencies, 14 require practicum experiences, and 8 require teaching experience in the regular classroom prior to teaching gifted students. As a result, teachers are not always the most reliable sources for identifying gifted learners (particularly culturally or racially diverse students) and then referring them for gifted education programs. Without training in gifted education, how qualified are teachers to recognize students with gifted characteristics?

Numerous studies have described the influence that teacher expectations have on student achievement. When making referrals, teachers often emphasize such behaviors as cooperation, answering correctly, punctuality, and neatness (Cox, Daniels, & Boston, 1985). These may not be the behaviors that gifted minority (and underachieving) students demonstrate. Likewise, such characteristics as race, gender, socioeconomic status, and family structure all influence teachers' perceptions of students (Good, 1981; Irvine, 1991; Winfield, 1986). Even when minority students have been identified as gifted, teachers may have low expectations (Ford, 1996; Jenkins, 1936). Although the nature and extent of teacher referral of minority students have been addressed in special education, only one study has examined teacher referrals and gifted minority students. High and Udall (1983) found that White teachers underreferred African American students for gifted education programs. Burstein and Cabello (1989) found that 38% of student teachers believed that poor academic achievement and performance among minority students was due to cultural deficits. These low teacher expectations and negative perceptions can result in the low referral rates of minority students for gifted education. It is an unfortunate reality that problems related to racism, segregation, and long-held beliefs concerning minority groups have resulted in dubious benefits for students whose rights the policies were designed to protect in the first place (Artiles & Trent, 1994).

Parent nominations. Forty-five states include parent nominations in the screening process and 38 use input from others (including parents) in making placement decisions (Coleman et al., 1994). However, many of these forms are complicated and cumbersome, thereby inhibiting some parents from completing them. Parents who have difficulty understanding the forms are likely to over- or underestimate their child's ability or refuse to complete the forms altogether.

Further, although parents represent important and essential sources of information, parent nomination forms and checklists can suffer from the same shortcomings as other instruments—lack of reliability and validity data, inattention to characteristics of underachievement, lack of cultural sensitivity, and an exclusive focus on intellectual or academic characteristics of giftedness. Parent nomination forms may also lack culturally specific characteristics of minority students, making it difficult for parents to recognize their children's strengths as listed on the forms. Equally important, a school's use of parent nominations assumes that all parents are informed about the parent nomination option. Minority parents who have little communication with schools are unlikely to be aware that a gifted education program exists or that they can nominate their children.

Self-nominations. Forty-two states use self-nominations in the screening process, and 38 use student nominations (Coleman et al., 1994). Negative peer pressure, however, may inhibit some minority students, particularly adolescents, from making self-nominations. Similarly, many gifted minority adolescents choose not to participate in gifted education programs. They often cite social-emotional variables—feeling isolated and alienated from White students and feeling rejected by minority peers—as reasons not to enter the gifted education program or not to remain there (e.g., Ford, 1996). Hence, self-nominations may not be a viable option for some minority group members.

Other nominations. Forty-three states use peer nominations as part of the screening process. Gagne (1989) concluded that the scientific foundation for peer nominations is fragile. For instance, peer nominations are frequently normed on a small sample; there is seldom reliability data (interjudger reliability, pre–post reliability); frequently, there are few or no data on construct and criterion validity. Although peer nominations are not sociograms, one must also consider the extent to which they are appropriate for minority students who attend predominantly White schools. The lack of heterogeneity in some schools calls into question the quality of data gathered from peers. Further, to what extent are White students sensitive to the many cultural characteristics and strengths of minority students? What perceptions do White students hold of minority students? To what extent are peer nomination forms culturally sensitive or biased? To what extent do they contain characteristics of gifted underachievers?

Composition and training of selection committee. To date, no national study has examined the racial and sociodemographic characteristics of selection committees in gifted education. In special education, Harry (1992) identified the lack of diversity among selection committee members as an important factor that increases the placement of minority students. Conversely, it is plausible that these characteristics may inhibit the placement of minority students in gifted education. That is, are members biased in favor of those students who share their racial background, socioeconomic status, and gender?

Characteristics and training of assessment personnel. School counselors and psychologists are heavily relied upon for identification and placement decisions. Yet, few counselors and psychologists are trained in gifted education, multicultural education, or urban education. Snyderman and Rothman (1987) found that more than half of the 661 measurement experts who responded to a 1984 survey on intelligence and aptitude testing believe that genetic factors contributed to IQ differences between African Americans and Whites. These beliefs carry significant implications. How do such attitudes affect their assessments with minority students?

Several studies have explored public school counselors' awareness of issues confronting gifted students, as well as their training to work with this student population. Findings indicate that few school counselors or psychologists are formally trained to work with gifted learners (Ford & Harris, 1994; Klausmeier, Mishra, &

Maker, 1987). They do not feel competent about identifying gifted students, and feel even less competent at identifying gifted minority students. Further, Frantz and Prillaman (1993) found that only 11 states required at least one course in special education for school counselor certification, 17 were changing certification requirements, and the remaining states neither required any courses nor were in the process of considering changes in certification. This lack of training among school counselors and psychologists might be contributing to misinterpretation of test data and to the underrepresentation of minority students in gifted education programs.

Retention Issues

Ford (1997) found that African American students who preferred not to be in gifted education programs expressed concerns primarily about feelings of isolation from White students. Thirty students (20%) agreed or strongly agreed with the statement "I would prefer to stay in a regular school program rather than be in a gifted program." Explanations related to socioemotional/affective issues: They do not want to be the only African American in the class; they fear feeling lonely, isolated, and different from White students; and they fear being negatively pressured by African American students. In addition, compared to gifted African American achievers, underachievers were more likely to report negative relationships with teachers (Ford, 1995). Finally, many of the African American students were underachieving (42%), mostly because of poor study habits and poor time management. Regardless of the reason, underachievers are less likely to be referred for screening and identification and to be identified as gifted than are achievers. Further, underachieving and socially isolated students are unlikely to persist in gifted education programs.

Recommendations for Recruiting and Retaining Minority Students in Gifted Education Programs

The majority of literature on minority students concentrates on recruitment—finding better ways to screen and identify minority students for gifted education programs and services. Few have focused on retaining these students once place. These recruitment and retention recommendations are described below.
1. *Use valid and reliable instruments.* All instruments used to screen and identify gifted students (including checklists, referral forms, and standardized instruments) must be valid and reliable, as well as culturally sensitive. In their study, Saccuzzo and colleagues (1994) reported that the

Raven's Matrices is more effective than the Wechsler Intelligence Scale for Children–Revised (WISC-R) at identifying gifted minority students. Other studies have reported similar findings. Whatever instruments are used, the issue of disparate impact must be considered. That is, if minority students consistently and disproportionately perform poorly on selected instruments, what rationale exists for those instruments' continued use?

2. *Collect multiple types and sources of information.* As advocated in special education, a holistic profile of students must be developed prior to making educational decisions. Both quantitative and qualitative information are necessary, as well as objective and subjective information. Information must be gathered from parents, teachers, and students. No one piece of information should be used to include or exclude a student from placement. A philosophy of assessment is essential if gifted minority students are to be identified and served. As Weschler (1991) noted, we must also consider multiple factors in the assessment process:

> It cannot be presumed that the array of tasks, standardized and presented as the WISC-III can cover all of an individual's intelligence. . . . other determiners of intelligence, nonintellective in nature, also help shape how a child's abilities are expressed. These nonintellective factors. . . . include attributes such as planning and goal awareness, enthusiasm, attitudes, field dependence and independence, impulsiveness, anxiety, and persistence. . . . [We] must consider an individual's life history (e.g., social and medical history and linguistic and cultural background) as part of any good assessment. . . . [It is] important to take into account factors other than intellectual or cognitive abilities. (pp. 2–3).

3. *Provide support services and educational opportunities.* The quality of students' educational experiences must be examined prior to identification and placement so that students will be successful in the gifted education program. For instance, as noted by Jenkins (1936) more than six decades ago, minority students coming from less academically rigorous schools and classrooms are likely to have difficulties in more academically rigorous gifted education programs. For underachieving students, preplacement educational experiences may be necessary, including study skills and time management skills.

4. *Provide extensive teacher and school personnel training.* The ability of teachers to work effectively with gifted minority students will increase based on staff development efforts and teacher education preparation. At a

minimum, preservice and practicing teachers need the following skills: (a) Teachers should gain substantive classroom experiences with minority students (e.g., during practica or internships); (b) teachers should be trained to understand and respect students' cultural heritage worldviews, values, and customs; (c) teachers need to understand minority students' communication skills, modalities, and behaviors (e.g., body language, facial expressions, eye contact, silence, touch, public space); (d) teachers must understand and decrease their stereotypes about and fears of minority students; (e) teachers need to learn outreach skills—how to work effectively with minority students, their families, and their community; and (f) teachers must gain a greater respect for individual and group differences in learning, achievement, and behavior. In general, teachers will need training to avoid cultural deficit and pathological models and to understand that intelligence and educability are matters of individual differences rather than racial differences (Jenkins, 1936).

5. *Increase family involvement.* Cultural, linguistic, and socioeconomic differences among schools, gifted education personnel, and minority groups have served as stumbling blocks to establishing effective home–school partnerships. The involvement of minority families in the recruitment and retention process is incomplete without early, ongoing, and substantive family involvement. This involvement must include participation in the screening, identification, and placement process to ensure that students are successfully identified and successful in the gifted education program. School personnel—not consumers (parents and children)—have the primary responsibility for ensuring equal participation and access for all families, which requires breaking down barriers to their involvement. Minority parents face numerous barriers to school involvement. As Marion (1981) noted, minority families remain apprehensive that school personnel may stereotype families that are less affluent, have different family values, have lower educational attainment levels, and have lower status occupations. These concerns, real or perceived, cause minority parents to fear that their children have little chance of being recognized as gifted.

    Equally important is that instruments completed by family members be culturally sensitive, as well as sensitive to all reading levels. In essence, policies and practices must be adopted that ensure meaningful minority family involvement and implementation of gifted education services. Ongoing and multiple modes of communication can increase family involvement (e.g., personal telephone calls, personal letters, newsletters, a minority liaison parent to families and community leaders).

6. *Increase and refocus research and literature.* More research and writing are needed to help unravel the complex issues surrounding minority students'

underrepresentation in gifted education. As noted in the beginning of this article, few studies have focused on gifted minority students. Without increased research and writing, there is the danger that school personnel will continue to base arguments about, and programs and services targeting minority students, on empirically unsupported information, which cannot result in improved educational outcomes for these students (see Artiles et al., 1997).

To avoid reaching erroneous conclusions about the minority underrepresentation problem, we must look not only at changes in figures, but also at contextual factors—both sociocultural and sociopolitical. We must examine the mosaic of factors affecting the placement of minority students in gifted education programs relative to policies, procedures, and practices (e.g., low teacher expectations, low teacher referral, poor home–school relations, definitions, standardized tests).

Also yet to be explored are the reasons Asian American students are overrepresented in gifted education, whereas other minority groups are underrepresented. That is, how do the factors discussed throughout this article differ for White, Asian American, and other minority students? Certainly, in reversing the underrepresentation dilemma, we must move beyond important but simplistic analyses that are race specific only. Too frequently, researchers assume that the main effects of race are superordinate to the influence of other sociopolitical and sociocultural factors, such as those described by Ford (1995) and Artiles and Trent (1994). Future analyses must consider data on race, gender, and socioeconomic status (SES). For instance, are African American males more likely to be underrepresented than African American females? Are middle SES Hispanic American students less likely to be underrepresented than their lower SES counterparts? How do representation trends differ across the racial minority groups? We cannot continue to treat minority students as a homogeneous or monolithic conglomerate of people (Artiles et al., 1997), for there is both within- and between-group diversity that cannot be ignored.

The underrepresentation of African American, Hispanic American, and American Indian students in gifted education requires a careful analysis that transcends merely contrasting ethnic group enrollment data. Thus, states and school districts must also collect data on the percentage of minority students served in the various gifted categories. It is noteworthy that no national studies or reports have described the representation of minority students in gifted education programs by categories of giftedness. This is surprising given that most states include specific references to gifted students from special populations in their policies, and many states identify gifted students in such areas as creativity and visual and performing arts. Are minority students underrepresented in intellectual and academic categories? Are they overrepresented in creative, artistic, and leadership categories?

More research is needed on referrals of minority students to gifted education. Who is the primary referral source (e.g., teachers, parents, peers, self)? What reasons are given for referral or lack of referral? What information is contained on the referral forms (e.g., do items lack cultural sensitivity)? Analyses of referral information must examine demographic variables, such as gender. Are minority females more likely to be referred than males? Equally important, to what extent are teachers trained in both gifted and cultural education more likely to refer minority students compared to teachers without such training'? Are minority teachers more likely than White teachers to refer minority students? What factors influence teacher referrals of Asian American students (given their overrepresentation in gifted education programs) versus other minority students?

As noted, most states report using multiple criteria and multiple sources of information when screening and identifying gifted students. More information does not guarantee changes in practices. Specifically, although more information is gathered, it is unclear how the information is used. For instance, are quantitative sources of information weighted more heavily than qualitative information? Are objective measures weighted more heavily than subjective measures? Are teacher nominations weighted more heavily than parent nominations?

Conclusions

Many school districts, policymakers, and researchers have endeavored to increase the representation of minority students in gifted education. A persistent finding, however, is that even with the best screening procedures and multiple identification criteria, minority students can be overlooked. As discussed in this article, the underrepresentation of minority students in gifted education programs must be examined in a contextual and comprehensive way because numerous factors affect the recruitment and retention of these students in gifted education. These factors include the definition and criteria adopted by states and school districts, as well as the validity and reliability of instruments adopted—tests, checklists, nomination forms. Also important are the many factors associated with referrals or nominations by teachers, parents, peers, and students themselves. And we cannot overlook the quality of students' educational experiences. The potential of students who are at educational disadvantage is likely to be hidden by such factors as poor quality of schooling and underachievement.

More research is needed in both gifted education and special education that examines how and why minority students are underrepresented in gifted education programs. Likewise, more efforts must focus on the recruitment and retention of minority students in gifted education programs. The persistent and pervasive underrepresentation of minority students represents a tragic and unnecessary waste of human potential and promise.

Author's Note

Preparation of this manuscript was supported in part by Grant No. H029J60006 from the U.S. Department of Education, Office of Special Education Programs, to the University of Virginia for the Center of Minority Research in Special Education.

Notes

1. The searches were conducted using the key words "gifted and Black or African American," "gifted and Asian American," "gifted and Indian," and "gifted and Hispanic" along with the journal title; thus, the searches located the key words in the title and abstract. Next, article titles and abstracts were reviewed for accuracy. For example, if the author's last name was Black, that article was excluded.
2. In their extensive analysis of the literature, Artiles, Trent, and Kuan (1997) found that few of the special education journals they reviewed focused on minority students—less than 6%.

References

Archambault, E. X., Jr., Westberg, K. L., Brown, S. W., Hallmark, B. W., Zhang, W., & Emmons, C. L. (1993). Classroom practices used with gifted third and fourth grade students. *Journal for the Education of the Gifted, 16*(2), 103–119.

Artiles, A. J., & Trent, S. C. (1994). Overrepresentation of minority students in special education: A continuing debate. *The Journal of Special Education, 27,* 410–437.

Artiles, J. J., Trent, S. C., & Kuan, L. (1997). Learning disabilities empirical research on ethnic minority students: An analysis of 22 years of studies published in selected refereed journals. *Learning Disabilities Research and Practice, 2*(2), 82–91.

Borland, J. H., & Wright, L. (1994). Identifying young, potentially gifted, economically disadvantaged students. *Gifted Child Quarterly, 38,* 164–171.

Boykin, A. W. (1994). Afrocultural expression and its implications for schooling. In E. R. Hollins, J. E. King, & W. C. Hayman (Eds.), *Teaching diverse populations: Formulating a knowledge base* (pp. 225–273). New York: State University of New York Press.

Burstein, N. D., & Cabello, B. (1989, September/October). Preparing teachers to work with culturally diverse students: Another educational model. *Journal of Teacher Education, 540*(5), 9–16.

Cassidy, J., & Hossler, A. (1992). State and federal definitions of the gifted: An update. *Gifted Child Quarterly, 15,* 46–53.

Chinn, P. C., & Hughes, S. (1987). Representation of minority students in special education classes. *Remedial and Special Education, 8,* 41–46.

Coleman, M. R., & Gallagher, J. J. (1992). *Report on state polices related to the identification of gifted students.* Chapel Hill: Gifted Education Policy Studies Program at the University of North Carolina at Chapel Hill.

Coleman, M. R., Gallagher, J. J., & Foster, A. (1994). *Updated report on state polices related to the identification of gifted students.* Chapel Hill: Gifted Education Policy Studies Program at the University of North Carolina at Chapel Hill.

Cox, J., Daniel, N., & Boston, B. (1985). *Educating able learners.* Austin: University of Texas Press.

Darling-Hammond, L. (1995). Inequality and access to knowledge. In J. A. Banks & C. A. M. Banks (Eds.), *Handbook of research on multicultural education* (pp. 465–483). New York: Simon & Schuster.

Ford, D. Y. (1992). Determinants of underachievement as perceived by gifted, above-average, and average Black students. *Roeper Review, 14,* 130–136.

Ford, D. Y. (1994). *The recruitment and retention of Black students in gifted programs.* Storrs: University of Connecticut, National Research Center on the Gifted and Talented.

Ford, D. Y. (1995). *A study of achievement and underachievement among gifted, potentially gifted, and average students.* Storrs: University of Connecticut, National Research Center on the Gifted and Talented.

Ford, D. Y. (1996). *Reversing underachievement among gifted Black students: Promising practices and programs.* New York: Teachers College Press.

Ford, D. Y. (1997). Black students' perceptions of gifted education and gifted programs. Manuscript submitted for publication.

Ford, D. Y., & Harris, J. J., III (1994). Promoting achievement among gifted Black students: The efficacy of new definitions and identification practices. *Urban Education, 29*(2), 202–229.

Frantz, C. S., & Prillaman, D. (1993). State certification endorsement for school counselors: Special education requirements. *The School Counselor, 40,* 375–379.

Frasier, M. M., Garcia, J. H., & Passow, A. H. (1995). *A review of assessment issues in gifted education and their implications for identifying gifted minority students.* Storrs: University of Connecticut, National Research Center on the Gifted and Talented.

Frasier, M. M., & Passow, A. H. (1994). *Toward a new paradigm for identifying talent potential.* Storrs: University of Connecticut, National Research Center on the Gifted and Talented.

Gagne, F. (1989). Peer nomination as a psychometric instrument: Many questions asked but few answered. *Gifted Child Quarterly, 33,* 53–58.

Gardner, H. (1983). *Frames of mind: The theory of multiple intelligences.* New York: Basic Books.

Good, T. L. (1981). Teacher expectations and student perceptions: A decade of research. *Educational Leadership, 38,* 415–421.

Hale-Benson, J. (1986). *Black children: Their roots, culture, and learning styles* (2nd ed.). Baltimore: Johns Hopkins University Press.

Harry, B. (1992). Restructuring the participation of African-American parents in special education. *Exceptional Children, 59*(2), 123–131.

High, M. H., & Udall, A. J. (1983). Teacher rating of students in relation to ethnicity of students and school ethnic balance. *Journal for the Education of the Gifted, 6*(3), 154–166.

Irvine, J. J. (1991). *Black students and school failure: Policies, practices, and prescriptions.* New York: Praeger.

Jacob K. Javits Gifted and Talented Students Education Act of 1988, 20 U.S.C. subsection 3061 et seq.

Jenkins, M. D. (1936). A socio-psychological study of Negro children of superior intelligence. *Journal of Negro Education, 5,* 175–190.

Jones, R. (Ed.). (1996). *Handbook of tests and measurements for Black populations.* Hampton, VA: Cobb & Henry.

Karnes, F. A., & Whorton, J. F. (1091). Teacher certification and endorsement in gifted education: Past, present, and future. *Gifted Child Quarterly, 35,* 148–150.

Klausmeier, K., Mishra, S. P., & Maker, C. J. (1987). Identification of gifted learners: A national survey of assessment practices and training needs of school psychologists. *Gifted Child Quarterly, 31*(1), 135–137.

Kozol, J. (1991). *Savage inequalities.* New York: HarperPerennial.

Marion, R. L. (1981). Working with parents of the disadvantaged or culturally different gifted. *Roeper Review, 4*(1), 32–34.

National Commission on Excellence in Education. (1983). *A nation at risk: The imperative for educational reform.* Washington, DC: U.S. Department of Education.

Oakes, J., & Guiton, G. (1995). Matchmaking: The dynamics of high school tracking decisions. *American Educational Research Journal, 32*(1), 3–33.

O'Connell, P. (1986). *The state of the states gifted and talented education.* Augusta, MN: Council of State Directors of Programs for the Gifted.

Raven, J. C., Court, J. H., & Raven, J. (1986). *Manual for Raven's Progressive Matrices and Vocabulary Scales.* London: Lewis.

Renzulli, J. S. (1986). The three-ring conception of giftedness: A developmental model for creative productivity. In R. J. Sternberg & J. E. Davidson (Eds.), *Conceptions of giftedness* (pp. 53–92). New York: Cambridge University Press.

Saccuzzo, D. P., Johnson, N. E., & Guerin, T. L. (1994). *Identifying underrepresented disadvantaged gifted and talented children: A multifaceted approach* (Vols. 1 & 2). San Diego: San Diego State University.

Samuda, R. J., Kong, S. L., Cummins, J., Lewis, J., & Pascual-Leone, J. (1991). *Assessment and placement of minority students.* Lewiston, NY: Hogrefe and ISSP.

Shade, B. J. (1994). Understanding the African American learner. In E. R. Hollins, J. E. King, & W. C. Hayman (Eds.), *Teaching diverse populations: Formulating a knowledge base* (pp. 175–189). New York: State University of New York Press.

Snyderman, M., & Rothman, S. (1987). Survey of expert opinion on intelligence and aptitude testing. *American Psychologist, 42*(2), 137–144.

Sternberg, R. J., Callahan, C., Burns, D., Gubbins, E. J., Purcell, J., Reis, S. M., Renzulli, J. S., & Westberg, K. (1995). Return gift to sender: A review of *The Bell Curve,* by Richard Herrnstein & Charles Murray. *Roeper Review, 39*(3), 177–179.

Thorndike, R. L., Hagen, E. P., & Sattler, J. M. (1986). *Stanford-Binet intelligence scale: Fourth edition.* Chicago: Riverside.

Tinsley, J. (1997, March 13). Access to advanced courses for blacks to be reviewed. *The Plain Dealer,* pp. 1-B, 4-B.

U.S. Department of Education. (1993). *National excellence: A case for developing America's talent.* Washington, DC: Author.

U.S. Department of Education. (1994). *Javits gifted and talented students education program.* (Grants Projects Abstracts, 1992–1993). Washington, DC: Office of Educational Research and Improvement, Programs for the Improvement of Practice.

U.S. Department of Education. (1996). *To assure the free appropriate public education of all children with disabilities: Eighteenth annual report to Congress on the Implementation of the Individuals with Disabilities Education Act.* Washington, DC: Author.

Weschler, D. (1991). *Manual for the Weschler Intelligence Scale for Children-Third Edition.* San Antonio, TX: Psychological Corp.

Winfield, L. F. (1986). Teacher beliefs toward academically at risk students in inner urban schools. *The Urban Review, 18,* 253–268.

CHAPTER 23

Recruitment Is Not Enough: Retaining African American Students in Gifted Education

James L. Moore III
The Ohio State University

Donna Y. Ford and
H. Richard Milner
Vanderbilt University

Abstract

In public school systems all around the country, educators—teachers, counselors, and administrators—have made significant progress in identifying and recruiting diverse populations in gifted and enrichment programs. Despite the efforts, too many African American students and other students of color (e.g., Hispanic Americans and Native Americans) are not faring well in gifted education. The social and cultural obstacles (e.g., racial and ethnic prejudice, negative peer pressure, poor parental involvement, negative teacher and counselor expectations, etc.) that students of color, particularly African Americans, face in gifted education are well known. In order to improve African American student retention, it is clear that public school systems must do more. Recruitment is an important component for increasing the number of African American students in gifted education, but retention is equally important. Using multiple frameworks, this article examines the notion of retention and its many challenges and offers recommendations for improving the retention of African American students in gifted education.

Reprinted from Moore, J. L., III, Ford, D. Y., & Milner, H. R. (2005). Recruitment is not enough: Retaining African American students in gifted education. *Gifted Child Quarterly, 49*, 51–67. Reprinted with permission of Sage Publications.

> **PUTTING THE RESEARCH TO USE**
>
> A litany of publications has focused on the persistent underrepresentation of African American students in gifted education programs. In response, school personnel (e.g., teachers, counselors, and administrators) have attempted to develop strategies to increase the representation of these students in gifted education programs. Efforts primarily target finding instruments and developing policies and procedures to recruit gifted African American students. Less often is there a focus on retaining diverse students in gifted programs once they have been recruited (that is, identified and placed). In this article, we extrapolate from the work of scholars and social scientists in higher education, many of whom bemoan the loss of diverse students who opt to withdraw from college, and draw implications for gifted education. Our thesis is that this underrepresentation problem will persist until educators more assertively focus on both the recruitment and retention of students of color. We argue, in other words, that recruitment is not enough to change the demographics of gifted education and otherwise increase access to these programs for African American students.

A recurring theme in education is the underrepresentation of African American, Hispanic American, and Native American students in gifted education programs. As discussed by numerous scholars (Bernal, 2002; Ford, 1998, 2002; Frasier & Passow, 1994), recruiting diverse students in gifted programs has been the primary focus for addressing their underrepresentation. Recruitment efforts—screening, assessment, and placement—have focused on: (a) finding appropriate instruments, namely culturally sensitive tests of intelligence and achievement, to assist with screening, referral, and placement decisions; (b) increasing teacher referrals of diverse students; and (c) creating or improving nomination forms and checklists that capture the strengths of diverse groups. In 1994, Ford argued that diverse students' representation can only increase when educators and other decision makers focus on "recruiting and retaining" diverse students in gifted education. Stated differently, Ford urged educators to go beyond the notion of referral, screening, and placement (i.e., recruitment) and find better ways to recruit students of color and more effective and innovative ways of keeping these students in gifted programs.

To date, few studies have focused on factors that affect the retention of students of color in gifted programs. However, from a conceptual perspective, Ford (1994, 1996, 2002) has maintained that African American students confront unique barriers to achievement that affect not only their recruitment into gifted programs, but also their retention. She categorized these barriers as social, cultural, and psychological inhibitors. For example, under the social barrier category, she and other scholars (Fordham, 1988; Fordham & Ogbu, 1986) have explored the role of negative peer pressures in hindering the desire of African American students to participate in gifted programs. Equally important have been unique psychological stressors related to racial identity issues that cause African American students to feel conflicted about racial identity and achievement. Specifically, national trends indicate that too many African American students do not wish to be involved in gifted education if there are few ethnic minorities in the programs, if they feel isolated from other gifted students, if they are teased by African American peers for achieving, and if they have poor (i.e., weak or negative) racial identities (Ford, 1996; Ford & Harris, 1996; Grantham & Ford, 2003). More recently, Harmon (2002) found similar results with elementary school students. African American students in her study emphasized the importance of student teacher relationships and the need for teachers to hold high expectations for African American students. Likewise, Corbett and Wilson (2002) reported that inner-city African American middle school students identified teacher-student relationships as fundamental to their interest and engagement in school, as well as school success. Flowers, Milner, and Moore (2003) also found similar results with high school seniors when investigating educational aspirations.

This article extrapolates from the research literature that has attempted to explore the myriad of factors affecting or hindering the participation and representation of African American students in gifted programs around the country. Rather than reiterate the many treatises on recruitment issues, this article focuses exclusively on the less explored, but equally important issue of retention. Why might African American students not persist in gifted education after being recruited (i.e., screened and placed)? What factors hinder their persistence and achievement? What can educators and other school officials do to retain African American students in gifted education?

The framework adopted in this article borrows from the extensive literature on retention and persistence of African American students who attend predominantly White educational institutions (PWEIs), specifically colleges and universities (Flowers & Moore, 2002; Fries-Britt & Tuner, 2001; Herndon, 2003; Herndon & Moore, 2002; Moore, 2001; Moore, Flowers, Guion, Zhang, & Staten, 2004; Moore & Herndon, 2003; Moore, Madison-Colmore, & Smith, 2003; Steele, 1997, 1999; Steele & Aronson, 1995). As in gifted programs, African American students are underrepresented in colleges and universities. The majority of studies on African American students' retention and persistence have focused on college-age students. Institutions of higher education have focused their attention on the recruitment and retention of African Americans and other students of color. On the other hand, gifted education has focused extensively—almost exclusively—on recruiting, rather than retaining, diverse students for gifted education programs.

It is quite likely that the research that has focused on retaining African American students in PWEIs has much to offer the field of gifted education because White students disproportionately comprise gifted education programs. Therefore, like colleges and universities, gifted programs can be considered PWEIs because they embody many of the same qualities and challenges that predominately White postsecondary institutions possess.

In 1998, Ford reviewed several reports to identify trends in the underrepresentation of diverse students in gifted education. Between 1984 and 1996, she found that diverse students were clearly underrepresented in gifted education and that the problem had gotten worse. It is possible that our historical and contemporary efforts to increase the representation of African American students in gifted education have failed, or been less than we desired, because educators and researchers have been looking at the wrong issues and the wrong solutions. Perhaps too little attention has been directed at the influence of social, cultural, and psychological variables on diverse students' persistence/retention in gifted education programs (Ford, 1994, 1996; Ford, Harris, Tyson, & Frazier Trotman, 2002).

MODELS OF DIVERSE STUDENT RETENTION/ PERSISTENCE IN PWEIs

Research on college persistence and retention among African American students is voluminous. Arguably, the most discussed and researched model is Tinto's (1975, 1987, 1993) model of persistence and departure, which provides a conceptual framework for examining how African American students become academically integrated into institutional life. Tinto (1987, 1993) suggests through his model that student departure is a function of individual and institutional factors that work together to promote, alter, or hamper a student's academic persistence or drive. Stated differently, it is hypothesized that certain individual and institutional factors impact the academic experiences of students and, in some cases, influence students' decision to persist or not persist in a given academic domain. In addition, Tinto (1987, 1993) notes that it is very difficult for educational researchers to understand student departure without first understanding the individual and institutional factors that lead to student attrition. For this reason, educational researchers "generally agree that what happens following entry is, in most cases, more important to the process of student departure than what occurs prior to entry" (Tinto, 1987, p. 47).

As in postsecondary education, academic persistence in gifted education programs requires commitment, as well as academic fortitude. The degree of individual commitment indicates whether or not the student is willing to invest the necessary "time, energy, and often scarce resources to meet the academic and social demands" (Tinto, 1987, p. 44) of gifted education. In most cases, the academic and social demands of these programs are imposed on gifted education students. The gifted education curriculum, unlike general education, typically reflects accelerated content, coursework, and assignments. In some cases, gifted education programs pose complex psychological, emotional, social, and academic problems for students. For example, it is not uncommon for academic learning environments in gifted education programs to breed social isolation, academic competition, and intellectual arrogance (Sapon-Shevin, 1994). Although some students are able to adjust to gifted educational learning environments, there are still many students who are not able to adjust. Those individuals who possess a relatively high degree of academic competence and commitment are the students who are more likely to adjust.

In gifted education programs, a number of African American students withdraw or disengage psychologically (Ford, 1996; Grantham & Ford, 1998; Harmon, 2002). Many students of color are not willing to remain in stressful gifted education programs. Because such programs are typically comprised of mostly White students, African American students often withdraw and opt for general educational tracks to be around more African American students. In other cases, teachers, school counselors, or parents recommend to African American students that they transfer out of gifted education because they are not faring well academically and socially. It is quite clear that students' goals and commitments play an integral role in their responses to gifted educational learning environments. As Tinto (1987) postulated with college students, "either lofty goals or strong commitments, or both, will lead individuals to persist in very difficult circumstances" (p. 49).

Collectively, Tinto's model (1975, 1987, 1993) insinuates that students' personal background characteristics, educational-occupational goals, commitment to their goals and the educational institution, and degree of academic and social involvement within the institution interact to help predict whether or not they will persist or not persist in the designated academic domain. The following variables comprise the primary make-up of the "student departure" model: preentry attributes, goals and commitments, institutional experiences, and personal and normative integration. Related to college students, the significance of preentry characteristics on educational outcomes is prominent in the research literature. In the case of gifted education programs, most students are usually identified for these educational enrichment initiatives after undergoing a battery of assessments and screening procedures. It is postulated that background factors are more closely linked with academic persistence than other factors.

Although students may possess the minimum academic requirements to participate in gifted education programs, it does not mean that their educational and occupational goals are well conceptualized or aligned with gifted education, nor does it mean that they are committed to doing well in the program. Similar to Tinto's (1987, 1993) findings with college students, several scholars (Ford, Grantham, & Harris, 1997; Ford & Harris, 1999; Hébert & Olenchak, 2000) believe that those gifted students who are committed to gifted education programs, are fairly satisfied with its academic and social environment, and have realistic goals related to achieving academic success are more likely to persist or remain in gifted education programs. The more students feel supported, the more they will feel that their goals and interests are reachable. Several researchers (Flowers et al., 2003; Howard, 2003; Moore et al., 2004; Moore et al., 2003) have found this to be especially true for African American students. These findings are also related to Tinto's (1987, 1993) model, which illustrates the importance of having goals and interests congruent with the mission of the educational environment.

As it relates to institutional experiences, it is important that teachers, counselors, and other school personnel monitor the educational experiences and progress of gifted education students in general and students of color in particular. Too often, gifted education programs do not take in consideration the cultural values, social experiences, and learning styles of students of color. As a result, students of color report feelings of discrimination, isolation, and lack of support from teachers, counselors, and other school personnel (Fordham & Ogbu, 1986; Howard, 2003; Ogbu, 2003). In gifted education programs, it is important that African American students are both academically and socially integrated. Similar to Tinto's model (1987, 1993), "academic and social integration" refers to the extent to which students are engaged and involved in the academic domain, adjusted to the academic learning environment, and integrated socially with peers (i.e., African American and non-African American students) and nonpeers (e.g., teachers, counselors, etc.) in the academic domain. Many scholars (Butler, 2003; Flowers et al., 2003; Grantham & Ford, 2003; Howard; Milner, Flowers, Moore, Moore, & Flowers, 2003; Moore, 2003) have recommended that teachers and counselors play a major role in facilitating learning and resiliency and providing encouragement to African American students.

The retention or persistence model, proposed by Tracy and Sedlacek (1982), has also been under extensive investigation. Tracy and Sedlacek, as well as Sedlacek (1983, 1987, 1989, 1991, 1998), maintain that the structural relations of eight noncognitive dimensions, along with traditional definitions of achievement and ability, effectively predict the academic persistence of African American students in PWEIs. They proclaim, based on their research, that the identified noncognitive variables more effectively predict persistence than achievement and performance variables (as measured by tests and grades) for African American students. These specific noncognitive variables are:

1. *positive self-concept or confidence*: has strong feelings about self, strength of character, determination, and independence;
2. *realistic self-appraisal*: recognizes and accepts deficiencies and works hard at self-development, especially academically; recognizes the need to broaden his or her individuality;

3. *understanding of and ability to deal with racism*: is realistic based on personal experience of racism; is committed to fighting to improve conditions; is not submissive to existing wrongs nor hostile to society; is able to handle a racist system; is assertive and encourages the school or organization to fight racism;
4. *preference for long-range goals over more immediate short term goals*: is able to respond to delayed gratification;
5. *support of others for academic plans*: has a person to whom he or she can turn for support;
6. *successful leadership experience*: has leadership experience in area(s) pertinent to his or her background (e.g., church, gang leader, sports, etc.);
7. *demonstrated community service*: is involved in his or her cultural community; and
8. *knowledge acquired in a field*: has unusual or culturally related ways of obtaining information and demonstrating knowledge (field may be nontraditional).

Table 1 contrasts the profiles of high and low scorers on the noncognitive variables.

Results from Sedlacek's (1991, 1998) studies also indicate that, while test scores are effective at predicting White students' persistence in PWEIs, they are less effective at predicting African American students' persistence. More succinctly, Sedlacek has found that, while noncognitive variables often predict the grades of White students, these variables predict the persistence of African American students. In essence, like Tinto's model (1987, 1993), Sedlacek's model contends that educators who are concerned with the success of African American students in PWEIs (including gifted programs) cannot afford to ignore the social and emotional qualities of life in these educational settings. These models provide convincing evidence that the educational experiences of diverse students cannot be relegated to predictions based on test scores, as is traditionally the case. Psychometric test scores of achievement and intelligence cannot fully or even adequately explain the complex issues related to diverse students' persistence and success.

The work of Van Gennep (1960) significantly influenced Tinto's model (1987, 1993). Furthermore, it provides insight on African American students' persistence in PWEIs. This rites-of-passage model focuses on issues surrounding the concepts of separation and academic and social integration as an individual interacts in different environments. According to Van Gennep, individuals go through a three-phase process of separation, transition, and incorporation when interacting in predominantly White settings. In the separation stage, the individual becomes separated from past associations and interacts less with his or her original group. In the transition stage, the individual begins to interact with the new group or culture and

Table 1
Profiles of High and Low Scorers on Noncognitive Variables

	High Score	Low Score
Positive self-concept or confidence	Feels confident in making it through graduation. Makes positive statements about him- or herself. Expects to do well in academic and nonacademic areas. Assumes he or she can handle new situations or challenges.	Can express reason(s) he or she might have to leave school. Not sure he or she has ability to make it. Feels other students are better than he or she. Expects to get marginal grades.
Realistic self-appraisal	Appreciates and accepts rewards as well as consequences of poor performance. Understands that reinforcement is imperfect, and does not overreact to positive or negative feedback. Has developed a system of using feedback to alter behavior.	Not sure how evaluations are done in school. Overreacts to most recent reinforcement rather than seeing it in a larger context. Does not know how he or she is doing in class until grades are out. Does not have a good idea of how peers would rate his/her performance.
Understanding of racism and able to deal with it	Understands the role of the "system" in his/her life and how it treats nontraditional persons, often unintentionally. Has developed a method of assessing the cultural and racial demands of the system and responding accordingly—assertively, if the gain is worth it; passively, if the gain is small or the situation is ambiguous. Does not blame problems or appear as a "Pollyanna" who does not see racism.	Not sure how the "system" works. Preoccupied with racism or does not feel racism exists. Blames others for problems. Reacts with same intensity to large and small issues. Concerned with race/culture. Does not have a method of successfully handling racism that does not interfere with personal and academic development.
Prefers long-range goals over immediate short-range goals	Can set goals and proceed for some time without reinforcement. Shows patience and accomplishing goals. Can see partial fulfillment of a longer term goal. Is future and past oriented, and does not just see immediate issues and problems. Shows evidence of planning in academic and nonacademic areas.	Likely to proceed without clear direction. Relies on others to determine outcomes. Does not have a "plan" for approaching a course, school in general, an activity, etc. Stated goals are vague and unrealistic.
Availability of strong support person	Has identified and received help, support, and encouragement from one or more specific individuals. Does not rely solely on his/her mentor. Willing to admit the need for help.	No evidence of turning to others for help. No single support person, mentor, or close advisor can be identified. Does not think he or she can handle things on his/her own. Is not aware of the significance of a support person.
Successful leadership experience	Has shown evidence of influencing others in academic or nonacademic areas. Comfortable providing advice and direction to others. Has served as a mediator in disputes or disagreements among peers. Comfortable taking action when called for.	No evidence that others turn to him or her for advice or direction. Nonassertive. Does not take initiative. Overly cautious. Avoids controversy. Not well known by peers.
Demonstrated community service	Is identified with a cultural, social, racial and/or geographic group. Has specific long-term relationships in a community. Has been active in community activities over a period of time.	No involvement in cultural, racial or geographic group or community. Limited activities. Fringe member of group(s). Engages more in solitary rather than group activities (academic or nonacademic).
Knowledge acquired in a field	Knows about a field or area that he or she has formally studied in school. Has developed innovative ways to acquire information about a given subject or field. Traditional in approach to learning.	Appears to know little about or has not studied in school. No evidence of learning from community or nonacademic activities. Has developed a nontraditional, possibly racially and culturally biased view of the field.

Note. From Employing Noncognitive Variables in the Admission and Retention of Nontraditional Students, by W. E. Sedlacek, n.d. Retrieved on November 15, 2002 from http://www.inform.ujd.edu/EdRes/Topic/Diversity/General/Reading/Sedlacek/book.html

seeks to acquire knowledge and skills to interact with them. In the incorporation stage, the individual takes on new patterns of interactions with the new group and becomes fully integrated into the culture of the new group. According to Pascarella and Terenzini (1991), "integration refers to the extent to which the individual shares the normative attitudes and values of peers and faculty in the institution and abides by the formal and informal structural requirements for membership in that community" (p. 51).

An underlying assumption of this model and those developed and theorized by Tinto (1987) and Sedlacek (1983, 1989, 1998) is that culturally diverse groups often find that they have to disassociate themselves from their native cultural group and realities in order to assimilate into PWEIs. Stated differently, the models suggest that diverse groups are often forced to abandon their culture and heritage (i.e., values and beliefs) to successfully integrate or incorporate the values and beliefs of the new culture. This notion is not new. For example, in his seminal book *The Souls of Black Folk*, W. E. B. DuBois (1903/1970) referred to this psychological dilemma as the "two warring souls"—double consciousness—whereby African Americans choose an allegiance to one culture over another and pay a social and psychological price in the process. This forced or false choice is something of a Pyrrhic victory in which gains are accompanied by losses. For instance, academic gains (e.g., improved grades) and economic gains may be accompanied by psychological losses (e.g., stress, identity conflicts) and social and cultural losses (e.g., friendships).

Carroll (1998) contended that, for many African American students at PWEIs, the environmental stress is very mundane and extreme. Such stress can be attributed to many types of transitions. When going from a familiar to an unfamiliar setting (e.g., PWEIs), there are at least four factors associated with adjustment: (a) academic adjustment to educational requirements; (b) institutional adjustment or commitment to academic pursuits, goals, and an eventual career; (c) personal-emotional adjustment or the need to manage one's own emotional and physical well-being; and (d) social adjustment to classmates, faculty, and other interpersonal relationships (Baker, McNeil, & Siryk, 1985; Herndon & Moore, 2002; Moore, 2001; Schwitzer, Griffin, Ancis, & Thomas, 1999). Moore (2001) further noted that "all of these adjustments play a tremendous role in causing students to question their academic ability, lose their motivation, and/or fail out of college" (p. 84).

Other retention models do not focus on assimilation—sacrificing or giving up one's original culture. Instead, they focus on biculturalism—adding to one's culture. Biculturalism occurs when individuals simultaneously enculturate and socialize in two different ways of life. The notion of giving up and making sacrifices is less salient in biculturalism than in assimilation. As described below, models of persistence developed in PWEIs, namely colleges and universities, can provide insight on how to better understand and improve retention in gifted education programs, which are PWEIs by definition.

Applying Retention/Persistence Models to Gifted Education

As stated earlier, diverse students are underrepresented in colleges and universities and in gifted programs. In the previous section, explanations for this problem were discussed, particularly the influence of noncognitive variables on academic persistent and retention using Sedlacek's model (1987, 1991, 1998). In this section, we explore these same explanations, focusing specifically on the influence of Sedlacek's eight noncognitive variables and their potential influence on African American students' retention in gifted programs. These noncognitive variables are grouped into two categories—social and psychological. Because of our focus on African American students in gifted programs, we utilized only the publications (i.e., articles, books, book chapters, etc.) on African American students identified as gifted, rather than research published with students in the general education population.

Noncognitive Variables—Social

The learning environment/climate is comprised of many factors, including social support systems that students have with teachers and other students. It is also comprised of teacher expectations and academic support systems (Flowers et al., 2003; Howard, 2003; Milner et al., 2003; Moore, 2003). When exploring diverse students' retention in gifted programs, it is necessary to examine thoroughly the learning environment relative to social relationships, supports, and social injustices (e.g., discrimination). Sedlacek (1987, 1991, 1998) referred to these noncognitive variables as "support of others for academic plans." In other words, these variables involve having a person to turn to for support. Two types of supports are described—peer and teacher. Also, included is a second variable, "understanding of and ability to deal with racism" (see Table 1).

Peer relationships and support. A significant body of research has found that the need to belong and peer allegiance often take precedence in the lives of African American students. African American students who feel alienated from, unaccepted by, and unconnected to their peers often become withdrawn, aggressive, or disruptive (Moore et al., 2004; Phelan, Yu, & Davidson, 1994; Steinberg, Dornbusch, & Brown, 1992). This sense of loneliness contributes significantly to underachievement and other maladjustments for African Americans.

Few studies have explored the perceptions gifted African American students hold of their peers. One exception is a study by Grantham and Ford (1998), who conducted a case study on a gifted African American female called Danisha who was underachieving. Danisha, who was 15 years old, expressed concern about having difficulty communicating with and relating to White students in the gifted program:

> In the fifth grade, I got into the [gifted] program and it seems like I was used to hanging around all Blacks students. I mean, there were a lot of Black students in [regular classes]. All of a sudden, I was just in a bunch of classes with a lot of White people, and it didn't matter to me, but I really didn't know how to converse with them. Because, like, Blacks [hang out] with the Blacks, and the Whites with the Whites, and the Jews with the Jews, and you conversate with this person because they are like you. But you don't conversate with the rest of the people in the classroom, 'cause they're not like you, and I had a real problem trying to conversate with them [White students]. (p. 98)

Danisha shared how uncomfortable she felt in classes where there were few African American students. She even mentioned how having more African American students in her classes provided academic support, moral support, and a sense of safety. Thus, Danisha felt alienated from White students in her gifted classes. This sense of alienation was also discussed by Van Gennep (1960), who argued that fitting into a new culture/environment can be difficult. In Harmon's (2002) study, African American students shared their frustrations and anger about being alienated from White classmates and teachers. They and other students of color reported being teased, taunted, and intimidated by some of the White students in their gifted education classrooms.

Danisha also confirmed what many scholars and researchers have noted. For example, many African American students equate achievement with "acting White," which often discourages and distracts gifted African American students (Ford, 1996; Fordham, 1988; Fordham & Ogbu, 1986). Like many African American students in gifted education programs, Danisha had few African American friends. There are a number of explanations for these occurrences. For example, few African American students have been identified as gifted and thus are not in her classes, and too many African American students have learned to shun achievement. In both instances, feelings of isolation and alienation can result.

Teacher relationships, support, and expectations. Hébert (2002a, 2002b) conducted several case studies with gifted African American males. He found that student-teacher relationships and expectations significantly impacted their achievement and motivation. Similarly, Ford and Harris (1996) found that most of the gifted African American students in their study did better in school when they had positive relationships with their teachers and when teachers tried to understand them. While all students can benefit from positive student-teacher relationships and expectations, these variables seem particularly important for African American students (Flowers et al., 2003, Howard, 2003, Grantham & Ford, 1998, 2003; Moore, 2003).

In Grantham and Ford's (1998) work, Danisha even discussed the influence of teacher expectations on students' motivation and achievement. She shared several examples of teachers accusing her of misbehaving. She noted that, when African American students act up, other African American students are considered "guilty by association" by teachers and other educators. Like teacher expectations, the relationships students hold with teachers influence their achievement (Flowers et al., 2003; Howard, 2003). Students in Harmon's (2002) study of elementary students reported that many teachers had low expectations of African American students, even those identified as gifted. For example, Jamaal stated: "They [teachers] expected you to never get anything right or to be the best. It was like they purposely did not want us [Black students] to succeed" (p. 71). Lamont stated: "The instruction she gave to White students seemed better than the instruction she gave to diverse students" (p. 71). Charles stated: "The teacher would encourage the other kids. He would give White students ideas about what to do, but he would just let us get in trouble." These African American students' comments were summed up as "They could have taught us, but they chose not to teach us" (p. 71). These students' comments parallel Sedlacek's (1991, 1998) noncognitive variable "understanding of and ability to deal with racism" because they relate to African American students' persistence at PWEIs.

Understanding and ability to deal with racism. According to Sedlacek (1991, 1998) and others (Fries-Britt & Tuner, 2001; Herndon, 2003; Moore, 2001; Moore et al., 2003), students who are able to cope with racism are more likely to persist at PWEIs. Several gifted African American students in Harmon's (2002) study complained about having to deal with racism. For example, Charday, a 4th grader, stated: "They would mostly hang out with their own color and talk about the kids of our race. . . . They would call us niggers and Black people and racial things. They would come up to us and say it in our faces and other things like that" (p. 71). Charday internalized racism and talked about "doing things" for herself because the teachers would not help or protect her.

On the other hand, Charles, a 5th grader, coped with racism from teachers and classmates by adopting an attitude of resilience: "I am really smart. And, like, I am proud of that. I feel good because I want to represent the Black people really good. Like, that is why I am trying to try for excellence and be a really smart person to show all White people that you all are not just the smart ones. We can be smart, too. We can be really successful, too!" (Harmon, 2002, p. 71). Students who "fight back" by working harder, and otherwise breaking stereotypes tend to persist in PWEIs (Moore, 2001; Moore et al., 2003), including gifted programs. Thus, the burden of challenging preconceived stereotypes points to enhanced emotional and psychological dilemmas (Moore, 2000a; Steele, 1997, 1999, 2003; Steele & Aronson, 1995). In essence, African American students who adopt the task of "proving Whites wrong" or portraying the African American race in a positive manner may find themselves emotionally and psychologically strained (Ford, 1996; Fries-Britt & Turner, 2001; Milner, 2002; Moore, 2001; Moore et al., 2003).

In addition, Ford et al. (2002) contended that deficit thinking by teachers and other school personnel (e.g., counselors and administrators) about African American students lie at the heart of the persistent and pervasive underrepresentation of such students in gifted education. Deficit thinking focuses on students' weaknesses. It is the belief that ethnic minority groups are in some way genetically or culturally inferior to Whites (Howard & Hammond, 1985). Ford (2003) provided concrete strategies on how teachers can transform their deficit thinking about practices to dynamic/positive thinking, especially where students of color are concerned.

On a final note, Danisha also wished that she had more African American teachers, particularly in classes where controversial and sensitive topics were discussed. For example, she stated: "I don't like social studies. I don't like reading about the past unless a Black teacher is teaching the class" (Grantham & Ford, 1998, p. 98). Ford et al. (1997) echoed Danisha's sentiments by advocating for diverse teaching staff in gifted education programs. Aligned with these beliefs, Milner et al. (2003) proposed that teacher education programs develop more effective ways (i.e., courses, field experiences, etc.) of preparing preservice teachers for teaching diverse student populations. Furthermore, they provided specific recommendations for improving preservice and in-service teachers' teaching competencies with diverse student populations.

Availability of academic supports. Social support for students is not limited to emotional support and relationships (Herndon, 2003; Herndon & Moore, 2002). The availability of academic support must also be examined. Ford (1996) and Ford and Harris (1996) shared research from various studies on underachieving gifted African American students. A significant finding was that they underachieved because of basic skill shortcomings and an antiachievement ethic. Few of the students studied a lot, and few understood the positive relationship between studying and achievement. Thus, they did not manage their time well, devoting little of it to academics. In essence, and to state the obvious, underachieving students are not likely to persist in gifted programs. Ford (1996) recommended tutoring, study skills, time management, and organizational skills for students as one way to increase the retention of African American students in gifted programs. Schools that do not focus on these skills deficits and shortcomings in students' work ethic are not likely to retain African American students in their gifted programs. Such students often find themselves in a quandary—academically capable but lacking the needed skills to be academically successful (Ford, 1996; Howard & Hammond, 1985).

Noncognitive Barriers—Psychological

An extensive body of research exists in education that highlights the critical role of self-esteem, self-efficacy, motivation, and attitudes of resilience. This article does not specifically reiterate these findings; however, it does illustrate that students who have confidence in their ability, who see the positive relationship between effort and achievement, and who are willing to "fight" to succeed tend to do well in school (Flowers et al., 2003; Fries-Britt & Turner, 2001; Howard, 2003; Moore, 2001; Moore et al., 2003). Sedlacek's (1987, 1991, 1998) model referred to two noncognitive variables—"positive self-concept or confidence" and "realistic self-appraisal" (see Table 1)—that have relevance when attempting to understand better the persistence or lack of persistence of African American students in gifted programs.

Research indicates that self-perceptions (e.g., self-concept and self-esteem) influence achievement; students who hold positive perceptions of themselves and their abilities are more likely to do well in school compared to other students (Flowers et al., 2003; Howard, 2003; Moore, 2001; Moore et al., 2003). When examining self-perception among culturally diverse students, numerous scholars argue that educators must not only consider self-concept and self-esteem, but they must consider racial identity, as well (Ford, 1996; Grantham & Ford, 2003; Rowley & Moore, 2002). In some respects, racial identity must be the central focus when working with culturally diverse students (Cross, 1995; Fordham, 1988; Rowley & Moore; Rowley, Sellers, Chavous, & Smith, 1998; Steele, 1999; Worrell, Cross, & Vandiver, 2001). Rowley and Moore stated that racial identity must be explored because it plays a protective role in students' lives. They further stated that students with strong or positive racial identities are better adjusted. An important question is, how do African American students' perceptions about being a Black person influence their motivation, achievement, and, ultimately, their retention/persistence in gifted education?

Cross' (1971, 1995) and Worrell et al.'s (2001) theory of Black racial identity has been used extensively in studies on self-perception and achievement. Many of these studies have found that African American students' racial identity is positively correlated with their achievement. The weaker or poorer their racial identity, the lower their achievement (e.g., grades in school) and work ethic (e.g., willingness to study, willingness to do school work and then to socialize). The following vignette, written by an African American female as a college freshman, illustrates the salience of racial identity to some African American students. The vignette also points out the trials and tribulations imposed upon African American students by society.

> When I look into the mirror, I see me. I see a beautiful, young woman who is multidimensional—spiritual, loving, caring, artistic, creative, and intelligent. I see a young lady who is learning and growing in many ways. I see a strong person that has come from a multi-cultural family that is well grounded in spirituality, morals, and social issues. When I look into the mirror, these things are what I see. I see the outside appearance of me, and I know the image staring back at me is a reflection of my identity. Once I walk away from the mirror to leave my friends, family and home, I enter the real world. The real world seems to have its own mirror. In that mirror, people often fail to recognize my beauty right away. They may not know that I am multi-talented. They may not understand my spirituality. They may not see that I am loving, caring, artistic, creative, and intelligent. They may not know anything about me, such as my family, the different cultures I have been exposed to, my religion, beliefs, or morals. They may not even care, because in this mirror of the world they do not first see me. The first thing they see is my color. Right away, when they see my darker, bronzed complexion, they may not care about what is inside. Or, they may just use my color to identify me with stereotypes in their minds.

Inevitably—and unfortunately—African American students are often confronted with racial injustices and negative stereotypes in their school experience that bring issues of racial identity to the forefront. Harmon's (2002) sample of elementary students is one such example, and, of course, there are many others. Racial prejudice, referred to as "encounters" by Cross (1971, 1995) and Worrell et al. (2001), wreaks havoc on African American students' self-efficacy, motivation, achievement, and identity. Many African American students internalize negative stereotypes and succumb to them (Howard & Hammond, 1985; Steele, 1997, 1999, 2003; Steele & Aronson, 1995). As Moore (2000b) found with African American male college students, African American secondary students are often difficult to recruit, as well as difficult to retain, in gifted education programs.

In a revised model of racial identity, Worrell et al. (2001) delineated three identity levels, all containing different identity types: (a) preencounter, (b) immersion-emersion, and (c) internalization. The *preencounter level* includes three identity types that involve either the belief that being White is more positive than being Black or preference for attaching low salience to race in one's life. These identity types have been referred to as "raceless" (Cross, 1995). The three identity types related to the *preencounter level* are the following:

1. *Assimilation*: For the assimilation type, the student's identity is organized around his or her sense of being an American and an individual. There is little salience accorded to racial group identity. More specifically, the individual tends not to be engaged in African American cultural and social issues.
2. *Miseducation*: For the miseducation type, the student accepts, as fact, stereotypical images and information about African Americans. He or she hesitates to engage in African American cultural and social issues. The individual often compartmentalizes and dissociates oneself from African Americans who are not doing well socially, economically, and academically.
3. *Self-hatred:* The self-hatred type is evident, when the student has negative thoughts and feelings about being African American. In turn, these thoughts and feelings may lead to extreme and detrimental behaviors to oneself and others that look like him (Madison-Colmore & Moore, 2002; Moore, 2000a).

Worrell et al. (2001) reported that changing one's racial identity, namely at the *preencounter level*, requires an encounter or series of encounters. Cross (1995) referred to this process as "Identity Metamorphosis," whereby the person experiences a major event or series of small events that are inconsistent with his or her frame of reference. The isolated episode or series of events tear away the raceless identity (Madison-Colmore & Moore, 2002; Moore, 2001). In the face of conflicting and startling information from an "encounter," the African American student reevaluates his or her self-image, thereby becoming vulnerable and otherwise uncertain about his or her identity. Anger, rage, guilt, and embarrassment surface as a result of encounters (Bailey & Moore, 2004; Madison-Colmore & Moore, 2002; Moore, 2001).

After confronting an encounter, individuals are thought to move to another level of racial identity called *immersion-emersion*, also referred to as the "vortex of psychological Nigresence" (Cross, 1995). This racial identity level is the antithesis of the *preencounter level*. At this level, all that is African American is cherished and glorified and all that is White is perceived as evil, oppressive, and inhumane. There are two *immersion-emersion levels*:

1. *Anti-White*: In the anti-White type, the person is consumed by hatred of White people and all that they represent. Furthermore, such individuals often harbor pent-up rage, anger, and resentment toward Whites. In turn, these feelings often manifest into aggression and confrontation with White America.

2. *Intense Black Involvement:* This individual tends to be obsessively dedicated to all things African American. He or she engages in Blackness in a "cult-like" fashion, may have "Blacker-than-thou" interactions with other African Americans, and sees every issue or situation in terms of Black and White or Black versus White.

The final level of Cross' racial identity theory is internalization. This level is considered the integration of a new identity, one that is more authentic and naturalistic. Social action (i.e., making a difference) is important. This new identity includes high salience for Blackness, which often takes on several manifestations:
1. *Nationalist*: This person tends to embrace an Afrocentric perspective or worldview about oneself, other African Americans, and the surrounding world. In addition, this individual often engages in African American community issues and liberation struggles.
2. *Biculturalist*: This individual tends to place equal importance on being Black and American. More specifically, this person usually possesses a comfortable affinity for both social identities.
3. *Multiculturalist*: This person usually gives equal importance to three or more social categories or frames of reference. Stated differently, this individual tends to see him- or herself, African Americans, and other groups in a global context.

Aligned with Cross' racial identity model, Ford (1994) found that gifted African American students who underachieved had lower levels of racial identity than those who achieved, when achievement was defined by grade-point average (GPA). The achievers were also more realistic about their abilities and the connection between work and effort. The underachievers were less likely to work hard to improve their achievement, and they relied on external motivators from teachers and parents for encouragement, rather than internal support. Rowley et al. (1998) had similar results.

These findings regarding different aspects of self-perception—more specifically, racial identity—are similar to those found by Sedlacek (1987, 1991, 1998) on African American student persistent at PWEIs. Teachers, counselors, and psychologists who are unfamiliar with theories of racial identity and the influence of racial identity on achievement are not likely to have success in recruiting and retaining gifted African American students (Grantham & Ford, 2003).

OTHER NONCOGNITIVE VARIABLES

Compared to the social and psychological variables just described, fewer studies have examined other noncognitive variables with gifted diverse students. An exception is the work of Hébert (2002a; 2002b). His collective research with gifted African American males demonstrates the importance of successful leadership experiences, having long-term goals, and demonstrated community service on academic persistence.

Leadership experiences and community service. The significance of these two noncognitive variables was explored by Hébert (2002a). When not studying, Claire spent a considerable amount of time in church. She was an Upward Bound student and three-sport athlete. She was chosen as a leader in a health program at her school and made presentations to younger females in her neighborhood about not becoming victims of their circumstances and about avoiding drugs and sex. The two other students in this qualitative study also participated in extracurricular activities.

Knowledge acquired in a field. The seventh noncognitive variable, discussed in the retention literature, is "knowledge acquired in a field." Relative to gifted African American students, studies on mentoring experiences are most relevant. Seminal studies (Kaufman, Harrel, Milam, Woolverton, & Miller, 1986; Torrance, 1984) in gifted education have noted the presence of mentors in the lives of highly successful people such as Presidential Scholars. Hébert and Olenchak (2000) examined how mentorships can increase African American students' achievement and engagement and, thus, retention in gifted programs. Their study included three gifted African American males who concerned teachers and administrators because of their low academic performance and poor social skills (e.g., behavioral problems). For example, Jackson, a 5th grader, refused to complete school assignments and was retained in the 1st grade; he was also being approached by gangs to become a member. Along with other interventions (e.g., contracts), Jackson was paired with a mentor who was a former NASA instructor. He eventually began to complete assignments, talk about his desire to stay out of trouble, and have a positive future. Mentoring seemed to be a significant factor in Jackson's changes.

Nathan, a 3rd grader identified as gifted, was frequently in trouble (e.g., for disrupting class and noncompliance) and had been referred to be evaluated for special education services because of persistent behavioral problems on two occasions; however, he did not qualify. Based on his interests in history and film, Nathan was paired with a professor of African American history, and he eventually showed improvements in achievement and behavior. Of his experiences, Nathan stated:

> It has been difficult for me to keep my end of the bargain. I have to bite my tongue a lot in class because I need to tell everyone what I think and what I feel. But, my teacher has really made school interesting for me. . . . This has really helped me. Oh, I'm not perfect, but my sister, Carole, has congratulated me on my success. (Hébert & Olenchak, 2000, p. 203)

Long-term goal orientation. The final noncognitive variable, long-term goal orientation, plays a major role in African American student retention at PWEIs. Studies in educational psychology (Kaufman et al., 1986; Moore, 2000b; Torrance, 1984) clearly demonstrate that setting future or long-term goals enhances students' achievement. For instance, Brown (2001) reported that African American students who set long-term goals were more likely to have higher academic achievement than those who did not. Ford (1996) noted that gifted African American achievers were more likely to have clear aspirations and goals than underachievers. With their goals in mind, the achievers were more likely to stay focused, complete school assignments, spend less time watching television, and spend less time socializing with friends. Claire, a gifted African American 10th grader, is the epitome of a student with a strong work ethic. She stated: "You have to work hard to get good grades. If you try and fail, that's good. If you don't try and you fail, that's stupid" (Hébert, 2002a, p. 133). Due to higher levels of achievement, these students are more likely to persist in gifted education and succeed. Related to this notion, in another qualitative study, Hébert (2002b) shared the experiences and dreams of Jermaine from grades 3 to 5. In the 3rd grade, Jermaine spoke often of his career goals. For example, he stated:

> Most of my day I spend daydreaming. In class, I daydream all the time. I think about my future plans for all the movie scripts I'm going to write when I become a movie producer. I just can't get over daydreaming. I read a book that explained it was normal for a kid my age to daydream a lot. At night, when I'm not daydreaming, I like to go out and stare out at the dark and think. I call it my "thinking in the dark time." It's my nighttime inspiration. I like to think about some of the movies I've watched. (Hébert, 2002b, p. 94)

This young man also talked about the importance of avoiding gangs and postponing dating because of their potential to affect his future negatively. Like Charles, described earlier in Harmon's study (2002), and Claire, in Hébert's study (2002a), Jermaine was described as resilient, having a keen ability to cope with adversity, and not being distracted from his dreams and future. Hébert (2002b) aptly concluded:

> Jermaine has spoken for children living in rural poverty by sharing his life story and his aspirations for the future with us. Whether the future remains bright for Jermaine and other gifted Black children will greatly depend on educational policy makers and the efforts of educators working with them to assure a better tomorrow for Jermaine and others like him. (pp. 100–101)

Recommendations

In early sections of this article, we applied Sedlacek's eight noncognitive variables to African American students in gifted education. Relying on studies specifically conducted with gifted African American students, we shared the results of studies that, while not using Sedlacek's model in its entirety, nonetheless examined one or more of his variables. For instance, Harmon (2002) explored African American students' relationships with White teachers and classmates, including the role of racial prejudice. Hébert (2002a, 2002b) examined how mentorships and leadership experiences in African American students' areas of interest can promote achievement. He also highlighted the importance of helping students to set goals and envision a future as a central way to promote achievement (Hébert, 1997; Hébert & Olenchak, 2000). Ford (1996) explored the relationship between racial identity and African American students' achievement. In their own way, the authors shed light on problems and promises for retaining African American students in gifted education. Having summarized these studies, we feel confident in concluding that noncognitive variables fundamentally influence the achievement and motivation of African American students in gifted programs. The magical question is "Where do we go from here?"

Based on the articles and studies reviewed, we present the following recommendations.

1. *In regard to research*, school personnel (i.e., teachers, counselors, administrators, etc.) must collect data on their recruitment and retention efforts. Such research should address the following questions: How many African American students have been identified as gifted? What variables positively and negatively influence African American students' recruitment (e.g., assessment instruments, cutoff scores, weighted matrices, teacher referral, etc.)? How many are placed and how many remain in gifted education programs? How many African American students persist in gifted education classes? What is the nature of their persistence? What specific factors affected those who persist versus those who do not persist? And, what gender differences, if any, exist in persistence/retention? Data collection can include interviews with graduating minority students and surveys of diverse students throughout their schooling. In particular, interviews with those who persist and those who do not should be conducted.

2. *In regard to monitoring*, teachers and other school personnel (e.g., counselors, administrators, etc.) must closely monitor the academic progress of gifted African American students and proactively approach and communicate with them about resources to improve their achievement. Struggling African American students must be provided academic support, such as

tutoring, study skills, time-management skills, and organizational skills (Ford, 1996). Mentoring programs should be used to help students refine their interests and examine career goals (Hébert, 2002b).

3. *In regard to relationship building*, two types of relationships must be improved: (a) student-teacher relationships and (b) student-student relationships. Teachers (and counselors) must work diligently to build relationships with African American students based on caring, trust, and positive regard. Fostering meaningful teacher-student relationships with African American students has rewarding effects on their academic achievement and persistence (Corbett & Wilson, 2002; Flowers et al., 2003; Harmon, 2002; Moore, 2001). Positive student-teacher relationships also help African American students to feel safe and have a sense of belonging, which decreases feelings of alienation and isolation (Ford, 1996; Hébert, 2002a; Howard, 2003; Moore, 2000b, 2001). Also, important are relationships between African American students and White students (Moore, 2000a, 2001). In the studies reviewed, African American students expressed numerous concerns about feeling disconnected with White classmates; they often felt as if they did not fit in and that they were misunderstood (Fries-Britt & Tuner, 2001; Herndon, 2003; Moore, 2000a, 2001; Moore et al., 2003). African American students also believed that White students had negative stereotypes about them. When teachers make home visits, attend community events, and hold consistent one-on-one conversations with students, it is likely that they can build positive relationships.

4. *In regard to learning environments*, teachers and counselors must create learning environments that are culturally responsive, rather than culturally neutral, culturally blind, or culturally assaultive (Butler, 2003; Flowers et al., 2003; Ford, 1996) Culturally responsive classrooms and schools capitalize on diverse students' cultural backgrounds, traditions, learning styles, and communication styles while also encouraging students to work with and support each other. This sense of "family" or "community" is psychologically important to numerous African American students (Corbett & Wilson, 2002; Harmon, 2002; Moore, 2001; Tatum, 1997). Having students work in cooperative groups, engage in peer tutoring, use study buddies, and participate in other social learning experiences can promote a sense of community and family for diverse students.

5. *In regard to counseling*, individual and group counseling may also be necessary for those African American students who are not adjusting well to gifted programs (Ford, 1994; Ford, Harris, & Schuerger, 1993). For example, students might act out to get attention. Counseling must center on addressing students' social-emotional, psychological, and academic

needs and development (Ford, 1994, 1995). More specifically, group counseling gives students an opportunity to share their experiences and concerns and to develop mutual coping skills and strategies. It also builds on African American students' preference for social learning and working in groups. A fundamental need also exists to nurture the racial identities of African American students (Ford, 1996). This need is related to developing students' self-concept; however, the focus on racial identity is essential when working with students of color, particularly African Americans. A multicultural curriculum (Ford & Harris, 1999) and mentoring programs in collaboration with minority professionals (Hébert & Olenchak, 2000) can improve African American students' academic achievement, as well as their racial identity.

6. *In regard to family involvement,* it is important that school personnel (e.g., teachers, counselors, and administrators) think of creative ways to get parents and other important family members intricately involved in the educational process of African American students. Although this article did not focus on the role of families in the retention process, families must be included as part of the discussion. Clearly, students whose families are involved in their education are likely to have positive school outcomes related to academic achievement and persistence in gifted programs. Like Herndon (2003) and others (Herndon & Moore, 2002; Hrabowski & Maton, 1995; Hrabowski, Maton, & Greif, 1998) found with African American college students, ongoing efforts need to be made to nurture relationships with African American families. Telephone calls, frequent notes, and family/social events effectively promote family involvement (Herndon & Moore; Moore, 2001).

7. *In regard to professional development*, it is an essential growth-enhancing process for teachers and other school personnel (e.g., counselors, administrators, etc.) who are working with culturally diverse gifted students. Teacher expectations and positive relationships significantly enhance African American students' achievement, motivation, and persistence, perhaps more so than for White students (Flowers et al., 2003; Harmon, 2002; Sedlacek, 1991, 1998; Tracy & Sedlacek, 1982). Ford (2003) argued that African American students are underrepresented in gifted education because of deficit thinking. Unless deficit thinking is eliminated, African American students will continue to remain underrepresented. Ford and Harris (1999) and others (Flowers et al., 2003; Milner et al., 2003) recommended that teacher training focus on such topics as (a) understanding culture and its impact on testing, learning, and teaching; (b) examining teachers' cultural biases and stereotypes and their influence on achievement and self-image; (c) understanding the needs and development of children

who live in poverty; (d) promoting positive racial identity among diverse students; (e) helping children cope with negative peer pressures and isolation; (f) understanding variables that promote the underachievement of diverse students and how to improve their achievement; (g) developing multicultural curricula that promote student achievement, motivation, and racial identities; and (h) working with culturally diverse families to promote student achievement.

Summary

Much attention has been devoted to recruiting culturally diverse students into gifted education, but too little attention has been devoted to retaining them. As noted from research extrapolated from higher education, African Americans and other students of color face unique and complex challenges in PWEI settings. Much of African American students' academic persistence—not grades or performance—is determined by noncognitive variables both internal (i.e., emotional and psychological) and external (i.e., institutional and social). Internal variables include self-concept, racial identity, motivation, and attitudes of resilience. External variables include social injustices, teacher and counselor expectations, social support systems (i.e., relationships with teachers, counselors, classmates, and parents), academic support systems (i.e., tutoring programs), leadership, and community service or involvement.

Not only do African American students need to learn how to manage these internal and external variables, they also need to be able to adjust to unfamiliar school settings and establish cross-cultural friendships (Moore, 2000b, 2001). They cannot make these adjustments alone; they need the support of teachers and other school personnel who are familiar with and willing to address their specific concerns and needs. Teachers, counselors, and administrators are needed who are willing and able to help diverse students adjust to gifted programs and who are willing to provide a supportive, caring, and culturally responsive learning environment. This requires building relationships with diverse students, showing students that they care, and being an advocate for students who tend to be marginalized in school settings.

References

Bailey, D. F., & Moore, J. L., III. (in press). Emotional isolation, depression, and suicide among African American men: Reasons for concerns. In C. Rabin (Ed.), *Linking lives across borders: Gender-sensitive practice in international perspective* (pp. 186–207). Pacific Grove, CA: Brooks/Cole.

Baker, R., McNeil, O., & Siryk, B. (1985). Expectations and reality in freshman adjustment to college. *Journal of Counseling Psychology, 32,* 94–103.

Bernal, E. M. (2002). Three ways to achieve a more equitable representation of culturally and linguistically diverse students in GT programs. *Roeper Review, 24,* 82–89.

Brown, W. T. (2001). Temporal orientation, ethnic identity, and perceptions of minority status: Examining ethnicity as a multidimensional construct and its relationship with African American high school students' academic engagement and performance. *Dissertation Abstracts International, 61,* 6697. (UMI No. AA19998731)

Butler, S. K. (2003). Helping urban African American high school students to excel academically: The roles of school counselors. *The High School Journal, 87,* 51–57.

Carroll, G. (1998). *Environmental stress and African Americans: The other side of the moon.* Westport, CT: Praeger.

Corbett, D., & Wilson, B. (2002). What urban students say about good teaching. *Educational Leadership, 60,* 18–22.

Cross, W. E., Jr. (1971). The Negro-to-Black conversion experience. *Black World, 20,* 13–27.

Cross, W. E., Jr. (1995). The psychology of Nigrescence: Revising the Cross model. In J. G. Ponterotto, J. M. Casas, L. A. Suzuki, & S. M. Alexander (Eds.), *Handbook of multicultural counseling* (pp. 93–122). Thousand Oaks, CA: Sage.

DuBois, W. E. B. (1970). *The souls of Black folk.* Greenwich, CT: Fawcett. (Original work published 1903)

Flowers, L. A., Milner, H. R., & Moore, J. L., III. (2003). Effects of locus control on African American high school seniors' educational aspirations: Implications for preservice and inservice high school teachers and counselors. *The High School Journal, 87,* 39–50.

Flowers, L. A., & Moore, J. L., III. (2002). Conducting qualitative research online in student affairs. *Student Affairs On-line, 4*(1). Retrieved October 24, 2004, from http://www.studentaffairs.com/ejournal/Winter_2003/research.html

Ford, D. Y. (1994). Nurturing resilience in gifted Black youth. *Roeper Review, 17,* 80–85.

Ford, D. Y. (1995). Underachievement among gifted African American students: Implications for school counselors. *The School Counselor, 42,* 94–106.

Ford, D. Y. (1996). *Reversing underachievement among gifted Black students: Promising practices and programs.* New York: Teachers College Press.

Ford, D. Y. (1998). The underrepresentation of minority students in gifted education: Problems and promises in recruitment and retention. *Journal of Special Education, 32,* 4–14.

Ford, D. Y. (2002). Creating culturally responsive classrooms for gifted students. *Our Gifted Children, 91,* 5–10.

Ford, D. Y. (2003). Changing deficit thinking to dynamic thinking. *Theory into Practice, 42,* 170–172.

Ford, D. Y., Grantham, T. C., & Harris, J. J., III. (1997). The recruitment and retention of minority teachers in gifted education. *Roeper Review, 19,* 213–220.

Ford, D. Y., & Harris, J. J., III. (1996). Perceptions and attitudes of Black students toward school, achievement, and other educational variables. *Child Development, 67,* 1141–1152.

Ford, D. Y., & Harris, J. J., III. (1999). *Multicultural gifted education.* New York: Teachers College Press.

Ford, D. Y., Harris, J. J., III, & Schuerger, J. M. (1993). Racial identity development among gifted Black students: Counseling issues and concerns. *Journal of Counseling & Development, 71,* 409–417.

Ford, D. Y., Harris, J. J., III, Tyson, C. A. & Frazier Trotman, M. (2002). Beyond deficit thinking: Providing access for gifted African American students. *Roeper Review, 24,* 52–58.

Fordham, S. (1988). Racelessness as a strategy in Black students' school success: Pragmatic strategy or pyrrhic victory? *Harvard Educational Review, 58,* 54–84.

Fordham, S., & Ogbu, J. U. (1986). Black students' school success: Coping with the burden of "acting White." *The Urban Review, 18,* 176–206.

Frasier, M. M., & Passow, A. H. (1994). *Toward a new paradigm for identifying talent potential.* Storrs: National Research Center on the Gifted and Talented, University of Connecticut.

Fries-Britt, S. L., & Tuner, B. (2001). Facing stereotypes: A case study of Black students on a White campus. *Journal of College Student Development, 42,* 420–429.

Grantham, T. C., & Ford, D. Y. (1998). A case study of the social needs of Danisha: An underachieving gifted African American female. *Roeper Review, 21,* 96–101.

Grantham, T. C., & Ford, D. Y. (2003). Beyond self-concept and self-esteem for African American students: Improving racial identity improves achievement. *The High School Journal, 87,* 18–29.

Harmon, D. (2002). They won't teach me: The voices of gifted African American inner city students. *Roeper Review, 21,* 68–75.

Hébert, T. P. (1997). Jamison's story: Talent nurtured in troubled times. *Roeper Review, 19,* 142–147.

Hébert, T. P. (2002a). Jermaine: A critical case study of a gifted Black child living in rural poverty. *Gifted Child Quarterly, 45,* 85–103.

Hébert, T. P. (2002b). Educating gifted children from low socioeconomic backgrounds: Creating a vision of a hopeful future. *Exceptionality, 10,* 127–138.

Hébert, T. P., & Olenchak, F. R. (2000). Mentors for gifted underachieving males: Developing potential and realizing promise. *Gifted Child Quarterly, 44,* 196–207.

Herndon, M. K. (2003). Expressions of spirituality among African American college males. *The Journal of Men's Studies, 12,* 75–84.

Herndon, M. K., & Moore, J. L., III. (2002). African American factors for student success: Implications for counselors. *The Family Journal: Counseling and Therapy for Couples and Families, 10,* 322–327.

Howard, J., & Hammond, R. (1985). Rumor of inferiority: The hidden obstacles to Black success. *The New Republic, 193,* 16–21.

Howard, T. C. (2003). "A tug of war for our minds": African American high school students' perceptions of their academic identities and college aspirations. *The High School Journal, 87,* 4–17.

Hrabowski, F. A., III, & Maton, K. I. (1995). Enhancing the success of African American students in the sciences: Freshman year outcomes. *School Science and Mathematics, 95,* 18–27.

Hrabowski, F. A., III, Maton, K. I., & Greif, G. I. (1998). *Beating the odds: Raising academically successful African American males.* New York: Oxford University Press.

Kaufman, F., Harrel, G., Milam, C., Woolverton, N., & Miller, J. (1986). The nature, role, and influence of mentors in the lives of gifted adults. *Journal of Counseling and Development, 64,* 576–577.

Madison-Colmore, O., & Moore, J. L., III. (2002). Using the H.I.S. Model in counseling African American men. *The Journal of Men's Studies, 10,* 197–208.

Milner, H. R. (2002). Affective and social issues among high-achieving African American students: Recommendations for teachers and teacher education. *Action in Teacher Education, 24*, 81–89.

Milner, H. R., Flowers, L. A., Moore, E., Jr., Moore, J. L., III, & Flowers, T. A. (2003). Preservice teachers' awareness of multiculturalism and diversity. *The High School Journal, 87*, 63–70.

Moore, J. L., III. (2000a). Counseling African American men back to health. In L. Jones (Ed.), *Brothers of the academy: Up and coming Black scholars earning our way in higher education* (pp. 248–261). Herndon, VA: Stylus.

Moore, J. L., III. (2000b). *The persistence of African American males in the College of Engineering at Virginia Tech.* Unpublished doctoral dissertation, Virginia Polytechnic Institute and State University, Blacksburg.

Moore, J. L., III. (2001). Developing academic warriors: Things that parents, administrators, and faculty should know. In L. Jones (Ed.), *Retaining African Americans in higher education: Challenging paradigms for retaining students, faculty and administrators* (pp. 79–90). Sterling, VA: Stylus.

Moore, J. L., III. (2003). Introduction. *The High School Journal, 87*, 1–3.

Moore, J. L., III, Flowers, L. A., Guion, L. A., Zhang, Y., & Staten, D. L. (2004). Investigating non-persistent African American male students' experiences in engineering: Implications for success. *National Association of Student Affairs Professionals Journal, 7*, 105–120.

Moore, J. L., III, & Herndon, M. K. (2003). Guest editorial. *Journal of Men's Studies, 12*, 1–3.

Moore, J. L., III, Madison-Colmore, O., & Smith, D. M. (2003). The Prove-Them-Wrong Syndrome: Voices from unheard African American males in engineering disciplines. *Journal of Men's Studies, 12*, 61–73.

Ogbu, J. U. (2003). *Black American students in an affluent suburb: A study of academic disengagement.* Mahwah, NJ: Erlbaum.

Pascarella, E. T., & Terenzini, P. T. (1991). *How college affects students: Findings and insights from twenty years of research.* San Francisco: Jossey-Bass.

Phelan, P., Yu, H. C., & Davidson, A. L. (1994). Navigating the psychosocial pressures of adolescence: The voices of high school youth. *American Educational Research Journal, 31*, 415–447.

Rowley, S. J., & Moore, J. A. (2002). Racial identity in context for the gifted African American student. *Roeper Review, 24*, 63–67.

Rowley, S. J., Sellers, R. M., Chavous, T. M., & Smith, M. A. (1998). The relationship between racial identity and self-esteem in African American high school and college students. *Journal of Personality and Social Psychology, 74*, 715–724.

Sapon-Shevin, M. (1994). *Playing favorites: Gifted education and the disruption of community.* Albany: State University of New York Press.

Schwitzer, A. M., Griffin, O. T., Ancis, J. R., & Thomas, C. R. (1999). Social adjustment experiences of African American college students. *Journal of Counseling & Development, 77*, 189–197.

Sedlacek, W. E. (1983). Teaching minority students. In J. H. Cones, III, J. F. Noonan, & D. Janha (Eds.), *New directions for teaching and learning* (pp. 39–50). San Francisco: Jossey Bass.

Sedlacek, W. E. (1987). Black students on White campuses: 20 years of research. *Journal of College Student Personnel, 28*, 484–494.

Sedlacek, W. E. (1989). Noncognitive indicators of student success. *Journal of College Admissions, 1,* 2–9.

Sedlacek, W. E. (1991). Using noncognitive variables in advising nontraditional students. *National Academic Advising Association Journal, 2,* 75–82.

Sedlacek, W. E. (1998). Admissions in higher education: Measuring cognitive and noncognitive variables. In D. J. Wilds & R. Wilson (Eds.), *Minorities in higher education 1997–98* (pp. 47–68). Washington, DC: American Council on Education.

Sedlacek, W. E. (n.d.). *Employing noncognitive variables in the admission and retention of nontraditional students.* Retrieved on November 15, 2002, from http://www.inform.ujd.edu/ EdRes/Topic/Diversity/General/Reading/Sedlacek/book.html

Steele, C. M. (1997). A threat in the air: How stereotypes shape intellectual identity and performance. *American Psychologists, 52,* 613–629.

Steele, C. M. (1999). Thin ice: "Stereotype threat" and Black college students. *Atlantic Monthly, 284*(2), 44–54.

Steele, C. M. (2003). Stereotype threat and African American student achievement. In T. Perry, C. Steele, & A. G. Hilliard III (Eds.), *Young, gifted, and Black: Promoting high achievement among African American students* (pp. 109–130). Boston: Beacon Press.

Steele, C. M., & Aronson, J. (1995). Stereotype threat and the intellectual test performance of African Americans. *Journal of Personality and Social Psychology, 69,* 797–811.

Steinberg, L., Dornbusch, S. M., & Brown, B. B. (1992). Ethnic differences in adolescent achievement: An ecological perspective. *American Psychologist, 47,* 723–729.

Tatum, B. (1997). *"Why are all the Black kids sitting together in the cafeteria?" and other conversations about race.* New York: Basic Books.

Tinto, V. (1975). Dropouts from higher education: A theoretical synthesis of recent research. *Review of Educational Research, 45,* 89–125.

Tinto, V. (1987). *Leaving college: Rethinking the causes and cures of student departure.* Chicago: University of Chicago Press.

Tinto, V. (1993). *Leaving college: Rethinking the causes and curses of student attrition* (2nd ed.). Chicago: University of Chicago Press.

Torrance, E. P. (1984). *Mentor relationships: How they aid creative achievement, endure, change and die.* Buffalo, NY: Bearly Limited.

Tracy, T. J., & Sedlacek, W. E. (1982). *Noncognitive variables in predicting academic success by race.* Paper presented at the annual meeting of the American Educational Research Association, New York.

Van Gennep, A. (1960). *The rites of passage* (M. Vizedon & G. Caffee, Trans.). Chicago: University of Chicago Press.

Worrell, F. C., Cross, W. E., Jr., & Vandiver, B. J. (2001). Nigrescence theory: Current status and challenges for the future. *Journal of Multicultural Counseling and Development, 29,* 201–213.

Endnotes

1. We distinguish between two kinds of poor racial identities. A weak racial identity exists when there is little salience attached to being a person of color. Being a person of color holds little significance in one's life such that other identities are given higher priority or significance. On the other hand, a negative racial identity can be interpreted in two ways: (a) the individual holds negative beliefs (e.g., stereotypes)

about being a person of color or (b) the individual rejects being a person of color (e.g., is ashamed of being a person of color). A strong racial identity is positive, and the individual typically shows pride in being a person of color, holding high regard for his or her racial heritage and identity.

CHAPTER 24

Culturally and Linguistically Diverse Students in Gifted Education: Recruitment and Retention Issues

Donna Y. Ford
Vanderbilt University

Tarek C. Grantham
University of Georgia

Gilman W. Whiting
Vanderbilt University

Abstract: *The field of gifted education has faced criticism about the underrepresentation of African American, Hispanic/Latino, and American Indian students who are culturally and linguistically diverse (CLD) in its programs. This article proposes that efforts targeting both recruitment and retention barriers are essential to remedying this disparity. Educators' deficit thinking about CLD students underlies both areas (recruitment and retention) and contributes to underrepresentation in significant, meaningful ways. The authors examine factors hindering the recruitment and retention of CLD students in gifted education, attending in particular to definitions and theories, testing, and referral issues, and offer recommendations for improving the representation of CLD students in gifted education.*

From Ford, D. Y., Grantham, T. C., & Whiting, G. W. (2008). Culturally and linguistically diverse students in gifted education: Recruitment and retention issues. *Exceptional Children, 74*, 289–306. Reprinted with permission of the Council for Exceptional Children.

A persistent dilemma at all levels of education is the underrepresentation of African American, American Indian, and Hispanic/Latino students in gifted education and advanced placement (AP) classes. Research on the topic of underrepresentation has tended to focus on African American students, starting with Jenkins' (1936) study, which found that despite high intelligence test scores African American students were not formally identified as gifted. For over 70 years, then, educators have been concerned about the paucity of Black students being identified as gifted. During this timeframe, little progress has been made in reversing underrepresentation. This lack of progress may be due in part to the scant database on gifted students who are culturally and linguistically diverse (CLD). In 1998, Ford reviewed trends in reports on underrepresentation spanning two decades and found that African American, Hispanic/Latino American, and American Indian students have *always* been underrepresented in gifted education, with underrepresentation increasing over the years for African American students. (Unlike African American, Hispanic/Latino, and American Indian students, Asian American students are well represented in gifted education and AP classes. For example, as of 2002, Asian American students represented 4.42% of students in U.S. schools but 7.64% of those in gifted education; see Table 1). Regardless of the formula used to calculate underrepresentation (see Skiba et al., 2008), the aforementioned three groups of CLD students are always underrepresented, and the percentage of underrepresentation is always greater than 40%. Also, as noted by Ford (1998), less than 2% of publications at that time focused on CLD gifted groups, resulting in a limited pool of theories and studies from which to draw.

The most recent data from the U.S. Department of Education's Office for Civil Rights (OCR; see Table 1) indicate that as of 2002, African American, Hispanic/Latino, and American Indian students remain poorly represented in gifted education, especially CLD males. Further, CLD students seldom enroll in AP classes (The College Board, 2002), the main venue for gifted education at the high school level. In both programs, underrepresentation is at least 50%—well beyond statistical chance and above OCR's 20% discrepancy formula stipulation (Ford & Frazier-Trotman, 2000). Several OCR *Annual Reports to Congress* (2000, 2004, 2005) and publications by Karnes, Troxlcair, and Marquardt (1997) and Marquardt and Karnes (1994) indicated that discrimination against CLD students continues in school settings and in gifted education. Kames et al. examined 38 complaints or letters of findings in gifted education, falling into four categories: (a) admission to gifted programs; (b) identification of gifted students; (c) placement in gifted programs; and (d) procedures involving notification, communication and testing of gifted students. Of these 38 complaints or letters, almost half ($n = 17$) pertained to discrimination against CLD students. Likewise, Marquardt and Karnes reported that most of the 48 letters of findings they reviewed related to discrimination against

Table 1
Racial and Gender Composition of Gifted Students in 2002

Race/Ethnicity	School Enrollment		Gifted Enrollment		Total	
	% Female	% Male	% Female	% Male	% School District	% Gifted & Talented
American Indian/ Alaskan Native	0.59	0.62	0.49	0.44	1.21	0.93
Black	8.46	8.7	4.78	3.65	17.16	8.43
Hispanic/Latino	8.67	9.13	5.36	5.05	17.80	10.41
Asian/Pacific Islander	2.14	2.28	3.65	3.43	4.42	7.64
White	28.81	30.61	36.71	35.88	59.42	72.59
Total	48.67	51.33	51.27	48.73	100.0	100.0

Note. Data from *Elementary and secondary school civil rights survey 2002*, U.S. Department of Education. 2002.

CLD students, mainly involving lack of access to gifted programs. They concluded that "unless a school district is constantly vigilant in monitoring its procedures for minority students' identification and admission to gifted programs, minorities report underrepresentation" (p. 164).

Compared to special education, gifted education is a small field; fewer publications are devoted to this area of study. And unlike special education, gifted education is not federally mandated, leaving much room for differences in definitions, identification, and programming across districts and states. Only 6 states fully mandate gifted education, and 10 states have neither funding nor a mandate (Davidson Institute, 2006). Proponents of gifted education argue that gifted students have exceptional or special needs, as do children in special education classes; without appropriate services, gifts and talents may be lost or not fully developed. Accordingly, the Javits Act of 1994 recognized this potential loss of talent, specifically among economically disadvantaged and CLD students. The major goal of the Javits Act is to support efforts to identify and serve CLD students and low socioeconomic status (SES) students.

This article first focuses on recruitment and retention issues (acknowledging that most of the scholarship has concentrated on recruitment) and then offers specific recommendations to guide educators in eliminating barriers and opening doors to gifted education for CLD students. We examine the education literature regarding the various conditions that hinder the representation of CLD students in gifted programs nationally, relying heavily on publications and studies that address the impact of perceptions on behavior, such as teacher expectancy theory and student achievement and outcomes (Merton, 1948; Rosenthal & Jacobson, 1968). We suggest that deficit thinking and the use of traditional tests (especially IQ tests) and lack of teacher referral of CLD students for gifted education screening and placement are the primary contributing factors to underrepresentation. In the process of reviewing the literature, we attend to the larger question of the impact of testing instruments and policies and procedures (particularly teacher referrals) on underrepresentation. Further, we consider what school personnel (teachers, school counselors, and administrators) can do to both recruit and retain CLD students in gifted education.

UNDERREPRESENTATION: RECRUITMENT AND RETENTION ISSUES

A lack of incentive and opportunity limits the possibility of high achievement, however superior one's gifts may be. Follow-up studies of highly gifted young African Americans, for instance, reveal a shocking waste of talent—a waste that adds an incalculable amount to the price of prejudice in this country (Educational Policies Commission, 1950).

To date, a disproportionate amount of the literature focuses on the recruitment aspect of underrepresentation, and particularly on intelligence tests and lack of teacher referral (Ford, 1994, 2004). The preponderance of research and scholarship indicate that poor IQ test performance by CLD students and low teacher expectations for these youngsters are the most salient reasons African American, Hispanic/Latino, and American Indian students are underrepresented in gifted education (Baldwin, 2005; Castellano & Diaz, 2001; Elhoweris, Kagendo, Negmeldin, & Holloway, 2005; Ford, 2004; Ford & Grantham, 2003; Frasier, Garcia, & Passow, 1995; Whiting & Ford, 2006).

Over a decade ago, Ford (1994) proposed that to improve the representation of African American and other CLD students in gifted education, educational professionals (i.e., teachers, school counselors, administrators, policy makers, etc.) needed to focus on retention as well as recruitment. She advocated following initiatives in higher education that went beyond the concept of "recruitment" (finding and placing students in gifted education) to focus on getting *and then keeping* CLD students in gifted education. Specifically, educators should: (a) find effective measures, strategies, policies and procedures to better recruit CLD students; (b) find more effective and inclusive ways of retaining these students in gifted programs once recruited; and (c) collect data on factors affecting both the recruitment and retention of CLD students in gifted education in order to more completely understand and redress the issue. Karnes et al. (1997) and Marquardt and Karnes (1994) offered similar recommendations after reviewing OCR letters of findings.

In 2004, Ford reported that the notion of retention continued to be neglected when considering underrepresentation. This lack of attention to keeping CLD students in gifted programs and AP classes contributes to underrepresentation (Ford, 1996). Retention issues often fall into three categories: (a) social-emotional needs expressed by students, including relationships between CLD students, and with their classmates and teachers (Harmon, 2002; Louie, 2005); (b) concerns expressed by CLD families regarding their children's happiness and sense of belonging (Boutte, 1992; Huff, Houskamp, Watkins, Stanton, & Tavegia, 2005); and (c) CLD students performing at acceptable achievement levels (Ford, 1996). For example, a Latino/a student may withdraw from an AP class for any number of reasons—including feelings of isolation from educators and/or classmates, the majority of whom are likely to be White. Similarly, African American parents may feel forced to withdraw their child from such classes because their child complains of being treated unfairly and not fitting in with other students. Another possible case would be one in which a teacher requests removal of an American Indian student from gifted education or AP classes, attributing the student's low grades to misidentification and error in placement.

Resolving the underrepresentation problem is not easy; there are no quick fixes. To begin this process, however, educators—teachers, school counselors, and administrators—must consider the following question: "How can we improve access to gifted education for CLD students, and once we successfully recruit them, how can we successfully retain them?"

Intentionally or unintentionally, gifted education and AP classes remain culturally, linguistically, and economically segregated (U.S. Department of Education, 1993, 2002; see also Table 1), still largely populated by White students in general and White middle-class students in particular. Recommendations regarding how to "desegregate" gifted education vary (Ford & Webb, 1994), but they share the goal of finding alternative ways—more valid and reliable instruments, processes and procedures—to equitably recruit and retain CLD gifted students. These options include culturally sensitive instruments (e.g., nonverbal tests), multidimensional assessment strategies, and broader philosophies, definitions, and theories of giftedness (Baldwin, 2005; Ford, 2005; Frasier, Garcia, & Passow, 1995; Milner & Ford, 2007; Naglieri & Ford, 2003, 2005; Sternberg, 2007).

Although most of the available literature focuses on recruitment, pointing to testing and assessment issues as primarily contributing to underrepresentation, we believe that underrepresentation is a symptom of a larger social problem, as discussed by Harry (this issue). More directly, the main obstacle to the recruitment and retention of CLD students in gifted education appears to be a deficit orientation that persists in society and seeps into its educational institutions and programs (Ford & Grantham, 2003; Ford, Moore, & Milner, 2005; Moore et al., 2006).

Deficit Thinking: Denying Access and Opportunity

The United States has a long history of fraudulent research, works, theories, paradigms, and conjecture that promotes deficit thinking about CLD groups, especially African Americans. Early in our history, African Americans and Latinos/as were deemed "genetically inferior"; later, they were viewed as "culturally deprived" or "culturally disadvantaged" (Gould, 1995; Valencia, 1997). The more recent and neutral nomenclature is that CLD groups are "culturally different." Unfortunately, the arguments have gone full circle, with some recent literature reverting to genetic inferiority and cultural deprivation (e.g., Herrnstein & Murray, 1994) as the primary or sole explanation for the achievement gap and lower test scores of CLD students. (For a detailed examination of this issue, see Valencia, 1997; Gould, 1995.)

Deficit thinking is negative, stereotypical, and prejudicial beliefs about CLD groups that result in discriminatory policies and behaviors or actions. Deficit thinking and resignation are reflected in the statement of two participants interviewed by Garcia and Guerra (2004) who believed that the success of some children is set early and it is irrevocable: "Some children are already so harmed by their lives that they cannot perform at the same level as other children," and "[i]f those neurons don't start firing at 8 or 9 months, it's never going to happen. So, we've got some connections that weren't made and they can't be made up" (p. 160).

According to Valencia (1997), "the deficit thinking paradigm posits that students who fail in school do so because of alleged internal deficiencies, such as cognitive and/or motivational limitations, or shortcomings socially linked to the youngster—such as familial deficits and dysfunctions" (p. xi). Such thinking inhibits individuals from seeing strengths in people who are different from them; instead, attention centers on what is "wrong" with the "different" individual or group, having low expectations for them, feeling little to no obligation to assist them, and feeling superior to them. Deficit thinking, subsequently, hinders meaningful educational change and reform because educators are unwilling to assume or share any responsibility for CLD students' poor school performance and outcomes (Berman & Chambliss, 2000; Garcia & Guerra, 2004).

Like other types of thinking, deficit thinking affects behavior: people act upon their thoughts and beliefs. Consequent behaviors include (but are not limited to) a heavy reliance on tests with little consideration of biases, low referral rates of CLD students for gifted education services, and the adoption of policies and procedures that have a disparate impact on CLD students.

As Harry (this issue) notes, deficit orientations go beyond thoughts, attitudes and values; deficit-based orientations are evident in behaviors and actions. Specifically, ideas about group differences in capacity and potential influence the development of definitions, policies, and practices and how they are implemented. Gould (1981, 1995) and Menchaca (1997) noted that deficit thinking contributed to past (and current) beliefs about race, culture, achievement, and intelligence. Gould's work helped to establish the reality that researchers or scientists are not objective, bias-free persons, and that preconceptions and fears about CLD groups (particularly African Americans) have led to polemical and prejudicial research methods, deliberate miscalculations, convenient omissions, and data misinterpretation among scientists studying intelligence. These prejudgments and related practices paved the way for the prevalent belief that human races could be ranked on a linear scale of mental worth (Gould, 1981, 1995).

Menchaca (1997) traced the evolution of deficit thinking and demonstrated how it influenced segregation in schools (e.g., *Plessy v. Fergusen*, 1896) and resistance to desegregation during the Civil Rights era and today. Some scholars have concluded that educators continue to resist desegregation, and use tracking and ability grouping to racially segregate students (e.g., Ford & Webb, 1994; Losen & Orfield, 2002; Oakes, 1985; Orfield & Lee, 2006). Accordingly, it seems reasonable to argue that much of the underrepresentation problem in gifted education stems from deficit thinking orientations. The impact of deficit thinking on gifted education underrepresentation should be clear when one considers how the terms *giftedness* and *intelligence* are used interchangeably, how both are subjective or social constructs (e.g., Sternberg, 2007), and how highly the educational elite and middle class prize gifted programs (e.g., Sapon-Shevin, 1994).

In this article we address four major symptoms or resultant behaviors of deficit thinking: (a) the reliance on traditional IQ-based definitions, philosophies, and theories of giftedness; (b) the dependence on identification practices and policies that have a disproportionately negative impact on diverse students (e.g., a reliance on teacher referral for initial screening); (c) the lack of commitment to helping educators become better prepared in gifted education; and (d) the lack of commitment among administrators to preparing educators to work competently with CLD students, which results in the inadequate training of teachers and other school personnel in multicultural education.

DEFINITIONS, TESTING, AND ASSESSMENT

IQ-BASED DEFINITIONS AND THEORIES

Debates are pervasive in education regarding how best to define the terms *intelligent*, *gifted*, and *talented*. A 1998 national survey of state definitions of gifted and talented students (Stephens & Karnes, 2000) revealed great differences and inconsistencies among the 50 states in their definitions. Most used the 1978 federal definition, which includes intellectual, creative, academic, leadership, and artistic categories. Other states have adopted either definitions derived from the Javits Act (1994), a definition created by Renzulli (1978), or the most recent federal definition (U.S. Department of Education, 1993). Some states do not have a definition (see Davidson Institute, 2006). Further, most states continue—despite recognizing more than one type of giftedness—to assess giftedness unidimensionally, that is, as a function of high IQ or achievement test scores. Such test-driven definitions may be effective at identifying middle-class White students (Sternberg, 2007), but they too infrequently capture giftedness among students who (a) perform poorly on paper-and-pencil tasks conducted in artificial or lab-like settings (Helms, 1992; Miller-Jones, 1989); (b) do not perform well on culturally loaded tests (e.g., Fagan & Holland, 2002; Flanagan & Ortiz, 2001; Kauffman, 1994; Sternberg, 2007); (c) have learning and/or cognitive styles that are different from White students (e.g., Hale, 2006; Helms, 1992; Hilliard, 1992; Shade, Kelly, & Oberg, 1997); (d) have test anxiety or suffer from stereotype threat (Aronson, Fried, & Good, 2002; Steele, 1997; Steele & Aronson, 1995;, 2004); or (e) have low academic motivation or engagement while being assessed (e.g., Wechsler, 1991).

Testing and Assessment Issues

The use of tests to identify and assess students is a pervasive educational practice that has increased with recent federal legislation such as No Child Left Behind Act of 2001. Test scores play the dominant role in identification and placement decisions. The majority of school districts use intelligence or achievement test scores for recruitment to gifted education (Davidson Institute, 2006; Davis & Rimm, 2003). This almost exclusive dependence on test scores for recruitment disparately impacts the demographics of gifted programs by keeping them disproportionately White and middle class. Although traditional intelligence tests, more or less, effectively identify and assess middle-class White students, they have been less effective for African American, Hispanic/Latino, and American Indian students (e.g., Helms, 1992; Miller-Jones, 1989; Naglieri & Ford, 2005; Skiba, Knesting, & Bush, 2002), including those at higher SES levels. This issue raises a fundamental question based on the Griggs Principle and the notion of disparate impact (see *Griggs v. Duke Power Co.*, 1971).

In *Griggs v. Duke Power Co.* (1971), African American employees at Duke Power's generating plant brought action pursuant to Title VII of the Civil Rights Act of 1964, challenging the company's requirement of a high school diploma or passing of intelligence tests as a condition for employment or transfer to jobs at the plant. African American applicants, less likely to hold a high school diploma and averaging lower scores on the aptitude tests, were selected at a much lower rate for these positions when compared to White candidates. This case called into question the validity and utility of using tests for employment decisions. Duke Power had not attempted to demonstrate that the requirements were related to job performance. The lower court ruled that because no evidence of intent to discriminate existed, Duke Power did not discriminate. On appeal, however, a unanimous Supreme Court sided with Griggs, concluding that if a test adversely impacts a protected class, then the company must demonstrate the job-relatedness of the test used. The Court ruling led to this question: "If certain groups do not perform well on a test, why do we continue to use the test so exclusively and extensively?"

There are at least three explanations for the poor test performance of CLD students: (a) the burden rests within the test (e.g., test bias); (b) the burden rests with the educational environment (e.g., poor instruction and lack of access to high quality education contributes to poor test scores); or (c) the burden rests with (or within) the student (e.g., he/she is cognitively inferior or "culturally deprived").

The first two explanations recognize the influence of the environment (including schools) on test performance and might suggest that we need to make changes in assessment and educational practices that pose barriers to the participation of CLD students in gifted education, eliminating tests, policies, and procedures that have a disparate impact on CLD students (Karnes et al, 1997; OCR, 2000, 2004, 2005; Marquardt & Karnes, 1994). However, the third explanation is positioned in deficit thinking. Those who support this view relinquish any accountability for CLD students' underrepresentation and lower test scores because of the belief that genetics or heredity extensively determines intelligence, that intelligence is static, and that some groups are simply more intelligent than others (see Herrnstein & Murray, 1994; Jensen, 1981; Rushton, 2003).

Decision makers must appreciate the impact of culture on test scores in order to use the scores in educationally meaningful and equitable ways (Ford, 2004; Ford & Frazier-Trotman, 2000; Helms, 1992; Miller-Jones, 1989; Sternberg, 2007). Educators need to understand how culturally loaded tests can lower CLD students' test scores (Fagan & Holland, 2002; Flanagan & Ortiz, 2001; Skiba et al., 2002). We must be conscientious in seeking to interpret and use test scores sensibly, to explore various explanations for the differential test scores, and to consider alternative instruments and assessment practices (American Educational Research Association, American Psychological Association, & National Council on Measurement in Education, 1999).

INEFFECTIVE POLICIES AND PRACTICES

Procedural and policy issues also contribute to underrepresentation; of these, teacher referral is particularly worthy of attention. The teacher referral process contributes significantly to the underrepresentation of culturally and linguistically diverse students in gifted education. Specifically, educators systematically under-refer CLD students for gifted education services (e.g., Saccuzzo, Johnson, & Guertin, 1994). Teacher referral (and its rating checklists and forms), intentionally or unintentionally, serves as a gatekeeper, closing doors to gifted education classrooms for CLD students. The importance of addressing teacher referral as a gatekeeper is not an insignificant matter, as most states rely on teacher referral or completed checklists and forms for selecting students for gifted education placement (Davidson Institute, 2006; National Association for Gifted Children and State Directors of Gifted Education, 2005). Likewise, according to the College Board (2002), access to AP classes is primarily dependent on faculty recommendations, accounting for almost 60% of eventual placement.

The topic of teachers as referral sources for gifted education assessment and placement falls under the larger umbrella of the teacher expectations or perceptions, and subsequent student achievement and outcomes (Merton, 1948; Rosenthal & Jacobson, 1968). This body of work refers to the extent to which a teacher's a priori judgment of a student's achievement corresponds to the student's achievement (e.g., grades) or performance on some formal and objective measure, such as a standardized or achievement-related instrument (Rist, 1996; Zucker & Prieto, 1977).

Since at least the 1920s, researchers have examined the efficacy of teacher judgment when making referrals for gifted education screening, identification, and placement (e.g., Cox & Daniel, 1983; Gagne, 1994; Gear, 1976; Hoge & Coladarci, 1989; Pegnato & Birch, 1959; Terman, 1925). Not surprisingly, results have been mixed; some studies find teachers to be accurate in their referrals, whereas others find them to be inaccurate. For example, Terman found that teachers overlooked up to 25% of students eventually identified as highly gifted on an intelligence test; however, Gagne argued that teachers are effective and that some of the previous studies were methodologically and conceptually flawed. At least four factors appear to contribute to the differential findings: (a) different instruments used to validate teacher's judgment; (b) different referral forms, checklists, and other forms used by teachers; (c) different populations of gifted students being judged (e.g., gifted vs. highly gifted; male vs. female; younger vs. older students; high vs. low SES); and (d) different methodologies (e.g., use of vignettes vs. actual student cases).

TEACHER REFERRAL AND CLD STUDENTS

Few studies or literature reviews have focused on teacher referral and identification of gifted students who are culturally and linguistically diverse. As previously noted, a body of scholarship has shown that some teachers have negative stereotypes and inaccurate perceptions about the abilities of CLD students—and their families (e.g., Boutte, 1992; Harmon, 2002; Huff et al., 2005; Louie, 2005; Rist, 1996; Shumow, 1997). Specifically, it is possible that teachers (the vast majority of whom are White) are more effective at identifying giftedness among White students, but less effective with CLD students. On this note, Beady and Hansell (1981) found that African American teachers held higher expectations of African American students than did White teachers (also see Ladson-Billings, 1994, and Irvine, 2002).

In 1974, Fitz-Gibbons studied different components of identification for intellectually gifted low-income minority students in California, including tests and teacher referral. Relative to teacher referral, she concluded:

> One might hazard the generalization that when teacher judgments are relied upon for placement or identification it is likely to be the child who does not relate to the teacher who gets overlooked, despite the fact that his achievements and ability are equal to or higher than those of the students recognized as bright. (pp. 61–62)

When CLD students were immature, taciturn, less comfortable with adults, or viewed as affable in some way, they were more likely to be overlooked by teachers.

Ford (1996) found that most of the African American students in one of her studies had high test scores—high enough to meet district criteria for identification and placement—but they were underrepresented in gifted education because teachers did not refer them for screening. For example, Dawn, an African American eighth grader, not only had high achievement scores (from the 95th to 99th percentile) each year tested, she had a perfect 4.0 cumulative GPA, and an IQ score of 143. Although Dawn had exceeded the identification and placement criteria (93rd percentile or higher on any subscale) since the third grade, she was not identified as intellectually or academically gifted, and she had not been referred for screening.

In a study of Hispanic and White students, Plata and Masten (1998) reported that White students were significantly more likely to be referred than Hispanic students, and White students were rated higher on a rating scale across four areas of giftedness—intelligence, leadership, achievement, and creativity (also see Pfeiffer, Petscher, & Jarosewich, 2007). Forsbach and Pierce (1999), in their sample of students in 199 middle schools in New York, found teacher referral ineffective as an identification tool for African American, Hispanic/Latino American, and Asian American students. After formal training, however, teachers were more effective at identifying gifted African American students only.

Two recent studies have continued this line of research on teacher referral and culturally diverse students. Elhoweris, Mutua, Alsheikh, and Holloway (2005) examined the effects of students' ethnicity on teachers' decision making using three vignettes of gifted students. Only the ethnicity of the student in the vignette changed. This impacted teacher referrals; specifically, "elementary school teachers treated identical information contained in the vignettes differently and made different recommendations despite the fact that the student information was identical in all ways except for ethnicity" (p. 29). Finally, in a study of referral sources using all elementary students in the state of Georgia, McBee (2006) reported that teacher referrals were more effective (accurate) for White and Asian students than for African American and Hispanic/Latino students. McBee concluded: "The results suggest inequalities in nomination, rather than assessment, may be the primary source of the underrepresentation of minority... students in gifted programs" (p. 103). Further, he noted that the findings could be interpreted in several ways, one being that "the low rate of teacher nomination could indicate racism, classism, or cultural ignorance on the part of teachers..." (p. 109).

Shaunessy, McHatton, Hughest, Brice, and Ratliff (2007) focused on the experiences of bilingual Latino/a students in gifted and general education. Several students in their study believed that being gifted was special, and being culturally diverse and bilingual added to that specialness. One of the students in their study stated:

> You're already special enough [because you are bilingual], but you are extra special because you are also gifted.... Latinos/as are not supposed to do well in school, and that's the expectation. So if you are gifted and Latino/a, then you've exceeded expectations. You feel a sense of pride, because you are doing better than even Americans are doing and you aren't even from here. (p. 177)

These Hispanic/Latino students appeared to believe, as proposed by Milner and Ford (2007) and Sternberg (2007), that cultural diversity cannot be ignored in our ideas, theories, and measures of giftedness, or in eventual placement. Despite the pride expressed by many of the students in the study by Shaunessy et al. (2007) about being gifted and culturally and linguistically diverse, all of these CLD youngsters had faced some form of discrimination; some students mentioned discriminatory school policies, and some did not feel accepted by White teachers and White students, both of whom made disparaging comments to them about their ethnicity (p. 179). When feeling isolated or rejected socially, CLD students and their parents may wish to withdraw their students from gifted education classes (Ford & Milner, 2006).

INADEQUATE TEACHER PREPARATION IN GIFTED EDUCATION AND MULTICULTURAL EDUCATION

VanTassel-Baska and Stambaugh (2006) recently reported that only 3% of colleges and universities offer courses in gifted education. With so few opportunities for formal preparation in gifted education, how can we expect teachers to effectively identify, refer, and teach gifted students? This problem is compounded by the lack of teacher training in multicultural education or cultural diversity. Too few educators, even at the time of this writing, receive formal and meaningful exposure to multicultural educational experiences, multicultural curriculum and instruction, and internships and practicum in urban settings (see Banks, 2006; Banks & Banks, 1999, 2006). Frequently, such preparation is limited to one course on diversity (Banks & Banks, 2006). This is a "double whammy" when students are gifted and culturally and linguistically diverse.

Essentially, future professionals, including education majors at both the undergraduate and graduate levels, frequently matriculate with a monocultural or ethnocentric curriculum that does not prepare them to understand, appreciate, and work with students who are culturally and linguistically diverse (Banks, 2006). They consequently misunderstand cultural differences among CLD students relative to learning, communication, and behavioral styles. This cultural mismatch or clash between educators and students contributes to low teacher expectations of students, poor student-teacher relationships, mislabeling, and misinterpretation of behaviors (along with other outcomes), as previously noted.

In the spring 2007 issue of *Roeper Review*, five of the nine articles focused on CLD gifted students (Chan, 2007; Milner & Ford, 2007; Pfeiffer et al., 2007; Shaunessy et al., 2007; Sternberg, 2007). Sternberg (2007) called for educators to be more proactive in understanding and making identification and placement decisions, placing culture at the forefront of our thinking and decisions. His article presents a forceful depiction of how culture affects what is valued as gifted and intelligence, how gifts and talents manifest themselves differently across cultures (also see Chan regarding leadership and emotional intelligence among Chinese students), and how our assessment instruments and the referral process should be culturally sensitive such that they do not hinder the recruitment and retention of CLD students in gifted education (Flanagan & Ortiz, 2001; Skiba et al., 2002; Whiting & Ford, 2006). Similarly, Milner and Ford shared cultural scenarios and models, and urged educators to assertively and proactively seek extensive training in cultural and linguistic diversity in order to become more culturally competent.

RECOMMENDATIONS FOR CHANGE

To recruit and retain more CLD students in gifted education and AP classes, school personnel and leaders must address low expectations and deficit thinking orientations, and the impact of such thinking on decisions, behaviors, and practice. This proactive attitudinal or philosophical shift increases the probability that educators will address all barriers to gifted education for CLD students. Figure 1 presents one model for reconceptualizing how educators can acquire the necessary dispositions, knowledge, and skills and competencies to work with students who are gifted and culturally and linguistically diverse. The Venn diagram suggests that teachers combine the best of research, policy, and theory in gifted education with the best of research, policy, and theory in multicultural education in order to meet

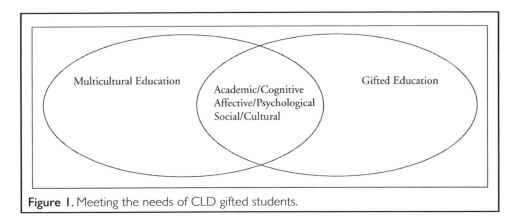

Figure 1. Meeting the needs of CLD gifted students.

the needs of gifted CLD students. Thus, we must study issues surrounding teacher referral of gifted students in general, as well as referral issues specific to culturally and linguistically diverse students.

In other words, a cultural lens or frame of reference must always be used to examine the status of gifted education for students who are gifted as well as culturally and linguistically diverse. Figure 2 presents an overview of recruitment and retention barriers, along with suggested recommendations for addressing them.

Adopt Culturally Responsive Theories and Definitions of Giftedness

Although the federal government does not mandate gifted education services, it does propose definitions. In 1993, the U.S. Department of Education offered its most culturally responsive definition of gifted to date:

> Children and youth with outstanding talent perform or show the potential for performing at remarkably high levels of accomplishment when compared with others of their age, experience, or environment. These children and youth exhibit high performance capacity in intellectual, creative, and/or artistic areas, and unusual leadership capacity, or excel in specific academic fields. They require services or activities not ordinarily provided by the schools. *Outstanding talents are present in children and youth from all cultural groups, across all economic strata, and in all areas of human endeavor.* (p. 19, emphases added)

This definition should appeal to those who are responsible for recruiting and retaining students into gifted education. First, the concept of talent development is a major focus of the definition. It recognizes that many students have had inad-

Barrier	Recommendation
Testing and assessment instruments that contain biases	Culturally sensitive measures that are reduced in cultural demand and linguistic demand
Policies and procedures that are both indefensible and have a disparate impact on CLD students	Policies and procedures examined for biases and negative impact, including teacher referrals, cut-off scores, weights assigned to items in matrices, and requirements associated with attendance, behavior, and GPA
Static definitions and theories of gifted that give little consideration to cultural differences and that ignore how students' backgrounds influence their opportunities to demonstrate skills and abilities	Culturally sensitive definitions and theories of gifted; definitions that recognize how differential opportunities result in poor outcomes for CLD students; definitions that recognize how differences can mask skills and abilities
Lack of teacher training in both gifted education and cultural diversity, which contributes deficit thinking about CLD students	Substantive, ongoing preparation of teachers in gifted education, cultural diversity, linguistic diversity, and economic diversity

Figure 2. Underrepresentation barriers and recommendations.

equate opportunities to develop and perform at high academic levels. For example, many students, especially those who live in poverty, lack exposure to books and other literature, they may not visit libraries or bookstores, and they often miss out on other meaningful educational experiences (Hart & Risley, 1995). Accordingly, the federal definition recognizes that students coming from high SES homes are likely to have such opportunities, which is likely to contribute to the fruition of their giftedness.

Further, the federal definition recognizes that some students face more barriers in life than others (including racial discrimination and prejudice). Discrimination and prejudice weigh heavily on the motivation, aspirations, and mental health (i.e., self-esteem, self-concept and racial identity) of CLD students and adults (e.g., Cross & Vandiver, 2001; Sue et al., 2007). Stated another way, discrimination places these students—at all levels of intelligence—at greater risk for low achievement, academic disengagement, school failure, and other social ills that have been described elsewhere (Allport, 1954; Constantine, 2007; Ford, Moore, & Whiting, 2006; Merton, 1948; Sue et al., 2007). Two theories of intelligence show potential for recruiting and retaining CLD students in gifted education; both theories assert that "gifted" is a social construct, that definitions and views of giftedness vary from culture to culture, and that giftedness is not easily quantifiable and easily measured by tests (see Sternberg, 2007; Whiting & Ford, 2006).

What is viewed as gifted in one culture may not be viewed and valued as gifted in another culture, and how giftedness is measured among different cultural groups varies as well. Our point here is to suggest that alternative theories and models of giftedness are needed that are sensitive to cultural differences.

Sternberg's (1985) Triarchic Theory of Intelligence proposes that intelligence is multidimensional and dynamic, and that no one type of intelligence or talent is superior to another. The theory holds that intelligence manifests itself in at least three ways: (a) componentially, (b) experientially, and (c) contextually. Componential learners are analytical and abstract thinkers who do well academically, and on achievement and standardized tests. Experiential learners value creativity and enjoy novelty. They often dislike rules and follow few of their own; they see rules as inconveniences meant to be broken. Contextual learners readily adapt to their environments (one of many skills that IQ tests fail to measure). They are street-smart and survivors, socially competent and practical, but they may not be high achievers in school. Gardner (1983) defined intelligence as the ability to solve problems or to fashion products valued in one or more cultural settings, a stipulation that does not get much attention in other definitions. In his Theory of Multiple Intelligences, Gardner differentiated seven types of intelligences: linguistic, logical-mathematical, interpersonal, intrapersonal, bodily kinesthetic, spatial, and musical. Each type of intelligence comprises distinct forms of perception, memory and other psychological processes.

Both of these theories are inclusive, comprehensive, and culturally sensitive; they are flexible and dynamic theories which contend that giftedness is a sociocultural construct that manifests itself in many ways and means different things to different cultural and linguistic groups. The theorists recognize the many-sided and complex nature of intelligence and how current tests (which are too simplistic and static) fail to do justice to this construct (Ford, 2004; Gould, 1995; Sternberg, 2007).

IDENTIFY AND SERVE GIFTED UNDERACHIEVERS

Related to this notion of talent development, it is important to consider gifted underachievers when discussing underrepresentation. Some perspectives specify that gifted students must be high achievers, equating giftedness with achievement or demonstrated performance. In schools that follow this philosophy, gifted students must demonstrate high achievement, otherwise they are unlikely to be identified or kept in gifted programs if their grades or test scores fall below a certain level. When one makes giftedness synonymous with achievement, gifted underachievers will be neither recruited nor retained. This has key implications for CLD students, too many of whom have lower grades and achievement scores than their White classmates. A wealth of reports under the topic of the achievement gap suggest that this problem cannot be ignored.

Adopt Culturally Sensitive Instruments

The most promising instruments for assessing the strengths of CLD students are nonverbal tests of intelligence, such as the Naglieri Non-Verbal Ability Test (NNAT; Naglieri, 1997), Universal Non-Verbal Intelligence Test (Bracken & McCallum, 1998), and Raven's Progressive Matrices (Raven, Raven, & Court, 2003). These tests are considered less culturally loaded than traditional tests (see Flanagan & Ortiz, 200l; Kaufman, 1994; Naglieri & Ford, 2003, 2005; Saccuzzo et al., 1994) and thus hold promise for more effectively assessing the cognitive strengths of CLD students. Saccuzzo et al., for instance, identified substantially more Black and Hispanic students using Raven's than using a traditional test, and reported that "50% of the non-White children who had failed to qualify based on a *WISC-R* qualified with the *Raven*" (p. 10), deciding that "the *Raven* is a far better measure of pure potential than tests such as the *WISC-R*, whose scores depend heavily on acquired knowledge" (p. 10). More recently, Naglieri and Ford (2003) reported that CLD students had comparable scores to White students on the NNAT, with IQs ranging from 96 to 99. This three-point difference is markedly less than the frequently reported 15-point gap that exists on traditional IQ tests between Black and White students. These nonverbal tests give students opportunities to demonstrate their intelligence without the confounding influence of language, vocabulary, and academic exposure. Fagan and Holland (2002) conducted several studies showing that CLD students get comparable scores to White students when there is an equal opportunity to learn the material, specifically vocabulary and language skills.

Provide Gifted Education Preparation for Educators

Few teachers have formal preparation in gifted education, leading us to question the extent to which teachers understand giftedness, are familiar with characteristics and needs of gifted students, are effective at referring students for gifted education screening and placement, and whether they can teach and challenge such students once placed.

We recommend that teachers take advantage of opportunities to become more competent in gifted education, by enrolling in any relevant courses at local colleges and by attending professional development workshops and conferences in gifted education, such as the National Association for Gifted Children, Council for Exceptional Children (Talented and Gifted SIG), and state and regional gifted conferences. Potential topics include definitions and theories of giftedness, identification and assessment, policies and practices, cross-cultural assessment, character-

> *Nonverbal tests give students opportunities to demonstrate their intelligence without the confounding influence of language, vocabulary, and academic exposure.*

istics and needs of gifted students (e.g., intellectual, academic, social/emotional), curriculum and instruction, programming options, gifted underachievers, talent development, working with families, and underrepresentation.

PROVIDE MULTICULTURAL PREPARATION FOR EDUCATORS

With forecasts projecting a growing CLD student population (Hochschild, 2005), teachers and other educators (e.g., school counselors and administrators) will have to bear a greater responsibility for demonstrating multicultural competence (Banks & Banks, 2006; Ford & Milner, 2006). Multicultural education preparation among all school personnel—teachers, school counselors, psychologists, administrators, and support staff—must focus on knowledge, dispositions and skills. Comprehensive preparation should help school personnel become culturally competent so that deficit orientations no longer impede diverse students' access to gifted education. This preparation can increase the recruitment and retention of CLD students in gifted education—if it permeates educational and professional development experiences.

Banks and Banks (2006) offer one model for infusing multicultural content into the curriculum. At the contributions and additive levels, diversity is addressed superficially: students are exposed to safe topics and issues, diversity permeates only a few courses, and alternative perspectives, paradigms, and theories are avoided. These two lower levels tend to promote or reinforce stereotypes about diverse groups. However, these shortcomings are rectified at the higher levels of transformation and social action. A transformational curriculum shares multiple perspectives; teachers are encouraged to be empathetic and to infuse multicultural teaching strategies, materials, and resources into all subject areas and topics as often as possible. Finally, teachers can be catalysts, agents of social change; if they are taught to be empowered, social justice is at the heart of their teaching. To become more culturally aware, sensitive, and competent, educators must:

1. Engage in critical self-examination that explores their attitudes and perceptions concerning cultural and linguistic diversity, and the influence of these attitudes and perceptions on CLD students' achievement and educational opportunities.
2. Acquire accurate information about CLD groups (e.g., histories, cultural styles, values, customs and traditions, child rearing practices, etc.) and use this information to support and guide students as they matriculate through school.
3. Acquire formal and ongoing multicultural preparation in order to maximize their understanding of and skills at addressing the academic, cognitive, social, psychological, and cultural needs and development of CLD students.

Ongoing Evaluation of Underrepresentation

Along with OCR (2000, 2004, 2005), we recommend that educators design racial equity plans to monitor gifted education data, including demographics, referrals, and instruments, all with the notion of disparate impact and eventual underrepresentation in mind. These data should be disaggregated by race, gender, and income level (Black males on free or reduced lunch vs. White males paying full price, teacher referral of American Indian males vs. all other males, patterns of referral by teacher demographics, patterns of representation across grade levels and school buildings, etc.) and should focus on both recruitment and retention barriers (e.g., What percentage of CLD students compared to White students leave gifted education and AP classes, and for what reasons? How many complaints are received about inequities in gifted education and what is the nature of these complaints?). Other recommendations include:

- Changing or eliminating any policies and practices that have a disparate impact on CLD students relative to their representation in gifted education (e.g., teacher referral, family referral, and peer referral, tests, definitions, checklists, nomination forms, views about underachievement);
- Setting concrete and measurable goals for changing the demographics of gifted education, and otherwise improving the experiences and outcomes of CLD students; and
- Reviewing these goals, plans, policies and practices annually, and making changes where necessary (i.e., retrain teachers and other school personnel who do not refer CLD students for gifted education screening, adopt alternative assessments, modify screening and placement criteria, provide different or additional support to CLD students and families, increase or modify professional development in gifted education and multicultural education).

Summary

Since its development, gifted education has failed to adequately provide access to gifted education and AP classes for students who are culturally and linguistically diverse. African American, Hispanic/Latino, and American Indian students have always been poorly represented in gifted education. We believe that the problem is complex, but not insoluble. Educators, particularly those in positions of authority, must explore this complex and pervasive problem, and then become proactive in eliminating all barriers that prevent CLD students from being recruited and retained in gifted education. Attitudinal changes are essential, as are changes in instruments, and policies and practices.

The underrepresentation problem is a result of both recruitment barriers and retention barriers; recruitment often receives greater attention because there is more data and information on this issue. A lack of preparation in and sensitivity to the characteristics of gifted students, a lack of understanding of needs and development of gifted CLD students, and a lack of attention to multicultural preparation all undermine educators' competency at making fair and equitable referrals and decisions. All educators—teachers, school counselors, and administrators—should seriously and honestly examine their respective school context to make changes, and seek the preparation and knowledge necessary to work with gifted students, CLD students, and gifted CLD students. The time to open doors to gifted education and AP classes is long overdue.

REFERENCES

Allport, G. (1954). *The nature of prejudice.* Boston: Beacon Press.

American Educational Research Association (AERA), American Psychological Association (APA), & National Council on Measurement in Education (NCME). (1999). *Standards for educational and psychological testing.* Washington, DC: American Psychological Association.

Aronson, J. Fried, C., & Good, C. (2002). Reducing the effects of stereotype threat on African American college students by shaping theories of intelligence. *Journal of Experimental Social Psychology, 38,* 113–125.

Baldwin, A. Y. (2005). Identification concerns and promises for gifted students of diverse populations. *Theory Into Practice, 44,* 105–114.

Banks, J. A. (1999). *Introduction to multicultural education* (2nd ed.). Boston: Allyn & Bacon.

Banks, J. A. (2006). *Diversity in American education: Foundations, curriculum and teaching.* Boston: Allyn & Bacon.

Banks, J. A., & Banks, C. M. (Eds.). (2006). *Multicultural education: Issues and perspectives* (6th ed.). Hoboken, NJ: John Wiley & Sons, Inc.

Beady, C., & Hansell, S. (1981). Teacher race and expectations for student achievement. *American Educational Research Journal, 18,* 191–206.

Berman, P., & Chambliss, D. (2000). *Readiness of low-performing schools for comprehensive reform.* Emeryville, CA: RPP International, High Performance Learning Community Project.

Boutte, G. S. (1992). Frustrations of an African-American parent—A personal and professional account. *Phi Delta Kappan, 73,* 786–788.

Bracken, B. A., & McCallum, R. S. (1998). *Universal Nonverbal Intelligence Test (UNIT).* Chicago: Riverside Publishing.

Casas, L. A., Suzuki, J., & Alexander, C. M. (Eds.). *Handbook of multicultural counseling.* Thousand Oaks, CA: Sage.

Castellano, J. A., & Diaz, E. (2001). *Reaching new horizons: Gifted and talented education for culturally and linguistically diverse students.* Boston: Allyn & Bacon.

Chan, D. W. (2007). Leadership competencies among Chinese gifted students in Hong Kong: The successful connection with emotion and successful intelligence. *Roeper Review, 29,* 183–189.

The College Board. (2002). *Opening classroom doors: Strategies for expanding access to AP; AP teacher survey results.* Washington, DC: Author.

Constantine, M. G. (2007). Racial microaggressions against African American clients in cross-racial counseling relationships. *Journal of Counseling Psychology, 54,* 1–16.

Cox, J., & Daniel, N. (1983). Identification: Special problems and special populations. *Gifted Child Today, 30,* 54–61.

Cross, W. E., Jr. & Vandiver, B. J. (2001). *Nigrescence theory and measurement: Introducing the Cross Racial Identity Scale (CRIS).* In J. G. Ponterotto, J. M. Casas, L. A. Suzuki, & C. M. Alexander (Eds.), *Handbook of multicultural counseling* (2nd ed.). Thousand Oaks, CA: Sage.

Davidson Institute. (2006). *State mandates for gifted programs as of 2006.* Retrieved August 4, 2006, from http://www.gt-cybersource.org/StatePolicy.aspx?NavID=4_0

Davis, G. A., & Rimm, S. B. (1997). *Education of the gifted and talented.* Boston: Allyn & Bacon.

Educational Policies Commission. (1950). *Education of the gifted.* Washington, DC: National Education Association and American Association of School Administrators.

Elhoweris, H., Kagendo M., Negmeldin, A., & Holloway P. (2005). Effect of children's ethnicity on teachers' referral and recommendation decisions in gifted and talented program. *Remedial and Special Education, 26,* 25–31.

Fagan, J. F., & Holland, C. R. (2002). Equal opportunity and racial differences in IQ. *Intelligence, 30,* 361–387.

Fitz-Gibbons, C. T. (1974). The identification of mentally gifted, "disadvantaged" students at the eighth grade level. *Journal of Negro Education, 43,* 53–33.

Flanagan, D. P., & Ortiz, S. (2001). *Essentials of cross-battery assessment.* New York: Wiley.

Ford, D. Y. (1994). *The recruitment and retention of African-American students in gifted programs.* Storrs, CT: University of Connecticut, National Research Center on the Gifted and Talented.

Ford, D. Y. (1996). *Reversing underachievement among gifted Black students: Promising practices and programs.* New York: Teachers College Press.

Ford, D. Y. (1998). The under-representation of minority students in gifted education: Problems and promises in recruitment and retention. *The Journal of Special Education, 32,* 4–14.

Ford, D. Y. (2004). Recruiting and retaining culturally diverse gifted students from diverse ethnic, cultural, and language groups. In J. Banks and C. A. Banks (Eds.), *Multicultural education: Issues and perspectives* (5th ed., pp. 379–397). Hoboken, NJ: John Wiley & Sons.

Ford, D. Y. (2005). Ten strategies for increasing diversity in gifted education. *Gifted Education Press Quarterly, 19*(4), 2–4.

Ford, D. Y., & Frazier-Trotman, M. (2000). The Office for Civil Rights and non-discriminatory testing, policies, and procedures: Implications for gifted education. *Roeper Review, 23,* 109–112.

Ford, D. Y., & Grantham, T. C. (2003). Providing access for culturally diverse gifted students: From deficit to dynamic thinking. *Theory Into Practice, 42,* 217–225.

Ford, D. Y., & Milner, H. R. (2006). Counseling high achieving African Americans. In C. C. Lee (Ed.), *Multicultural issues in counseling: New approaches to diversity* (pp. 63–78). Alexandria, VA: American Counseling Association.

Ford, D. Y., Moore, J. L., III, & Milner, H. R. (2005). Beyond cultureblindness: A model of culture with implications for gifted education. *Roeper Review, 27,* 97–103.

Ford, D. Y., Moore, J. L., III, & Whiting, G. W. (2006). Eliminating deficit orientations: Creating classrooms and curriculums for gifted students from diverse cultural backgrounds. In M. G. Constantine & D. W. Sue (Eds.), *Addressing racism: Facilitating cultural competence in mental health and educational settings.* (pp. 173–193). Hoboken, NJ: John Wiley & Sons, Inc.

Ford, D. Y., & Webb, K. S. (1994). Desegregation of gifted educational programs: The impact of Brown on underachieving children of color. *Journal of Negro Education, 63,* 358–375.

Forsbach, T., & Pierce, N. (1999). *Factors related to the identification of minority gifted students.* Paper presented at the Annual Conference of the American Educational Research Association, Montreal, Canada. (ERIC Document Reproduction Service No. 430 372)

Frasier, M. M., Garcia, J. H., & Passow, A. H. (1995). *A review of assessment issues in gifted education and their implications for identifying gifted minority students.* Storrs, CT: University of Connecticut, National Research Center on the Gifted and Talented.

Gagne, F. (1994). Are teachers really poor talent detectors? Comments on Pegnato and Birch's (1959) study of the effectiveness and efficiency of various identification techniques. *Gifted Child Quarterly, 38,* 124–126.

Garcia, S. B., & Guerra, P. L. (2004). Deconstructing deficit thinking: Working with educators to create more equitable learning environments. *Education and Urban Society, 36,* 150–168.

Gardner, H. (1983). *Frames of mind: The theory of multiple intelligences.* New York: Basic Books.

Gear, G. H. (1976). Accuracy of teacher judgment in identifying intellectually gifted children: A review of the literature. *Gifted Child Quarterly, 20,* 478–489.

Gould, S. J. (1981). *The mismeasure of man.* New York: Norton.

Gould, S. J. (1995). *The mismeasure of man* (Rev. ed.). New York: Norton.

Griggs v. Duke Power Co., 401 U.S. 424 (1971).

Harmon, D. (2002). They won't teach me: The voices of gifted African American inner-city students. *Roeper Review, 24,* 68–75.

Harry, B. (2008). Family-professional collaboration in special education: A review of research on the participation of culturally and linguistically diverse families. *Exceptional Children, 74,* 372–388.

Hart, B. H., & Risley, T. R. (1995). *Meaningful differences in the everyday experience of young American children.* Baltimore: Paul H. Brookes.

Helms, J. E. (1992). Why is there no study of cultural equivalence in cognitive ability testing? *American Psychologist, 47,* 1083–1101.

Herrnstein, R. J., & Murray, C. (1994). *The bell curve: Intelligence and class structure in American life.* New York: Free Press.

Hilliard, A. G., III. (1992). Why we must pluralize the curriculum. *Educational Leadership, 49*(4), 12–16.

Hochschild, J. L. (2005). Looking ahead: Racial trends in the U. S. *Daedalus, 134*(1), 7–81.

Hoge, R. D., & Coladarci, T. (1989). Teacher-based judgments of academic achievement: A review of literature. *Review of Educational Research, 59,* 297–313.

Huff, R. E., Houskamp, B. M., Watkins, A. V, Stanton, M., & Tavegia, B. (2005). The experiences of parents of gifted African American children: A phenomenological study. *Roeper Review, 27*(4), 215–221.

Irvine, J. J. (2002). *In search of wholeness: African American teachers and their culturally specific classroom practices.* New York: Palgrave/St. Martin's Press.

Jacob K. Javits Gifted and Talented Students Education Act of 1994, 20 U.S.C. ~ 8031 *et seq.* (1994)

Jenkins, M. D. (1936). A socio-psychological study of Negro children of superior intelligence. *Journal of Negro Education, 5,* 175–190.

Jensen, A. R. (1981). *Straight talk about mental tests.* New York: Free Press.

Karnes, F. A., Troxclair, D. A., & Marquardt, R. G. (1997). The Office of Civil Rights and the gifted: An update. *Roeper Review, 19,* 162–165.

Kaufman, A. S. (1994). *Intelligent testing with the WISC-III New* York: John Wiley & Sons, Inc.

Ladson-Billings, G. (1994). *The dreamkeepers: Successful teachers for African-American children.* San Francisco: Jossey-Bass.

Losen, D., & Orfield, G. (Eds.). (2002). *Racial inequality in special education.* Boston: Harvard Education Publishing Group.

Louie, J. (2005). *We don't feel welcome here: African Americans and Hispanics in metro Boston.* Cambridge, MA: The Civil Rights Project at Harvard University.

Marquardt, R. G., & Karnes, F. A. (1994). Gifted education and discrimination: The role of the Office of Civil Rights. *Journal for the Education of the Gifted, 18,* 87–94.

McBee, M. T. (2006). A descriptive analysis of referral sources for gifted identification screening by race and socioeconomic status. *Journal of Secondary Gifted Education, 17,* 103–111.

Menchaca, M. (1997). Early racist discourses: The roots of deficit thinking. In R. R. Valencia (Ed.), *The evolution of deficit thinking: Educational thought and practice* (pp. 13–40). New York: Falmer.

Merton, R. K. (1948). The self-fulfilling prophecy. *Antioch Review, 8,* 93–210.

Miller-Jones, D. (1989). Culture and testing. *American Psychologist, 44,* 360–366.

Milner, H. R. & Ford, D. Y. (2007). Cultural considerations in the under-representation of culturally diverse elementary students in gifted education. *Roeper Review, 29,* 166–173.

Moore J. L., III, Ford, D. Y., Owens, D., Hall, T., Byrd, M., Henfield, M., et al. (2006). Recruitment of African Americans in gifted education: Lessons learned from higher education. *Mid-Western Educational Research Journal, 19,* 3–12.

Naglieri, J. A. (1997). *Naglieri Nonverbal Ability Test: Multilevel technical manual.* San Antonio, TX: Harcourt Brace.

Naglieri, J. A., & Ford, D. Y. (2003). Addressing under-representation of gifted minority children using the Naglieri Nonverbal Ability Test (NNAT). *Gifted Child Quarterly, 47,* 155–160.

Naglieri, J. A., & Ford, D. Y. (2005). Increasing minority children's participation in gifted classes using the NNAT: A response to Lohman. *Gifted Child Quarterly, 49,* 29–36.

National Association for Gifted Children and Council of State Directors of Programs for the Gifted. (2005). *State of the states 2004–2005.* Washington, DC: Author.

Oakes, J. (1985). *Keeping track: How schools structure inequality.* New Haven, CT: Yale University Press.

Orfield, G., & Lee, C. (2006). *Racial transformation and the changing nature of segregation.* Cambridge, MA: The Civil Rights Project at Harvard University.

Pegnato, C. W., & Birch, J. W. (1959). Locating gifted children in junior high schools: A comparison of methods. *Exceptional Children, 48,* 300–304.

Pfeiffer, S. I., Petscher, Y., & Jarosewich, T. (2007). The Gifted Rating Scales–Preschool/Kindergarten Form: An analysis of the standardization sample based on age, gender, and race. *Roeper Review, 29,* 206–210.

Plata, M., & Masten, W. G. (1998). Teacher ratings of Hispanic and Anglo students on a behavior rating scale. *Roeper Review, 21,* 139–144.

Plessy v. Ferguson, 163 U.S. 537 (1896).

Raven, J., Raven, J. C., & Court, J. H. (2003). *Manual for Raven's Progressive Matrices and Vocabulary Scales. Section 1: General Overview.* San Antonio, TX: Harcourt Assessment.

Rist, R. C. (1996). Color, class, and the realities of inequality. *Society, 33,* 2–36.

Renzulli, J. S. (1978). What makes giftedness? Reexamining a definition. *Phi Delta Kappan, 60,* 180–184, 261.

Rosenthal, R., & Jacobson, L. (1968). *Pygmalion in the classroom: Teacher expectation and pupils' intellectual development.* New York: Rinehart and Winston.

Rushton, J. P. (2003). Brain size, IQ and racial-group differences: Evidence from musculo-skeletal traits. *Intelligence, 31,* 139–155.

Saccuzzo, D. P., Johnson, N. E., & Guertin, T. L. (1994). *Identifying underrepresented disadvantaged gifted and talented children: A multifaceted approach, Vols. 1 & 2.* San Diego, CA: San Diego State University.

Sapon-Shevin, M. (1994). *Playing favorites: Gifted education and the disruption of community.* Albany, NY: State University of New York Press.

Shade, B. J., Kelly, C., & Oberg, M. (1997). *Creating culturally responsive classrooms.* Washington, DC: American Psychological Association.

Shaunessy, E., McHatton, P. A., Hughest, C., Brice, A., & Ratliff, M. A. (2007). Understanding the experiences of bilingual Latino/a adolescents: Voices from gifted and general education. *Roeper Review, 29,* 174–182.

Shumow, L. (1997). Daily experiences and adjustment of gifted low-income urban children at home and school. *Roeper Review, 20,* 35–8.

Skiba, R. J., Knesting, K., & Bush, L. D. (2002). Culturally competent assessment: More than nonbiased tests. *Journal of Child and Family Studies, 11,* 61–78.

Skiba, R. J., Simmons, A. B., Ritter, S., Gibb, A. C., Karega Rausch, M., Cuadrado, J., et al. Achieving equity in special education: History, status, and current challenges. *Exceptional Children, 74,* 264–288.

Steele, C. M. (1997). A threat in the air: How stereotypes shape the intellectual identities and achievement of women and African Americans. *American Psychologist, 52,* 613–629.

Steele, C. M., & Aronson, J. (1995). Stereotype threat and the intellectual test performance of African-Americans. *Journal of Personality and Social Psychology, 69,* 797–811.

Stephens, K. R., & Kames, F. A. (2000). State definitions of the gifted and talented revisited. *Exceptional Children, 66,* 219–238.

Sternberg, R. J. (1985). *Beyond IQ: A triarchic theory of intelligence.* Cambridge, England: Cambridge University Press.

Sternberg, R. J. (2007). Cultural concepts of giftedness. *Roeper Review, 29,* 160–165.

Sue, D. W., Capodilupo, C. M. Torino, G. C., Bucceri, J. M., Holder, A. M. B., Nadal, K.L., et al. (2007). Racial micro aggressions in everyday life: Implications for clinical practice. *American Psychologist, 62*(4), 271–286.

Terman, L. M. (1925). *Genetic studies of genius. Vol. 1. Mental and physical traits of a thousand gifted children.* Stanford, CA: Stanford University Press.

U.S. Department of Education. (1993). *National excellence: A case for developing America's talent.* Washington, DC: Author.

U.S. Department of Education. (2000). *Office for civil rights, annual report to Congress.* Washington, DC: Author.

U.S. Department of Education. (2002). *Elementary and secondary school civil rights survey 2002*. Retrieved September 10, 2007, from www.demo.beyond2020.com/ocrpublic/eng

U.S. Department of Education. (2004). *Office for civil rights, annual report to Congress*. Washington, DC: Author.

U.S. Department of Education. (2005). *Office for civil rights, annual report to Congress*. Washington, DC: Author.

Valencia, R. R. (Ed.). (1997). *The evolution of deficit thinking: Educational thought and practice*. New York: Falmer.

VanTassel-Baska, J., & Stambaugh, T. (2006). *Comprehensive curriculum for gifted learners* (3rd ed.). Needham Heights, MA: Allyn & Bacon.

Wechsler, D. (1991). *Wechsler Intelligence Scale for Children–Third Edition*. San Antonio, TX: The Psychological Corporation.

Whiting, G. W., & Ford, D. Y. (2006). Under-representation of diverse students in gifted education: Recommendations for nondiscriminatory assessment (part 2). *Gifted Education Press Quarterly, 20*(3), 6–10.

Zucker, S. H. & Prieto, A. G. (1977). Ethnicity and teacher bias in educational decisions. *Journal of Educational Psychology, 4*, 2–5.

ABOUT THE AUTHORS

DONNA Y. FORD (CEC TN Federation), Professor of Special Education, Peabody College of Education, Vanderbilt University, Nashville, Tennessee. **TAREK C. GRANTHAM** (CEC GA Federation), Associate Professor and Gifted & Creative Education Program Coordinator, College of Education, University of Georgia, Athens. **GILMAN W. WHITING** (CEC TN Federation), Assistant Professor and Director of Undergraduate Studies, African American Diaspora Studies Program, Vanderbilt University, Nashville, Tennessee.

Address correspondence to Donna Y. Ford, Professor, Department of Special Education, Peabody College of Education, 230 Appleton Place (Peabody Box 228), Vanderbilt University, Nashville, TN 37203 (e-mail: donna.ford@vanderbilt.edu).

Manuscript received September 2006; accepted August 2007.

SECTION VII

The Future of Gifted Education for Black Students

Donna Y. Ford, Tarek C. Grantham, and Malik S. Henfield

For professionals and laypersons, considering the future is simultaneously challenging, frightening, and even threatening. Questions run rampant about how we and our families and community members will be impacted. How will our personal and professional lives change? Fears and anxieties aside, one thing is clear: Considering the increasing diversity of our nation and public schools, change is inevitable. It is an unfortunate reality that too few people like change. However, it is a likely reality that we will need to work together and recognize the importance of interdependence to evoke change in a positive way for gifted Black students.

When considering the future, readers must consider several definitions. The dictionary defines future as:
- the time yet to come
- undetermined events that will occur in that time
- the condition of a person or thing at a later date
- the likelihood of later improvement. (n.d.)

As we have previously stated/asserted, mainly in other sections, educators and decision makers can and must learn from the past in order to equitably address the present and future. We must question and challenge the efficacy of living in the past, and we must question and challenge the efficacy of living in the present—without considering the future. We—students, educators, communities, and all of us in this global society—cannot live in a time warp that is blind to inevitable and constantly changing demographics regarding students today and the manner in which we educate today and in the not too distant future.

In essence, everyone must be proactive rather than reactive in working with our racially and culturally diverse student population. We must be proactive to ensure that Black students have unlimited, unqualified opportunities to gifted education—no exceptions, no excuses! Too few students (Black and others), schools, and communities benefit when educators accept bystander behavior, burying their heads in the sand, choosing to live in the past, and choosing to succumb to the status quo. The declining state of education for Black students in many schools across the country presents a state of emergency. Educators must change from being bystanders to upstanders, which involves being proactive and committed to equity and excellence for gifted Black students.

As one saying goes, the only way to predict the future is to invent it. As the authors of this section question in their own way, what do we want the future to hold for gifted Black students, our communities, and our nation? At what point will educators see that their future is at stake when gifted Black students fail to be identified as gifted and fail to experience school success? When will our attitudes change about giftedness and intelligence in Black students, and what are we willing to do to change it so that more gifted Black students are best positioned to contribute their gifts to society and we are best able to enjoy, celebrate, and benefit most from their accomplishments? These are questions we ask you to ponder as you read the articles in this section and as your purpose in the quest for excellence and equity for gifted Black students continues or begins to unfold.

REFERENCE

Future. (n.d.) In *The free dictionary*. Retrieved from http://www.thefreedictionary.com/future

CHAPTER 25

Underrepresentation in Gifted Education: How Did We Get Here and What Needs to Change?
Straight Talk on the Issue of Underrepresentation: An Interview With Dr. Mary M. Frasier

Tarek C. Grantham

Dr. Mary Frasier is the founder and director of The Torrance Center for Creative Studies. The Torrance Center conducts research and provides instructional programs specifically concerned with the identification and development of creative potential. She earned the M.Ed. in Guidance and Counseling from South Carolina State University and the Ph.D. in Educational Psychology from the University of Connecticut. She has also taught in the public schools of South Carolina at the middle and high school levels. Dr. Frasier has been at The University of Georgia since 1974, where she is currently a professor in the Department of Educational Psychology, providing instruction in the gifted and creative education degree program and conducting research, specifically in the area of gifted identification and program planning.

Dr. Frasier has conducted research and presented numerous workshops, invited lectures, and seminars at the state, national, and international levels concerned with the identification and education of gifted and creative individuals. Her special focus is on gifted minority and economically disadvantaged children. She is the

---

From Grantham, T. C. (2002). Underrepresentation in gifted education: How did we get here and what needs to change? Straight talk on the issue of underrepresentation: An interview with Dr. Mary M. Frasier. *Roeper Review, 24,* 50–51. Reprinted with permission of *Roeper Review.*

author of the Frasier Talent Assessment Profile (F-TAP) (1983), a comprehensive assessment system used by school districts across the United States to identify and develop educational programs, especially for gifted minority and economically disadvantaged children. She served on the Georgia Department of Education Task Force, a committee charged with establishing procedures to apply multiple criteria in identifying those Georgia children and youth who would be eligible for participation in the state's programs for gifted children.

From 1983 to 1991, Dr. Frasier served as president of the National Association for Gifted Children; from 1979 to 1985 as governor for The Association for the Gifted (TAG); and from 1976 to 1979 as president of Georgia Federation Council for Exceptional Children. She has also served as one of the associate directors of the National Research Center on the Gifted and Talented, and was the primary investigator for the National Research Center project at Georgia, a five year, $7.5 million grant provided to four universities (The University of Connecticut, The University of Georgia, The University of Virginia, and Yale University) by the U.S. Department of Education's Office of Educational Research to study gifted and talented children.

Selected honors and awards include Leadership Georgia, 1981; Who's Who in Black America, 1981; Who's Who Among American Women, 1982; Pallischeck Visiting Distinguished Professor Lecturer, University of Northern Iowa, 1988; and EVE Award for Achievement in Education, Athens Daily News/Banner Herald, Georgia National Bank, WNGC/WGAU, 1990; and the Distinguished Service Award of the National Association for Gifted Children, 1991. In March of 1998, Dr. Tarek Grantham, assistant professor of Educational Psychology at the University of Georgia, interviewed Dr. Frasier for the National Association for Gifted Children Task Force on Advocacy, for which he served as a case researcher collecting data from those who had effectively participated in advocacy efforts that addressed underrepresented groups. The data/interview was revisited and Dr. Frasier was reinterviewed regarding her thoughts in November, 2001. The *Roeper Review* is pleased to publish Dr. Frasier's valued opinions as part of this special issue on underrepresentation among ethnically diverse students.

Grantham: You have been a long-time advocate for underserved populations of gifted students in Georgia and across the country. Your work with assessment issues has helped to transform ways in which we approach the problem of underrepresentation.

Frasier: One of the things that I have always been aware of is that you do not solve problems of underrepresentation in one fell swoop. It takes time. If it was simply a matter of finding the right tests, then this would not be a difficult problem to solve. You know, you just come up with a test, a test that will fit Black kids, poor kids, whomever, that will give you the number. But, it is not just a test. Even if you have the best test and the best procedures in mind for getting referrals and nominations, there are those ingrained attitudes about the abilities of poor and minority children that will somehow thwart the efforts that you want to make. So, you have to deal with all those feelings around this issue of underrepresentation without being threatened.

Grantham: *What are some of the attitudes that create barriers?*

Frasier: Things like poor kids and gifted programs just don't go together. I mean, I think that people in their heart of hearts really think that when kids are poor they can't possibly perform at the level of kids that are advantaged because they haven't had certain kinds of advantages in their home. There is such a cause-effect relationship in gifted programs that create barriers, you know, I call them my list of prerequisites to being gifted. You must have two parents; they must be college educated. You must be White. You must be in the suburbs. I know this sounds a little bit facetious, but if you look at the enrollment in gifted programs, it's not facetious. And any time you have any of those factors missing, then it is very difficult for people to grasp this whole issue of giftedness in other groups.

Grantham: *How do you define giftedness?*

Frasier: I define giftedness as that potential to excel at the upper end of any talent continuum. That is my simple definition. That ability to excel. I also look at giftedness as a developmental phenomenon. I think that kids show you their potential, but they don't show you all of their gifts. It is our job as an educator, as a teacher, as a mentor to help bring those gifts to fruition. I am not willing to be bound just by the U.S. Office of Education's six categories or by the recent National Excellence report's categories or by any theorist's categories of multiple intelligences. I don't think mankind knows enough to be able to say that they have ever been able to categorize all of the areas in which people can express their gifts. Giftedness is not just about excelling in the ways that we have already discovered. Giftedness is about developing new pathways that we have not taken because we didn't know that they existed. So, anytime we feel like we have cornered the market on what the categories are or the areas are in which people can express their gifts, we have somehow not been honest and true to the concept of giftedness.

Grantham: *How do you work with people who hold views of giftedness that create barriers for underrepresented groups?*

Frasier: My philosophy is that you cannot make a person gifted. In my advocacy efforts, I tell people that I want them to clearly understand that I am not there to help them get ten Black students because they have only identified one. I am here to help them identify gifted Black students or underrepresented students, period! I am not here to help you meet a number quota. If that's their goal, then I tell them that I can't help them. You really cannot help school districts or educators who hold these views because they are going to be so distracted by focusing on the number that they want and not look for quality of the student. I will not let my people, or any group for which I advocate, be insulted like that. When I have worked to address Black student underrepresentation in predominantly White schools, I maintain that you can't make Black people gifted if they aren't, and you can't make White people gifted if they aren't. You really can't. And if you really want me to work with you, you have to understand this. The second thing that I say is that, if you really want to look at the gifted potential in your school population, then some of the students who are in the program now will not be in it when we finish the identification process. I mean, schools need to know that. I feel that advocacy cannot just be about increasing representation unless people clearly understand that the way they are now defining giftedness for participation and identifying some kids for programs is flawed.

Grantham: *This is a very touchy situation, isn't it?*

Frasier: Touchy is not the word. You are dealing with a very sensitive social problem. There is no one who would say to you, "Well, the reason that these kids aren't in the program is because I am prejudiced. I discriminate. I am biased in my opinion about giftedness." But what you do get from people is, "I am very interested in finding more gifted Black kids, gifted minority kids, but I can't. I have never discriminated against kids in my life." It would be unheard of for people to say, "I am biased" or "I am prejudiced" or "I don't think Black kids are gifted." People just won't say that.

Grantham: *What do people say?*

Frasier: "Well, the problem is these parents don't value education; the problem is that these parents don't come to school enough; the problem is these parents don't take these kids to the library; the problem is so and so." When I hear these kinds of things, I know what the problem is. The problem is they feel like these parents are not doing those kinds of things to support education the way they do. Mind you, they never think about the fact that they really don't see these people in their daily routines, they don't see them in church or any other activities where their talents are being displayed and nurtured. So they really don't know whether these parents value education or not. And they don't know what parents do in their homes to support their kids. I know that when I get this litany of excuses and reasons for underrepresentation, that I've got to help people get past them.

Grantham: *What should be some of the goals in addressing underrepresentation in gifted program?*

Frasier: One of the goals should be to continue to provide a quality gifted program. Agree philosophically and practically on what a gifted program is. It is not a program to satisfy some social need. It is a program to satisfy the needs of children who have the potential to excel in some talent continuum that can be addressed by the program. A second goal is to understand that addressing underrepresentation is not going to be a task that can be solved in one or two steps; that it is going to take a lot of educating of teachers, of parents, and the community. And the third thing is that whatever we do to resolve problems requires us to make choices that will help us focus on finding the gifted child who has been unrecognized. And whatever choices we make must not insult the intelligence of that child.

Grantham: *What are key components that can make these goals a reality?*

Frasier: One key is that you have got to work together in small groups. I would say no more than fifteen—no more than you can sit around a conference table. You do not get momentum in trying to deal with large audiences. In small groups, everyone can get comfortable enough to put their problems and their concerns on the table and not feel embarrassed to do so. I prefer not to speak to a large group, say 500 people, because I am not going to be able to do anything for them to change their minds. I don't consider myself to be an entertainer. Another key is having a committed administrator, not necessarily a strong administrator. Strong by itself doesn't do it. The administrator has to be somebody who is truly committed to going beyond the surface, who truly wants to make this happen, who truly believes that gifted kids from underrepresented groups are out there. A final key is for administrators to work through and implement a design without any apologies. There should be no apologies for using nontraditional methods and procedures. As soon as advocates start apologizing for and/or overexplaining anything, then they have opened the process up to unwarranted criticism. The focus must always be on recognizing gifted potential, however it comes packaged.

CHAPTER 26

African American Experiences
Conducting Cross-Cultural Research: Controversy, Cautions, Concerns, and Considerations

*Donna Y. Ford, James L. Moore III,
Gilman W. Whiting, and Tarek C. Grantham*

In this article, the authors share concerns and considerations for researchers conducting cross-cultural research in gifted education. They contend that researchers should be mindful of the need to consider their own humanness—their beliefs, assumptions, attitudes, values, paradigms—and the limitations of their humanness when working with research participants from racially, culturally, and linguistically diverse backgrounds, especially those backgrounds that differ from their own. Furthermore, the authors assert that research is culture bound and that it is very difficult to conduct research where circumstances, demographics, and context can be ignored, minimized, negated, or in any way trivialized. Examples are presented of racially, culturally, and linguistically responsive researchers.

Over the last 5 years, we have directed our efforts toward both gifted education and urban education. Much of this work has focused on the critical need for educators (e.g., teachers, school counselors, psychologists, and administrators) to create culturally responsive learning environments, assessments, and curricula for gifted students who are racially, culturally, and linguistically diverse. To this end, this dis-

From Ford, D. Y., Moore, J. L., III, Whiting, G. W., & Grantham, T. C. (2008). African American experiences: Conducting cross-cultural research: Controversy, cautions, concerns, and considerations. *Roeper Review, 30,* 82–92. Reprinted with permission of *Roeper Review*.

course has centered almost exclusively on instruction, curriculum, assessment, and subsequent learning. Similar to other scholars (e.g., Au & Jordan, 1981; Banks & Banks, 1995; Sue & Sue, 1990), we have urged educators to seek knowledge, skills, and dispositions to become racially, culturally, and linguistically competent professionals. We have also strongly suggested that professionals, such as teachers, researchers, school counselors, and others, be proactive, creative, and assertive in this educational journey. They must prepare themselves now for today's diversity and for tomorrow's increasingly diverse student population and society (Ford, Grantham, & Harris, 1998; Ford, Grantham, & Moore, 2006; Ford & Harris, 1999; Ford & Moore, 2004; Ford, Moore, & Harmon, 2005; Ford & Whiting, 2006; Moore, 2006; Moore, Ford, & Milner, 2005a, 2005b; Moore et al., 2006). The heart of our work has been the belief that educators who lack cultural competence (knowledge, skills, and dispositions) are not likely to refer racially, culturally, and linguistically diverse students for gifted-education screening, identification, and service (Ford et al., 1998; Moore et al., 2005a; Moore et al., 2006). Thus, this dearth of cultural competence contributes to the underrepresentation of racially, culturally, and linguistically diverse students in gifted education.

An abandoned or overlooked topic in this discussion has been the issue of educators and other social scientists conducting research on or with diverse student populations. Little attention, if any, has focused on the concept of "racially, culturally, and linguistically responsive research." What knowledge, skills, and dispositions are needed by social scientists and practitioners (e.g., teachers, school counselors, psychologists, and administrators) involved in cross-cultural research? What problems exist when researchers, the majority of whom are White and middle-class, conduct research on African American, Asian American, Hispanic American, and Native American student populations and their families?

These questions are not new. According to W. H. Tucker (1994), it was not until the 20th century that the linkage between science (epistemology) and politics was made clear. W. H. Tucker (1994) and Gould (1981, 1995), for example, have written extensively on the socio-political nature of research, both historical and contemporary research, and how, when conducting research on race, self-interests have tainted cross-cultural research. It is difficult to locate a more polemic, contentious, and impassioned debate than the debate about research on race/culture and intelligence. Like many other researchers, Tucker and Gould urged social scientists in all disciplines to consider seriously and reflectively the science and politics of racial or cross-cultural research. As Sue and Sue (1999) noted, "One issue has bedeviled psychology for many decades—namely, the relationship between racial and ethnic bias and the practice of psychology" (p. 1070). Specifically, they noted that issues over race and intelligence, test bias, the design and interpretation of research about ethnic minority groups are prominent and contentious themes. Aligned with this notion, Thomas and Sillen (1972) discussed *scientific racism* and the ways in which theories and empirical research perpetuate a biased view of African Americans and other diverse populations. Yet, during our graduate training preparation, little if any discussion was given to this notion. Instead, we recall readings and discussions matter-of-factly, presenting researchers as neutral, objective, and impartial. Further, many statistical models abound that endeavor to demonstrate that researchers can be professionally unbiased. Karl Pearson, one of the greatest contributors to contemporary statistics, wrote this in 1925: "We firmly believe that we have no political, no religious, and no social prejudices. We rejoice in numbers and figures for their own sake" (as cited in W. H. Tucker, 1994, p. 7).

We disagree with this image of researchers being superhuman paragons of virtue, as does Banks (2006), who stated that "social scientists are human beings who have both minds and hearts" (p. 4). The researcher is an integral part of the research process. It is the researcher who chooses, has access to, and establishes rapport with the population under study. With this in mind, we ask what makes researchers so different from other professionals that they can be so objective and impartial? We have speculated about the implications of White researchers conducting research with racially, culturally, and linguistically diverse groups in terms of the conceptual framework adopted, the instrument selected, how the data are interpreted, and how the results or findings are used. We cannot see how so many social scientists can believe that research on race, culture, and class is free of politics, social policy, and legal mandates.

In this article, we share concerns and considerations for researchers studying cross-cultural populations in gifted education. We contend that researchers should be ever mindful of the need to consider their humanness—their beliefs, assumptions, attitudes, values, paradigms—and the limitations of their humanness when working with diverse participants. Several assumptions guide this article and should be noted. Like Banks (2006), we assume that the cultural communities in which researchers are socialized are also epistemological communities that have shared beliefs, values, and paradigms. Thus, we are products of our environment. Second, research is influenced by life experiences, values, and personal biographies of researchers. Thus, we cannot disconnect our personal and professional beliefs from our lives and lived experiences. Third, how researchers interpret their experiences and work is the result of many complex factors, mediated by such variables as race, gender, language, political affiliation, religion, region, age, and/or sexual orientation. Thus, the social lenses that we use to see the *other* are influenced by who we are as individuals. Finally, all research is culture bound. Thus, it is not possible to conduct research where circumstances, demographics, and context can be ignored, minimized, negated, or in any way trivialized. These propositions are discussed in more detail below. First, we present two major problems inherent in conducting cross-cultural research. Following this discussion, we present more concrete examples of how these two major problems influence all aspects of the research process.

No Epistemology Is Context Free

Numerous scholars of all racial, cultural, and linguistic backgrounds have suggested that research is not an objective, neutral science: that all aspects of research are influenced by researchers' experiences and beliefs. Stated differently, all knowledge is relative to the context in which it is generated. Thus, when academics construct knowledge, they are influenced by the ideas, assumptions, and norms of the cultures and subsocieties in which they are socialized (Banks & Banks, 1995). From the research focus to the research questions, to the research design and methodology, to the theoretical orientation, and to data interpretation, research is riddled with subjectivity. Researchers come to their work, as do other professionals, with beliefs and attitudes that affect their work. Hence, Scheurich and Young (1997) maintained that the epistemologies we typically use in educational research may be culturally biased.

Both a cursory and an in-depth look at America's most influential scholars reveal a predominant European orientation (Stanfield, 1985). In 1997, Scheurich and Young observed that the major influential writers, philosophers, social scientists, and educational leaders (e.g., Dewey, Kant, Descartes, Weber, and others) all have been White. They are the common script writers and researchers who have developed the ontological and axiological categories or concepts (e.g., individuality, truth, education, free enterprise, and good conduct) that we use to conceptualize children and their cognitive, social, and emotional development. This racially exclusive group also has developed the epistemologies that we use. Thus, White scholars, most of them males, have defined the standards used to judge what is normal, right, and healthy. Deviations from these norms are considered abnormal, wrong, and unhealthy. It is little wonder that racially, culturally, and linguistically diverse scholars argue that too many studies with diverse groups operate from a deficit or pathology orientation (e.g., Ford & Moore, 2004; Ford et al., 2005; C. M. Tucker & Herman, 2002). The result is what Scheurich and Young (1997) refer to as "epistemological racism" (p. 4).

Statement of the Problem

Researchers conducting cross-cultural research should not only be mindful of issues surrounding epistemologies but also those affecting generalizability or external validity. As Sue and Sue (1999) explained, science is used to describe, explain, predict, and modify phenomena. Through the soundness of scientific methodology, rigor, and theoretical coherence, one gains confidence that the findings are valid and that they have external validity. A persistent problem in research relates to beliefs regarding universals. Sue and Sue further suggested that researchers often assume generality of findings when it is not warranted. This raises the questions: To what extent can the findings from one population or sample be generalized to another population? How do our epistemologies impact us when conducting cross-cultural research? How do assumptions influence our work with people whose cultural or racial backgrounds differ from our own? In 2002, C. M. Tucker and Herman observed that most theories and interventions for children and adolescents are based on research with mainly White, middle-class samples[1]. This includes research in gifted education. About two decades ago, Ford et al. (1988) examined the number of articles published on gifted students and found that less than 2% focused on culturally diverse gifted students. To what extent are theories and interventions in the remaining studies appropriate for other groups, such as racially, culturally, and linguistically diverse students and/or children who live in poverty?

Several researchers report that too few studies discuss the racial background or ethnicity of participants, resulting in a type of colorblindness where race is ignored and/or where explorations by race are viewed as trivial or not worth studying. According to Case and Smith (2000), 40% of the articles published in major clinical, counseling, and school psychology journals between 1993 and 1997 failed to report the race or ethnicity of the participants. Sue and Sue (1999) expressed the concern this way:

> In psychological research with human beings, we seem to deemphasize background characteristics and to draw broad conclusions about human beings in general rather than about the particular human beings in the study. In other words, our modus operandi is to assume that the work is universally applicable; the burden of proof is placed on researchers concerned about race, ethnicity, and bias to show that there are ethnic differences . . . we have not followed good scientific principles in assuming that findings from research on one population can be generalized to other populations. (p. 1073)

In their summary of this issue, Sue and Sue (1999) stated that ethnicity should not be treated as a *nuisance variable*, because the United States is one of the most diverse societies in the world. The two researchers also asserted that social scientists should take full advantage of this ethnic diversity by promoting external validity and by testing the generality of theories.

---

[1] Graham's (1992) detailed examination of trends in research on African Americans, published in APA journals between 1970 and 1989, revealed that most of the subjects were White and middle class.

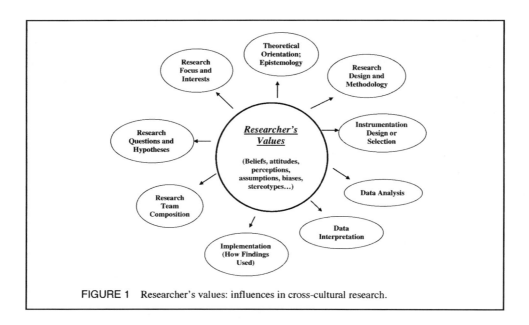

FIGURE 1 Researcher's values: influences in cross-cultural research.

IMPLICATIONS FOR GIFTED EDUCATION RESEARCHERS

Cross-cultural research poses both challenges and promise for researchers. Given the heavy reliance on White, middle-class epistemologies as just discussed, it is essential that researchers consider seriously the impact of their experiences and beliefs on their work. As presented in Figure 1, all aspects of the research project should be evaluated from a cross-cultural perspective.

RESEARCH FOCUS

A large and disproportionate percentage of the studies on racially diverse groups, such as African Americans, operates from deficit perspectives rather than assumptions of strengths (see Graham, 1992; W. H. Tucker, 1994). Journal articles, book chapters, books, and monographs are full of articles/chapters on "at risk," "disadvantaged," and "impoverished" racially, culturally, and linguistically diverse groups. Most studies have focused on the educational and social problems of racially, culturally, and linguistically diverse students and their families, particularly those living in poverty, and virtually ignore those diverse students who are educationally and socially successful. Thus, many of the studies focus on racially, culturally, and linguistically diverse students in special education, but few focus on those students in gifted education. Further, studies on intelligence and ethnicity consistently focus on the lower IQ scores of African Americans compared to the scores of Whites. Studies on the achievement gap consistently focus on the low academic achievement of African American students compared to White students.

Taken as a whole, a potential, mistaken image is that there are few if any high-IQ African American students and few academically successful African American students. What drives this consistent focus on only "at risk" racially, culturally, and linguistically diverse students, economically disadvantaged diverse students, low-performing diverse students, and low-IQ diverse students?

Theoretical Orientation

Our beliefs and experiences influence the theoretical orientation we adopt in our work. For example, the senior author has devoted her professional life to studying gifted African American students because that is who she is. She grew up in poverty and, thus, focused on children who live in poverty. She is concerned about students who do not test well because of her personal and professional knowledge of many intelligent racially, culturally, and linguistically diverse students who perform poorly on tests. The research interests of the authors are personal. Toward this end, our work has been influenced by the theoretical researchers, such as Fordham (1988), Ogbu (1992), Boykin (1994), Mickelson (1990), and Banks (2006); therefore, we can relate to and identify with how peer pressure undermines students' motivation (Fordham); how one racially diverse group might have different beliefs about achievement than another (Ogbu); how cultural styles influence teaching and learning (Boykin); how beliefs, concrete and abstract, influence motivation and achievement (Mickelson); and how curriculum should be multicultural, relevant, and meaningful to students (Banks). According to W. H. Tucker (1994), George Albee, a professor of psychology at the University of Vermont, offered the following opinion in his address to an American Psychological Association conference as the recipient of the Award for Distinguished Contribution to Community Psychology:

> Instead of facts being useful as the objective building blocks of theories, rather it is more accurate to say that people, and especially social scientists, select theories that are consistent with their personal values, attitudes, and prejudices and then go out into the world or into the laboratory, to seek the facts that validate their beliefs about the world and about human nature, neglecting or denying observations that contradict their personal prejudices. (p. 2)

Literature Review

One of the many dangers of being human is the propensity to present or highlight points of view that are consistent with our own views. The work of Herrnstein and Murray (1994) comes to mind. The main premise of their scholarship is that Whites are smarter than African Americans and that high IQ is strongly correlated with academic success and low IQ is closely associated with deviance, poverty, crime, and other problems. Although there are many shortcomings in Herrnstein and Murray's work, the one that stands out the most is that they focused extensively on African Americans who performed poorly on intelligence tests and ignored those who scored high and/or those who were identified as gifted. Thus, this is not surprising given that, "for over a century, there have been scientists obsessed with proving that minorities, poor people, foreigners, and women are innately inferior to upper-class White males" (W. H. Tucker, 1994, p. 4; also see Gould, 1995). Put another way, social scientists have furnished the ammunition with no reservations about its use (W. H. Tucker).

In reading articles in gifted education journals, we have noted four types of studies: Type 1 studies focus exclusively on a White sample; Type 2 studies focus on predominantly White samples; Type 3 studies focus on more than one group of diverse participants; and Type 4 studies focus on one diverse group, with most studies focusing on African Americans rather than other racially diverse groups. In looking at these four groupings, most studies are conducted with White students (Type 1). If racially diverse students are included in the sample, this fact is seldom noted. And if diverse students (Types 2 and 3) are included, group differences such as socioeconomic status, gender, and level of acculturation/assimilation are seldom explored (see Table 1).

When researchers focus their work on racially, culturally, and linguistically diverse students (Type 4), between-group studies outnumber within-group studies. Thus, racially, culturally, and linguistically diverse students are compared to White students on some construct or another (e.g., peer pressures or self-concepts between gifted White and diverse students are compared and beliefs about giftedness are compared between Puerto Rican students and White students). However, when the sample is racially or culturally homogeneous, little attention is given to gender differences or socioeconomic status differences. Further, if gender and socioeconomic status are considered, they are done so in isolation, such as: (a) in a sample of Latino students, only low-income students are studied; (b) in a sample that contains both high- and low-income African American students, results for high-income, gifted African American students are not compared to low-income, gifted African American students; and (c) in a sample with representative percentages of males and females, gifted Japanese boys are not compared to gifted Japanese girls.

Table 1
Sample of External Validity Issues

Demographics of Participants	Sample Scenarios With External Validity in Question
Types 1 and 2: Findings from exclusively/ predominantly White gifted sample generalized to other gifted students	Study finds that the gifted students sampled prefer to work independently as opposed to being in cooperative learning groups. Researcher recommends that educators avoid using cooperative learning with gifted students. Potential Issues: Researcher fails to mention that all or most students are White. Researcher does not compare the White students by gender, age, or area of giftedness. Researcher does not note that the findings may not apply to diverse gifted students, or older/younger gifted students, other types of giftedness, etc.
Type 3: A study with more than one group of diverse participants does not conduct analyses by racial group	Study is conducted primarily with Mexican American and Black gifted students. Researcher finds that the majority of the sample has faced negative peer pressure. Researcher concludes that peer pressure is pervasive among diverse gifted students. Potential Issues: Researcher fails to compare the responses of Mexican American students with those of Black students to see whether differences exist. Researcher does not analyze the data by other demographic variables, such as gender, age, or SES. Researcher fails to note that findings from Mexican American students may not generalize to other Hispanic Americans (e.g., Puerto Rican or Cuban students). Researcher fails to consider issues of acculturation among diverse students (e.g., first- vs. second-generation immigrants).
Type 4: Study with one minority group fails to consider within group differences.	Study is conducted with sample containing only African Americans. Findings indicate that the sample tends to dislike lecture-based instructional methods. Research recommends that teachers decrease their reliance on this instructional style. Potential Issues: Researcher does not compare responses by gender, age, type of giftedness, or SES.

RESEARCH DESIGN AND METHODOLOGY

One of the contributions of qualitative research is the attention devoted to the realities and effects of researcher biases. Qualitative researchers often discuss the notion of "researcher as instrument" and discuss the limitations of their work in the context of the biases they bring to all aspects of the study. Several strategies are utilized to avoid contaminating the data. When analyzing interview transcripts, for example, researchers conduct reliability checks using interrater reliability. Researchers may also ask participants to read their notes to determine whether interpretations are accurate. This process is referred to as member checking (Merriam, 2002).

Researchers with a quantitative orientation must be equally vigilant or conscientious about their design and methodology. The first author recalls helping a colleague to design a survey several years ago. This person was conducting research in a low-income, inner-city community and focusing on some aspect of parent involvement. Having grown up in a similar community, the first author offered him two suggestions: (a) change the study to "family" involvement, and (b) when asking students who they live with, expand the choices from "mother, father, both, and other" to "mother," "father," "both," "grandmother," and "other." But, the person refused. Further, when the researcher analyzed the data, it was found that 40% of the students reported living with their grandmother only or with their mother and grandmother.

INSTRUMENTATION

In gifted education, we have grappled with how to increase the representation of culturally diverse students. We have found that African American and Hispanic students tend to score lower on traditional intelligence tests than White students. However, on nontraditional tests, the scores are more comparable (see extensive research by Jack Naglieri on this topic and others who advocate for the use of nonverbal intelligence tests). Given this finding, we wonder why professionals continue to rely so extensively or exclusively on traditional tests—and on any test or measure that has a disparate impact? Other questions arise as well: What notions about intelligence and tests affect our continued reliance on traditional tests? How do our personal beliefs and paradigms affect this decision? What literature do we rely on to support this decision? What research do we ignore to support this decision?

DATA ANALYSIS AND INTERPRETATION

As noted herein and elsewhere, racially, culturally, and linguistically diverse students are poorly represented in gifted education. Most studies have concluded that diverse students are underrepresented because of low test scores. Several questions come to mind:
1. If tests are one of the culprits, why do we continue to use them?
2. If traditional tests are the culprit, why do we not adopt alternative tests?
3. What are the explanations for this low performance on traditional tests?
4. If tests are not the culprit, what are other possible explanations for underrepresentation?

In essence, when analyzing data, researchers should consider alternative explanations for findings. They should contextualize findings. In addition, they should provide enough demographic and contextual information to assess external validity or generalizability.

Data Use and Dissemination

Much of the research on racially, culturally, and linguistically diverse groups has been pathological (Gould, 1995). There exists a body of historical and contemporary work conducted by ethnocentrists, social Darwinists, or epistemological racists whose motives are suspect and whose orientations seem sociopolitical and value-laden. Their work often seems less than objective, neutral, and free of bias. The work on intelligence, as already stated, is a prime example (see Ford, 2004). The nature-nurture stalemate and attendant assumptions about racial cultural, and linguistic inferiority, along with the perceived superiority of one group over another, have gone on ad nauseam (e.g., Herrnstein & Murray, 1994). Results from these works have been used for social and political reasons to support the Holocaust, slavery, segregated schools and communities, denial of marriages across race, special education (mis)placement, and gifted education denial. Skeptics have looked only at the work of Herrnstein and Murray, a contemporary form of social Darwinism.

Before their book (i.e., *The Bell Curve: Intelligence and Class Structure in American Life*), there was a similar controversy about Putnam's (1967) *Race and Reason: A Yankee View*. Nevertheless, both works conveyed a resounding message that African Americans were second-class and genetically inferior. Further, Hernstein and Murray's book contributed to the American Association of Physical Anthropologists adopting a resolution deploring "the misuse of science to advocate racism. We condemn such writings as *Race and Reason* that urge the denial of basic rights to human beings and we affirm that there is nothing in science that justifies the denial of opportunities or rights to any group by virtue of race" (as cited in W. H. Tucker, 1994, p. 161).

A Vision of Racially, Culturally, and Linguistically Responsive Research in Gifted Education: Considerations and Recommendations

Racially, culturally, and linguistically responsible research is within the four authors' reach as is becoming racially, culturally, and linguistically responsive researchers. In this section, we present a vision of racially, culturally, and linguistically responsive researchers and investigations, paying attention to issues presented in Figure 1, discussed earlier.

Characteristics of Culturally Responsive Researchers

Elsewhere, we have described characteristics of racially, culturally, and linguistically responsive researchers. Drawing on that work, we contend that racially, culturally, and linguistically responsive researchers have self-awareness, cultural awareness and understanding, strong feelings about social justice, and a range of skills and strategies.

Self-awareness and self-understanding. The first step to becoming a racially, culturally, and linguistically responsive researcher is to be self-reflective. This quality requires researchers to think seriously, critically, and honestly about their own views about racial diversity and diverse racially groups (Pang, 2001). Racially, culturally, and linguistically competent researchers seek greater self-awareness and understanding regarding their biases, assumptions, and stereotypes. Self-awareness comes from understanding one's own cultural beliefs, values, and norms and recognizing that everyone is a product of his or her culture. It is also imperative that researchers understand that their race, culture, and language are not superior to another. Additionally, it is important that they recognize that self-awareness helps researchers to recognize how their assumptions and biases influence their work and relationships with diverse groups. In this process of self-reflection and self-appraisal, researchers should ask themselves the following questions:

1. How do I feel about working with individuals or groups that are different from me? What stereotypes, biases and fears do I hold of other groups? How do these views affect my work, including research questions, hypotheses, literature review, instrument development or selection, data interpretation, and data use?
2. What aspects of my research skills and strategies might hinder building rapport with diverse participants and data collection procedures?
3. How are the expectations that I hold of diverse individuals/groups different from those of White individuals/groups?
4. How much time and effort am I willing to devote or have I devoted to studying and learning about acculturation/assimilation, within group differences versus between group differences, biculturalism, monoculturalism, and transculturalism?
5. How much time and effort am I willing to devote to learning about alternative theories and models associated with diverse groups (e.g., their views about intelligence, giftedness, achievement, and creativity? Their childrearing practices? Their views about education?)
6. Am I willing to change, to adapt and add to my ways of thinking about those who are different from me?
7. When presented with data, will I change my thinking and behavior?

Cultural awareness and understanding. After examining the previous questions and confronting their beliefs, attitudes, and values, researchers should learn as much as they can about the populations that they plan or hope to study. To this end, it is essential that researchers interact with and observe diverse populations, particularly those who they plan to include in their research studies. In doing so, the following questions might be useful:

1. What is "race/culture" and how does it affect teaching and learning, self-concept, and racial identity (and the construct under investigation)?
2. Where can I go and who can I turn to for more information and resources on diverse cultures?
3. What are the cultural beliefs, values, norms and traditions of the diverse participants represented in my sample? What cultural beliefs, values, norms, and traditions of the diverse participants are not represented in my sample?
4. What data collection strategies/procedures are culturally compatible with and to the participants in the study? (e.g., Do participants feel more comfortable with surveys or interviews? Do they prefer telephone calls or face-to-face meetings? Would participants prefer to be interviewed at their home or at a neutral site? Do males tend to respond to questions rather than females?)
5. How comfortable am I when working with diverse groups? Am I comfortable going into their homes and community to collect data?

Racially, culturally, and linguistically competent researchers, as the questions suggest, attempt to understand the worldviews (i.e., values and norms) of diverse groups. Researchers who fail to consider these views may undermine the investigation in some way.

Socially responsive and responsible. Socially responsive researchers attempt to increase multicultural or cross-cultural awareness and understanding within the larger society. They seek to conduct cross-cultural research even in racially, culturally, and linguistically homogenous settings (e.g., predominantly or all-White classrooms, schools, and communities). The shortage or absence of ethnic minority students in a gifted program, school, community, or state is not an excuse for inattention to cross cultural research. Socially responsible researchers feel that it is their duty to always include diverse groups in their studies and to draw externally valid conclusions.

Racially, culturally, and linguistically sensitive techniques and strategies. Racially, culturally, and linguistically competent researchers recognize the importance of acquiring communication and other skills (e.g., data collection and instrument development) to work effectively with diverse groups. In their efforts to develop and conduct an effective study, cross-culturally, racially, and linguistically competent researchers adopt principles and epistemologies that address the academic, social-emotional, and psychological needs of diverse groups. Much of their effort is directed at achieving the highest levels of multicultural competence, as described by Storti (1998). That is, researchers have an increased sensitivity to

Table 2
Levels/Stages of Cultural Awareness

	Incompetence	Competence
Unconscious	Blissful Ignorance 1 You are not aware that cultural differences exist between you and another person. It does not occur to you that you may be making cultural mistakes or that you may be misinterpreting much of the behavior going on around you.	Spontaneous Sensitivity 4 You no longer have to think about what you are doing in order to be culturally sensitive (in a culture you know well). Culturally appropriate behavior comes naturally to you, and you trust your intuition because it has been reconditioned by what you know about cross-cultural interactions.
Conscious	Troubling Ignorance 2 You realize that there are cultural differences between you and another person, but you understand very little about these differences. You know there's a problem but don't know the magnitude of it. You are worried about whether or not you'll ever figure out these differences in others.	Deliberate Sensitivity 3 You know there are cultural differences between people. You know some of the differences and you try to modify your own behavior to be sensitive to these differences. This does not come naturally but you make a conscious effort to behave in culturally sensitive ways. You are in the process of replacing old intuitions with new ones.

Note. From *Figuring Foreigners Out: A Practical Guide*, by C. Storti, 1998, Yarmouth, ME: Intercultural Press.

diversity and feel compelled to avoid promoting social injustices. Storti presented four levels of multicultural or cross-cultural competence/awareness worth considering (see Table 2).

At the highest level, called *spontaneous sensitivity*, professionals are unconsciously competent. Thus, they no longer have to think about what they are doing in order to be culturally sensitive (in a culture you know well). Culturally appropriate behavior comes naturally, and they trust their intuitions because they have been reconditioned by what they know about cross-cultural interactions.

FEATURES OF RACIALLY, CULTURALLY, AND LINGUISTICALLY RESPONSIVE RESEARCH

Being a racially, culturally, and linguistically responsive researcher is not necessarily synonymous with conducting racially, culturally, and linguistically responsive research. More specifically, such research entails (a) diverse groups included in studies, and (b) cross-cultural communication and research strategies. Further, the following characteristics are associated with racially, culturally, and linguistically responsive research.

- ❖ *Racially, culturally, and linguistically relevant research topics.* A central feature of racially, culturally, and linguistically responsive research is a focus on topics that carry important implications for diverse groups. Thus, researchers focus on prevailing social injustices and their influence on diverse groups and their situation. Social injustices are explored when interpreting findings and making recommendations, for example.

- *Racially, culturally, and linguistically informed theories and paradigms.* Another feature of racially, culturally, and linguistically responsive research is the use of theories and paradigms that have been developed with diverse student populations. These theories have high external validity or degree of relevance to the population that is under study.
- *Multiple explanations examined.* In research, knowledge is far from a scarce resource; knowledge is power. However, racially, culturally, and linguistically responsive researchers recognize that knowledge is subjective, value-laden, and reciprocal (i.e., researchers and participants learn from each other). Just as important, at every level or phase of the research, multiple worldviews and explanations are considered.
- *Relationship building with participants.* Collecting data from racially, culturally, and linguistically diverse groups often necessitates, first and foremost, seeking partnerships with participants. At the heart of this relationship is taking time to allow research participants to build trust and confidence in the researchers and their motives. Relationship building might consist of visiting homes, community centers, and places of worship.
- *Respect for participants' primary language.* Racially, culturally, and linguistically responsive researchers build upon the language of diverse participants. They use appropriate communicative strategies and philosophies that affirm their participants' native languages or dialects. This need to accommodate language may be evident when students speak Spanish, Creole, Japanese, or Chinese, for example. It may be less obvious when students speak "Ebonics" or the Black English vernacular. No language is negated, criticized, or devalued in the process of research; instead, forms and data collection instruments are translated, and interpreters are members of the research team.
- *Racially, culturally, and linguistically congruent research practices.* When research is racially, culturally, and linguistically responsive, research procedures undergo modifications to become more congruent or compatible with the study's participants (e.g., translate the survey instrument in Spanish for Spanish-speaking students, where English is their second language). Stated differently, researchers should capitalize on the communication styles of diverse groups when conducting face-to-face interviews, small group interviews, interviews in neutral settings, and direct versus indirect questioning strategies.

❖ *Racially, culturally, and linguistically sensitive assessments.* Racially, culturally, and linguistically responsive research is not possible without culturally sensitive (bias-reduced) assessment. Perhaps the most common criticism of standardized tests is that they underestimate the abilities of diverse students, but many schools continue to use these tests as the primary or sole criterion for placement in gifted programs and services. Consequently, many racially, culturally, and linguistically diverse students, already at risk for reluctant teacher referrals, remain underrepresented in gifted education programs that rely heavily on tests. Racially, culturally, and linguistically responsive researchers recognize that students have many strengths that intelligence tests may not measure. They also use a variety of measurements to collect data to ensure that they are able to capture students' strengths.

❖ *Diverse research team.* In racially, culturally, and linguistically responsive research, investigators understand the importance of having a diverse team of researchers. For example, while it may be uncomfortable for us to admit, some diverse participants may feel more comfortable being interviewed by researchers with similar racial, cultural, and linguistic backgrounds. To this end, diverse members can often (a) shed valuable light on potential problems with research protocols/instruments (e.g., questions being asked and the wording of questions/items); (b) inform the literature review from a cross-cultural perspective; (c) shed light on the values, beliefs, and customs of participants from diverse backgrounds; (d) offer alternative interpretations of the findings; and (e) offer culturally sensitive interventions strategies and plans. The learning is also reciprocal in that both researchers become—or should become—knowledgeable of the other.

Conclusion

Many White scholars have devoted their lives to combating racism and other forms of oppression (e.g., classism); they have worked diligently to change ethnocentric or race-based paradigms. However, it is worth noting that "a researcher could be adamantly anti-racist in thought and deed and still be using a research epistemology that could be judged to be racially biased" (Scheurich & Young, 1997, p. 5). Thus, we should aggressively and proactively seek to become racially, culturally, and linguistically competent researchers. Our nation and schools are more diverse than ever before. If projections come true, in the not-too-distant future, racially diverse groups will be the overwhelming majority in our schools. How will this affect our research paradigms, sampling procedures, designs, and instruments? Will we continue to conduct business as usual? Will we continue to profess that scientists are neutral, value-free professionals? Will we continue to be overly generous with generalizations, assessing external validity, and making universal assumptions? Will we continue to conduct research on White gifted students and apply the findings to racially diverse gifted students? Will we continue to apply theories of intelligence and giftedness developed by White scholars and based on White populations to diverse populations? Will we continue to downplay the need to disaggregate the findings by race? Will we continue to practice this form of colorblindness? The authors' fear is that researchers will make these mistakes unless they acquire the knowledge, skills, and dispositions to become racially, culturally, and linguistically competent. Just as colorblindness has no place in teaching, it has no place in research. No time is better than now to become racially, culturally, and linguistically competent researchers. The integrity of our work depends on it.

References

Au, K. H., & Jordan, C. (1981). *Culture in bilingual classrooms.* New York: Newbury House.

Banks, J. A. (2006). *Cultural diversity in American education.* Boston: Allyn & Bacon.

Banks, J. A., & Banks, C. A. M. (Eds.). (1995). *Multicultural education: Issues and perspectives.* Boston: Allyn & Bacon.

Boykin, A. W. (1994). Harvesting culture and talent: African American children and educational reform. In R. Rossi (Ed.), *Schools and students at risk* (pp. 149–164). New York: Teachers College Press.

Case, L., & Smith, T. B. (2000). Ethnic representation in a sample of the literature of applied psychology. *Journal of Consulting and Clinical Psychology, 68,* 1107–1110.

Ford, D. Y. (2004). *Intelligence testing and cultural diversity: Concerns, cautions, and considerations.* Storrs: University of Connecticut, National Research Center on the Gifted and Talented.

Ford, D. Y., Grantham, T. C., & Harris, J. J., III. (1998). Multicultural gifted education: A wakeup call to the profession. *Roeper Review, 19,* 72–78.

Ford, D. Y., Grantham, T. C., & Moore, J. L., III. (2006). Essentializing identity development in the education of students of color. In H. R. Milner & E. W. Ross (Eds.), *Race, ethnicity, and education: Racial identity in education* (pp. 3–18). Westport, CT: Greenwood/Praeger.

Ford, D. Y., & Harris, J. J., III. (1999). *Multicultural gifted education.* New York: Teachers College Press.

Ford, D. Y., & Moore, J. L., III. (2004). The achievement gap and gifted students of color. *Understanding Our Gifted, 16,* 3–7.

Ford, D. Y., Moore, J. L., III, & Harmon, D. A. (2005). Integrating multicultural and gifted education: A curricular framework. *Theory Into Practice, 44,* 125–137.

Ford, D. Y., & Whiting, G. W. (2006). Underrepresentation of diverse students in gifted education: Recommendations for nondiscriminatory assessment (part 1). *Gifted Education Press Quarterly, 20,* 2–6.

Fordham, S. (1988). Racelessness as a strategy in Black students' school success: Pragmatic strategy or pyrrhic victory? *Harvard Educational Review, 58,* 54–84.

Gould, S. J. (1981). *The mismeasure of man.* New York: Norton.

Gould, S. J. (1995). *The mismeasure of man* (rev. ed.). New York: Norton.

Graham, S. (1992). "Most of the subjects were White and middle class": Trends in published research on African Americans in selected APA journals, 1970–1989. *American Psychologist, 47*, 629–639.

Herrnstein, R. J., & Murray, C. (1994). *The Bell Curve: Intelligence and class structure in American life*. New York: Free Press.

Merriam, S. B. (2002). Assessing and evaluating qualitative research. In S. B. Merriam & Associates, *Qualitative research in practice: Example for discussion and analysis* (pp. 18–33). San Francisco: Jossey-Bass.

Mickelson, R. A. (1990). The attitude-achievement paradox among black adolescents. *Sociology of Education, 63*, 44–61.

Moore, J. L., III. (2006). A qualitative investigation of African American males' career trajectory in engineering: Implications for teachers, counselors, and parents. *Teachers College Record, 108*, 246–266.

Moore, J. L., III, Ford, D. Y., & Milner, H. R. (2005a). Recruitment is not enough: Retaining African-American students in gifted education. *Gifted Child Quarterly, 49*, 51–67.

Moore, J. L., III, Ford, D. Y., & Milner, H. R. (2005b). Underachievement among gifted students of color: Implications for educators. *Theory Into Practice, 44*, 167–177.

Moore, J. L., III, Ford, D. Y., Owens, D., Hall, T., Byrd, T., Byrd, M., et al. (2006). Retention of African-Americans in gifted education: Lessons learned from higher education. *Mid-Western Educational Researcher, 19*, 3–12.

Ogbu, J. (1992). Understanding cultural diversity. *Educational Researcher, 21*, 5–24.

Pang, V. O. (2001). *Multicultural education: A caring-centered, reflective approach*. Columbus, OH: McGraw-Hill.

Putnam, C. (1961). *Race and reason: A Yankee View*. Washington, DC: Public Affairs Press.

Scheurich, J. J., & Young, M. D. (1997). Coloring epistemologies: Are our research epistemologies racially based? *Educational Researcher, 26*, 4–16.

Stanfield, J. H. (1985). The ethnocentric basis of social science knowledge production. *Review of Research in Education, 12*, 387–415.

Storti, C. (1998). *Figuring foreigners out: A practical guide*. Yarmouth, ME: Intercultural Press.

Sue, D. W., & Sue, D. (1999). *Counseling the culturally different* (3rd ed.). New York: John Wiley.

Thomas, A., & Sillen, S. (1972). *Racism and psychiatry*. New York: Brunner/Mazel.

Tucker, C. M., & Herman, K. C. (2002). Using culturally sensitive theories and research to meet the academic needs of low-income African American children. *American Psychologist, 57*, 762–773.

Tucker, W. H. (1994). *The science and politics of racial research*. Champaign, IL: University of Illinois Press.

Author Bios

Donna Y. Ford, PhD, is a professor of education in the Peabody College of Education at Vanderbilt University. Her scholarship focuses on closing the achievement gap, increasing the representation of Black and other culturally diverse students in gifted education, reversing underachievement among Black students, and creating culturally responsive learning environments. Dr. Ford consults with school districts and families nationally on these and other topics. She is also the author of numerous articles and books and is a member of numerous professional organizations, including the National Association for Gifted Children. E-mail: donna.ford@vanderbilt.edu

James L. Moore III, PhD, is an associate professor in counselor education in the College of Education and Human Ecology and is the coordinator of the School Counseling Program at Ohio State University. He also holds a faculty appointment as a senior researcher associate at the Kirwan Institute for the Study of Race & Ethnicity and has a faculty affiliation with the Ohio Collaborative and The John Glenn Institute at The Ohio State University. In 7 years, Dr. Moore has published more than 70 publications and given more than 100 lectures, presentations, and keynote addresses around the world. Currently, he serves as the senior associate editor for the *Journal of the Professoriate* and is also a member of numerous editorial boards (i.e., *Exceptional Children, Gifted Child Quarterly, Journal of Advanced Academics, Urban Education, Journal of Counseling* & *Development*, and others). E-mail: moore.1408@osu.edu

Gilman W. Whiting, PhD, is an Assistant Professor of African American and Diaspora Studies and the Director of Undergraduate Studies at Vanderbilt University. He also teaches in Vanderbilt University's Peabody College of Education in the Department of Human and Organizational Development. He consults with school districts nationally on various issues related to psychosocial behavior and motivation among young students. He is the creator of the Scholar Identity Model™ and co-directs the summer Scholar Identity Institute for young Black males. E-mail: g.whiting@vanderbilt.edu

Dr. Tarek C. Grantham is an associate professor in the Department of Educational Psychology and Instructional Technology at the University of Georgia. He also serves as the program coordinator and teaches courses in the Gifted and Creative Education Program. His research focuses on recruitment and retention of underserved students in gifted and advanced programs and addresses the problem of underrepresentation and underachievement among diverse youth (particularly African Americans). In his area of research, Dr. Grantham directs his attention to mentoring, multicultural education, motivation, and effective advocacy for recruitment and retention of diverse youth. He has published on these issues and presented to local, state, and national audiences (e.g., Georgia Association for Gifted Children and American Educational Research Association) to encourage proactive efforts that aim to reverse underrepresentation and underachievement. Further, Dr. Grantham currently serves on the Diversity Committee for the National Association for Gifted Children (NAGC). E-mail: grantham@uga.edu

Received 8 May 2007; accepted 6 July 2007.

Address correspondence to Donna Y. Ford, PhD, Department of Special Education, 230 Appleton Place (Box 228), Peabody College of Education, Vanderbilt University, Nashville, TN 37203. E-mail: donna.ford@vanderbilt.edu

EPILOGUE

Tarek C. Grantham, Donna Y. Ford, and Malik S. Henfield

We, the coeditors, began developing this series of readings with several assumptions and propositions; all of them share the belief that underrepresentation is a problem that can be and must be interrogated and addressed. Business must not continue as usual. At the heart of each assumption and proposition is our unwavering belief that gifted education has yet to adequately address inequity related to Black students, and Black students continue to be victims of benign neglect in our field. We, and the scholars in this anthology, believe that:

- underrepresentation is inequitable and unnecessary;
- all groups are equally endowed in intelligence, academic ability, and creativity; thus, no group should have a monopoly on being identified and served as gifted;
- underrepresentation can decrease when the focus is on recruitment and retention;
- teachers/educators (due to low expectations and deficit thinking) are the major contributors to underrepresentation, but substantive and purposeful professional development and courses can change this;
- creative strengths reveal gifted potential;
- traditional tests and instruments are a major contributor to underrepresentation, but alternative tests and instruments can increase representation;
- policies and procedures that contribute to and sustain underrepresentation must be interrogated and changed; and
- underrepresentation can be corrected.

The 26 articles and 20 authors in this anthology told the stories of where we have been and where we are. Also of importance is where we want to go, with an eye toward not being bystanders when Black students are severely underidentified and underrepresented.

Section I provided a historical context and background regarding Black students, gifted education, and underrepresentation. Akin to a clarion call for attention to real issues, as well as dialogue and change, the collective voices of Frasier,

Baldwin, and Ford set the stage. Sadly, what Frasier and Baldwin discussed in the 1970s and 1980s was also discussed by new scholars entering the field, such as Ford, Grantham, Harmon, and others, some 20 years later! Given what we now know and the consequences of not acting on what we know, resistance to change is unacceptable. Accepting slow change or applauding snail-paced progress is unacceptable.

Section II focused on creativity, intelligence, and Black students, with attention to the impressive and visionary work of E. Paul Torrance. We argued that the field's focus on Torrance's contributions in creativity—through a colorblind lens—has neglected his contributions to improving the lives of gifted Black students. Initially writing during the 1960s and 1970s, Torrance was a forerunner, a proactive advocate for gifted Black students in general and low-income gifted Black students in particular. Prior to writing this anthology, none of the members of CAAS fully understood or embraced the depth of Torrance's commitment to racial justice and equity. His commitment was neither common nor popular during this time. Torrance left a legacy that will hopefully be addressed exclusively in a future anthology by CAAS, under the leadership of Tarek C. Grantham.

Section III, Discovering Gifted Potential in Black Students, shared what must be done to move beyond deficit thinking in order to discover, value, and nurture gifts and talents in Black students. Unlike some other scholars and practitioners, we do not waste our time quibbling about the role of genetics versus the environment in the development of giftedness. Instead, we and those in this section advocate for and believe in the power of education, delivered by trained professionals, to discover and nurture gifts and talents in all students—but Black students in this case.

Highly gifted Black students were the focus of Section IV, in which Martin D. Jenkins' extensive and neglected body of work was presented. At a time when segregation was the reality, when *Brown v. Board of Education* (1954) did not exist, Jenkins conducted his work—breaking myths and stereotypes by letting all educators and families know that Blacks are not only gifted but also highly *gifted*! Unfortunately, Jenkins has been the only scholar with this focus. His work cannot and must not continue to collect dust.

As should be expected, there was a section on the assessment of Black intelligence. In Section V, we tackled the thorny, sometimes polemic issue of the pros and cons of testing and assessing Black students. The writers gave specific attention to equitable assessments and nonverbal measures. Section VI focused on a concept that Donna Y. Ford introduced to the field in the early 1990s—recruitment *and* retention. Her rationale remains clear: We must not only find ways to increase access to gifted education, we must also ensure Black students' success once identified and placed. Recruitment and retention is comprehensive; it covers *all* aspects of underrepresentation: prescreening strategies, instruments and forms, referral, policies and procedures, learning environment, philosophy, placement, curriculum, and instruction.

The final section built upon and went beyond our past and current status to focus on future considerations in educating gifted Black students. Here, contributors urged us to learn from the past and present—to deeply consider what has not worked, what is not working, and what are promising possibilities for research, policy, and practice focusing on gifted Black students. We urged readers and decision makers to partake in honest self-reflections, to desire change, and to take bold but necessary steps to make gifted education better (i.e., excellent and equitable) for Black students. When this happens, everyone wins.

ABOUT THE EDITORS

Tarek C. Grantham, Ph.D., is an associate professor in the Department of Educational Psychology and Instructional Technology at the University of Georgia (UGA). He teaches courses in the Gifted and Creative Education Program and has served as program coordinator for its on-campus and online graduate programs. Dr. Grantham is an alumnus of the University of Virginia in Charlottesville, VA, earning three degrees from his alma mater. In 1991, Dr. Grantham graduated from the Curry School of Education Five-Year Dual-Degree BA/MT Program. He earned his bachelor's degree in Spanish from the Department of Spanish, Italian, and Portuguese and his Master of Teaching Degree (MT) in secondary education-foreign language from the Department of Curriculum, Instruction, and Special Education. In 1997, Dr. Grantham pursued doctoral research as a graduate student in the Department of Educational Leadership, Foundations, and Policy, majoring in administration and supervision and specializing in the area of gifted education.

His research addresses the problem of underrepresentation and underachievement among diverse youth (particularly African Americans) in programs for gifted students. In his area of research, Dr. Grantham emphasizes mentoring, multicultural education, and "upstander" attitudes to enhance motivation, leadership, and talent development among diverse youth. He has published on these issues and presented to local, state, and national audiences to encourage proactive efforts that aim to recruit and retain culturally and linguistically diverse students in gifted programs.

Dr. Grantham has served as a board member of the Education Commission for the National Association for Gifted Children and as a co-coordinator of the UGA Preparing Future Faculty Program in Psychology, sponsored by the American Psychological Association, working to recruit, train, and retain diverse faculty in colleges and universities in the field of educational psychology. Dr. Grantham has served as a guest editor of a special issue of *Roeper Review* entitled "Underrepresentation Among Ethnically Diverse Students in Gifted Education," along with service to editorial review boards of professional and academic journals, including *Exceptional Children, Gifted Child Quarterly, Journal of Advanced Academics, and Urban Education.*

Dr. Grantham is the husband of a wonderful woman, Dr. Kimberly Dillon Grantham, and the proud father of Kurali, Copeland, and Jovi Grantham.

Donna Y. Ford, Ph.D., is Professor of Education and Human Development at Vanderbilt University. She teaches in the Department of Special Education. Dr. Ford conducts research primarily in gifted education and multicultural/urban education. Specifically, her work focuses on: (a) minority student achievement and underachievement; (b) recruiting and retaining culturally diverse students in gifted education; (c) multicultural and urban education; and (d) family involvement. Dr. Ford is cofounder of the Scholar Identity Institute for Black Males.

Dr. Ford's work has been recognized by various professional organizations. She has received the Research Award from the Shannon Center for Advanced Studies; the Early Career Award and the Career Award from the American Educational Research Association; the Senior Scholar Award and the Early Scholar Award from the National Association for Gifted Children; and the Esteemed Scholarship Award from the National Association of Black Psychologists. She is the author of several books and more than 100 articles and chapters, and she presents nationally at professional conferences and school districts. She has served as a board member of the National Association for Gifted Children and on numerous editorial boards.

Malik S. Henfield, Ph.D., is an assistant professor in the counselor education program in the College of Education at The University of Iowa. Dr. Henfield teaches courses in school counseling and gifted education in elementary, middle, high school, and postsecondary settings. He received a B.A. in biology from Francis Marion University, an M.Ed. and an Ed.S. in K–12 school counseling from the University of South Carolina, and a Ph.D. in counselor education from The Ohio State University.

Dr. Henfield's research agenda is focused most generally on the academic, personal, social, and career success of Black students in grades K–12 and postsecondary settings. More specifically, his scholarship pertains to the following areas: (a) recruiting and retaining Black students, particularly males, in gifted education programs, Advanced Placement (AP) programs, and science, technology, engineering, and math (STEM) majors and careers; (b) increasing the multicultural competence of pre- and in-service educators working with Black students; (c) recruiting and retaining Black students in Counselor Education programs; and (d) studying social, cultural, and psychological factors related to the achievement gap between Black and White students in urban-, suburban-, and rural-specific settings.

In 2010, Dr. Henfield was named North Central Association for Counselor Education and Supervision (NCACES) Deanna Hawes Outstanding Mentor for his mentorship of master's and doctoral students. He has published multiple refereed and editor-reviewed scholarly publications and delivered many national, regional, state, and local keynote addresses and professional presentations.

Deborah A. Harmon, Ph.D., is a professor of curriculum and instruction in the Department of Teacher Education at Eastern Michigan University. She is also the director of the Office of Urban Education and Educational Equity in the College of Education at Eastern Michigan University. Dr. Harmon earned her doctor of philosophy degree in educational leadership and human resource development (1999) with a specialization in multicultural education, urban education, and gifted education and a bachelor of science degree in psychology and child development (1975) from Colorado. She is creator of the Minority Achievement, Retention and Success (MARS) program model and the Developing Resiliency and Education Achievement in Minority Students program. Dr. Harmon conducts research primarily in multicultural/urban education and gifted education. Specifically, her work focuses on: (a) recruiting and retaining culturally diverse students in gifted education and teacher education; (b) multicultural and urban education; (c) reducing the achievement gap; and (d) teacher preparation for urban education. She consults with school districts and educational and legal organizations in the areas of multicultural/urban education, reducing the achievement gap, and gifted education.

Dr. Harmon has authored and coauthored chapters and books including *Elementary Education: A Reference Book* (2005), "The Underachievement of African American Males in K–12 Education" in *The State of African American Males in Michigan: A Courageous Conversation Monograph* (2010), and "The Underachievement of African American Females in K–12 Education" in *Nurturing Our Future as African American Females: A Courageous Conversation* (in press).

Michelle Trotman Scott, Ph.D., is an assistant professor at the University of West Georgia. She teaches in the Department of Collaborative Support and Intervention. Michelle has been an adjunct professor at The Ohio State University, a superintendent of a charter middle school in Dayton, OH, and a director of a charter elementary school in Columbus, OH. She also taught and coached in the Columbus Public School System. Dr. Trotman Scott earned her doctor of philosophy degree in applied behavior analysis with an emphasis on special, gifted, and urban education; her master of arts degree in technology education; and her bachelor of science degree in education from The Ohio State University.

Dr. Trotman Scott's research interests include the achievement gap, special education overrepresentation, gifted education underrepresentation, creating culturally responsive classrooms, and increasing family involvement. She has conducted professional development workshops for urban school districts and has been invited to community dialogues with regard to educational practices and reform. She has written and coauthored several articles and has made numerous presentations at professional conferences.

Sonya Porchèr, Ed.D., is a Language Learner Director (LLD) with Disney English in Hanghzou, China. She serves as center support for Chinese students ages 2–12 in their acquisition of the English language. Dr. Porchèr was formerly the gifted program coordinator in a large metro Atlanta school system for 6 years. She also worked as a sixth-grade assistant principal for 4 years and an elementary teacher for 10 years. Dr. Porchèr earned her doctorate of education in school reform at the University of West Georgia (2007) and her master's of education degree in elementary instruction (1991) and her bachelor of arts degree in educational studies and psychology (1990) from Emory University.

Dr. Porchèr's focus is school improvement and program development in gifted education. Her work involves professional development and teacher training that encompasses gifted certification with an emphasis on differentiated instruction. She has presented at both the national and local levels. Dr. Porchèr is a National Board Certified teacher and the recipient of a Fulbright scholarship to the United Kingdom. She is also a recipient of the Phi Delta Kappa READ Scholarship, in which she received an opportunity to visit schools in Finland and present the instructional practices at the local level.

Cheryl L. Price is currently assistant program director of the Minority Achievement, Resiliency and Success (MARS) program that supports talented minority students enrolled in teacher certification programs. She is also a doctoral candidate in educational leadership at Eastern Michigan University and has a master's degree in educational leadership with an emphasis on higher education administration. Her research focuses on the impact of cultural competency on developing effective educational leaders. Ms. Price has been involved in professional development with teachers and administrators focusing on the development of cultural competency, multicultural education, and effective strategies that address the achievement gap.

She has coauthored a book chapter with Dr. Vernon Polite in *The State of African American Males in Michigan*. Ms. Price was the recipient of Eastern Michigan University's Woman of the Year award.